The Sociology of "Structural Disaster"

How and why did credible scientists, engineers, government officials, journalists, and others collectively give rise to a drastic failure to control the threat to the population of the Fukushima disaster? Why was there no effort on the part of inter-organizational networks, well-coordinated in the nuclear village, to prevent the risks from turning into a disaster?

This book answers these questions by formulating the concept of "structural disaster" afresh. First, the book presents the path-dependent development of structural disaster through a sociological reformulation of path-dependent mechanisms not only in the context of nuclear energy but also in the context of renewable energy. Second, it traces the origins of structural disaster to a secret accident involving standardized military technology immediately before World War II, and opportunistic utilization of the Great Kanto Earthquake of 1923, thus reconstructing the development of structural disaster within a long-term historical perspective. Maintaining distance from conflicts of interest and cultural essentialisms, this book highlights configurations and mechanisms of structural disasters that are far more persistent, more universal, but less visible, and that have turned risk into suffering. The book seeks to cast light on an important new horizon of the science-technology-society interface in the sociology of science and technology, science and technology studies, the sociology of disaster, the social history of the military-industrial-university complex, and beyond.

Miwao Matsumoto is a Professor Emeritus of Sociology at the University of Tokyo, Japan.

Routledge Studies in Science, Technology and Society

33 **The Ethics of Ordinary Technology**
   Michel Puech

34 **Imagined Futures in Science, Technology and Society**
   Edited by Gert Verschraegen, Frédéric Vandermoere, Luc Braeckmans and Barbara Segaert

35 **Adolescents and Their Social Media Narratives**
   A Digital Coming of Age
   Jill Walsh

36 **Scientific Imperialism**
   Another Facet of Interdisciplinarity
   Edited by Uskali Mäki, Adrian Walsh and Manuela Fernández Pinto

37 **Future Courses of Human Societies**
   Critical Reflections from the Natural and Social Sciences
   Edited by Kléber Ghimire

38 **Science, Africa and Europe**
   Processing Information and Creating Knowledge
   Edited by Patrick Harries, Martin Lengwiler and Nigel Penn

39 **The Sociology of "Structural Disaster"**
   Beyond Fukushima
   Miwao Matsumoto

40 **The Cultural Authority of Science**
   Comparing across Europe, Asia, Africa and the Americas
   Edited by Bauer, MW, Pansegrau, P and Shukla, R

For the full list of books in the series: www.routledge.com/Routledge-Studies-in-Science-Technology-and-Society/book-series/SE0054

The Sociology of "Structural Disaster"
Beyond Fukushima

Miwao Matsumoto

LONDON AND NEW YORK

First published 2021
by Routledge
4 Park Square, Milton Park, Abingdon, Oxon OX14 4RN
605 Third Avenue, New York, NY 10017

First issued in paperback 2023

Routledge is an imprint of the Taylor & Francis Group, an informa business

© 2021 Miwao Matsumoto

The right of Miwao Matsumoto to be identified as authors of this work has been asserted by him in accordance with sections 77 and 78 of the Copyright, Designs and Patents Act 1988.

All rights reserved. No part of this book may be reprinted or reproduced or utilised in any form or by any electronic, mechanical, or other means, now known or hereafter invented, including photocopying and recording, or in any information storage or retrieval system, without permission in writing from the publishers.

Trademark notice: Product or corporate names may be trademarks or registered trademarks, and are used only for identification and explanation without intent to infringe.

British Library Cataloguing-in-Publication Data
A catalogue record for this book is available from the British Library

Library of Congress Cataloging-in-Publication Data
A catalog record for this book has been requested

ISBN: 978-1-03-256992-5 (pbk)
ISBN: 978-1-138-23034-7 (hbk)
ISBN: 978-1-315-38618-8 (ebk)

DOI: 10.4324/9781315386188

Typeset in Galliard
by Apex CoVantage, LLC

Publisher's Note
The publisher has gone to great lengths to ensure the quality of this reprint but points out that some imperfections in the original copies may be apparent.

Contents

List of figures and tables ... ix
List of abbreviations ... xii
Preface and acknowledgments ... xiii

1 "Structural disaster" behind extreme events: sociological reflection on Fukushima and beyond ... 1
   What is undetected behind risk society? 1
   Dual underdetermination 3
   "Structural disaster": beyond risk sociology 6
   Institutionalized secrecy: a SPEEDI story 9
   The chain of institutionalized secrecy and institutional inertia 12
   Sociological implications of structural disaster as a new framework 14
   Disaster matrix 19
   Structure of the book 21
   Broader sociological implications of "structure" 26

2 The theory of structural disaster: sector model and sociological path-dependency in the science-technology-society interface ... 28
   Intermingling of epistemological and ontological dimensions: the first step toward a sector model based on the foundation of the sociology of science and technology 29
   Basic terminologies to specify aspects of science, technology, and society: the second step to sector model 33
   Snapshot of what the sector model can reveal: a view through types of actors 41
   Sociological path-dependency as a dynamic theory of structural disaster 42

Following a precedent leads to non-rationality 45
Integration of static and dynamic frameworks: why has structural disaster been neglected for so long? 50

3 Institutionalized inaction by compliance: from the Great Kanto Earthquake to the nuclear village 53

Dual organizational structure of the governmental investigation committee 54
Quick fixes for problems at hand and lack of structural reform 58
Big subsidy in expectation of something unusual 59
After the Great Kanto Earthquake: a national research institute that works by inertia 63
Advanced defense nation versus high economic growth nation: recurring structural disaster 67
How nuclear power bills are drafted 74
The academic sector and institutionalized inaction: what comes at the end of long-standing structural disaster? 82
How to discern the credibility of expertise in the science-technology-society interface 84

4 Secrecy throughout war and peace: structural disaster long before Fukushima 87

Structural similarities between the Fukushima accident and little-known pre-war accident: from the perspective of structural disaster 87
Development trajectory of the Kanpon type and its pitfalls 90
The serious accident undisclosed: institutionalized secrecy during the wartime mobilization of science and technology 93
The hidden accident and outbreak of war with the United States and Britain: deciphering institutionalized secrecy 96
Sociological implications for the Fukushima accident: beyond dichotomous understanding of success or failure 102
SPEEDI revisited: from the perspective of structural integration and functional disintegration 105
Structural disaster across pre-war/military and post-war/non-military regimes 108

5 A structural disaster in environmentally friendly oceanic energy development: the hidden link between renewable energy and stratospheric ozone depletion 112

Social background of "new energy" technology development in Japan: the origin of the Sunshine project 112

Ocean energy development and global environmental assessment: the complex case of ocean thermal energy conversion (OTEC) 116
Subtler aspects of the complex relationship between OTEC and the global environment: an unexpected path revealing structural disaster 122
Feedback-for-learning channels inactivated 127
Reversible technological development and irreversible environmental change: decision-making process exhibiting structural disaster 129
Structural disaster, the precautionary principle, and "mild freezing" 135

6 **Structural disaster and the wind power regime: myth creation, myth destruction, and relevant outsiders**   139
The connection between structural disaster and path-dependency: select perspectives from important cases 140
Sociological path-dependency and the other side of the wind power regime: resolutions discordant with the realization of public interest 142
Relevant outsiders breaking the myth of wind power generation infeasibility: the case of M Project 154
Relevant outsiders creating a path to exporting domestically produced wind turbines: the case of N Project 156
Relevant outsiders after a mega-disaster: the case of Hokudan-machi 158
Fair public participation based on local knowledge: relevant outsiders versus choreographed outsiders 160
The quality of social decision-making processes 164

7 **To understand or not to understand?: infinite responsibility for HLW disposal, or ongoing structural disaster**   166
How to make visible and share the horizon of extreme events 167
Revealing the way to fix type-two underdetermination in HLW disposal 168
Hidden social model implicating infinite responsibility for HLW disposal: the Toyocho case 175
The hidden social model failed in HLW disposal: resistance in Toyocho 178
Subtler configurations of intra-sector and inter-sector relationships 182
Sociological implications of an ongoing structural disaster 186
Prospects for moving away from ongoing structural disaster 189

8 **Conclusion: renovating the principle of symmetry beyond a pre-established harmony between expertise, policy, and democracy** 192

Overall structure of the arguments developed throughout the book 192
A renovated principle of symmetry 199
Three proposals within the multiple-assumptions approach to structural disaster 201
A focus on drastic structural reform 208
The "certainty trough" and the distribution of power in social decision-making 209
Circular arguments in the science-technology-society interface 212
Looking toward the future 214

Appendix A: policy formulation and revision-related administrative documents prior to the establishment of the Agency of Technology (June 1940 to October 1941) from the Kokusaku Kenkyukai Archives 216
Appendix B: the results of gas chromatography analysis of a working fluid for OTEC 222
Notes 223
Bibliography 247
Index 271

Figures and tables

Figures

1.1	Two Types of Underdetermination: Scientific Knowledge and Policy	5
1.2	The Structure of Diverging Estimations of Risks	7
2.1	One-dimensional Narrative of Airfoil Development Trajectory	43
2.2	Alternative Narrative of Airfoil Development Trajectory	44
2.3	The Logical Skeleton of Path-Dependency Theory	48
2.4	Sociological Reformulation of Path-Dependency Theory	50
3.1	Organizational Structure of the Governmental Investigation Committee	57
4.1	Plane View of the Kanpon Type Turbine	92
4.2	Broken Part of a Blade in the Rinkicho Accident	99
4.3	Flow of SPEEDI-Related Information	106
5.1	Social Shaping of the Sunshine Project	114
5.2	Budgetary Evolution for the Sunshine Project: 1974–1984	115
5.3	The Concept of OTEC	118
5.4	Results of Quantitative Analysis of a Working Fluid for OTEC	119
5.5	The Concept of the First Working OTEC Pilot Plant	120
5.6	The First Evidence of an Ozone Hole	125
6.1	Fair Public Participation in the Selection of Technology	163
7.1	Configuration of Internal Structure within Sectors and the Intersectoral Relationships between Subsectors	183
7.2	Configuration of the New Relationships between Governmental and Citizen Subsectors	185
8.1	Multiple-Assumptions Transparent Communication Design in the Science-Technology-Society Interface	203
8.2	Multiple-Assumptions Transparent Expert Advice Design in the Science-Technology-Society Interface	205
8.3	Multiple-Assumptions Transparent Design for Public Funding for Academic Research in the Science-Technology-Society Interface	207
8.4	Certainty Trough	210
8.5	Power Distribution	211
8.6	Mismatch between Power and Certainty	211

Tables

1.1	Case Categories Presumed in the Original Guideline for Monitoring Environmental Radiation during Emergency Situations	10
1.2	Disaster Matrix for Comparison	20
2.1	Four Configurations of the Sociological Exploration of Science and Technology	34
2.2	Types of Actors	40
3.1	Different Investigation Committees Related to the Fukushima Accident	54
3.2	Items of Public Expenditure for the Siting of Nuclear Power Stations	60
3.3	Public Facilities Built by the Grants-in-Aid for the Promotion of the Power Source Location	62
3.4	Estimated Economic Effects from Subsidy and Grants-in-Aid on Power Source Siting Laws	63
3.5	Examples of Technological Swords to Plowshares (Excerpt)	68
3.6	Summary of Policy Formulation and Revision-Related Administrative Documents Prior to the Establishment of the Agency of Technology (June 1940 to October 1941)	69
3.7	The Government Sector's Process of Building Nuclear Energy Development and Utilization Regime	75
3.8	Composition of the Five Groups in the Nuclear Energy Industry at the Time of Formation	76
3.9	Nuclear Energy-Related Departments and Graduate Schools Founded in the 1950s	81
4.1	Nuclear Reactor Specifications at the Fukushima Daiichi Nuclear Power Plant	89
4.2	Geared Turbine Failures of Naval Vessels from 1918	91
4.3	References to the Rinkicho Accident	93
4.4	Discussions about Naval Vessels in the Imperial Diet: January 1930 – March 1940	95
4.5	Members of the Special Examination Committee by Section	97
4.6	Naval Turbine Failures Classified by Location: 1918–1944	98
4.7	Brief List of Military Secret Instructions Issued to Deal with the Rinkicho Accident: January 1938–December 1941	101
5.1	Sea Wreck Statistics in the Expected Sea Areas for OTEC Siting: 1976–1980	122
5.2	Patents Related to OTEC	123
5.3	Production Capacity of CFC Manufacturers in Japan: 1980–1990 (thousand tons)	124
5.4	OTEC-related Patents Granted since 1990	132
6.1	Wind Power Generation Capacity in Select Countries (2016)	144
6.2	List of Wind Turbine Failures by Cause	147
6.3	Sales of Major Wind Turbine Manufacturers Worldwide (2004)	149

6.4	Number of Wind Turbines Introduced by Imported versus Domestic Units (cumulative)	151
6.5	Relevant Outsiders Who Proved the Feasibility of Wind Turbines in Japan	155
6.6	Relevant Outsiders in Creating a New Path to Exporting Domestically Produced Wind Turbines to Africa	157
7.1	Subjects of Papers Pertaining to Risk Sciences in *Transactions of the Atomic Energy Society of Japan*, 2002–2011	173
7.2	Economic Effects Expected from HLW Disposal Estimated by NUMO	176
7.3	Financial State of Local Governments Showing Interests in the Geological Survey for HLW Disposal	177
7.4	Timelines of HLW Siting Failure in Toyocho in 2007	178
7.5	Articles in Local and Commercial Papers and Leaflets Created by Opposition Movements: 2006–2007	179

Abbreviations

AIT	(Agency of Industrial Technology, currently the National Institute of Advanced Industrial Science and Technology)
ANT	(Actor Network Theory)
HLW	(High-level Radioactive Waste)
JAEC	(Japanese Atomic Energy Commission)
JSPS	(Japan Society for the Promotion of Science)
METI	(Ministry of Economy, Trade and Industry)
MEXT	(Ministry of Education, Culture, Sports, Science and Technology)
MHI	(Mitsubishi Heavy Industries, Ltd.)
MITI	(Ministry of International Trade and Industry, currently METI)
NAIIC	(National Diet of Japan Fukushima Nuclear Accident Independent Investigation Commission)
NEDO	(New Energy and Industrial Technology Development Organization)
NISA	(Nuclear and Industrial Safety Agency)
NRC	(Nuclear Regulatory Commission)
NUMO	(Nuclear Waste Management Organization of Japan)
OTEC	(Ocean Thermal Energy Conversion)
SCJ	(Science Council of Japan)
SKB	(Swedish Nuclear Fuel and Waste Management Company)
SPEEDI	(System for Prediction of Environmental Emergency Dose Information)
SSK	(Sociology of Scientific Knowledge)
STA	(Science and Technology Agency, currently MEXT)
TEPCO	(Tokyo Electric Power Company)

Preface and acknowledgments

The spring weather was fine and everything was perfect. I was talking on the phone in my workroom when a huge tremor shook the building. I told myself that it would gradually decrease, so I kept talking. Contrary to my expectation, however, the tremor quickly increased in strength. I told my colleague, "You had better evacuate." "We have already," she answered. At this knowledge, I ran out onto the campus road and saw the huge, old trees swinging like pendulums along the side of the road, a sight like none other I had ever seen in my life.

This is my memory of experiencing the Great East Japan Earthquake. Next, the Fukushima Daiichi nuclear accident occurred, followed by rescue, recovery, and rebuilding. An uneasy feeling about the entire process stuck with me, even after the earthquake and accident, and it was related to these "after-events" themselves. If we could control the situation with the aim of getting back to the earlier state, it would be helpful for everyone; however, my intuition and the facts I ascertained during the process revealed that, in reality, it was quite different. Because of this, as a sociologist I was forced to face indecision and frustration in the middle of an extraordinary disaster. One day, I happened to recall that I had presented the concept of "structural disaster" in my book published in 2002 (Matsumoto 2002), and I hoped that it might be able to shape my persistent unease about the situation following the Great East Japan Earthquake and the Fukushima Daiichi nuclear accident (hereafter, abbreviated to just the Fukushima accident). While this book is based on an intense personal experience, the points herein far exceed the local issues involved in the Fukushima accident; on the contrary, the content in this book can be interpreted in a much more general context by any reader.

In the years since, various news outlets in Japan have reported that many evacuated children became targets of harassment in schools. Suppose you are one of these victimized children, and you find that the local accent, housing, food, and even the trees and plants are somehow different from those you have been used to seeing. Your parents might be far away, still living in Fukushima. When those children grow up and have their own children, in what words will they explain what they went through to the next generation?

Whatever the response of the Japanese government to the Fukushima accident may be from now and into the future, the untold but lived experiences of those who suffered from the Fukushima accident and of their families will be transmitted from generation to generation and accumulated in the social memory of the people. This is what was in my mind during the process of writing this book. Driven by this incentive, I have tried to "look through" the Fukushima accident to see what is beyond it.

Some parts of this book are based on talks and papers that I have given on various occasions; for example, Chapter 4 is a revised version of my paper given at the Advanced Summer School of Nuclear Engineering and Management with Social Scientific Literacy, held between July 31 and August 6, 2011, at the University of California, Berkeley. I would like to sincerely thank the late Joonhong Ahn, who lives on in my vivid memory as a productive organizer and excellent intellectual. The UT-SNU Joint Meeting, held on November 23, 2012, at the University of Tokyo also provided an opportunity to discuss portions of the ideas in Chapter 4. I am grateful to all participants of these meetings for their helpful comments.

The core idea of Chapter 5 was first presented at the United States – Japan seminar on mathematical sciences in 1996. Since then, revised versions of the paper have been read at seminars such as the Science and Technology Policy Research Unit, University of Sussex; the Center for Research into Innovation, Culture, and Technology, Brunel University; and the Center for the Sociology of Innovation (CSI), École des Mines. I thank the participants of these seminars for their useful comments. Particular thanks are due to Michael Lynch and Bruno Latour for their helpful suggestions and advice. Part of Chapter 6 was presented at the International Workshop on Social Decision-Making Process for Energy Technology Introduction, held on December 12–13, 2003, University of Tokyo. I thank all of these participants as well for their helpful comments.

In an effort to cross-check critical information obtained from some source materials, independent interviews were carried out in accordance with a modified Chatham House Rule in Chapter 6, wherein the names of some interviewees have been changed to initials only in order to obtain firsthand information from these insiders who required anonymity before consenting to share. In other cases, full names are given for interviews. In both cases, all information from these interviews is included in endnotes. Responsibility for any errors therein is entirely mine. I thank Kohta Juraku for his helpful comments on the manuscript of Chapter 7. I also thank Ryuma Shineha for his insightful arrangements for my visit to Fukushima. In preparing figures and tables, Chisato Katsuki, Ken Kawamura, Atsushi Sadamatsu, Yuji Tateishi, and Naomi Kaida provided much-appreciated assistance. Last but not least, I owe a lot to my wife Yasue, to whom I offer my profound thanks.

A part of the research for the book was funded by Grants-in-Aid for Scientific Research of Japan Society for the Promotion of Science, No. 26285107. I would like to express gratitude to the publishers for their permissions related to rewriting and reusing my articles and books for this current work, the full bibliographical information of which is acknowledged below.

Chapter 2

"Theoretical Challenges for the Current Sociology of Science and Technology: A Prospect for Its Future Development," *East Asian Science, Technology & Society: An International Journal* (Durham, NC: Duke University Press), 4(1), 2010: 129–136.

Chapter 4

"'Structural Disaster' Long before Fukushima: A Hidden Accident," *Development & Society* (Seoul: Seoul National University), 42(2), 2013: 165–190.

"The 'Structural Disaster' of the Science-Technology-Society Interface: From a Comparative Perspective with a Prewar Accident," in J. Ahn, C. Carson, M. Jensen, et al. eds. *Reflections on the Fukushima Daiichi Nuclear Accident.* New York: Springer, 2014, p. 189–214.

Technology Gatekeepers for War and Peace. London: Palgrave Macmillan, 2006, p. 159–172.

Chapter 5

"The Uncertain but Crucial Relationship between a 'New Energy' Technology and Global Environmental Problems," *Social Studies of Science* (London: Sage), 35(4), 2005: 623–651.

I would also like to express gratitude to MIT Press for their permissions to reuse a relevant figure from their publications for this book, the full bibliographical information of which is acknowledged below.

Figure 7.2, in Donald MacKenzie. *Inventing Accuracy: A Historical Sociology of Nuclear Missile Guidance.* Cambridge, Massachusetts: The MIT Press, 1990. p. 372.

1 "Structural disaster" behind extreme events
Sociological reflection on Fukushima and beyond

Extreme events are typically placed outside the range of sociology and social sciences literature, as researchers attempt to explore risk as well as decision-making under uncertainty (Clarke 2008). The term "extreme events" indicates severe incidents with a low probability of occurrence; however, when extreme events actually occur and when resulting damage is suspected to be incurred and amplified by social factors in addition to and/or in combination with natural disasters, relevant sociological frameworks to discern and specify these social factors should be explored. This book presents a new sociological framework to explore extreme events occurring within the nature-artifacts-society interface, such as the Fukushima nuclear accident, that focuses on the intersection of risk sociology and the sociology of science and technology.

The concept of a risk society, as well as the various arguments developed from this concept, is one of the most influential intellectual resources in a post-Fukushima world. In practical terms, recovery from the accident has required urgent and ongoing support for the victims of the accident, utilizing all available intellectual resource. Behind the serious and urgent questions regarding recovery and resilience, however, are subtle yet important sociological stories that have not been told and are difficult to reveal without devising a new narrative that differs from those typically used in the sociology of both risk and science and technology. Extreme events leading to a disaster can be a "melting pot," where anything heterogeneous – be it modern, post-modern, or non-modern – is mixed together, creating a new output that is difficult to identify via the use of earlier intellectual resources. This book seeks to take the lid off of this melting pot in a scholarly fashion in order to create a new horizon for reconciling techno-science and democracy in a fruitful way.

What is undetected behind risk society?

Various risk-related arguments are thriving today: the risk of economic calculations in fund management, epidemiological risk, the risk of natural disasters, and risk factors of incurring cancers. Among these, arguments based on the concept of risk society (Beck [1986]1992, 1987) have been the most conspicuous in sociology over the past 30 years. Since the occurrence of the Fukushima accident, considerably widespread use of the concept of risk society has been observable, appearing for the first time in 1986, the year of the Chernobyl nuclear accident. It is often difficult, however, for the concept of risk society to explain the sociological causes of the Fukushima accident, detect the precursors of a future one, or identify effective preventive measures, because most arguments that are based on this concept assume the pre-existence of risk society before investigating the characteristics of risk in a particular case; for example, Beck states: "In contrast to all earlier *epochs* (including industrial society), the risk society is characterized essentially by a *lack*: the impossibility of an *external* attribution of hazards" ([1986]1992: 183).

While the concept of risk society significantly contributed to a sociological distinction between danger and decision-related risks,[1] arguments mobilizing the concept of risk society have a tendency to find elements relevant to the Fukushima accident, which could be ascribed to and derived from risk society in an almost tautological manner.[2]

Beck's method of argument is exemplified as follows: "One can *possess* wealth, but one can only be *afflicted* by risks; they are, so to speak, *ascribed* by civilization; Risk society is a *catastrophic* society. In it the exceptional condition threatens to become the norm" ([1986]1992: 23–24). This argument is one step away from a view wherein severe accidents like Fukushima could be explained (and even predicted) by the transformation of an industrial society to risk society. In fact, in 2015, the following observation was made:

> When people begin to talk about the unforeseeable future of Japan, somebody will quickly mention the 'risk society' even though they don't necessarily understand what that concept actually means. Needless to say, such phenomenon increased after the huge earthquake, concomitant tsunami and the horrible disasters caused by the nuclear plant's meltdown in Fukushima in March of 2011.
>
> (Abe 2015)

In this way, the concept of risk society could justify, in a sense, ad hoc interpretations of an extreme event via hindsight, which perpetuates the self-reinforcing loop of risk society arguments.[3] What is missing, then, is theoretical specification of the conditions within which extreme events happen and, thereby, risk is turned into disaster, as the concept of risk society is too general to explain an individual extreme event. This kind of relevant specification is required to break the self-reinforcing loop of such risk society arguments and link the general concepts of risk and risk society with an individual extreme event in a meaningful way.

From such a viewpoint, the concept of "secrecy" embedded in the behaviors of heterogeneous agents before, during, and after accidents such as Fukushima have prompted us to re-examine the basic assumptions of prior sociological frameworks to treat the social dimensions of uncertainty and risk. This is because prior sociological frameworks have trended toward using scientific uncertainty and the associated risk as the noteworthy factors in understanding all kinds of uncertainty and risk and dismiss other types, such as those complicated by secrecy. This is not a matter of "naturalizing" or "sociologizing" risks (Murphy 2009: 32); rather, an extreme event like the Fukushima nuclear accident is so extraordinary that it reveals the irrelevance of ordinary assumptions embedded in former sociological discourse due to its hitherto unnoticed factors (for example, secrecy).

This chapter critically examines the sociological concept of risk and related arguments in view of the salient features present in the circumstances of the Fukushima accident. Based on this critique, requirements for new sociological frameworks for reconsidering uncertainty and risk are examined, and, in particular, the new concept of "structural disaster" is presented as a framework for properly understanding extreme events and for seeking feasible and pertinent solutions to crucial problems relating to them. This chapter then illustrates the power and implications of this new concept with reference to the System for Prediction of Environmental Emergency Dose Information (SPEEDI), the report on the High-level Radioactive Waste (HLW) disposal of the special committee of the Science Council of Japan (SCJ), and the governmental decontamination policy enacted after the Fukushima accident. The applicability of this new concept is then investigated with a comparative perspective for independent disasters that occurred in different times, places, and social contexts; based on this, a disaster matrix is formulated to systematically categorize different types of disasters. Based on the arguments developed above, this chapter lays out the overall plan of this book by summarizing each of the main points of subsequent chapters and offers prospects for the exploration of the still-unnoticed social dimension of uncertainty and risk.

Dual underdetermination

Understanding how indetermination can be due to the following factors can help to uncover the hidden social dimension of uncertainty and risk: the fragile nature of relationships between experts and the general public, changing budgetary limits, the need for "face-saving" in the public sphere, and the particularistic interests of a public body that need to be handled across the entire social process of policy-making, implementation, and evaluation. New sociological frameworks are required for the exploration of uncertainty and risk due to such factors in extreme events; for example, the unnoticed social dimension of uncertainty and risk in the Fukushima accident is related to the factors above.

This exploration concerns the extension of "underdetermination," which means the difficulty of strict one-to-one correspondence between scientific statements and empirical evidence. The concept is well-known and originated with the formulation of the Duhem-Quine thesis (Quine 1951) and Strong Program (Bloor 1976: 2–5); since then, the subsequent development of social constructionist studies on technology has enabled underdetermination to proliferate in a sociological way.[4] As a result, there are now many empirical studies on well-specified sociological accounts of underdetermination of expertise, which could ultimately lead to underdetermination of scientific knowledge.[5] If the latter occurs, this would mean that people are more likely to see the underdetermination of the entire process of policy-making, implementation, and evaluation in the science-technology-society interface. This is not only because indeterminate scientific knowledge is one of the key elements involved in the process but also because the process includes a different kind of underdetermination due to parameters such as the fragile nature of relationships between experts and the general public, changing budgetary limits, and others, as noted above.

This book refers to the underdetermination of scientific knowledge as "type-one underdetermination" and all other underdetermination involved in the process of policy-making, implementation, and evaluation as "type-two underdetermination" (see Figure 1.1).

This dual underdetermination has previously escaped scholarly attention, likely due to complications caused by its association with dichotomous phrases, such as the "technocratic way" of decision-making versus the "participatory way." As a result, various important questions posed by underdetermination have been neglected, failing to capture the subtler realities of relationships between experts, including scientists and engineers, and the general public in the context of their day-to-day activities.

To remedy this, examination of the unexplored realities of type-two underdetermination should be sought separately from those of type-one. In particular, the exploration of type-two underdetermination could answer questions in complicated borderline cases in the nature-artifacts-society interface. For example, the allocation of responsibility based on a clear distinction between victims and perpetrators is often impossible because in some cases there is a vast "gray zone" in which victims can also be perpetrators and vice versa. Examples of such cases may relate to global environmental problems (Matsumoto 2005; Edwards 2010), the political ecology around the sites of nuclear weapon arsenals (Masco 2006), and, more generally, "the tragedy of the commons" (Hardin 1968; Ostrom 1990; Buchanan and Yoon 2000; Dolsak and Ostrom 2003). However, human-caused extreme events in the public sphere necessitate distinct allocation of responsibility for incurring and/or aggravating the events. In this way, the sociological categorization of social actors, networks, groups, institutions, organizations, and systems can enable a better understanding of the reality beyond the dichotomous categories of perpetrators and victims.

Considering such a gray zone, it is crucial for new sociological frameworks to employ symmetrical categorization of agents both in the description and analysis of type-two underdetermination (and its associated risks) and the allocation of responsibility if it turns into a disaster during an emergency situation. To be more specific, the sociological categories of social actors, networks, groups, institutions, organizations, and systems should be equally assumed both in description and analysis and in the allocation of responsibility. The concept of structural disaster can further illuminate this point.

"Structural disaster" behind extreme events 5

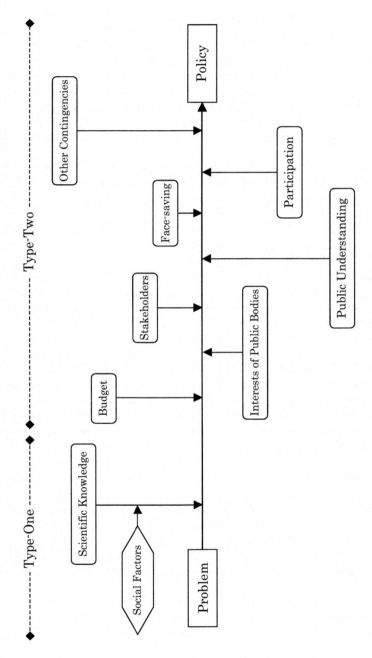

Figure 1.1 Two Types of Underdetermination: Scientific Knowledge and Policy

Note: This figure does not necessarily imply that factors take effect in this particular sequence nor such an effect is linear.

"Structural disaster": beyond risk sociology

Since risk is usually uncovered by estimating directly unobservable parameters, such as safety coefficients or the breakdown rate of novel components, the estimation of risk accompanies a considerable range of uncertainty, which can be corrected by introducing assumptions that could, in turn, be influenced by the social situations of those in charge of estimation. In its extreme, for example, the introduction of ad hoc assumptions could give rise to mutually opposite estimations of risk (for example, estimation *within* safety versus estimation *without*). In addition, it is not unusual that different assumptions leading to such disparate estimations are due to heterogeneous social situations among those who made them (see Figure 1.2).

A divergence in the risk assessment of the "Cambrian sheep" case (Wynne 1987, 1996) during the aftermath of the Chernobyl accident, the heavily context-dependent safety assessment of the nuclear reactors of electrical companies in the context of restarting them after the Fukushima accident, as well as other nuclear-related estimations (Eden 2004), can effectively illustrate this. Ultimately, the identification of a particular risk could be dependent not only on scientific knowledge but also on heterogeneous social situations; therefore, a particular social decision made in a particular social situation could be responsible for generating a particular kind of risk. Apart from risk society arguments, previous sociological studies on risk have focused on the subtler relationships between the responsibility of social decision-making, the contents of risk, and scientific knowledge.

Conversely, in the context of the allocation of responsibility for risk incurred as a result of decision-making, the agents in question have tended to be reduced either to human beings as a whole or to dichotomous agents, such as victims who are exposed to risk versus perpetrators who caused it (and can often escape from it) (Worm 1996; Connelly 2008). To explore extreme events within the nature-artifacts-society interface, it is necessary to sidestep such a bipolar categorization of agents, as the patterns of behavior among agents involved in extreme events who exist in the gray area between the victims versus perpetrators dichotomy could provide an in-depth look at the structural factors involved.

Here, the new concept of "structural disaster" can provide a deeper understanding of the social backgrounds of extreme events, detect a previously unforeseen precursor of similar events, and devise appropriate measures against future events. The term "structural disaster" is defined as a state consisting of one or more of the following characteristics (Matsumoto 2012: 46, 2014: 191):[6]

1. Adherence to erroneous precedents, which can cause problems that are carried over and reproduced.
2. The complexity of a system under consideration and the interdependence of its units, which can aggravate problems.

"Structural disaster" behind extreme events 7

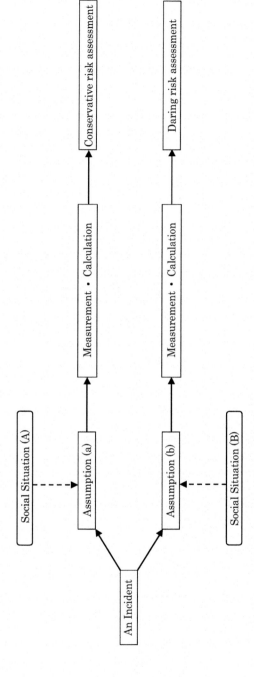

Figure 1.2 The Structure of Diverging Estimations of Risks

Note: "Conservative" and "Daring" represent a mutually diverging risk assessments of an incident. Dotted lines indicate the possibility of external influences from heterogeneous social situations.

3 The invisible norms of informal groups, which essentially hollow out formal norms.
4 Quick fixes to the problems at hand, which lead to further such fixes as temporary counter measures.
5 Secrecy developing across different sectors, which blurs the locus of those agents responsible for the problems that need to be addressed.

The concept of structural disaster in the science-technology-society interface was developed to provide a sociological account of the repeated occurrence of similar type failures (Matsumoto 2002: 25–27). Structural disaster can clarify a situation in which novel and undesirable events have happened but where there is no single agent to blame and no way to prescribe remedies. The reason for denominating a disaster as a failure of the science-technology-society interface rather than that of science, technology, or society independently is critical to understanding the development of this book's primary argument. For example, if nuclear physics is completely successful in explaining a chain reaction, then how did technology such as nuclear engineering fail in controlling the reaction, as in the case of Chernobyl and its aftermath (Wynne 1996)? Similarly, if nuclear engineering is nearly successful in containing radioactive materials within reactors, then how did social decision-making fail, as in the case of Three-Mile Island (Perrow 1984, 1999, 2007; Walker 2004)? If society is completely successful in setting goals for the development of renewable energy technologies, then how could science and/or technology fail, as in the case of Ocean Thermal Energy Conversion (Matsumoto 2005)?

In short, the success or failure of science, technology, and society are intimately interwoven but cannot be overlapped (Latour [1993]1996; Hecht 2012). In particular, there seems to be something missing "in between" that has unique characteristics of its own; for example, institutional arrangements (Fricke and Moore 2006), organizational routines (Vaughan 1996; Eden 2004), tacit interpretations of a formal code of ethics or protocols (Jobin 2013), invisible customs and semantics behind real-time logics (Perin 2005), or the networks of different organizational interests. The failure to interface can be an indicator of one or more of these states of affairs.

This book focuses on, among other things, structural similarity in the patterns of behavior of heterogeneous agents that interact in the science-technology-society interface under a specific social condition. Of course, "structural" here does not privilege commensurability and/or pure formality without corrosive elements. What is described through the concept of structural disaster could be either commensurable or incommensurable; it could have more or fewer corrosive elements depending on the time, place, and social contexts of a disaster (Fortun 2001: 366–367). Rather, what is asserted is that if structural similarity is observed among heterogeneous agents within and without disasters, this could have its own clarifying power to observers apart from its meanings to the agents involved. By focusing on persistent secrecy before, during, and after the Fukushima accident, this chapter explores the power of the concept of structural disaster.

Institutionalized secrecy: a SPEEDI story

One of the most salient patterns of behavior among heterogeneous agents before, during, and after the Fukushima accident is "institutionalized secrecy." The concept of institutionalized secrecy does not concern personal attitude but rather the outcomes of institutional interactions between science, technology, and society. Specifically, institutionalized secrecy is defined as a legitimate way to keep public knowledge within the boundaries of institutional design, often to the detriment of the general public.[7] The SPEEDI exemplifies this pertinently.

The SPEEDI was developed in 1984 to make the early evacuation of potentially affected people smoother and safer. The first recommendation from the government for evacuation following the Fukushima accident was made on March 12, 2011, immediately after the accident; however, the prediction obtained from the SPEEDI was not made public until April 26. As a result of this secrecy, the people who were affected were advised by the government to evacuate without being given critical information during the initial phase, when they were exposed to a high-level dose of radiation.

A similar behavioral pattern of government secrecy and subsequent suffering can be observed in various other cases associated with the accident, such as the delayed venting of the nuclear reactors in the Fukushima Daiichi Nuclear Power Plant, the deregulation of using decontaminated mud for concrete production, the rise and fall of dosage levels allowed for children in primary schools or station workers, and others. In particular, the SPEEDI provides helpful indicators to uncover and explore in depth the ways in which organizational errors were hidden and then revealed in this particular case, all of which were institutionally legitimized in the science-technology-society interface.

The SPEEDI is the first system in Japan designed to "predict the diffusion of radioactive materials emitted in the atmosphere and the amount of dose due to nuclear accidents." The end of this prediction is the early evacuation of potentially affected people; however, this bit of information was not revealed at the critical moment of the actual evacuation. Contrary to a popular story about the SPEEDI, this was not due to a lack of helpful prediction; in fact, according to a statement made by the Nuclear and Industrial Safety Agency (NISA) that was made public after the accident (NISA 2012), the SPEEDI carried out an estimation to predict the effect of the venting of reactor No. 2 at 21:12 on March 11, the day of the accident. According to the *ex post* confirmation of the estimation by SPEEDI, the estimation showed that the contaminated area could be concentrated in the area northwest of the power station, including Namiecho and Futabacho, both of which were ultimately found to be heavily contaminated.[8]

When the government advised people to evacuate, however, only a wide area (indicated by a concentric circle) was given as a guideline to those affected, without information on the distribution of contamination. As a result, many people around the Fukushima Daiichi Power Plant evacuated from their residences in a northwest direction, toward the heavily contaminated area. This reveals a sharp contradiction between the purpose of the evacuation for which the SPEEDI was originally developed and the actual behavior of the ministry in charge – the Ministry of Education, Culture, Sports, Science and Technology (MEXT) – which withheld critical information. The lack of accurate and observational data was inexcusable, particularly because the SPEEDI's prediction, roughly matching the observational data,[9] could have indicated something helpful in terms of the distribution of contamination.

Thus, there exists a contradiction between the end of the SPEEDI prediction and its actual utilization, one that makes the situation difficult to understand in integrated terms. The concept of structural disaster, however, enables a view of this disintegrated state of affairs to be the result of a common mode failure of the science-technology-society interface caused by institutionalized secrecy. To prove the grounds for this assertion, it is necessary to discuss additional details regarding the ways in which matters are kept secret in accordance with a particular institutional design.

The key to this burden of proof is the Guideline for Monitoring Environmental Radiation prepared by the Nuclear Safety Commission before the Fukushima accident, which stipulated in detail the utilization of the SPEEDI. According to the guideline, the goal of monitoring during an ordinary situation is "protecting the health and safety of the inhabitants around nuclear facilities" (Nuclear Safety Commission 2008: 3), and that the goal of monitoring during emergency situations is to "collect necessary information for estimating the effects of radioactive materials and radiation on the inhabitants around nuclear facilities" (Nuclear Safety Commission 2008: 15). As such, the goal of "protecting health and safety" clearly transforms to "estimating the effects of radioactive materials and radiation." When the goal is "protecting health and safety," damage to health and safety would indicate failure of the guideline, and when the end is "estimating effects," such damage can occur without challenging the success of the guideline because the possibility of "estimating effects" at the cost of "health and safety" is not excluded.

This is significant because the divergence between estimation and protection was derived from the guideline itself. Not utilizing the predicted diagrams of the SPEEDI for the evacuation of people around nuclear facilities like the Fukushima plant is stipulated as fully permissible in the original institutional design (see Table 1.1).

Table 1.1 Case Categories Presumed in the Original Guideline for Monitoring Environmental Radiation during Emergency Situations

Estimating effects \ Health & safety	Protect	Not protect
Contribute	Permissible	Permissible
Not contribute	Irrelevant	Impermissible

Note: "Irrelevant" means the case that is outside the goal of the guideline.

Source: Produced based on Nuclear Safety Commission (2008).

Secrecy coupled with inaction was a by-product of an anticipated institutional design. Suffering that resulted from the Fukushima accident was not due to the complexity of the nature-artifacts-society interface and the associated risk and uncertainty; rather, it was due to, primarily, structural characteristics such as institutionalized secrecy that underlie individual behaviors and were embodied in the institutional design.

This is the locus wherein the concept of structural disaster has power, because suffering is not caused by breaking rules but rather by compliance with a particular institutional design. In the current stipulation of laws and ordinances and the unduly limited utilization of the SPEEDI, secrecy is neither rule-breaking nor ethically questionable; instead, it is institutionalized as appropriate behavior to fix the type-two underdetermination between policy and reality.

Institutionalized secrecy presumes a fairly long duration of time for the process of various secrecies to institutionalize. In other words, different cases of secrecy throughout the past make up "institutionalized secrecy" and therefore have direct impact on cases taking place over a fairly long duration of time. Structural disaster, then, is a theoretical framework wherein institutionalized secrecy is a particular type of secrecy, so the relationship between theoretical frameworks and historical cases constitutes a strategic research problem in terms of the organization of this book, one that could distinguish the book from others related to the Fukushima accident.

There are two major intersections where theoretical frameworks and historical cases are systematically integrated within the general theme of structural disaster in this book:

1   The sociologically reformulated path-dependent mechanism can explain the emergent process leading to over-reliance on nuclear power generation as well as the process leading to under-reliance on generation by renewable energy (Chapters 5 and 6); opposite historical processes which, respectively, paved the way for the social background behind the Fukushima accident. This explanation focuses on the mechanism that gives rise to structural disaster via different historical cases and has two important meanings: first, the seemingly opposite ways in which a given purpose could be dominated by a similar social mechanism such as a "nuclear village" and the renewable energy regime, which eventually led to devastating and extreme events; second, such a structural similarity is not the outcome of intended social action, but rather an unintended outcome of purposive social action of rational agents maximizing their own benefit within the bounds of contingent local conditions. To illustrate these meanings of structural disaster, it is necessary to couple historical cases with a sociologically reformulated path-dependent mechanism.
2   Institutionalized secrecy, another mechanism of structural disaster – or, more generally, institutionalized inaction in the Fukushima accident – can and should be illustrated by historical case studies because this mechanism originated in a long-term accumulation of ad hoc institutional design in

energy policy starting in the 1950s in Japan, which shows a strong structural similarity in wartime mobilization process of science and technology in pre-war Japan (Chapters 3 and 4). In particular, institutionalized inaction culminating in collective irresponsibility for crucial national decision-making penetrates both processes, either the outbreak of war or radioactive contamination, as is detailed in Chapter 4.

Thus, the coupling of theoretical frameworks such as sociologically reformulated path-dependency and institutionalized inaction within historical cases is essential to explaining structural disaster. This coupling also enables the book to cut across the long-standing dichotomy of nuclear versus renewable, wartime versus peacetime, and, more generally, techno-science versus society.

The chain of institutionalized secrecy and institutional inertia

As stated, this book discusses secrecy as an institutionally legitimated state rather than the personal attitude of particular individuals in an effort to expand the sociological implications of structural disaster. Because inertia resulting from the past track record of an institution is much greater than that of an individual, introducing a "secret" to fulfill an institution's accountability is likely to yield something that is difficult to explain consistently; in turn, this will necessitate another secret to disguise the inconsistency and the same could follow in perpetuity.

A significant sociological implication of the chain of institutionalized secrecy from the viewpoint of structural disaster can be illuminated by the role of "lay experts" (Collins and Evans 2002; Collins, Evans, and Weinel 2017). These lay experts are often invited to participate in the social decision-making process regarding sensitive public issues, such as high-level waste (HLW) disposal, as a high degree of type-one underdetermination affects experts' ability to provide unique or optimum solutions. The term "lay experts" here indicates not only non-specialists, such as politicians, bureaucrats, and local residents, but also specialists in other fields who have little expertise regarding the particular issue.

The key question to be posed with lay experts is as follows: "Who will take responsibility for anything detrimental to the lay people when they are invited to participate in situations where there could be institutionalized secrecy and its chain?" In the post-Fukushima context, the Report of the Special Committee on HLW disposal of SCJ is an excellent illustration of this scenario (SCJ 2012). HLW disposal is a persistent problem, particularly regarding diffusion of radioactive materials through eco-systems, such as the underground water system, and (as after the Fukushima accident) even if it is "under control."[10]

What is noteworthy and important is that a rudimentary report error was suspected by an expert: the report was assumed to have "rediscovered" the concept of temporary storage without correct expertise from the experts of HLW disposal" (Ahn 2013). For example, no conceptual distinction between retrievability and reversibility is made in the report, despite the fact that retrievability and geological disposal have been unduly dichotomized without reference to the fact that, in many cases, retrievability is part of geological disposal (SCJ 2012: 16–17; Lehtonen 2010).

Because it was not until this external evaluation from abroad was made that such an error was detected in the report (that is to say, after the report was made public following review by the members of the due committees of the SCJ), it can be assumed that there were few experts on HLW disposal in the committees who drafted and approved the report. This means that the SCJ self-negates the academic sector because the special committee may have skipped substantially relevant peer reviews and neglected expertise. It should be noted that since 1986, the criterion for membership in SCJ was changed to nomination by the prime minister; in addition, without external evaluation, the report error would have remained secret from the members of the committees as well as from the general public.[11] Such secrecy is devastating not only to the SCJ, as it is purported to be "the representative organization of the Japanese scientist community ranging over all fields of sciences subsuming humanities, social sciences, life sciences, natural sciences, and engineering" (SCJ 2015), but also to affected local residents, who would be invited to participate in the social decision-making process regarding the areas to be nominated as candidates for HLW disposal, unaware of the chain of institutionalized secrecy occurring. As posed above: "Who will take responsibility for such a situation?" Without breaking the institutional inertia that reinforces the kind of tribalism within and without a nuclear village such as this example, it is conceivable that collective irresponsibility would emerge as a manifestation of structural disaster.

The governmental policy of encouraging affected people in Fukushima to return to their original residences through decontamination provides another example of merging lay experts, the chain of institutionalized secrecy, and the possibility of collective irresponsibility caused by institutional inertia. The governmental policy was intended to encourage people in the designated evacuation areas to return to their original residences within a few years by decontaminating said areas, though the scientific evidence of the safety of this plan has not been made public. If evidence-based policy is advocated by the government, it is required that everyone, as a lay expert, is able to ascertain the evidence for the policy whenever necessary. As far as the concept of evidence is correctly understood, the provision of such for examination in the public sphere is not the end state but rather the initial state from which decision-making should begin. For example, in the case of the decontamination policy, lay people's understanding of contamination would require revision of scientific evidence in order for it to align with the reality of the situation (Nakanishi et al. 2013; Ahn et al. 2014; Nakanishi and Tanoi 2016).

A decontamination policy that is designed under the expectation that the evacuated local inhabitants would return to their original residences within a few years (Ministry of the Environment 2012: 3–5) must be built on sufficient evidence from the start; however, in the case of Fukushima, the governmental decontamination policy predated the release of scientific evidence that is still in the process of being updated. For example, it is highly probable that there is tremendous inequality in the distribution of radioactive materials and dose levels across areas; similarly, the total quantity of radioactive material may gradually decrease over a longer period of time, possibly extending over several dozen years. This indicates that the policy was made and implemented without the assistance of scientific evidence, whether it was the best available or not.

While the Environmental Agency reported in December 2013 that the term of the governmental evacuation policy should be extended for another three years due to difficulty during decontamination, there is no widely acknowledged scientific evidence made public that endorses this extension (Tateishi 2016). Introducing additional secrecy of this kind in the governmental decontamination policy that cancels a repopulation of those affected could invite suspicion about the Ministry of Environment's capability to create a valid roadmap of decontamination with fair compensation throughout the affected communities. Since Chernobyl, however, compensation could be considered "an attempt to balance or neutralize opposing forces" (Petryna 2013: 218). In addition, most governmental officials of the former NISA were transferred to the Environmental Agency for undisclosed reasons (an example of yet another level of institutionalized secrecy).[12]

A retroactive introduction of institutionalized secrecy might occur to "save the face" of the governmental sector and retain legitimacy of one created policy and implementation of another. In such a situation, evidence-based policy could be used to confirm the social legitimacy of stakeholders – such as the governmental sector before, during, and after the Fukushima accident – rather than scientific evidence for the evacuated residents. When a self-legitimation loop of this kind cuts across different sectors, multiple tribalism including the nuclear village, will coexist without confronting and tackling structural disaster. In such a situation, the chain of institutionalized secrecy could continue in tandem with institutional legitimacy, the state in which structural disaster could be the common mode failure of the science-technology-society interface.

Sociological implications of structural disaster as a new framework

It is appropriate in this context to examine the applicability of structural disaster to other kinds of disasters from a comparative perspective. If the elements of structural disaster can be substantiated in other independent cases, then pertinent sociological implications from the Fukushima accident (as a structural disaster) can be obtained, and these implications can be extended to potential future extreme events. To this end, an almost unknown accident that happened long before Fukushima deserves mention because it epitomizes the sociological nature of the institutionalized secrecy that is involved in structural disaster.

The accident involves standard military technology developed by the Imperial Japanese Navy that occurred immediately before the outbreak of World War II

(WWII). Looking through the lens of structural disaster, this accident reveals that the science-technology-society interface was already sustained by institutionalized secrecy in critical, national decision-making during the pre-war period. The sociological implications of this accident originate within a social context, in which organizational errors arose and were kept secret in relation to wartime mobilization of science and technology. As will be detailed in Chapter 4, the accident was classified as top secret and was never disclosed either within or without the military-industrial-university complex at the time of the submitted final reports on November 2, 1938. Neither the Imperial Diet nor other agents of the military-industrial-university complex were aware of the accident or remediation measures.[13]

This functional disintegration of the relationships between the military and other sectors was occurring at this time, when the structural integration of the military-industrial-university complex was formally being reinforced by the Wartime Mobilization Law and the Research Mobilization Ordinance. Such a coupling of structural integration and functional disintegration could provide a suitable perspective for understanding structural disaster in the current context. For example, if the Fukushima accident can be considered a structural disaster from such a perspective, it should also contain the coupling of structural integration and functional disintegration. In this case, functional disintegration of the relationships linking Tokyo Electric Power Company (TEPCO) officials and the reactor designers of heavy electric equipment manufacturers could have been taking place at the time when the structural integration of the government-industrial-university complex was formally reinforced by the laws revolving around the "double-check" system within a single ministry in the past and between the Ministry of Economy, Trade and Industry (METI), and the Ministry of the Environment today.

By comparing the pre-war social context of wartime mobilization of science and technology and the current social and historical context of the Fukushima accident through the concept of structural disaster, basic questions about the concept are due to be re-examined. First, what constitutes a "disaster" and what makes it "structural"? In light of the five characteristics of structural disaster defined earlier as well as the historical perspective mentioned above, the concept implies that an institutionally legitimized collective action can generate and/or amplify devastating outcomes. Institutionalized secrecy bears on institutional interaction between science, technology, and society through the exchange of money, information, goods, and human resources. What makes a situation a "disaster" is the sharp contrast between the legitimate working of institutionalized collective action and unintended but devastating outcomes imposed on individuals. Relatedly, this book highlights the coexistence of the legitimate working of institutionalized collective action and unintended but devastating outcomes whose damage tends to surpass the institutional capability of the relevant systems. This book uses the term "disaster" in this connotation.[14]

What makes a disaster structural is the state in which devastating outcomes result not from outside but from within. The possibility of functional disintegration through structural integration coupled with the suppression of negative information under the guise of communication activities could manifest the symptom of "structural" in the current context of the Fukushima accident. While Café Scientifique was designed to facilitate communication between science, technology, and society well before the Fukushima accident,[15] it turns out only one previous Café Scientifique event series had been held on anything nuclear (held on July 24, 2010) out of the 253 carried out in the Tohoku district, including the Fukushima prefecture, and had nothing to do with the risks of nuclear power plants (Matsumoto 2012: 166–167, 2014: 211).[16] The institutionalized activities designed to facilitate communication between science, technology, and society, then, played no active role in early warning, nor in managing the social factors that influenced responses to the warning (Mileti 1999: 191–192).

The intention of comparing the pre-war social context of wartime mobilization of science and technology and the current social context of the Fukushima accident through the lens of structural disaster is not to associate the nuclear village with pre-war Japanese militarism; rather, the intent of this book is to clarify the structural similarity of the behavior patterns among heterogeneous organizations and social factors interacting with techno-scientific systems by employing the comparative perspective of a nuclear village in the current context and the military-industrial-university complex in the context of wartime mobilization in pre-war Japan.

The nuclear village in this book indicates that the governmental-industrial-university complex functions to blur the conflicts of interest between the promotion and regulation of nuclear power generation through the institutionally legitimized bureaucratic control that is specific to Japanese customs and traditions, such as retired government officials landing jobs in the governmental and/or industrial sector (*amakudari*) (Congressional Research Service 2011). However, cross-cutting heterogeneous agents (for example, nuclear village in this sense), the renewable energy regime, and the military-industrial-university complex through the concept of structural disaster does not provide an explanation by appealing to Japanese culture. On the contrary, this book shows that the concept can serve as a tool to go beyond cultural essentialism into factors that are intrinsic to the agents involved, by delving into much deeper socio-historical factors for explanation.

As to the usage of the term "structural disaster," focusing on the Fukushima accident alone will not, in itself, prove this book's primary argument. Rather, focusing on what the Fukushima accident means is dependent on singling out conceptual frameworks. According to the conceptual framework of structural disaster, not only the coverage of arguments but their depth could be made richer by using more than a single issue-oriented approach due to the integration of seemingly heterogeneous issues within the common conceptual framework of structural disaster. For example, the concept allows a significant and meaningful link to other structural disasters after the Great Kanto earthquake in 1923 (see Chapter 3), the above-mentioned hidden military accident in pre-war Japan (see Chapter 4), renewable energy issues such as ocean energy (see Chapter 5) and wind turbines (see Chapter 6), as well as HLW disposal issues (see Chapter 7), among others.

The reason why the concept of structural disaster can enrich such links is that there is a strong structural similarity of the social mechanisms throughout nuclear villages and other social institutions such as renewable energy regimes, long-standing national research institutes, the military-industrial-university complex, and others. For example, regarding the renewable energy regime, wind turbine development and generation was deemed infeasible in Japan, and this myth was reinforced through a subsequent path-dependent social process. A similar social mechanism can be detected in the myth of safety in nuclear power generation and the subsequent path-dependent social process that reinforces this myth. The result is a state of "lock-in" where retreat from renewable energy occurs and a trend toward nuclear power coexisted, which eventually formed the primary social background of the devastating Fukushima accident. However, there are dimensions to be carefully considered before drawing sociological implications from structural disasters, such as the distinction between slow and fast; dynamic and static; short-term and long-term; universal and local; and equilibrium and non-equilibrium.

As to the distinction between slow and fast,[17] what is structural corresponds more naturally to the "slow"; however, this designation is dependent on whether the process in which events unfold is accumulative or not. If accumulative, the essential features of events that happened in the past provides social context in which other, subsequent events occur so that the features will be remembered/accumulated and form a structure for the process. In such a case, structural disaster corresponds to slow, extreme events. If each event, however, happens and develops independently of one another to form a random stochastic process, then slowness simply means that events happen and develop slowly without accrued meaning of the formation of structure in the process. In addition, as far as the mode in which extreme events happen and develop is concerned, the concept of structural disaster is presented here in such a way to simultaneously include "explosive" and "creeping" as different aspects of a single disaster (Matsumoto 2002, 2012).[18] In the aftermath of Fukushima, the above discrimination deserves careful attention with deliberate reflection on multiple socio-historical factors involved in order to investigate and understand the long-term outcomes of the Fukushima accident.

As to the distinction between dynamic and static categories, structural disaster contains both, as is detailed in Chapter 2. When the term "structural" is interpreted in the sociological context, it means relatively stable patterns of interaction of agents, which tend to crystalize in a configuration of social roles in a given social situation. Thus, "structural" corresponds to the static aspect, as exemplified above by the institutional design that stipulated the social role of the utilization of SPEEDI in an emergency situation. Conversely, because such an institutional design is not pre-ordained but rather created by due social process, we can ask what kind of social process is involved in creating a particular institutional design. In this context, "structural" means a dynamic social process and related social conditions, through which relatively stable patterns of agents' interactions emerge and crystalize in a particular institution. For this reason, "structural" in this book signifies both static and dynamic categories depending on the phase being discussed within the broader process in which events unfold. The patterns of behavior among heterogeneous agents, which are the key to disclosing a structural similarity across heterogeneous cases, are structural in this sense.

Another meaning of the term "structure" is relevant due to the way in which static aspects get coupled with dynamic ones. If a static aspect of structure indicates relatively stable patterns of agents' interactions together with a tendency to crystalize in a configuration of social roles in a given social situation, structure, then, should function as a guiding rule to condition the behaviors of the agents involved. Since the possible courses of behavior are omnifarious from one particular social situation to another, structure provides agents with "heuristics" (Martin 2009: 16–20) that enable them to find a plausible course of behaviors and associated meaning in exchange for accepting constraints on the vast meaning of lived experience. In other words, the wide range of meaningful lived experience is repressed by structure in a static sense and therefore will inevitably seek an outlet for expressing itself.

Going back to the example of using the SPEEDI, those in charge of utilizing this tool must have faced a virtual dilemma: whether to help people in designated areas evacuate by immediately making public the prediction of SPEEDI, even though such a behavior would deviate from the stipulated institutional design for which they were working. Under such a dilemma, the repressed meaning of a lived experience could provide potential energy for justifying a course of behaviors already taken, rather than soliciting a reflexive way of thinking that would change the institutional design under which many stakeholders are obliged to work. Namely, the static aspect of structure tends to generate a significant amount of energy from the lived experience of agents involved, and the energy tends to be dynamically mobilized to reinforce the given structure rather than to change it. This is another reason why the path-dependent process could be regarded as a basic social mechanism that would eventually lead to structural disaster. The overall foundation of this mechanism is described in detail in Chapter 2.

There are also two different ways to understand structure when referring to the distinction between something universal and something local. The way to regard structure as universal is evident in structuralism ranging from the social sciences, such as anthropology (Lévi-Strauss 1958), sociology (Merton 1957), linguistics (Saussure 1916; Chomsky 1975), to physics (Poincaré 1902; Kuhn 1962), among others. In anthropology, observers can deduce the kinship structure that spans different communities; in sociology, the configuration of expectations, roles, and statuses constitute social structures throughout different societies; in linguistics, the distinctive features of particular words in phonology or the transformational and/or generative grammar at the syntactical level can determine linguistic structures; in physics, the structure of symbolic generalization is preserved from one operation to another in the deduction process or in multiple problem areas. The common thread throughout this way of understanding structure is the idea that the concept indicates something universal being constant throughout time, space, and/or the rules of transformation. In this understanding, structural disaster means that universal characteristics are observable over time, space, and social contexts even in abstract forms, which represent the unfolding process of a series of events taking place in these contexts.

At the other end of the spectrum, locally contingent and specified senses of structure can be found in relational sociology that can be traced back to Georg Simmel ([1908]1950). Contrary to a popular perception of formal sociology, "relationships" in relational sociology make sense only in a setting where an individual has a specific interaction with another particular individual in a specific social situation, as exemplified by friendships and patronage. Structure, then, is understood within the particular patterns of concatenation of concretely bound relationships that can change incessantly over a relatively short period of time only within localized settings (that is to say, within a microscopic world). Network analysis based on graph theory (Gould 1991) and/or ethnomethodological conversation analysis (Suchman 1987) can provide tools to depict a snapshot of such a structure bound within a relatively short period of time.[19]

In addition, a universal structure entails abstract features appearing throughout a relatively long time period, while local structure entails concrete features detectable within a relatively short time period. The usage of such concepts in this book verges on universal structure rather than local with a couple of modifications: first, structure is universal but not pre-ordained, so that it has its own process by which it can emerge; second, structure is open to change over a long time period. Therefore, structure in this book has both a universal and dynamic nature; for the latter, this means that it is open to change and is quite different from the adjustment process from a non-equilibrium to equilibrium state.

To further clarify the nature of the arguments asserted in this book, the sociological standpoint employed implies that it is difficult to make a distinction between the science-technology-society interface in wartime and that in peacetime by appealing to the contrastive purposes of war and commercialism. Evidence to support this includes the institutional design of the science-technology-society interface created during the wartime mobilization of science and technology, which has undergone a spin-off to accommodate nuclear energy generation in post-war Japan (Matsumoto 2012) as well as a complex combination of "spin-on and de facto spin-off" (Matsumoto 2006: 111), which can be observed in different social contexts.

Based on this confirmation and elaboration of the sociological implications of structural disaster, heterogeneous historical cases will be examined, and the common features and differences of the relevant social processes involved will illustrate social mechanisms generating and working with structural disaster. The reason for investigating the nature of structural disaster in such a scrupulous manner is because a failure to break the social mechanisms can lead to structural disaster because of face-saving measures taken in the public sphere, where a higher type-two underdetermination resides. This could generate a devastating event that is uncontrollable and irreversible for all agents.

Disaster matrix

The concept of structural disaster is thus applicable to an independent case and has implications that exceed the straightforward understanding of a single

20 *"Structural disaster" behind extreme events*

Table 1.2 Disaster Matrix for Comparison

Dimension \ Relevant factors	Adherence	Complexity	Invisible norms	Quick fix	Secrecy
Individual action					
Social relation					
Social group					
Institution/organization					
Social system					

Note: "Adherence" means adherence to erroneous precedents; "Complexity" means the complexity of a system under consideration; "Invisible norms" means the invisible norms that hollow out formal norms; "Quick fix" means quick fixes for problems at hand for temporary countermeasures; "Secrecy" means secrecy blurring the locus of agents responsible.

extreme event such as the Fukushima accident. Here, it is important to focus on both the dimensions of the disasters and the relevant factors involved concurrently; the former should express symmetrical sociological categorization of agents, and the latter should include the elements of structural disaster (see Table 1.2).[20]

Major concepts that could explain disasters can be located in applicable cells. For example, the concept of "normal accidents" (Perrow 1984, 1999), which is based on the case of Three-Mile Island, can be regarded as underlining the probability of catastrophic techno-scientific system accidents by way of "complexity" and the unexpected "coupling" of system elements. This concept, however, also tends to pay little attention to the dimensions of inter-organizational relations and relationships between organizations and the social system as a whole.

The concept of "normalization of deviance" (Vaughan 1996) that is based on a nearly ten-year investigation of the space shuttle *Challenger* disaster can be seen as highlighting the invisible yet formal norms hollowed out by informal groups within organizations, with little attention to the dimensions of inter-organizational relations and the intricate relationships between organizations and the social system as a whole.[21] The concept of ritualized "procedural rationalism" (Wynne 1982: 172–176), which is based on the case of Britain's Windscale fire in 1957 and its aftermath, can be understood as a tool for clarifying the danger of using quick fixes as more than just temporary countermeasures, but the concept does not consider the intricate relationships between individual organizations and the social system as a whole. Concepts that could be included in the matrix could be enlarged with an almost similar tendency: the relative lack of attention to the dimensions of inter-organizational relations and/or their intricate relationships with social systems as a whole when exploring extreme events.

There have been many single issue case studies on disasters conducted on both dimensions of individual action through institutions and organizations. These provide an in-depth understanding of important features of disasters, such as the effects of following in the footsteps of erroneous precedents in extreme events such as the Chernobyl accident (Kuchinskaya 2014; Schmid 2015). There are also case studies on the particular organizations that make up the nuclear regime, such as the Lawrence Livermore Laboratory (Gusterson 1996) and the Atomic Energy Commission (Balogh 1991), which provide exemplars of a "normal state" amidst the risk of nuclear warfare. There seem to be few studies, however, with an explicit theoretical perspective for examining the applicability of insights into single issues that could apply to the multiple dimensions and/or factors within the disaster matrix. A considerable portion of these single issue case studies focus on "organizational tragedy" (Weick 2009: 209–221), such as mistakes, vulnerability, and spontaneous occurrences within organizational boundaries.

Against the background of this general mapping, structural disaster could redress a bias that favors the internal structure of an organization by opening the boundaries of organizations to incorporate relevant heterogeneous organizations. Such inclusiveness would indicate a higher degree of complexity – including both "intended rationality" (Jones 2001: 54) and "bounded rationality" (March and Simon 1993: 157–192, 225–226) – within organizational boundaries. Conversely, structural disaster can reduce such complexity by illustrating the common behavior patterns among heterogeneous organizations along with specifying the relevant social factors that interact with techno-scientific systems.

This is not to say that the general concept of structural disaster can work without due consideration of the different times, places, and social contexts of particular cases. Underlying all cases is the deconstruction of a variety of disasters into generalizable elements through the lens of structural disaster. To test the applicability of the concept to various independent cases considering multiple local conditions such as differences in time, place, and social context, and to modify boundary conditions would be promising tasks for future studies on extreme events other than the Fukushima accident.

Structure of the book

Based on what is mentioned above, the structure of this book is as follows.

Grounded on the concept of structural disaster, Chapter 2 not only defines and examines the concept but also develops the theoretical foundation of structural disaster, which is made up of two parts: static and dynamic. The static part of the theory presents a model that maps the configuration of heterogeneous agents within the science-technology-society interface and lays the foundation for describing and analyzing what is structural in extreme events. The dynamic part presents the sociologically reformulated model of path-dependency to show the social mechanisms that generate structural disaster.

In particular, three theoretical focal points warrant further explanation. First, what differentiates the concept of structural disaster from prior usages of the concept of structure in sociology is that "structure" here indicates the stable patterns of interaction *within* pre-existing constraints that are observable at the sector level such as government, industry, and academia.

Second, the concept of "structure" defined here implies that structural disaster is not caused by perturbation taking place somewhere else other than the science-technology-society interface, but by the multiple layers of the interface itself. Chapter 2 critically reviews the merits and demerits of related theories, including the sociology of scientific knowledge, actor network theory, and sociological studies on public knowledge; in addition, it determines the locus of the concept of structural disaster in relation to prior related concepts. Through such specification, structural disaster incorporates natural and human-caused disasters to explain the "lock-in" mechanism of the path-dependent process that leads to extreme events. Third, by integrating static and dynamic aspects of structural disaster, the chapter examines the overall theory in the view of empirical references; in doing so, it clarifies the reason why structural disaster has been dismissed for such a long time, and illustrates the presupposed hypotheses to develop substantial arguments for exploring structural disaster.

Based on the key concepts and theoretical frameworks formulated and developed in Chapters 1 and 2, subsequent chapters explore the sociological nature of structural disaster. Chapter 3 examines the social mechanism through which institutionalized inaction by compliance occurs, with a focus on strategically targeted cases such as the SPEEDI example given earlier in this chapter, where suffering during the process of evacuation following the Fukushima accident was caused not by rule-breaking but rather by rigid compliance with a particular institutional design. If such a state is institutionalized as appropriate behavior, it should be reconfirmed from the perspective of structural disaster by relevant, independent cases. Chapter 3 will examine three independent cases: METI's Report on Severe Accidents in 1992 and its connection to the framework of post-Fukushima policy measures; the dual organizational structure of the Governmental Investigation Committee; and procedural legitimization of nuclear-related matters by power source siting laws.

Chapter 3 then investigates the origins of structural disaster by tracing back to the behavior patterns of a national research institute damaged by the Great Kanto Earthquake in 1923. These behavior patterns may reveal structural similarities to the combination of institutionalized inaction by compliance, localized action, and devastating outcomes from the Fukushima accident. Within this structural similarity, the emerging process of nuclear village in post-war Japan is analyzed by unfolding the socio-historical background of the post-war nuclear power generation's institutional design in Japan. The concept of structural disaster will enable an analysis of heterogeneous extreme events within a common framework as well as the extrapolation of in-depth sociological implications.

Chapter 4 scrutinizes the little-known accident in pre-war Japan as compared to the Fukushima accident. The chapter focuses on institutionalized secrecy within structural disaster and shows structural similarities between the Imperial

Japanese Navy accident in pre-war Japan and the Fukushima accident in a manner that is free from an opportunistic "narrative-in-hindsight." In doing so, the chapter goes beyond common dichotomous narratives that make a distinction between the pre-war social context of wartime mobilization of science and technology (resulting in nuclear bombing) and the post-war promotion of science and technology for commercialization in peacetime (manifested in nuclear reactors). In particular, the chapter probes the behavior patterns of agents involved in the pre-war accident that was kept secret and then compares these behavior patterns to those of agents involved in the Fukushima accident. By posing the questions of why and how the well-intended interests of scientists and engineers led to disaster, the chapter presents a unique perspective that does not take a single-issue-oriented approach to extreme events, but rather a comparative perspective for extreme events taking place in different times, places, and social contexts. By focusing on the restriction of critical information following the pre-war accident and in the Fukushima accident, the chapter reveals that the structural adaptation of heterogeneous agents is carried out in a path-dependent manner, and that such an adaptation transforms structural integration into functional disintegration.

In contrast to the common dichotomous distinction between two seemingly contrastive regimes, Chapters 5 and 6 will, in turn, highlight the structural similarities between the nuclear regime and the renewable energy regime in Japan. Chapter 5 uses the example of an oceanic renewable energy development project called "Sunshine" to discuss structural disaster by delineating a hidden link to stratospheric ozone depletion. The project was launched in the 1970s to develop renewable energy technology and continued through the early 1990s, around the time when the nuclear village established itself in Japanese society. From the viewpoint of structural disaster, this chapter analyzes the complex social process involved in the development of renewable energy technology, which is typically thought to be quite different from nuclear energy projects.

Particular attention is given to the complex relationship between the project's oceanic thermal energy conversion technology and stratospheric ozone depletion. Chapter 5 shows that development of this supposedly environmentally friendly energy technology had the unintended consequence of potentially aggravating global environmental problems. The chapter then explains the discrepancy between the intended purposes and actual consequences of the technology by analyzing the Sunshine project's blind spots activated by a path-dependent social mechanism. The complex relationship between the development of renewable energy technology and irreversible environmental change can thus be regarded as constituting a kind of structural disaster in situations that have an inherent degree of uncertainty that is difficult to detect and address proactively. Sociological implications are discussed with reference to principles that allocate responsibility for problems related to this uncertainty.

Chapter 6 discusses collective decision-making by heterogeneous agents involved in the process of wind turbine development and diffusion in Japan. This chapter reconsiders the path-dependent trajectory of renewable energy technologies and re-examines new implications of structural disaster by focusing on the haphazard process of initial technology development and diffusion. Particular attention is paid to the social process that changed the trajectory from domestic development and diffusion of renewable energy technologies to an alternative trajectory that promotes diffusion by importing foreign technologies. The chapter underlines network effects and constraints of shared belief as key factors contributing to such a path-dependent social process: network effects refer to the way in which an agent's decision-making process can be influenced by that of others with whom the agent has some link (weak or strong, formal or informal); and constraints of shared belief refer to the existence of a cognitive framework (evidence-based or not) that continues to influence subsequent thinking and behavior of agents who are not involved with the formation of the framework. This chapter shows that, despite the lack of evidence proving the discouraging effect of local wind conditions on wind turbines, these two effects generated the myth of infeasibility of wind power generation in Japan, which resulted in significantly understated national goal setting for energy generation by wind turbines.

Chapter 6 then analyzes the sociological mechanisms that could break this path-dependent stagnation of wind turbine development and diffusion in Japan by focusing on the social process at the local level that triggered the initial interest. To reconsider this decision-making process from the perspective of structural disaster, the chapter examines unique roles played by relevant outsiders who were excluded from the closed inner circle of governmental, industrial, and academic sectors on renewable energy development and diffusion. Based on the sociological reformulation of path-dependent mechanisms developed in Chapter 2, this chapter illustrates the existence of a fixed trajectory of initial wind turbine technology development and analyzes the behavior patterns of agents who were able to break that trajectory. Chapter 6 argues that the initial breakthrough of the fixed trajectory of technology was made by relevant outsiders who were marginal both in terms of access to expertise and to the decision-making process overall. If there are structural similarities between nuclear and renewable energy regimes from the perspective of structural disaster, relevant outsiders could be instrumental in destroying the myth of nuclear power as a harbinger of sustainability as well as the myth of the infeasibility of wind turbines in Japan.

Chapter 7 focuses on radioactive waste disposal as another issue of electricity production by nuclear power. The chapter attempts to justify the structural similarities between the Fukushima accident (the "front-end" of nuclear power generation) and Japan's radioactive waste disposal (the "back-end" of nuclear power generation) from the perspective of structural disaster. In particular, the chapter examines the possibility of infinite responsibility resulting from HLW disposal as an ongoing structural disaster beyond Fukushima. There are also salient characteristics that distinguish HLW disposal from ordinary risk allocation issues; for example, due to the long half-life of radioactive-wastes, the handling of HLW necessitates a time period spanning 10,000 to millions of years. However, intermediate storage utilized as a temporary measure can realistically only continue for a limited period due to space and capacity issues of disposal sites.

Dual underdetermination mentioned in this chapter is key to identifying the sociological implications of structural disaster in the extreme case of radioactive waste disposal. This is because the problem of knowledge distribution cannot be self-contained, as it is entangled with the allocation of responsibility for what is collectively decided upon under strong uncertainty. As such, dual underdetermination plays a crucial role. Even if the current solution of geological disposal of HLW contains no scientific uncertainty, there can be no unique solution when it comes to social decision-making involving such a long time frame. This chapter delves into the difficulty of finding a meaningful way to take responsibility for the results of a social decision made at a particular moment whose implications continue to exist for such a long period of time. Because no agent can take infinite responsibility, this chapter asks how infinite responsibility can be made finite so that the settings of social decision-making can fall within boundaries where responsibility for results are socially meaningful.

To illustrate the current mechanisms that define the boundaries of responsibility for HLW disposal in Japan, Chapter 7 uncovers implicit assumptions that address dual underdetermination – assumptions that tend to be embedded, naturalized, and taken for granted in day-to-day social settings where policies are made, implemented, and evaluated. Two different mechanisms are singled out. First, the prevalent and shared social model addresses dual underdetermination in fixing the procedures of HLW disposal. Second, the chapter analyzes the Toyocho case, which was the first instance in which the critical financial deficit of a town influenced the mayor to break the behavior pattern of Not in My Backyard (NIMBY). This case illuminates how monetary compensation works in HLW disposal. Since these two mechanisms have been widely observed in the "front-end" processes of siting nuclear power stations in Japan since the 1970s, similar mechanisms can be used in a path-dependent manner for the "back-end" processes in the post-Fukushima phase. In an effort to illuminate a new path to structural reform of social decision-making processes, this chapter examines the reasons why these path-dependent mechanisms could be regarded as an ongoing structural disaster.

Chapter 8 is the concluding chapter that integrates the key points of the book and discusses the overall implications of its findings that are applicable to the currently under-researched but critical issues involving the science-technology-society interface in an effort to provide impulses for future research. This chapter presents a renovated principle of symmetry to provide a more realistic and fair configuration of socially responsible agents when allocating responsibility for decisions (for example, those related to HLW disposal) that are crucial yet uncertain. In addition, this concluding chapter presents a multiple-assumptions approach for intellectual interactions among experts and other agents, scientific advice for government agencies, and public funding of research. To address strong uncertainties in the science-technology-society interface, the multiple-assumptions approach will make extensive policy options available to the public sphere so that those who are obliged to be engaged in decision-making are able to sidestep potential pitfalls of simplistically assuming that there is a pre-established harmony between expertise, policy, and democracy in the science-technology-society interface.[22]

Broader sociological implications of "structure"

The following points have been made in this chapter to prepare a new sociological framework for investigating structural disaster.

1   To break the self-reinforcing loop of risk society arguments via a critical examination of prior sociological discourse about uncertainty and risk, two requirements are presented: exploration of type-two underdetermination separately from type-one; categorizing agents along the principle of symmetry in the analysis of type-two underdetermination and the allocation of responsibility.
2   Structural disaster is the key to incorporating the above two requirements into the exploration of extreme events, detecting precursors of similar events, and mapping preventive measures.
3   Through the concept of structural disaster, the nature and reach of institutionalized secrecy can be illustrated with reference to the utilization of the SPEEDI, the report on HLW disposal by the SCJ, and governmental decontamination policy in the post-Fukushima situation.
4   The applicability of the concept of structural disaster to an independent case of a hidden but serious naval accident in pre-war Japan suggests the coupling of structural integration with functional disintegration. This case shows that failures of the science-technology-society interface could trigger uncontrollable and irreversible effects in the current context. To obtain a systematic mapping of different extreme events, a disaster matrix is devised as a heuristic device.

Ultimately, a broader sociological implication of structural disaster would include the locus of "structure" in two different contexts. First, since the concept of structure can apply to individual social action as well as the social system as a whole, there are two ways to explain its emergence: one is through the aggregation of relevant individual social action, and the other is through the embodiment mechanism of a social system's particular characteristics. Though the two ways may appear contrastive, both have commonalities with respect to bracketing cultural essentialism and explanation by endogenous culture as the cause, such as in the narrative of "made in Japan" in the National Diet of Japan Fukushima Nuclear Accident Independent Investigation Commission Report (NAIIC 2012a: 9). Both ways attempt to explain the process through which structural disaster occurs without appealing to any holistic explanation (for example, culture).

Second, if we regard structure as penetrating different dimensions throughout the disaster matrix described in this chapter, it follows that institutionalized secrecy and structural integration coupled with functional disintegration can affect individual social action through social systems in a fractal manner. For example, institutionalized secrecy can hide human errors in an individual social action, hide organizational errors, or authorize the hiding of multiple items within the social system as a whole. Similarly, impression management in an individual social action could function to hide human error in a broad sense (Downer 2014) or to crowd out the recognition of threats (Steinberg 2000) when they are too serious. By extension, to combine various agents and stakeholders in an investigation of structural disaster could also involve institutionalized secrecy if such a combination functions to blur the due social responsibility of a particular institutional design for incurring and/or amplifying disasters.[23]

Thus, an explanation of structural disaster implies keeping a proper distance from holistic explanations and requires a scale-free application of the concept from social action through social system with an appropriate variety of interpretations of the term "structural disaster." Scale-free here means that the arguments within the following chapters are seen as valid to analyze structural disaster at any level of description, ranging from individual social action to social system. There could be, then, multiple snapshots of structural disaster so that the common sociological basis on which the integrated portrayal of the disaster is depicted (see Chapter 2). A focus on accurate comparisons of similar structures – ranging from individual social actions to a social system, and of the different functions of similar structures throughout – could provide a significant clue to preventing collective irresponsibility when extreme events occur.[24]

2 The theory of structural disaster

Sector model and sociological path-dependency in the science-technology-society interface

Chapter 2 lays the theoretical foundation for the sociology of structural disaster, which is made up of two parts: static and dynamic. The static part of the theory presents a sector model that can be used to map the configuration of heterogeneous agents within the science-technology-society interface and sets the foundation for analyzing what is "structural" throughout extreme events. The dynamic part presents the sociologically reformulated model of path-dependency that is designed to show the social mechanisms that generate structural disaster.

Three theoretical focal points warrant further explanation. First, in sociology, the concept of structure is understood as the stable patterns of interaction between individual agents generated from purposive social action, as well as pre-existing constraints (for example, informal ties, institutionalized norms). What differentiates the concept of structural disaster from these prior usages is that "structure" here indicates the stable patterns of interaction generated *within* pre-existing constraints that are observable at the sector level such as military, government, industry, and academic, as exemplified by the nuclear village.

Second, the concept of "structure" defined here implies that structural disaster is not caused by perturbation taking place somewhere else other than the science-technology-society interface, but by the multiple layers of the interface itself. Chapter 2 critically reviews the merits and demerits of related theories, including the sociology of scientific knowledge, actor network theory, and sociological studies on public knowledge, in order to determine their locus. Through such specification, the sociology of science and technology presented in this book incorporates natural and human-caused disasters to explain the "lock-in" mechanism of the path-dependent process that leads to extreme events.

Third, by integrating both static aspect of structural disaster (via the sector model) and the dynamic aspect (via the sociologically reformulated model of path-dependency), this chapter examines the sociological theory of structural disaster with empirical references and clarifies the reason why the concept has been dismissed in previous research. "Explosive" and "creeping" aspects within the context of extreme events are also illustrated as being intertwined, with reference to the Fukushima accident.

The sector model developed in this chapter is founded on a basic need to reformulate the discourse regarding the sociology of science and technology. Then what is indispensable to fixing this universe of discourse? To answer this question, it is necessary to first distinguish between epistemological and ontological dimensions.

Intermingling of epistemological and ontological dimensions: the first step toward a sector model based on the foundation of the sociology of science and technology

> While the approach seems, on the one hand, radical and shocking, on the other hand it does not provide any countercommonsensical surprises.
> (Collins and Yearley 1992a: 310)

> It is like a child's toy clock face, the hands may be set anywhere, but it is not of much use for telling the time.
> (Collins and Yearley 1992a: 320)

> As long as social scientists safely stuck to social relations – power, institutions, classes, interactions, and so forth – they might have considered artifact making as a sort of borderline case which could be put out of the picture of society. But how can we do this with sociotechnical imbroglios where every case is a borderline case?
> (Callon and Latour 1992: 360)

The above extracts are from the "epistemological chicken" dispute between the sociology of scientific knowledge (SSK) and actor network theory (ANT). While the traditional sociology of knowledge has argued for a sociological explanation of knowledge that specifies its origins rather than assuming a "social vacuum" in the explanation, science and technology have escaped this coverage. SSK first challenged this limited scope and laid the theoretical foundation called "strong program" for the sociology of science, which has since accumulated detailed case studies on mathematics (Bloor 1976), pseudo-science (Wallis 1979), mathematical statistics (MacKenzie 1981), particle physics (Pickering 1984), and natural philosophy (Shapin and Schaffer 1985), and others. SSK also repudiated a long-standing, simplistic assumption that technology could be understood as a mere application of science (Barnes 1982); in particular, studies on the process by which one type of technology is singled out from other types of almost equal performance proliferated under the name of "social construction of technology" (SCOT). A variety of quite disparate technologies such as the inertial guidance system of nuclear missiles (MacKenzie 1990), bicycles (Bijker 1995), simulation models to estimate the degree and range of nuclear bombing (Eden 2004), synthesizers (Pinch and Trocco 2004) and others were brought under scrutiny by the SCOT perspective.[1]

Conversely, ANT has provided the sociology of science and technology with a different theoretical framework that requires science, technology, and society to have equal weight. According to Michel Callon, one of the founders of ANT, the strong program principle of reflexivity within SSK is not consistently applied to sociological explanations of SSK; as such, a kind of sociological imperialism ensues. The theoretical framework of ANT is constituted by the following three principles (Callon 1986a; Latour 1991):

1   Generalized reflexivity: An agnostic or skeptical attitude applied to the social sciences, including sociology, in an effort to explain society; no particular framework is given a privileged position, and an equal distance from any framework should be retained in the explanation.
2   Generalized symmetry: Terminologies employed for describing science and technology should be consistently employed for describing society.
3   *Libre association*: Any kind of *a priori* distinction between natural and social events should be abolished; equally, any kind of *a priori* connection should be abolished in associating actors in nature with those in society.

From these principles, it follows that society resides in everything; there is no need to detect society externally, as in the case of SSK's identification of relevant social groups.[2] ANT enables the translation of a microscopic description of research sites, such as laboratories, to a macro-sociological description of society as a whole by explaining the networks of actors. Of course, the working of these networks accompanies the transformation of meanings (*déplacement* [Callon 1986a]) through the dynamics of continuous boundary setting and resetting between nature and society.

The ANT perspective is unique and yet also convenient in the sense that society can be found in any object under investigation. It has also generated intensive case studies on bacteriology (Latour [1984]1988), electrical vehicles (Callon 1986b), underground control systems (Latour [1993]1996), jet engines (Law 2002), and others. In the process of applying ANT to such examples, the epistemological chicken dispute arose (Pickering 1992: Part 2) over the explanatory power of SSK and ANT.[3] However, this chapter discusses the dispute as it pertains to the intermingling of epistemological and ontological dimensions because the crux of these dimensions is in defining the universe of discourse of the sector model.

Michel Callon, in his seminal paper on scallop-raising technologies, found – as an observer – a social association among scallops, government researchers, scientists, and fishermen, with government researchers as the agents dynamically negotiating heterogeneous problems among the various actors, both human and non-human (Callon 1986a). While sharing the intent to embody the symmetry between science, technology, and society, SSK criticized ANT's dependence on scientists in describing things, including artifacts and nature:

> C & L [Callon and Latour], we think, will always be the puppets while the scientists remain the puppet masters . . . either their grand ambitions will be subverted in their practice, or their claims to speak on behalf of things will be superficial.
>
> (Collins and Yearley 1992b: 385)[4]

The epistemological question remains, however, of how it is possible for ANT scholars to gain understanding of objects without the help from relevant scientists. Strangely, a reply from Callon and Latour to this question seems to lack an epistemological dimension:

> As long as he is in the laboratory looking for replication procedures, Collins is . . . stressing the indefinite pliability and endless negotiability of everything – but when he wishes to finish his book and closes Weber's story, he has no other issues but to jump to an Edinburgh type of interest theory: the winner will be the one who reverberates less (or more) through the entrenched interests of the wider society.
>
> (Callon and Latour 1992: 364)

To clarify, it is better to make a supplementary remark to eliminate possible confusions and bolster the argument for a distinction between epistemological and ontological dimension; in other words, at issue is not the dispute regarding the axes of dependence on scientists in the description of things versus the interest theory as espoused by both parties. Such axes result from the rhetorical demand in dispute because interest theory of any type does not endorse total independence from scientists in the description of things and vice versa.[5] This chapter takes a critical examination of the theoretical foundation of the sociology of science and technology. From such a perspective, the dispute is between the entity model and the network model in framing the working of the science-technology-society interface. As will be further discussed, particular entities – such as 19th-century middle-class professionals in England – embody the workings of society in the former model (MacKenzie 1981: 91–93), whereas there is no need to do so in the latter model because "network" always implies the working of society through the actions of heterogeneous agents with *déplacement* (Callon 1986a). Entities lead and networks follow in the former model, while networks lead and entities follow in the latter model.

Callon and Latour state that ANT is "an ontological manifesto" (1992: 358) in their reply to criticism from SSK. In other words, SSK posed an epistemological question to ANT, and ANT gave an ontological answer, revealing an intermingling of epistemological and ontological dimensions within the dispute. If the intermingling is consciously made, the discourse is intellectually unfair; if unconsciously made, the discourse is confusing. In either case, it is difficult to see productivity in scholarly discourse. To sidestep this intermingling, it is important to distinguish between epistemological and ontological dimensions before making use of them in combination in order to formulate a sector model.

Epistemological and ontological dimensions in the science-technology-society interface are defined in this book as follows:

- The epistemological dimension reveals how the perception of society plays a role in scientists' and engineers' cognition process regarding nature and/

or artifacts, and how the perception of science and technology plays a role in non-scientists'/non-engineers' cognition process of society.
- The ontological dimension reveals how funds, information, human resources, and goods are exchanged among science, technology, and society, resulting in a sustained, changed, or collapsed interface.[6]

Epistemological and ontological dimensions in this sense are independent of both technological and social determinism, each being occasionally presupposed in the science-technology-society interface. If technological determinism is the general idea that a state of science and technology determines the state of society, then science and technology are responsible for social problems arising in the science-technology-society interface; conversely, if social determinism is the general idea that a state of society determines the state of science and technology, then the former is responsible for any problems arising with the latter. In each of the above contexts, both epistemological and ontological dimensions are valid; both dimensions are fundamentally independent of technological and social determinism in the discourse that analyzes the interaction between science, technology, and society.[7]

Epistemological and ontological dimensions are also independent of whether the science-technology-society interface is regarded as knowledge or activity because the two dimensions precede the distinction between knowledge and activity in the interface. When epistemological questions are posed, science and technology and society each contain a particular type of knowledge; for example, in epistemological problematics, science and technology could serve as a knowledge system that ignores qualitative characteristics; conversely, society could serve as a capitalist system working toward exchange value while ignoring use value. In such problematics, correspondence among the types of knowledge in science and technology and society should be sought.[8]

In contrast, when we ask ontological questions, science, technology, and society are regarded as activity rather than knowledge. Here, science and technology can be regarded as problem-solving activities, such as how to determine latitude and longitude by a chronometer through obtaining funds from patrons, getting information on competitors, contacting craftsmen who can develop an accurate chronometer, and finding collaborators. Society in this context is a kind of warehouse of resources that enables scientists and engineers to mobilize funds, information, human resources, and goods necessary for problem-solving.[9]

As such, science, technology, and society can serve as knowledge or activities depending on whether we ask epistemological or ontological questions, as these two dimensions provide one of the most fundamental rudiments that penetrates science, technology, and society. Since coherent criteria should be employed when analyzing the science-technology-society interface – to avoid double standards, as required by the principle of generalized symmetry of ANT – epistemological and ontological dimensions with such a fundamental penetration should be the first rudiment employed when defining the universe of discourse.

Basic terminologies to specify aspects of science, technology, and society: the second step to sector model

The next element to assist in defining the universe of discourse to analyze the science-technology-society interface relates to the terminology denoting the aspects of science, technology, and society on which the analysis will focus. This terminology, which will enable the specification of coherent criteria, is indispensable to a consistent and thorough argument. This book employs the following six basic terminologies to specify the different aspects of science, technology, and society in order of complexity, where "a" indicates the simplest and "f" the most complex. The terms within parentheses indicate the social characteristics that differentiate the concept from simpler concepts:

a   Individual agents
b   Action (motivation, goal, situation)
c   Social relationships (continuity)
d   Groups (boundary)
e   Institution/Organization (norm, legitimacy, reward system)
f   Social system (interaction)

Although most of the terms are well-known in sociology, two are being used here in unique ways. First, "reward system," as one of the social characteristics of institution/organization, means that the system in which individual members' performance is evaluated within the institution/organization determines honorific rewards and resources (for example, money, information, human resources, and goods) according to the performance.[10] Second, "interaction" here is stated as being one of the social characteristics of a social system but does not refer to the interaction of individuals; rather, that of multiple different institutions/organizations through the exchange of money, information, human resources, and goods.

These basic terminologies meet the requirement for coherent criteria mentioned above; for example, when applied to science, individuals mean scientists, action means the purposive social action of scientists (for example, publication of scientific papers), network means the social network of scientists within the scientific community, group means the scientific community, and institutions/organizations mean the scientific institutions and/or scientific organizations. Similarly, when applied to a bureaucracy, individuals mean bureaucrats, action means the office work of bureaucrats, network means the social network of bureaucrats within a particular department, group means a particular ministry, and institutions and/or organizations mean the bureaucratic system.

By deconstructing the different aspects of science, technology, and society with these six terminologies, heterogeneous agents within the science-technology-society interface can be consistently analyzed across all three realms. Therefore, problems related to the sociological exploration of the interface can be defined by the following four types, within which the issue type related to the sociology of science and technology can be properly expressed (see Table 2.1).

Table 2.1 Four Configurations of the Sociological Exploration of Science and Technology

---
1. a • b
2. a • b • f
3. f → (a • b) ∨ (a • b • c) ∨ (a • b • c • d) ∨ (a • b • c • d • e)
4. [f → (a • b) ∨ (a • b • c) ∨ (a • b • c • d) ∨ (a • b • c • d • e)] • [(a • b) ∨ (a • b • c) ∨ (a • b • c • d) ∨ (a • b • c • d • e) → f]

Note: Letters used in this table correspond to those used to denote the six basic terminologies on page 33

Type 1 focuses on the actions of scientists with no regard for other aspects of science or social system. The description of science given by Alfred Schutz is appropriate when this type of discourse is convened; he depicted the world of scientific theory by saying "science becomes again included in the world of life" (Schutz 1962b: 259).

Type 2 can analyze both the actions of scientists and social systems simultaneously, though it lacks substantial social theory to meaningfully link them. When Max Weber refers to the "external conditions" of Wissenschaft at the outset of *Wissenschaft als Beruf*, this type of discourse is embodied in his description of Wissenschaft's economic status (Weber [1922]2004: 1–7).

Type 3 can analyze both the actions of scientists and social system simultaneously and does contain a substantial social theory to meaningfully link them; however, the social theory has a peculiar inclination to social determinism in analyzing the science-technology-society interface. When J. D. Bernal, one of the leading socialist scientists in the 1930s and known for "Bernalism" (Werskey 1978: 185–199), maintained the following argument in the context of science and social transformation that enunciates this type of discourse: "Science is predominantly a transforming and not a conserving influence, but the full effect of its action has not yet to be seen . . . criticism of the present state of man and . . . its indefinite improvement . . . depends on social force outside science" (Bernal 1939: 385).

Type 4 can analyze the actions of scientists and social systems simultaneously and contains a substantial social theory to meaningfully link them by way of social relations, groups, and institutions/organizations in the realms of science, technology, and society. This is the type of discourse that this book defines as the most relevant to the sociology of science and technology.

For the sake of simplicity, science and technology/scientists and engineers are indicated as science/scientists in the above illustrations. While the texts and authors quoted above do not ensure a one-to-one correspondence to the types of discourse classified here, they are provided to display an approximate interpretation of each type. For example, when we look at *Wirtschaft und Gesellschaft* (1921–1922) by Max Weber, his arguments of bureaucracy went far beyond Type 2 and rather well demonstrated Type 3, such that a trend toward bureaucracy in social systems has a significant influence on the social status and action of scientists:

> In the field of scientific research and instruction, the bureaucratization of the inevitable research institutes of universities is also a function of the increasing demand for material means of operation. Liebig's laboratory at Giessen University was the first example of big enterprise in this field. Through the concentration of such means in the hands of the privileged head of the institute the mass of researches and instructors are separated from their "means of production" in the same way as the workers are separated from theirs by the capitalist enterprises.
> (Weber [1921–1922]1978: 983)

In any case, the configurations presented above reveal an extension of the sociological exploration of science and technology, within which the task of analyzing the sociology of science and technology as conceived in this book is appropriately placed.

Level, type, and plan of the sector model

Based on the above theoretical assumptions and basic terminologies, the sector model can be established, with the concept of sector as being in-between institutions/organizations and social systems (that is to say, sector here does not indicate a single institution/organization but rather the amalgam of heterogeneous institutions/organizations, which roughly corresponds to business circles in daily languages).[11] Since the levels of analysis of sectors are in-between institutions/organizations and social systems, the motivation, goal, and situation of agents – together with their social relationships, groups, legitimacy, norms, and reward systems – can be found within a particular sector. In this sense, the working state of a social system as a whole is based on the state of sectors.

While identifying the boundary between one sector and another is sometimes obvious/intuitive, it does not guarantee that the analysis will be theoretically consistent and sociologically meaningful. To achieve theoretical consistency and relevant sociological interpretation, it is critical to typify a select number of sectors that appear to represent the reality of the science-technology-society interface in-between institutions/organizations and social systems as a whole. From such a viewpoint, this book typifies military, governmental, industrial, academic, and citizen sectors.

- The military sector is directly and indirectly concerned with the production and deployment of weapons for warfare and national security. Air force, navy, army, and related defense agencies exemplify this sector.
- The governmental sector is directly and indirectly concerned with the ordainment and enforcement of laws designed to protect public interest. Parliament and the bureaucratic systems of central and local governments exemplify this sector.

- The industrial sector is directly and indirectly concerned with the production of goods, artifacts, and services. Manufacturers and related private companies exemplify this sector.
- The academic sector is directly and indirectly concerned with the production of public knowledge, particularly scholarly expertise. Universities, learned societies, and research institutes exemplify this sector.
- The citizen sector is directly and indirectly concerned with the production of voices against the actions and discourse of the military, governmental, industrial, and academic sectors as the agents suffering from these activities. Non-profit organizations, non-governmental organizations, and private citizens exemplify this sector.

Thus, sectors in this book are defined not by a particular entity but by the roles they play in the science-technology-society interface. According to such roles, the achievements of individuals are evaluated and rewards are allocated among them within a sector. In this sense, sectors fulfill the expected social function of sustaining social systems as a whole and providing individuals within these sectors with continuous and stable economic opportunities. Thus, sectors have an ontological dimension, as they are determined by their problem-solving activities in two contexts: the context of fulfilling the expected social function, and the context of enabling individuals to earn a living.[12]

Sectors also have an epistemological dimension because there are different ways of thinking among each of the different sectors (Wynne 1982: 11–14). For example, ways of thinking over unexpected uncertainties in the science-technology-society interface (a regular event within type-one underdetermination) can typically exhibit noticeable differences. The military sector, in seeking the maximum performance of a novel weapon, should regard uncertainty as an unexpected opportunity to gain ground or necessary loss, both resulting from a high risk-high return strategy. The governmental sector should regard uncertainty within the context of precedent-following, or to carry it forward into the future when there is no precedent to follow at the present time. The industrial sector should regard uncertainty as one of the conditions to be either considered or avoided when analyzing the maximum expected pay-off. The academic sector should regard uncertainty as something to be deliberately evaluated to determine whether it leads to the acquisition of another fund for research. The citizen sector should regard the same uncertainty as a basis to become mobilized in criticism of the discourse and actions of other sectors, and to present alternative discourse and actions. Thus, the accumulation of ways of thinking crystalize in different ways among sectors, even when analyzing the same issue.

Therefore, sectors intrinsically have both ontological and epistemological dimensions, which form the rudiments of the universe of discourse for the sociology of science and technology. The sector model aims to gage how ontological features of a sector correspond to or contrast with the epistemological features of the same sector; for example, how the cognition of a sector represents the interest of the sector as an occupational group, or how some features deviate from it.

At the same time, similarities and differences can be seen among sectors over a single issue in the science-technology-society interface; for example, when the cognition of a sector represents its own interest, different cognition among the sectors will result; in addition, when the cognition of a sector deviates from its own interest, similarities across different sectors will appear. When the cognition among sectors over a controversial issue in the epistemological dimension differs so greatly that the cognition is mutually incommensurable (for example, pro- versus anti-nuclear energy), amalgamation of substantially incommensurable cognition, even with the assistance of the rhetoric of consensus, is not logical. The analyses of incommensurable cognition by the sector model in terms of epistemological and ontological dimensions, instead of the juxtaposition of incommensurable cognition in the epistemological dimension alone, enables the portrayal of incommensurable issues within the science-technology-society interface in a multi-dimensional way.

To illustrate the sociological implications of such a multi-dimensional analysis of controversial issues in this interface, it is pertinent here to broaden our perspective and look at the dilemma of "knowledge commons" with reference to sociological studies on public knowledge.

Dilemma between epistemological and ontological dimensions in the public sphere: dilemma of knowledge commons

Public goods are defined as goods that have low subtractability and exclusion (Hess and Ostrom 2007: 9), or that these goods are immune from deterioration in quantity and quality by common and widespread use and therefore are difficult or virtually impossible to make exclusive. The provision of sunlight, defense/police, and public health services are examples of public goods. There are also goods referred to as common-pool resources, which have low exclusion but relatively high subtractability, such as irrigation facilities. Goods that have low subtractability but relatively high exclusion (for example, day-care centers,) are called club goods. Goods that have both subtractability and exclusion are considered private goods.[13]

According to this definition, scientific and technological knowledge is considered a public good.[14] Since there is no deterioration in terms of quantity and quality after being widely used, scientific and technological knowledge has very low subtractability. In addition, since scientific and technological knowledge is essentially made public for replication and open use, there is very low exclusion.[15] With this understanding, it is logical that policy goals would provide scientific and technological knowledge as a public good by way of museums, public education, adult education, and other available means of distribution or provision. One of the primary goals of such endeavors is to enhance science and technology literacy in the public sphere.

Policies oriented toward this goal originated in public understanding of science movement in Britain in the 1980s;[16] however, what does enhancing science and technology literacy actually mean in relation to society? For example, suppose that a questionnaire is designed to measure the degree of science and technology literacy and asks the following question to a randomly sampled population group: Is astrology science? According to ordinary procedures of social research, three categories of answer would be presented: "Yes," "No," "Don't Know"/"No Answer" ("DK" or "NA"). Those who answer "Yes" are categorized into the "wrong answer" group, comprised of those who do not have science literacy; those who answer "No" are categorized into the "right answer" group considered to have science literacy. Those who answer "DK" or "NA" are considered missing values and their responses are omitted. The ratio of the group giving the right answer in the entire sample, or aggregation of such ratios calculated from multiple questions, is used for measuring the degree of science literacy. However, while standard procedures were used in our example in terms of social research, is it reasonable to regard those who answer "DK" or "NA" as yielding truly missing values and eliminate them from the sample that is meant to determine the degree of science literacy?

For example, the law of constant areal velocity introduced by Johannes Kepler as a landmark of modern astronomy was inextricably coupled with his thoughts on astrology (Koestler 1960). If the "right" or "wrong" answer dichotomy employed in measuring the degree of science literacy is strictly followed, relevant experts such as historians of science who are familiar with the emerging process of modern science may provide answers that do not fall within a valid sample.[17]

At issue are not the measurement techniques and/or the wording of questionnaires; rather, the problem lies in the fact that there could be a case where "DK" or "NA" has positive relevant meaning in relation to society. The requirement of accurate transmission of scientific and technological knowledge to society is logical only when the right answer is already known. Questions arising within the science-technology-society interface typically include questions that are difficult to answer with a straight "Yes" or "No"; rather, they lend themselves to "DK" or "NA." The closer to the latest research in scientific and technological knowledge, such as the triggering mechanism of earthquakes around plate boundaries, the more acute and urgent the issues in the science-technology-society interface. In these instances, expected answers tend to have a non-dichotomous answer. Conversely, acute, and urgent questions necessitate the earliest possible disclosure of the reasons for answering "DK" or "NA" to the public sphere, in which people live who are directly concerned.

People within the citizen sector typically have a distaste for "DK" or "NA" answers and there could be two reasons for this. First, ordinary people have a low probability of ascertaining the truth or falsehoods of scientific and technological knowledge by themselves. Second, as a result, they tend to dislike "DK" or "NA"; as such, they seek "Yes" or "No" answers to scientific and technological questions, to help them determine what is true or false. Because the truth or falsehood of scientific and technological knowledge (that is to say, its validity) is almost completely unavailable to them unassisted, the desire for straight answers is rooted in the belief among the general public that scientific and technological knowledge is clear and undisputable.

Considering these conditions, there always exists the risk that science and technology literacy provides the right answer in response to the expectation from the citizen sector where there is no other way than saying "DK" or "NA." The more faithful to the demand for ensuring the quality of scientific and technological knowledge scientists and engineers are, the more obliged to deliberately distance themselves from such a dichotomous way of answering. In contrast, the more acute and urgent the questions arising in the science-technology-society interface are, the simpler the answers, including the dichotomous way of answering by scientific and technological knowledge, are expected to be prioritized. This exemplifies the dilemma between the epistemological demand for guaranteeing the quality of scientific and technological knowledge as public goods and the ontological demand for the fastest possible transmission of information to the public sphere when acute and urgent issues are emerging.

This chapter identifies this as the dilemma of knowledge commons because the above-mentioned two demands stem from the nature of scientific and technological knowledge as a public good. The epistemological demand is embodied by relevant experts, who are expected to commit to ensuring the quality of knowledge commons, and the ontological demand is embodied in the commitment to securing the swift transmission of knowledge commons to society when necessary. These two demands could be mutually contradictory in an emergency situation.

Since the endeavor to enhance the degree of science literacy in the context of public understanding of science has not yet underlined this dilemma as it would stem from a potential tension or conflict between epistemological and ontological dimensions, nor has the endeavor identified a solution to the dilemma, new tools through which to find provisional solutions to this dilemma are required. What is expected for such tools is twofold: first it is better to sharpen the awareness of the dilemma rather than covering it up under the guise of public consensus; second, it is better to pinpoint the locus of the dilemma to clarify due responsibility for social decisions made under the dilemma rather than to blur this responsibility. The sector model is designed with these principles in mind, and the multi-dimensional analyses mentioned earlier have sociologically important implications, particularly when the sector model is applied to complicated controversial issues in the science-technology-society interface. To carry out such a multi-dimensional analysis, however, the supplementary conceptual distinction between actors and sectors must be articulated.

Sectors and actors

In addition to the concept of sectors, it is necessary to introduce another set of concepts, particularly to help clarify complicated controversial issues emanating from extreme events such as the Fukushima accident, within the science-technology-society interface. As such, this section discusses actors, which are conceptualized by appealing to three criteria: first, how far can actors to engage in defining current problems (the possibility of problem definition); second, to what extent can actors gain or lose as a result of the current problems (expected effects); third, to what extent are actors expected to take responsibility for the results of current problems (expected responsibility). Based on these three criteria, this section conceptualizes the following five types of actors:

- Parties concerned: Actors that should be engaged in problem definition but actually have only limited possibility of such engagement; actors that are expected to be highly affected by the consequences of the problem – either direct or indirect – and indefinite responsibility (sometimes there is no way to take responsibility due to little engagement in problem definition; even so, sometimes this type of actor is obliged to take its own responsibility).
- Stakeholders: Actors that are usually engaged in problem definition and are expected to experience indirect effects from the consequences of the problem and have considerable possibility of taking responsibility for the consequences.
- The third party: Actors that are fully engaged in problem definition but are expected to experience little direct or indirect effects from the consequences of the problem and have little possibility of taking responsibility for the consequences.
- Ones to profit: Actors that are engaged in problem definition only when having gain from the consequences of the problem and take no responsibility for the consequences.
- Bystanders: Actors that have no relation to problem definition, will not experience effects from the consequences, and will not be held liable for the consequences.

These types of actors are summarized in Table 2.2.

What, then, is the relationship of actors with sectors? Since the definition of an actor is given independent of the sectors and of the six terminologies, the five types of actors can be assumed at any level of analysis ranging from individuals, actions, social relationships, groups, institutions/organizations, sectors, and social systems as a whole. For example, the sociologists of science and technology (academic sector) are engaged in problem definition so that they should be considered stakeholders or the third party.

Table 2.2 Types of Actors

Criteria \ Types of actors	Parties concerned	Stakeholders	The third party	Ones to profit	Bystanders
Possibility of problem definition	+	++	+++	+	–
Expected effects	+++	++	–	+	–
Expected responsibility	+	++	–	–	–

Note: +++: Strong commitment; ++: Commitment; +: Partial commitment; –: No commitment.

In particular, the articulation of these types of actors is significant in analyzing the nature of the citizen sector in the science-technology-society interface because there has been no previous effort to breakdown by these types of actors within the context of citizens' participation in the interface. For example, when participating citizens groups are comprised of stakeholders and those who stand to profit with no concern for affected parties, the reality of the groups is much closer to an interest group rather than representing the will of concerned parties. Conversely, citizens groups are comprised of those within the concerned party (absent of stakeholders, the third party, ones to profit, or bystanders), which means that the groups are like endogenous communities bound together by common concern and destiny.

Labeling interest groups and endogenous communities as being within the same sector (for example, the citizen sector) would be misleading and make it difficult to reflect on the substantial quality of participatory decision-making.[18] Therefore, it is advisable to use the concept of actors as a supplementary device, when necessary, in employing the sector model to avoid such misleading analysis. Of course, which sectors correspond with which actors depends on the nature of individual issues within the science-technology-society interface, and also on time, place, and social contexts in which the issue arises. This book assumes intricate relationships among stakeholders and the third party as an example of scrutiny. The next section illustrates this by using the academic sector as an empirical reference.

Snapshot of what the sector model can reveal: a view through types of actors

> I am a professor of the Imperial University who has devoted most of his life to academic research aloof from the mundane world. The man having the career path of this kind now dares to say "Yes" to the request from the state to contribute to the businesses of national defense under the aegis of the military sector. I am not the only man who says so. All fifteen members of my laboratory are ready to say so and at least four of my colleagues have determined to say "Yes."
> (Kotake 1941: 65)

Munio Kotake, an organic chemist, made the above statement one year after the enactment of the National Mobilization Ordinance for Research, one year before the outbreak of war with the United States of America and Britain. Kotake called this particular phase a "critical phase for the nation." Within the social context at the time, it would be hard to argue for the prioritization of research for the public; however, one cannot suppose that this kind of macroscopic social context such as "critical phase for the nation" could serve as a wide-ranging explanation. For example, Kotake clarified the following as his incentive for cooperation with wartime mobilization:

> When I entered the university, I was truly devoted myself to research alone . . . after more than ten years flied after graduation and around a time

when I came to be mid-forties of age, I became discouraged because I found it difficult to achieve originally intended research goal . . . after passing forty years of age when I realized I had been unsuccessful in academic research, conciliatory attitude sprang up in my heart. With that attitude it comes to my mind that if I could not catch up with scientific progress, it is good for society and for myself to contribute to the nation as far as possible utilizing my past experience.

(Kotake 1941: 56–58)

In terms of relationships between stakeholders and the third party, the above vividly expresses the process of change from the latter to the former in relation to wartime mobilization within the same academic sector actor. Tetsu Hiroshige, a historian of science, called this type of change a "conversion springing from discouragement in academic research" (Hiroshige 1973: 165). Sociologists of science and technology once called a similar type of change "role attrition" (Allison and Stewart 1974) in the context of accumulative advantage (Owen-Smith 2003). The reason for calling attention to this type of change is to clarify its sociological mechanism, rather than its psychological one. The change clearly suggests the possibility that activities and cognition are made possible by committing to a particular type of actor, and that this can change drastically within any sector or dimension (epistemological or ontological).

The multi-dimensional analyses enabled by the sector model could enrich their sociological implications along with the articulation of types of actors. In particular, as illustrated above, the change in type of actor from the third party to stakeholders could have telling implications for the analyses of complicated controversial issues regarding extreme events, such as war, that have various deeply committed stakeholders. Similar changes could also provide an important focal point for the analysis of the Fukushima accident as a structural disaster. Common patterns running through the dynamic process in which extreme events such as war and the Fukushima accident unfold should be specified as what is structural in characterizing the process of change.

After devising a basic conceptual framework of the sector model to map what is structural in the science-technology-society interface together with the conceptual tools of actor types and defining the universe of discourse as the static part of structural disaster analysis, the argument now focuses on where the dynamic part of the theory of structural disaster should be constructed.

Sociological path-dependency as a dynamic theory of structural disaster

One of the key differentiators between the dynamic and static parts of the structural disaster concept is in how the duration of time is treated. Particularly in cases of extreme events, such as a structural disaster that unfolds within the science-technology-society interface, it is crucial to pay careful attention to the virtual impossibility for the agents involved to make *ex ante* predictions of the course of

The theory of structural disaster 43

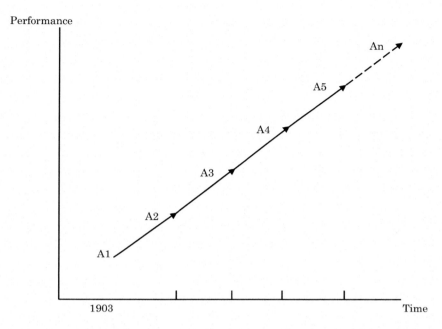

Figure 2.1 One-dimensional Narrative of Airfoil Development Trajectory

Notes: 1903 indicates the year when the Wright brothers made their first flight. A1 ... An indicate a particular type of airfoils that enabled the top performance measured by various indexes such as lift-to-drag ratio in each stage of the technological development. A linear image is employed only for the sake of simplification.

events due to dual underdetermination. To cite a simpler example, the development trajectory of airfoil (airplane wing) embodies one-dimensional development of technology; however, this is only possible based on *ex post* narratives such as leading from the airfoil of the first aircraft to those airfoils effectuating top-ranked performance in each stage of development (Figure 2.1).[19]

Hindsight makes this kind of one-dimensional narrative possible. In contrast, no single agent involved is privileged to obtain *ex ante* predictions from the future. No agent knows which airfoil will be the best solution in advance. This requires an alternative and more realistic narrative, which establishes the social process of singling out one type of airfoil among mutually competing types with almost unknown performance at a given time (Figure 2.2).

This narrative adopts the viewpoint of actual agents who undergo dual underdetermination and, therein, get involved in the social process in which they single out one particular type of technology from among other alternatives available at a given time. When the scope is widened to incorporate the science-technology-society interface, stronger dual underdetermination occurs because the development trajectory of science and the course of social change must be considered simultaneously with the development trajectory of technology. Therefore, the

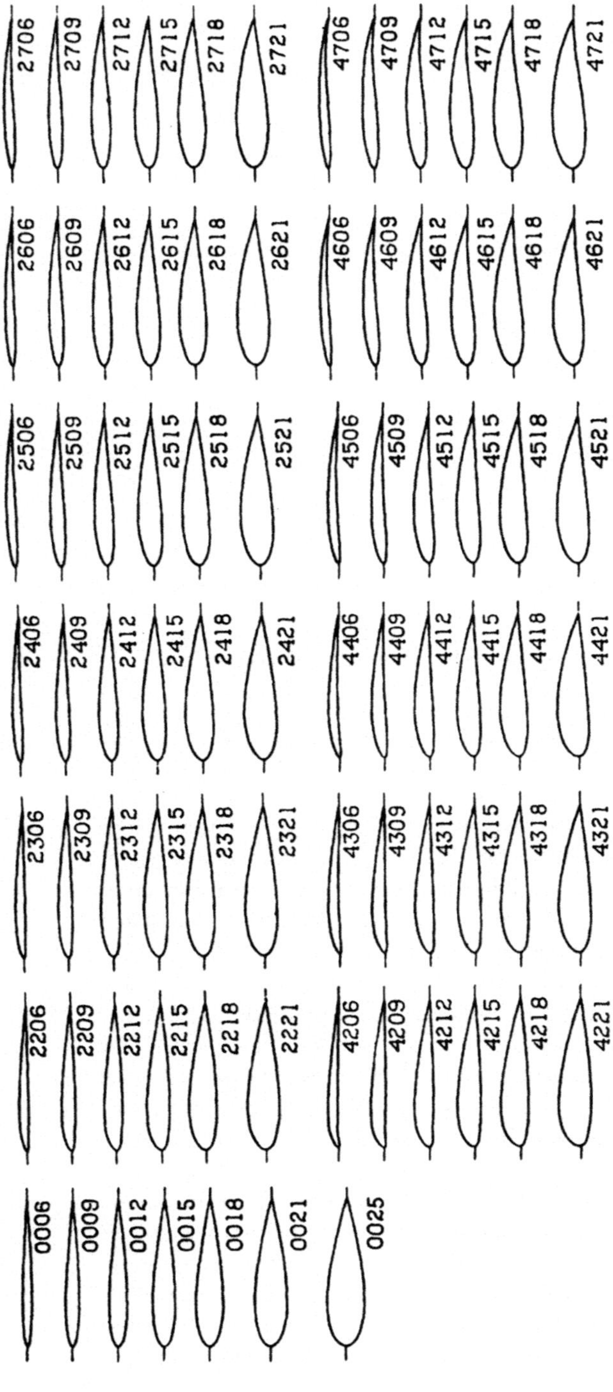

44 *The theory of structural disaster*

Figure 2.2 Alternative Narrative of Airfoil Development Trajectory
Source: Jacobs, Ward, and Pinkerton (1933).

adoption of the viewpoint of actual agents who undergo dual underdetermination in the science-technology-society interface is more logical when portraying the dynamic aspect of structural disaster in the interface. How, then, is it possible for such a complex viewpoint to be part of the dynamic aspect of structural disaster rather than as part of the static aspect? The answer can be found by shifting the focus away from a single cause/single incident that corresponds to some elements of the disaster to tracking down a generalized mechanism at work within structural disaster.

Following a precedent leads to non-rationality

The dynamic part of the structural disaster concept examines how such a disaster occurs in terms of a generalized dynamic mechanisms.[20] To use the terminologies defined in Chapter 1, the generating mechanism of structural disaster that will be theoretically formulated with relatively general logic means focusing on the universal and dynamic aspects of structural disaster, as "structure" here does not refer to static properties at any given time but rather to patterns of change that penetrate the dynamic process in the science-technology-society interface.

A clue in path-dependency theory

Untangling the general mechanism of structural disaster will require sociologically reformulating path-dependency theory and expanding its scope. Path-dependency theory is a framework to describe and explain the process through which an unstructured state ultimately becomes a tightly structured state. An example would be a state that hosts multiple types of technologies in different formats but with almost the same performance then becomes a state in which a particular type of technology dominates, leaving almost no room for other types of technology to enter. In other words, path-dependency is illustrated by a process through which the dominant technology is determined independently of its performance, because once a given type of technology gains even a slight expanding momentum, it will start to dominate the market at an accelerated pace.

In general, path-dependency theory is characterized by a gap between an ordinary initial state and an extraordinarily structured end state; in addition, there can be uncertainty introduced in the theory, such that agents are unable to make an *ex ante* prediction at a given time. One important implication of path-dependency theory is that once a technology begins developing along a certain path while uncertainty exists, it can lead to a state called "lock-in." In this state, it becomes difficult to shift to another development path, even if it would be more rational to switch technologies in terms of net pay-off. This corresponds to adherence to erroneous precedents as an element of structural disaster in the sense that continuing to follow an erroneous path results in amplification of negative effects.

This theoretical framework suggests that a variety of technology selection processes – for example, the light water reactor gradually becoming a standard nuclear reactor for power generation, or the process of selecting between

46 The theory of structural disaster

Betamax and VHS for video recording/playback systems – could be explained as a state of lock-in determined by past technological development trajectories. Lock-in has also been illustrated more broadly, often as a phenomenon related to institutional inertia and used as a key concept for explaining the dynamics of institutional formation, development, continuation, and decline. For example, an institution that is saddled with vested interests survives even after losing its mission, the mission to which it was originally designed to serve; this is regarded as a result from the inertia of the institution.[21]

From the viewpoint of path-dependency theory, structural disaster could be understood as a state of lock-in in the following two senses:

- A state in which the technology development path is fixed without rational consideration of other potential technologies, even when the agents are assumed to be rational in the sense that they behave to maximize their own pay-off. As a result, the introduction of other technologies after such a fixation becomes virtually impossible.
- A small yet contingent disturbance to the agents in the initial stage when the technology development path is about to be determined can have a decisive effect on the subsequent development trajectory of the technology.

The characterization given by the first sense implies that the aggregation of behaviors by rational agents yields non-rational outcomes; for example, technological lock-in includes cases in which, once a given technology is chosen by the majority, choosing a different and even superior technology (for example, in net pay-off or superior cost-performance in the future) becomes virtually impossible due to precedent. Suppose there are two types of almost equal performance technologies, A and B, and Technology A happens to have a slightly larger initial advantage than Technology B. Also suppose that the rate of benefit increase is larger for Technology B than for Technology A. In this case, it is initially more beneficial to choose Technology A; however, both technologies should at some point become equally beneficial; after this point, the relative benefits from the two technologies are reversed, so that the benefit of choosing Technology B becomes greater.

Nevertheless, if Technology A becomes locked in due to external contingent factors before the benefits of both technologies equalize, the agents will ultimately continue to choose the less beneficial technology.[22] For example, according to David (1985) and Arthur (1989), the keyboard layout designed to slow typing speed to prevent a mechanical typewriter's bars from entangling is still used even after the advent of computers eliminated the need to worry about such physical entanglement. In this case, it is a mistake to think that Technology A is the most suitable technology because it was chosen and survived. In this setting, the winner is not necessarily the fittest. To further investigate this enigma, it is necessary to specify what kinds of conditions cause a technology to become locked in.

When the threshold between relative benefit for the agents is crossed, and the counter-beneficial technology continues to be chosen at an accelerated pace, this is attributed to accidental factors working before the two technologies come into play. Brian Arthur, an advocate of this theory, calls these factors "random historical events" (Arthur 1989), which could be a specific business relationship at a given time in the past, an effect of the institutional design or convention, or a result of governmental/political influence through personal connections.

Such events are random for two reasons. First, they are factors introduced almost independently of a technology's performance. Second, they are difficult to anticipate because they come from outside the agents' perspective at the time of choosing a technology. Path-dependency theory regards uncertainties in such technology selection and diffusion processes as situational disturbances. In other words, if one assumes that agents behave in a rational way in terms of being sensitive to pay-off, or more broadly, cost-benefits, the initial contingent factor to bring on a lock-in state that can yield a non-rational situation for those agents becomes a major pillar supporting path-dependency theory.

Speaking technically, path-dependency theory rests on assumptions such that the overall process in question can be expressed as a stochastic process (that is to say, a collection of random variables);[23] however, when disregarding these auxiliary assumptions and revealing a substantially meaningful framework, the basic prerequisite that leads to a lock-in state in path-dependency theory can be attributed to the unexpected effects arising from the behavior of agents who are sensitive to maximizing benefits in uncertain situations in which contingency could intervene in the initial stage (see Figure 2.3).[24]

Sociologically reformulating and expanding path-dependency theory

As discussed, path-dependency, which results from a disturbance due to random external events in the initial stage of technology development, ultimately leads to a state of lock-in; however, this approach provides no room to question how the external events that cause the lock-in might occur. This is because what initially causes a lock-in is subsumed within uncertainty as represented by random disturbances coming from outside of the theory's framework. This makes it impossible to pose further questions about the components of external situations themselves.

The key to expanding path-dependency theory to represent the generating mechanism of structural disaster lies in how this problem is formulated. Instead of viewing a situation caused by such disturbances to fall under the realm of external uncertainties, this book adopts the sociological viewpoint that the individual agents are affected by the situation while also creating it, as clarified by the basic terminologies in the static part of structural disaster. Thus, incorporating a mutual relationship between the individual agents and the situation, and also understanding how past events can affect or influence current situations can offer insights into the mechanism through which a structural disaster occurs.

48 *The theory of structural disaster*

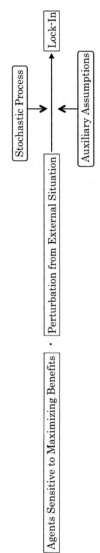

Figure 2.3 The Logical Skeleton of Path-Dependency Theory
Source: Matsumoto (2009: 96).

The theory of structural disaster 49

What kinds of mechanisms, then, are at work in the mutual relationship between individual agents and the situations caused by past events? If we follow the logic leading to a lock-in state based on path-dependency theory, the following four different mechanisms are known. (1) The *initial cost effect* refers to situations in which the original cost spent on a particular type of technology (before it becomes dominant) is so large that to switch from this type of technology to another type becomes virtually impossible because the cost to do so becomes unjustifiable. (2) The *learning effect* refers to cases in which users develop skills specific to a particular type of technology as they use it; thus, it becomes difficult to switch to another type of technology. (3) The *network effect* refers to cases in which a given agent's decision-making is affected by formal and informal relationships with other agents. Finally, (4) the *belief effect* refers to situations in which the details of a particular perception affect how an agent thinks and behaves, regardless of the existence of evidence.[25]

Both (1) and (2) develop based on the premise of the market. In contrast, (3), which is an effect of the social relationships the individual agent creates with other agents, and (4), which is an effect of the perceptional details that the individual agent shares with other agents, represent more general mechanisms that work both within and without the market.[26] Therefore, the network and belief effects are useful in describing a general mechanism that gives rise to structural disaster, which occurs in the science-technology-society interface, surpassing the boundaries of the market.

The assumption that the process that leads to a lock-in state is a stochastic process must also be examined, and the kind of empirical state to which it corresponds should be clarified. To regard something as a stochastic process, the states constituting the process must be predetermined and comprised of mutually exclusive cases. Interpreting the stochastic process within the context of the development trajectory of technology, implies a situation in which multiple types of technologies aimed at the same purpose have emerged and are competing. Such a situation can often be seen in the initial stages of technological development after a scientific principle produces the basic concept of the technology, in which stage the tasks of empirical specification for making the technology actually work remain to be resolved; therefore, various types of technologies designed for serving the same purpose are released in close succession, in a trial-and-error manner. Hereafter, such a state is referred to as "initial divergence." Thus, the sociologically expanded mechanism that holds path-dependency theory as prime for reformulation can be expressed as follows (see Figure 2.4).

According to this mechanism, even if certain agents are attuned to maximizing benefits at a given time and are considered rational in this sense, lock-in could still occur due to the path of past technology development, which is affected by factors such as the network effect, belief effect, and the initial divergence of technology.[27] If such a possibility does exist, what are the empirical details of the network effect, belief effect, and initial divergence of technology? In light of these specific questions to interpret the contents of the sociologically reformulated path-dependent theory, in what sense can a process leading

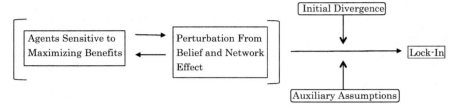

Figure 2.4 Sociological Reformulation of Path-Dependency Theory
Source: Matsumoto (2009: 99).

to a lock-in be regarded as a social process that substantiates structural disaster? The answers will be given in the following chapters; for now, however, it is important to integrate the static and dynamic parts of the sociological theory of structural disaster and confirm the presuppositions for developing substantial arguments.

Integration of static and dynamic frameworks: why has structural disaster been neglected for so long?

As mentioned, the theoretical foundation for analyzing structural disaster can be outlined as follows:

1 Pulling apart multiple elements involved in the epistemological chicken dispute between SSK and ANT, where epistemological and ontological dimensions are abstracted as rudimentary elements in defining the universe of discourse for examining the sociological theory of structural disaster based on the sociology of science and technology. Six basic terminologies, ranging from individual agents to social systems, are defined to categorize the universe of discourse into four types.

2 As to the static aspect of structural disaster, the sector model shows the importance of a multi-dimensional analysis of such issues within the science-technology-society interface as illustrated in extreme events encompassing war and the Fukushima accident, among others. The term "multi-dimensional" here means overlapping as well as deviance between the state of the epistemological dimension and the ontological one together with the similarities and differences among sectors. In addition, five types of actors are introduced to articulate multi-dimensionality of extreme events within the science-technology-society interface in order to reveal the dilemma of knowledge commons.

3 The sociologically expanded theory of path-dependency is reformulated to show the generating mechanism and dynamic aspect of structural disaster. In particular, the social process leading to a lock-in state could provide an

important focal point of the analysis of the dynamic aspect of the disaster as well as the social process in which network effect, belief effect, and the initial divergence of technology could arise as key factors.

To integrate the static and dynamic parts of structural disaster, it is important to identify presuppositions that will form more elaborate arguments in the following chapters. There are four postulates germane to the integrated analysis of static and dynamic aspects of structural disaster. First, although five elements of structural disaster, ranging from adherence to erroneous precedents to secrecy, can be applied to both static and dynamic aspects, in the following chapters, the five elements are assumed to be basic features of the dynamic process of structural disaster. Associated with this attention to the dynamic process is the end state of structural disaster, which is not confined to events such as the Fukushima accident and the post-Fukushima situation, but rather can include a variety of extreme events taking place across different times, places, and social contexts.

Second, to enable the systematic consistency on mutually heterogeneous cases throughout the exploration of the dynamic aspects of structural disaster, the arguments in the following chapters presuppose the theoretical frameworks presented in this chapter. This does not mean, however, that mechanical application of the frameworks has been made in individual cases; rather, the theoretical frameworks will be embedded in the analyses in the following chapters. In particular, the sector model formulated in this chapter for the static aspects of the sociological theory of structural disaster will be presupposed as the basic ground against which dynamic processes of structural disaster will be discussed. For example, when the sector model is mobilized in Chapter 4, the military sector will be collectively scrutinized via analysis of a hidden accident that happened during mobilization of science and technology in the pre-war period. In other chapters, the governmental, industrial, academic, and citizen sectors will be assumed within the analyses. Third, all of the individual agents will be assumed to be stakeholders in terms of the types of actors, except when otherwise stated.

Finally, although both explosive and creeping aspects of the discussed issues will be equally expected, the focus of attention will be placed on the creeping aspect. The explosive aspect here refers to events constituting causes and effects that happen within well-defined boundaries and within a relatively short time frame, so it is relatively easy to delineate the problem area. Since accidents in various types of plants tend to manifest this aspect, it is named after the often-resulting explosions. What is characteristic of the aspect is that the parties directly concerned, stakeholders, and the third party are responsible for clearly communicating with each other because everything must work in tandem within such small and well-defined boundaries. Conversely, the creeping aspect means that it is difficult to clearly delineate the problem area from other defined areas. Since links between causes and effects in the creeping aspect tend to require an extended time period (sometimes over several generations) and have much more global extension, it is difficult to discern the parties concerned, stakeholders, and the third party because there is no particularly well-defined problem area every actor is clearly involved. In addition, a higher degree of uncertainty is usually present in the creeping aspect, as exemplified by HLW disposal issues, global environmental issues, GMO-related issues, and genomic therapy-related issues. Because the inherent higher uncertainty could generate problems developing over an extended period of time, and therein any sector and/or actor in the science-technology-society interface could become involved at any time, this aspect is named for the often slow process.

Even though the above differentiates both types of aspects, a single extreme event is usually of a bit of both. For example, when looking at a hydrogen explosion, the Fukushima accident appears to exhibit the explosive aspect in this regard, but when looking at the diffusion of radioactive materials, the creeping aspect is involved. Because the explosive aspect of problems is more visible than the creeping aspect, from the viewpoint of the sociology of science and technology, it is important not to dismiss the existence and functioning of the creeping aspect even if it is not as visible as the explosive aspect. This point is critical to the exploration of structural disaster when the disaster is analyzed through the layers running through heterogeneous cases in this book.

Thus, the arguments in the following chapters have a broad scope and include heterogeneous cases and systematic and in-depth treatment that enables thorough analysis that cuts across different times, places, and social contexts (namely, covering both width and depth). This kind of approach has been rarely explored in previous studies and is considered outside of the general rules of case analysis,[28] a fact that could provide one of the key reasons why the existence and functioning of structural disaster has been neglected despite evidence of many unexpected extreme events within the science-technology-society interface, both past and present. When structural disaster occurs, devoting energy to an in-depth case analysis situated in a single time, place, and social context, can make the unexpectedly broad extension of the disaster less invisible. By the same token, confining ourselves to far-reaching conceptual arguments without in-depth case analyses could result in discarding the unexpectedly deep layers of the disaster. Neither approach can help us to have a well-balanced and full realization of the events and their implications. This is why this book dares to present the concept of structural disaster,[29] with arguments that are based on the postulates mentioned above.

3 Institutionalized inaction by compliance
From the Great Kanto Earthquake to the nuclear village

This chapter illustrates the sociological implications of structural disaster through unfolding the social background of institutionalized inaction as exemplified by the prediction made by SPEEDI that was never released to the general public, including people concerned with Fukushima at the critical moment of evacuation. A particular focus is placed on the actual workings of institutionalized inaction that pervades different individual behaviors. For example, as discussed in Chapter 1, the Nuclear Safety Commission's Guideline for Monitoring Environmental Radiation that stipulated most details about the utilization of SPEEDI included no stipulation on "protecting the health and safety" of inhabitants around nuclear power stations in emergency situations. Thus, secrecy, coupled with the inaction that resulted from institutional design itself, made real the extent of suffering that resulted from the Fukushima accident. Suffering was brought on by the disaster not by rule-breaking but rather by rigid compliance with a particular institutional design.

This chapter extends these insights across different cases in different time periods in Japan and, in doing so, presents a broader perspective to trace the genealogy of structural disaster and generalizes its sociological implications over a longer time span. First, institutionalized inaction as a cardinal implication of structural disaster should be reconfirmed by independent cases within the same context as the Fukushima accident to set the basis for analyzing the genealogy of structural disaster and generalizing its sociological implications. Three independent cases will be discussed in this chapter: the dual organizational structure of the Governmental Investigation Committee on the Fukushima accident; METI's Report on Severe Accidents in 1992 and its connection with policy measures to deal with the post-Fukushima situation; and procedural legitimation of siting nuclear power stations based on existing power source siting laws.

Additional evidence to illustrate the implications of structural disaster in the context of institutionalized inaction by these independent cases will provide important clues to elaborating the two different types of institutionalized inaction. First, institutionalized inaction can allow the nuclear village to save face in the public sphere by blurring the responsibility of stakeholders;[1] second, institutionalized inaction can use extreme events to enable stakeholders to utilize something that is unusual to gain in a normal state. In either case, institutionalized inaction serves as a tool to realize pay-off, be it face-saving or material gain, at the cost of endangering public interest (including the safety of society). While it can be argued that the devastation of society is too high of a price for the pay-off of local stakeholders, the genealogy of structural disasters reveals that institutionalized inaction can manifest itself at the cost of public interest by taking advantage of extreme events, expected or real, depending on situations.[2]

Dual organizational structure of the governmental investigation committee

The first example that can reconfirm institutionalized inaction of the first type involving the nuclear village implied by structural disaster is the organizational structure of different investigation committees following the Fukushima accident (see Table 3.1).

Of these, the relationships between the National Diet of Japan Fukushima Nuclear Accident Independent Investigation Commission (set up by the Parliament and abbreviated to Parliamentary Investigation Committee) and the Investigation Committee on the Accident at the Fukushima Nuclear Power Stations set up by the government (abbreviated to Governmental Investigation Committee) hold the key to reconfirming and elaborating the institutionalized inaction that has enabled those concerned to save face in the post-Fukushima context.

On January 16, 2012, Kenzo Ohshima, a member of the Parliamentary Investigation Committee, posed a question directly to the chair of the Governmental

Table 3.1 Different Investigation Committees Related to the Fukushima Accident

Founder of investigation committee	Diet	Government	Rebuild Japan Initiative Foundation	TEPCO	Atomic Energy Society of Japan
Chair of Investigation Committee	K. Kurokawa	Y. Hatamura	K. Kitazawa	M. Yamazaki	S. Tanaka
Institutional Affiliation of the Chair	Past President of SCJ	Professor Emeritus of University of Tokyo	Former President of JST	Vice President of TEPCO	Professor of University of Tokyo
Date of the Final Report	7/5/2012	7/23/2012	2/27/2012	6/20/2012	3/14/2014

Source: Produced from Library of Congress (2012) and Atomic Energy Society of Japan (2014).

Investigation Committee, Yotaro Hatamura, under the auspices of whom the Interim Report had just been made public three weeks earlier:

> The Parliamentary Investigation Committee has the right to investigate state affairs while the Governmental Investigation Committee has not. Investigation by the Parliamentary Committee is carried out in public while that by the Governmental one is not. Considering these differences, do you feel something to limit and/or constrain your investigation? If the answer is yes, could you tell us what kind of problems are involved therein?
> (NAIIC 2012c)

The following statement was the answer given:

> The question makes me embarrassed because it makes me aware whether I am able to really tell the truth or not. We have been able to obtain full cooperation from the interviewees. On the other hand, there are some cases in which we feel like checking plans of components in question and, of course, real things.
> (NAIIC 2012c)

This suggests that there is no way to prove what was told by the interviewees independently. The settings in which the investigation was conducted by the committee illustrate the factors working behind the situation. According to the Interim Report of the Governmental Investigation Committee, an agreement on July 8, 2011, among the members of the Governmental Investigation Committee was such that "the interviews are to be made behind closed doors, in principle." Furthermore, according to the same agreement, it is stated that "the secretariat of the committee is to summarize the contents of the interviews and report them to the committee only when necessary." As such, the committee members could participate in the interviews, but the results were to be released only to the committee members within the bounds deemed necessary by the secretariat.[3]

From the viewpoint of the committee members, the traceability of the interview results on which this conclusion was drawn was restricted by various modifications imposed on the members by the secretariat. The secretariat of the Governmental Investigation Committee belongs to the Cabinet Secretariat; as such, the traceability of the interview results is restricted by the government itself, which is the most obvious stakeholder.

On May 24, 2011, however, the cabinet decided that the Governmental Investigation Committee would carry out the investigation "from the neutral and well-balanced standpoint of the people with attention to various different viewpoints"; accordingly, a structural tension would exist between the "neutral standpoint" announced in public and the fact that the Committee was set up by and collaborating with the governmental Secretariat, both being the stakeholders. The restriction imposed on the Committee members by the Secretariat to utilize interview results could thus be construed as one of the means to mitigate such tension; in fact, the above-mentioned agreement among the members of the Governmental Investigation Committee of July 8, 2011, states that all results from interviews made by the committee are "not to be used for searching due responsibility of stakeholders involved in the accident" (The Governmental Investigation Committee 2011b). Thus, the organizational structure of the Committee manifests in the way in which its investigation proceeds without "searching due responsibility of stakeholders in question."

According to the rule of May 31, 2011, ordained by the Cabinet in setting up the Governmental Investigation Committee, the Cabinet Secretariat is authorized to assist the Committee. For example, there is a one-to-one correspondence between the specialized investigation teams of the Committee and the teams of the Secretariat, which are sustained by abundant human resources comprised of team leaders, experts, sub-team leaders, and team members (see Figure 3.1).

When considering the magnitude of the Fukushima accident and its aftermath, it may seem logical that such a well-organized and well-staffed Secretariat would be created in the period following. From the viewpoint of structural disaster, however, there can be differing viewpoints for the roles played by the Secretariat. Because of the above-mentioned structural tension between a supposedly independent third party and stakeholders within a single organization of the Governmental Investigation Committee, the Secretariat of the Committee (as a stakeholder) could play the role of controlling the committee's behavior to fall within the agreement of not "searching due responsibility of stakeholders" under the name of "assisting the Committee."[4]

Such a dual organizational structure as mixing third parties with stakeholders renders responsibility for the Fukushima accident invisible in the public sphere and therefore enables the governmental sector to save face in the post-Fukushima situation. In fact, the Japanese government has made it a rule without exception that government officials are to establish all committees, including the Governmental Investigation Committee. Thus, adherence to such procedures could function as a tool of institutionalized inaction to defocus and/or disguise the due responsibility of the governmental sector.

This is noticeable in two ways when we view the Fukushima accident as a structural disaster. First, fulfilling such a function is an institutionalized result rather than the result of a personal attitude or the behavior pattern of a particular individual. The institutionalized secrecy enabled by the dual organizational structure of the Governmental Investigation Committee, as mentioned above, together with adherence to erroneous precedents, gave rise to the institutionalized inaction. As such, structural reform in institutional design should be mandatory. Second, the chain of institutionalized inaction, when introduced into remedial measures to save face in the public sphere, can give rise to a "reverse salient" (Hughes 1983, 1986) that is difficult to secure without structural reforms. In turn, this invites another institutionalized inaction through employing a quick fix for problems at hand, which is also an element of structural disaster. If this occurs, there is no structural reform at the extreme of this chain of institutionalized inaction, as discussed in the next section.

Institutionalized inaction by compliance 57

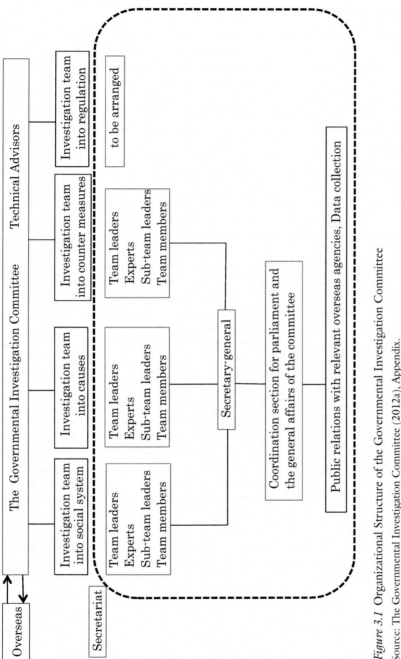

Figure 3.1 Organizational Structure of the Governmental Investigation Committee
Source: The Governmental Investigation Committee (2012a), Appendix.

Quick fixes for problems at hand and lack of structural reform

Another example that reconfirms institutionalized inaction is the relationship between quick fixes for problems at hand and lack of structural reform, which can be seen in the issue of restarting the nuclear power stations after the Fukushima accident. The declaration of safety for nuclear reactors No. 3 and No. 4 at the Ohi nuclear power station by the Japanese government was utilized as the grounds for restarting the reactors in the post-Fukushima situation.[5] The declaration was based on a primary "stress test" comprised of 35 items that assess safety. This stress test, however, was only a simulation by computers conducted within the framework of an event-tree analysis. Although the framework was improved after its failure in the WASH 1400 report to predict the severe accident of Three-Mile Island, basically, the results of the test can change considerably in accordance with the initial conditions assumed and auxiliary presumptions introduced to fix various different parameters, as is often the case with simulations.

This creates a fitting example to examine the relationship between quick fixes for problems at hand and the lack of structural reform in the post-Fukushima situation. What had provided the substantial basic ground for the safety of nuclear reactors was the framework of severe accidents management created by the government (such as METI 1992). However, this framework was made nearly 20 years earlier, when Japan had no experience of severe accidents. This old-fashioned framework clearly stated that "the safety of Japan's nuclear power stations is secured. Speaking engineeringly, the probability of severe accidents is so low that it is unthinkable" (METI 1992: 5). As a severe accident actually happened in Fukushima, however, there is no justification for relying on such a framework in the post-Fukushima situation. Nevertheless, despite the lack of an updated framework, the declaration of safety for nuclear reactors Nos. 3 and 4 at the Ohi nuclear power station was made and the decision to restart the two nuclear reactors was taken. The declaration of safety by the government was made on June 8, 2012 and the restarting of the Ohi nuclear reactors No. 3 and No. 4 was decided on June 16, 2012 (Prime Minister's Office n.d.) Conversely, it was not until September 19, 2012 that the newly established Nuclear Regulatory Authority took over NISA or still later that the old-fashioned framework of severe accidents management was updated.

In this situation, the above-mentioned stress test was utilized as a quick fix for the declaration of safety and restarting of the Ohi nuclear reactors No. 3 and No. 4. Quick fixes for problems at hand as an element of structural disaster justified the state that lacked structural reform such as the updating of the old-fashioned framework of severe accidents management. The question then becomes: Who will take responsibility for the results expected from the decision to restart nuclear power stations decided on such a weak basis?

This reliance on stress test as a quick fix for the declaration of safety and restarting of the nuclear reactors could save face of the nuclear village in the post-Fukushima situation. However, on the other hand, it is obviously unreasonable to put off updating the old-fashioned framework of severe accidents management after the declaration of safety and restarting in practice, when already experiencing a severe accident that demonstrated the devastating failure of the framework. Thus, a quick fix for problems at hand for temporary countermeasures is one of the decisive barriers against drastic structural reform that compels the first type of institutionalized inaction.[6]

Big subsidy in expectation of something unusual

The other type of institutionalized inaction is the utilization of an extreme event by stakeholders in order to obtain something that is typically difficult to gain in a normal state while making no direct action relevant to the risk of the extreme event. This type of institutionalized inaction does not represent the results of the purposive social action of a particular agent with a conscious intention to utilize the extreme event; rather, this type of inaction too is deeply embedded in institutional design.

The success in persuading local residents in more than 50 areas to accept the locations of nuclear power stations prior to the Fukushima accident is a fitting example of this. The siting process of nuclear power stations was made by legitimate law enforcement (rather than being a conspiracy of a particular agent) and is enacted based on a formal process that encompasses three laws ordained in 1974: The Electric Power Development Taxation Law, the Special Budget Law for the Development of Electric Power, and the Law for the Adjustment of Areas Adjacent to Power Generating Facilities. If the items of expenditure authorized to be paid for by the local governments that accepted the siting are deconstructed, the following items in Table 3.2 are articulated. The use of these expenditures under the name of subsidy and/or grants-in-aid has extended over most public goods even if the expenditures are itemized only by Grants-in-Aid for the Promotion of Power Source Location, as shown in Table 3.3.

These expenditures are made within a special account that has a higher degree of freedom in execution, and the basic ground for the expenditures is compensation by money allocated for unusual risk, such as that expected from nuclear power plant siting (for example, toxic spent fuel storage, damage by heated effluents, terrorist attack). Behind the scenes and out of the public purview, there is an unbalanced distribution of merits such that large nuclear power stations and related facilities often provide the sited areas with no electricity. This creates an imbalance between populated areas that consume the electricity produced by nuclear power stations and the unpopulated areas that accept the siting of these stations that supply electricity to the populated areas. As a model case, according to METI (2016: 3–4), the siting of a nuclear power station with an output of 135 million kW is estimated to bring to the sited areas 1,240 billion yen out of the special account of the national treasury based on power source siting laws, with the assumption that it will take seven years to build the plant and another 10 years to begin operation, which will then continue to operate for 35 years (see Table 3.4).

Table 3.2 Items of Public Expenditure for the Siting of Nuclear Power Stations

Grants/subsidies	Relevant projects	Areas	Upper limit and term of grants
Grants for the Initial Measures for Power Source Siting	(1) Promotion of public understanding of power source facilities and promotion of siting power source facilities (2) Project for improving welfare of local citizens (3) Project for industrial promotion (4) Project for fisheries promotion (5) Prefectural project for promoting fisheries around nuclear power facilities	City, town, village, and prefecture	For nuclear power facilities: Period I: From the second year of feasibility studies to the starting year of environmental impact assessment; 1.4 billion yen/each fiscal year Period II: 10 years from the second year of environmental impact assessment; 9.8 billion yen/each fiscal year, up to 51.5 billion yen within the period Period III: Following fiscal year of the last year of Period II to commencement of power generation; 0.8 billion yen/each fiscal year
Grants for PR/Safety Measures	(1) Dissemination of knowledge concerning nuclear power utilization and coordination concerning research and safety (2) Research and assessment of the impact of warm wastewater around siting area, and maintenance of facilities and equipment's for the research and assessment (3) Maintenance of PR training facilities for nuclear power	(1) City, town, village, and prefecture, and neighboring municipalities (2) Prefecture (3) Prefecture	(1) In accordance with the number of siting facilities: Prefecture 18~42 million yen/year Neighboring municipalities 6.3~18.9 million yen/year (2) In accordance with the number/contents of projects, 5 million yen/year~ (3) 389.2 million yen/year for a PR training facility
Subsidies for Industrial Development in Power-Source Siting Areas	Making industrial development plan within the power source siting area, Promoting technological introduction into the area	City, town, village, and neighboring municipalities	Applied for power stations over one million kW. Subsides 3/4 of running cost. The upper limit is set by business type.

Grants for Power Plant Siting Promotion	Public facilities in actual power generating facility's siting municipality, and neighboring municipalities, maintenance of facilities for the promotion of industrial development	City, town, village, and neighboring municipalities	For nuclear power stations, grant is calculated by the following equation, and granted to the sited communities and neighboring municipalities. Total cost = 750yen/kW × output power(kW) × coefficient7
Special Grant for Power Plant Siting (Grants for Nuclear Power Plant Facilities Siting Neighboring Areas)	Grant for local citizens and local companies (electricity charge discount), and company introduction/industrial modernization in commutable area	City, town, village, and neighboring municipalities	Number of local citizens contractor × kW of company contractor × unit costs of nuclear power facilities
Special Grants for Power Plant Siting (Grants for Power Supplying Prefectures)	Industrial location and industrial modernization within commutable area in neighboring municipalities	City, town, village, and neighboring municipalities	(1) Under 50 billion kWh 0.75 billion yen ~ over 1,200 billion kWh 36 billion yen (2) For the installing of first reactor over 500 thousand kW, 10 billion yen for 5 years from the second year of construction
Grants for Long-Term Development in Nuclear Power Facilities Siting Areas	Industrial location, industrial modernization, and promotion of welfare in nuclear facilities' siting municipalities	City, or town, and village	(1) From second year of operation till the end of operation of a nuclear power facilities: 1 billion yen/1 million kW/year (2) After 15 years of operation, 50 million yen/ 1 million kW/year will be added.

Source: METI (2008a).

Table 3.3 Public Facilities Built by the Grants-in-Aid for the Promotion of the Power Source Location

Public facilities	Examples of public facilities
Roads	Prefectural roads, municipal roads
Harbors	Waterways and basins for small crafts, protective facilities for harbors, mooring facilities
Fishing ports	Small fishing facilities in ports for coastal fisheries
Parks	Disaster prevention green belt, parks (children's playgrounds, community parks, neighborhood parks, athletic parks)
Water supply	Waterworks, small-scale water supply system
Communication facilities	Wire broadcasting facilities, radio broadcasting facilities, cable television facilities, and other similar facilities
Sports facilities	Gymnastic halls, swimming pools, athletic grounds, parks, green fields, ski sites, skate rinks, campsites, cycling paths, and other related facilities
Environmental hygienic facilities	Domestic waste disposal facilities (waste disposal facilities, excrement treatment facilities), public sewage systems, urban drainage systems, drainage canals, environmental monitoring facilities, industrial waste disposal facilities, graveyards, crematories, road cleaning vehicles, snowplow vehicles, wagons for collecting waste, hearses, pollution detecting vehicles, and other related equipment
Educational and cultural facilities	Schools, training centers, community centers, libraries, museums, accommodations for youth, other social education facilities, halls for workers, school lunch preparation centers, Judo/Kendo training halls, meeting halls, cultural halls, and other related facilities
Medical facilities	Hospitals, public health centers, health centers for children, medical devices and equipment, ambulances, and other related facilities
Social welfare Facilities	Children's recreational facilities, nursery centers, children's park, welfare facilities for mothers and children, welfare facilities for the elderly (community centers for the aged, recreation centers for the aged), public baths, and other related facilities
Fire-fighting facilities	Fire-fighting stations
Land conservation facilities	Facilities for the prevention of landslips, facilities for the prevention of collapsing steep slopes, forest preservation facilities, coastal protection facilities, river erosion control facilities
Traffic safety facilities	Traffic signals, traffic signs, traffic safety PR vehicles, other traffic safety-related facilities
Heat supply facilities	Area cooling and heating systems, and other related facilities
Industrial development facilities	Agricultural roads, forestry roads, drainage facilities for agricultural wastewater, industrial parks, job training facilities, buildings for the promotion of commerce and industry, and other related facilities

Source: METI (2008b).

Table 3.4 Estimated Economic Effects from Subsidy and Grants-in-Aid on Power Source Siting Laws

Item	Amount of grant (billion yen)
Grant for the Initial Measures for Power Source Siting	52
Grant for Power Plant Siting Promotion	142
Grant for Nuclear Power Stations Located in Region	597
Grant for Power Supplying Prefectures	275
Grant for Long-Term Development in Nuclear Power Facilities Siting Area	149
Grant for Harmonious Coexistence with Power Source Located Region	25
Total	1,240

Source: Produced from METI (2016).
Note: The estimation is made for 35 years since the start of construction.

Thus, this type of institutionalized inaction originates from the utilization of expected risk from potential extreme events by stakeholders to gain something that is typically difficult to gain in a normal state. The gains in the example used above are the immense subsidies and grants-in-aid resulting from sited areas of nuclear power stations, and what differentiates this gain from that in a normal state is the unusual risk expected from the siting of these stations, the expectation of which actually authorizes and legitimates the input. The elements of structural disaster relevant to this case are adherence to erroneous precedents that, in turn, cause problems to be carried over and reproduced, and quick fixes for current problems that lead to further such fixes as temporary countermeasures, both of which are embodied in the power source siting laws. As to adherence to erroneous precedents, it is not certain whether the institutional design to invite the siting of nuclear power stations can be considered erroneous at a time when the laws were originally promulgated back in 1974. However, because there was no change to these laws after the Fukushima accident, this poses a question about the validity of inviting the siting via compensation involving money enabled by the laws; as such, adherence to erroneous precedents can be assumed.

Based on these examples what kind of genealogy of institutionalized inaction can we envisage, and in what sense can we say that this genealogy features the characteristics of structural disaster? The next section will provide answers to these questions by examining Japan's past science-technology-society interface in the pre-war period.

After the Great Kanto Earthquake: a national research institute that works by inertia

Another example of the second type of institutionalized inaction (coupled with the utilization of extreme events by stakeholders to gain something unusual) is a past case that occurred during the time period immediately after the Great Kanto Earthquake of 1923.

> At the time of the earthquake . . . perhaps a day or two after the earthquake . . . anyway, we wrote down even the items that didn't exist, you see. I confess now. Speaking of the machines . . . we only had a 30-ton Amsler, an Olsen impact tester, and a Brinell. That's all we had, but we wrote down a lot of things and multiplied them into 67 pages of items taking advantage of the earthquake. . . . He undertook sort of thing without any hesitation. He exhibited . . . how should I put it . . . a surprising political skill to negotiate without a qualm. I have much respect for him for that. Not only that, he said "go find a piece of vacant land somewhere because we now have tentative prospects for a temporary building," we answered, "perhaps the lot where the undersecretary's official residence used to be might work." Then he told us to just go ahead and rope off the place. So we roped off where the Postal Savings Bureau was and went ahead with building a house.
> (National Institute for Ship Experiment 1956: 134)

The above statement was made on November 7, 1946, at the National Institute for Ship Experiment of the Ministry of Transport (the current National Maritime Research Institute) during a ceremony for the Institute's 30th anniversary, where a recollection roundtable was held. The remark was extracted from the Commemoration History of the Institute (National Institute for Ship Experiment 1956), which compiled talks and related documents from this event.

Yakebutori – becoming more prosperous by taking advantage of disasters: the case of the National Institute for Ship Experiments before and after the Great Kanto Earthquake

In the extract quoted above, "earthquake" refers to the Great Kanto Earthquake, which occurred on September 1, 1923. "Amsler" is a material testing machine for tensile strength; "impact tester" gages material strength; and "Brinell" refers to a hardness tester for the hardness of materials. The individuals who attended the roundtable included 14 former employees of the Institute, the current director, and the current section chief directors of the National Institute for Ship Experiment.

The quote reveals how those who worked in the national research institute lacked adequate testing equipment, but nevertheless successfully expanded the facilities – both the building and equipment – by taking advantage of a restoration budget that was granted after they lost the entire building as a result of the Great Kanto Earthquake. An attendant at the roundtable said: "The building of the institute was burned down by the Great Kanto Earthquake . . . We put everything in one location that is closer to Onhamagoten where we constructed a larger building thanks to *yakebutori*, making huge progress" (National Institute for Ship Experiment 1956: 132).

Institutionalized inaction by compliance 65

Yakebutori, in this context, corresponds to the type of institutionalized inaction in which stakeholders utilize an extreme event to gain something that would be typically difficult to gain in a normal state with no relevant action to the recovery from the extreme event. What is gained here is the expansion of space, buildings, and equipment for the Institute. What differentiates this gain from that in a normal state is an unusual post-disaster situation where no evidence was left to prove that damages resulted from the Great Kanto Earthquake except for self-declaration and the general, visible devastation after the earthquake.

As suggested above, there was certainly a particular agent with an intention to utilize the devastation after the Great Kanto Earthquake for self-benefit; however, this type of institutionalized inaction was not the result of the purposive social action of only this one agent, because this type of inaction is deeply embedded in the institutional dimension. For example, taking advantage of the earthquake to achieve *yakebutori* seems to have been widespread at the time, almost as if it were a success story such that those taking advantage of the disaster were persons rendering a distinguished service (National Institute for Ship Experiment 1956: 131–139). The given accounts and recollections that made up these claims have a due social background that is related to the institutional dimension; in particular, the elements of structural disaster involved in this case are adherence to erroneous precedents that, in turn, cause problems to be carried over and reproduced, and quick fixes for current problems that lead to further such fixes as temporary countermeasures.

At the time, establishing a ship experimental station was an ardent wish of the government officials involved, because the ship model basin that was planned to be installed at the station was an integral testing facility for determining optimal hull form through model experiments. Other countries at the time were also constructing such facilities for use in building merchant vessels and warships. Although establishing a ship model basin that could be used to build merchant vessels had long been expected in Japan as contributing to the public interest, the plan was not easy to materialize.

The Ministry of Communication, which was in charge of ships and watercrafts at the time, finally allocated a portion of the fiscal year 1921 budget for building a towing tank and initiated construction after obtaining the approval of the Imperial Diet. The tank was not completed until 1930, however, after being interrupted by deferred spending in the aftermath of the Great Kanto Earthquake. The situation the quote at the beginning of this section represents is the interruption caused by the Great Kanto Earthquake during this process of development. On one hand, the officially stated objective clearly contributed to the public interest; on the other, the confusion caused by the earthquake seems to have been taken advantage of to achieve the objective. The reason for mentioning this anecdote is to highlight the fact that the behavior of the actors in *yakebutori* to take advantage of the disaster – a social action that is generally frowned upon – is actually noted as something to be respected within this governmental organization. In fact, the Institute went on to say:

> Meanwhile . . . the Postal Savings Bureau belatedly came by and said "this is scandalous conduct, this land belongs to the Postal Saving Bureau," but we

already had the house built anyhow, you know . . . I've heard they had to deal with very persistent harassment from the Postal Savings Bureau, but, his efforts were meritorious. In fact, several different individuals voiced praise, such as noting "powerful influence" and "demonstrating his ability."

(National Institute for Ship Experiment 1956: 134)

As stated previously, this type of inaction is deeply embedded in the institutional dimension, meaning that "good people" who made contributions to a given sector or organization could play a role in utilizing extreme events such as the Great Kanto Earthquake for the self-benefit of a given sector or organization that would not be apparent to the public. Because this example of the construction of the ship model basin is merely a "storm in a teacup," so to say, between the National Institute for Ship Experiment and the Postal Savings Bureau within the same governmental sector, it is unclear whether the Ministry of Communications' proceeding with its construction could be considered structural disaster, without clearer implications for the failure in the science-technology-society interface.

However, if a similar situation were to occur between a governmental sector and the public interest of the citizen sector, for example, and the agents responsible for *yakebutori* elicited praise via institutional legitimation in the same way while the public interest was compromised, then this would mean that "good people" who contribute to a particular organization and/or a particular sector are playing a role of contributing to a structural disaster by containing the problem within the bounds of the organization and/or the sector in question and hiding it from the public.

Such a state cannot be observed by a third party in the public sphere. The mechanism of following an erroneous precedent within a locally "agreeable" equilibrium state and continually reproducing this within a particular organization and/or sector presumes this type of condition. The below comment (which was also part of the same celebration and roundtable) reveals how a problem can be reproduced when following precedent:

Old-timers taught me to be persistent enough . . . you just have to become dumb and stay persistent because everyone will bring up a reasonable argument so that it is extremely difficult to persuade others by reason. Since then, I played dumb and got by because I was told there is no other way.

(National Institute for Ship Experiment 1956: 141)

Thus, in terms of adherence to erroneous precedents and secrecy, structural disaster may be traced back to the case of the National Research Institute after the Great Kanto Earthquake. If everyone acted based on such a precept in a situation in which a structural disaster was already occurring in terms of adherence to erroneous precedents and secrecy, the disaster would be repeatedly perpetuated using the existing institutions as steppingstones. In view of this possibility, how was Japan's science-technology-society interface developed with respect to the nuclear regime (for example, the government-industrial-university complex of nuclear power)? The answer to this question concerns both the continuity and discontinuity between Japan's pre-war science-technology-society interface and this same interface in the post-war period.

Advanced defense nation versus high economic growth nation: recurring structural disaster

> Having hit rock bottom . . . we have only one path to follow: resolving to build a new, cultivated Japan with the power of education, instead of having the armed forces, to contribute to the advancement of the world.
> (The History of Science Society of Japan 1964: 45)

The above remark was made by Tamon Maeda, then-Minister of Education, during a radio broadcast on September 9, 1945. When WWII ended, Japan's production capacity in terms of the industrial production index (IPI) had fallen to about half of what it had been in 1940, as almost one-third of the country's industrial machinery, one-quarter of its buildings, and more than 80 percent of its merchant ships had been destroyed (Bank of Japan 1966). The post-war Japanese society began after the country's national wealth was completely destroyed, and veering toward peace (as quoted above) was the basic policy at the time.

Swords to plowshares after defeat in WWII

In an effort to build a new, more cultivated Japan, there was enthusiastic hope for the promotion of science and technology. Calls for improved public welfare through the promotion of democratic science and technology had also risen, indicating remorse over war that promised to effect change. Ultimately, it was the aim of economic recovery (which would later lead to high economic growth), that gave the idea of reconstruction in Japan its main purpose through the use of science and technology for non-military purposes. From this perspective, the dichotomy of a pre-war militaristic nation and post-war economic nation is often referred to; indeed, the goal had changed.

Gained experience that would contribute to this goal, however, had been developing prior to and during the war, and this was passed down after the war in different forms. For example, the seeds of science and technology – particularly in areas such as warplanes, warships, radio wave weapons, and optical weapons – developed before and during the war had led to various other product development within major companies that were instrumental in the reconstruction of Japan's economy. Cases such as those listed in Table 3.5 are excerpted from a study conducted by the 149th Committee of the Japan Society for the Promotion of Science (JSPS 1993, 1996).

If structural disasters already existed in terms of adherence to erroneous precedents and secrecy well before WWII, as suggested in the previous section, it is

68 Institutionalized inaction by compliance

Table 3.5 Examples of Technological Swords to Plowshares (Excerpt)

Areas	Core technology	Pre-war status of the inventors	Post-war status of the inventors
Warplanes	Supercharger	Nakajima Airplane Ltd., Deputy manager	Nissan, Senior managing director
Warplanes	Vibration control	Naval aeronautical engineer	IHI, Managing director
Warplanes	Aerodynamics	Tachikawa Aiaplane Co., an employee	Toyota, Senior managing director
Warships	Hydro-dynamics	Tokyo Imperial University, Associate Professor	Hitachi Shipbuilding Ltd., President
Warships	High-tensile steel	Imperial Japanese Navy, Major	NKK Co., Chief of Technical Laboratory
Radio waves weapons	Magnetron	Nihon Musen Ltd., an employee	Nihon Musen Ltd., Senior managing director
Radio waves weapons	Television	NHK, Technical Laboratory, Staff member	Victor Company of Japan, Chief of the Central Research Institute
Optical weapons	Calculators for fire control	NIKON Ltd., an employee	NIKON Ltd., Vice president
Torpedo	Automatic control techniques	Imperial Japanese Navy, Major	The Cannon Inc., Vice president
Fire balloon	Composite materials	Imperial Japanese Navy, Major	Mitsubishi Acetate Co., Managing director
Fuel	Coal liquefaction	Nihon Chisso Ltd., an employee	Asahi Kasei Ltd., Managing director

Source: Produced from JSPS (1993, 1996).

Note: All private companies appearing in pre-war status of the inventors were military designated factories.

possible that such elements that form structural disaster were also passed down. For example, adherence to erroneous precedents and secrecy could, in combination with each other, defocus the locus of agents responsible for WWII and could be passed down to trigger a structural disaster in the post-war period in a different form. For example, when we broaden our perspective to embrace an institutional spin-off from the governmental sector's experience during the wartime mobilization of science and technology, such a spin-off can be observed in the post-war period.

Science- and technology-driven nation and structural disaster during the wartime mobilization period

In particular, the institutional spin-off from the pre-war experience of establishing the Agency of Technology (Gijutsu In) in 1942, which aimed to create a

Table 3.6 Summary of Policy Formulation and Revision-Related Administrative Documents Prior to the Establishment of the Agency of Technology (June 1940 to October 1941)

Classification	Number of documents
Top secret	59
Secret	3
Reference	2
Others	21
Total	85

Source: Calculated based on Kokusaku Kenkyukai Archives.

comprehensive policy for the wartime mobilization of science and technology, to the post-war institutional design, which was oriented toward economic recovery, reveals that such a spin-off accommodates the elements of structural disaster.[7] According to the archives of the Kokusaku Kenkyukai (referred to as Kokusaku Kenkyukai Archives hereafter), 85 administrative documents related to the establishment of the Agency of Technology were issued during the period from June 1940 through October 1941 (see Appendix A). This translates to a frequency of one document per five to six days. A summary of these documents is shown in Table 3.6.

As shown in the table, there were numerous top secret proposals, secret proposals, reference information, and revisions, negotiations, and arrangements for these items. The process of establishing the Agency of Technology was a large-scale experiment of administrative reform to conduct subtle yet complicated interactions across governmental agencies under an emergency situation during the wartime mobilization of science and technology. In particular, this allowed the governmental sector to experience firsthand how a science- and technology-driven nation (namely, one that positions science and technology as a primary means to achieve social goals and approves its promotion) could become critical in various situations. Furthermore, it provided an opportunity for the sector to learn how to coordinate the local interests of the different ministries and agencies, and ultimately to gain consensus under this mobilization. The elements of structural disaster such as adherence to erroneous precedents and secrecy detected before wartime mobilization of science and technology within the bounds of the governmental sector's national research institute after an extreme event (the Great Kanto Earthquake) could be preserved through such experience and gained skills of the governmental sector in another extreme event: WWII.

Regarding the institutional legacy passed down to the post-war era, programs such as the Ministry of Education's research grant program established in 1939 and institutions such as the JSPS, which was established in 1932 by pooling donations from the business community, an imperial donation of 1.5 million yen, and government grant of 1 million yen, are influential. Compared to these, the above-mentioned administrative experience and gained skills are less visible; however, in these institutional spin-offs, adherence to erroneous precedents coupled with secrecy as elements of structural disaster could be easily overlooked by many people. In addition, this invisibility makes it possible that they activated other elements of structural disaster and that these additional elements were preserved after WWII.

To ascertain this possibility, I split the following argument into two parts; first, ascertaining the elements of structural disaster in the science-technology-society interface with a focus on the wartime mobilization of science and technology in the pre-war period; and second, ascertaining whether similar elements can be found in the post-war period. In particular, quick fixes as temporary countermeasures as an element of structural disaster are suspected to have been activated through the idea of a science- and technology-driven nation as being a sacred cause in the wartime mobilization of science and technology during and after WWII. In fact, the idea is clearly observed in the proposal to expand technology research agencies, dated June 25, 1940, which is the first top secret document listed in Table 3.6 and is excerpted below:

> In order to successfully carry out the ethnic mission of founding a new order in East Asia . . . and handle the rapid transformation of international political situations, the national defense force must be strengthened and the production capacity must be increased foremost. . . . For that, the matters to be settled first are the independence of our country's technology, improvement of its standards, and streamlining the technology mobilization structure. . . . In addition to planning for international technological independence, having our country's industry to outgrow the colonial status of Western countries, and improving the international standards of Japanese technology . . . try to organize government agencies and research institutions in preparation for the forthcoming stage of leaps and bounds of total war.
> (Kokusaku Kenkyukai Archives)

Based on this view, they offered quick fixes as temporary countermeasures to re-inspect research institutions in Japan and correct their perceived shortcomings. The same document summarized those shortcomings into 10 items, five verbatim examples of which are as follows (Kokusaku Kenkyukai Archives):

- Corporate research institutions have degraded to profit-oriented research while government research institutions have fallen to preparing irresponsible research papers, and since there is actually a tendency to honor those, they fall short of industrial research.
- The current research institutions do not have any principle for establishing priorities in the researches, which are being conducted based on personal preference and curiosity.
- Researchers are not aware of the issues the government and industry want investigated. There is no communication between researchers and practitioners.

- It is difficult to hire excellent researchers because rewards for researchers are quite poor.
- In terms of human resource management of research institutions, there are only so-called "factions" but no principle of merit system.

These points might pre-empt the issues that are identified when the research environment for innovation is discussed in post-war Japan. In addition, these points could serve to encourage the modernization of the academic sector; however, what actually emerged was a scheme in which the governmental sector required science and technology to provide quick fixes for cooperating with predetermined national goals. For example, "Outline for Establishing a New Science and Technology Structure" of August 23, 1940, states the following:

> In order to enhance and expand the national defense strength and the production capacity through a comprehensive use of modern science and technology, we are determined to establish a military state by promoting science and technology research, taking measures to proactively utilize their results, establishing technology with Japanese characteristics grounded on the resources within the Greater East Asia self-sufficient zone, and encouraging the improvement of technology standards, in addition to developing and strengthening an advanced science and technology structure.
> (Kokusaku Kenkyukai Archives)

It is worth noting that, in addition to the governmental sector being proactive toward quick fixes for cooperating with predetermined policies, the movement to support these quick fixes from the bottom up through nationwide science and technology education emerged simultaneously. The movement aimed to improve scientific knowledge in the citizen sector through the spread of school-age education, adult education, and scientific thinking among the general public, which is illustrated in "Summary Measures for the Outline for Establishing a Science and Technology Structure" of September 5, 1940:

> The popularization of science in people's lives can be achieved through school and social education by trying to improve scientific knowledge of people and spread scientific thinking in order to arouse interest in science and technology among people and infiltrate science into their lives.
> (Kokusaku Kenkyukai Archives)

Given that Japan had just enacted the National Mobilization Law in 1938 and the war with Britain and the United States was about to break out, it could be assumed that the inclination toward quick fixes for current problems was unavoidable;[8] however, this is nearly the same idea as within a science- and technology-driven nation that supports post-war reconstruction, where the goal to build an advanced military state is replaced with the goal to achieve high economic growth.

72 Institutionalized inaction by compliance

Continuity of the science- and technology-driven nation from the pre-war to the post-war period

According to the House of Representatives' resolution on the promotion of science and technology, stated on March 11, 1950:

> In order for our country with its excessive population to truly gain independence and [rebuild], we must seek our foundation in science. That is, the development of industrial economy and the improvement of culture can be achieved only by promoting science and technology and cultivating scientific intelligence.

In addition, *Keidanren Geppo (Keidanren Monthly Report)*, the journal of the Keidanren (currently the Japan Business Federation) established in 1948, published "Requests Related to the Development of a Comprehensive Research Institution" on August 31, 1954. The idea of a science- and technology-driven nation that emerged during the wartime mobilization of science and technology supported post-war reconstruction as quick fixes for current problems, the element of structural disaster which seems to have been passed down and works effectively even when goals are swapped.

Regarding the wartime mobilization of science and technology in the pre-war period, the strategies to determine policies, schedule centrally, and coherently mobilize competent human resources and materials in a focused, well-timed manner were absent because of the "quick-fix" strategy and the arbitrary assumptions needed to produce such quick fixes. For example, the United States Military's scientific intelligence investigation team, which remained in Japan from September to October of 1945, investigated the realities of Japan's wartime mobilization of science and technology and prepared a confidential military report consisting of five volumes. The first volume mentions that the lack of such strategies led Japan to "run out of time" to efficiently mobilize science and technology (GHQ/SCAP 1945a). The very strategies used to effectively determine policies, schedule centrally, and coherently mobilize competent human resources are currently referred to as research and development. Therefore, what the United States military's scientific intelligence investigation team was saying was that Japan was defeated in terms of wartime mobilization of science and technology because quick fixes superseded systematic research and development. Conversely, the successful wartime mobilization of science and technology that was normalized in peacetime immediately after the war (Bush 1946) led to what is called the "linear model" of research and development, such that scientific research precedes technological development, which in turn precedes the successful achievement of social goals.[9]

The idea of a science- and technology-driven nation that supports pre-war wartime mobilization of science and technology was passed down as the precedent for the support of post-war reconstruction. As far as adherence to erroneous precedents is concerned, this succession, as well as the reliance on quick fixes for current problems in given social contexts, are considered elements of structural disaster. As such, there is a possibility that the post-war period began with a combination of the two elements of structural disaster: adherence to erroneous precedents and quick fixes for current problems as temporary countermeasures.

The simplistic idea of viewing science and technology only as quick fixes for current problems remains and is evident in the idea of techno-nationalism through promotion of science and technology via innovation and creation of intellectual property, as defined by the Basic Law on Science and Technology ordained in 1995 in Japan (Ministry of Internal Affairs and Communications 2014). From the Fukushima nuclear accident itself through the responses to the event, including the disputes over resuming the operation of the Ohi nuclear power station, it is evident that this idea is not relevant to solving problems for the actual victims.[10]

The idea that a science- and technology-driven nation represents one form of the quick fixes for current problems can occur regardless of the characteristics or the ideology of the bearer, which can be located in different time periods and across different social contexts. One typical example of this is cooperation with war efforts by Haruki Aikawa, a pre-war Marxist theorist on technological development who served as the assistant secretary for the second and third subcommittees of the Greater East Asia Co-Prosperity Sphere Science and Technology Structure Research Team established on October 26, 1942 (Kokusaku Kenkyukai 1945). Because the materialization of the Greater East Asia Co-Prosperity Sphere was the paramount objective of the wartime mobilization of science and technology at the time, the idea that a science- and technology-driven nation could have a wartime purpose was promoted by Marxist scholars as one quick fix for current problems.[11]

If structural disaster was passed down from the pre-war to the post-war period, viewing such an event as merely as "turnaround" would obscure the essential issue. This is because there were innumerable cases of turnarounds that were incorporated into the Greater East Asia Co-Prosperity Sphere to act as their instruments in terms of wartime mobilization in general (Baba 1971; Kawamura 1996). There were also reverse cases in which government officials from various ministries and related bodies during the wartime mobilization (for example, Ministry of Commerce and Industry, Agency of Technology, and Ministry of Communications) played a positive role in mobilizing science and technology turnarounds for the post-war reconstruction of Japan (Oyodo 1989; Sawai 2012). It was possible to share the benefits of such actions among the general public after the high economic growth period occurred.

This is a social phenomenon that can be recognized almost independently from the ideologies and individual characteristics of those who uphold the idea. If this continues even after a dramatic social change, such as the change from a militaristic state in the pre-war period to an economic state in the post-war period, this reveals that the idea of a science- and technology-driven nation is a quick fix for current problems as a temporary countermeasure, and that since this idea displays an element of structural disaster in different social contexts, it is historically robust and could continue to survive in the future. Intellectual imagination is required to identify these types of elements of structural disaster that transcend the boundaries of time and then translate them into the situation following the Fukushima nuclear accident as well.

Part of forgetting or ignoring "bad" traditions in the past and devoting efforts into more constructive nation-building for the future is certainly uniting under a common grand purpose. However, structural disaster is deeply related to the idea of a common grand purpose rather than the minor differences among the bad traditions of the past, which justifies this book's interest in the dynamic aspects of structural disaster. This book does not take a broad view of multi-sectored entities such as the nuclear village; rather, it examines such entities through their formation and transformation mechanisms within the science-technology-society interface. From such a viewpoint, the nuclear village has its own *raison d'être* as a kind of governmental-industrial-academic complex, which will be demonstrated in the next section with particular reference to the emergence of the post-war nuclear regime in Japan.

How nuclear power bills are drafted

> As far as I can see in the development of the basic framework for nuclear power research and development, the academic sector in Japan mostly cannot be called responsible nor instrumental in reality, regardless of promotion of or criticism against nuclear power . . . they are excluded from a substantial decision-making process by the governmental and industrial sectors. As a result . . . this is equivalent to citizens being excluded from the process.
> (Matsumoto 1998: 252)

While the above view was voiced in 1998, it remains relatively unchanged in the present day, even after experiencing the Fukushima nuclear accident, because the governmental and industrial sectors still lack a serious interest in deriving lessons from the structural disaster aspects of that event to serve in constructive nation rebuilding. A clue to this problem lies in the characteristics of the nuclear energy development and utilization regime, as they exclude the academic and citizen sectors. The regime is led by the governmental and industrial sectors, and all others must react *ex post facto* to the situation.

Proactive and reactive parties in the creation of nuclear energy bills

In post-war Japan, the nuclear energy development and utilization system evolved under the leadership of the governmental and industrial sectors.[12] On March 3, 1954, a budget proposal of 252 million yen for nuclear energy research was submitted to the Budget Committee of the House of Representatives. Following, the governmental sector immediately began building the nuclear energy development and utilization regime (see Table 3.7).[13]

On March 1, 1956, the industrial sector founded the Japan Atomic Industrial Forum (JAIF), an integrated nuclear energy-related industrial association with

Table 3.7 The Government Sector's Process of Building Nuclear Energy Development and Utilization Regime

Date	Item
1954/5/11	Cabinet set up the investigation committee into the preparation for nuclear utilization
1954/6/19	MITI set up a preliminary meeting for nuclear-related budget
1955/12/13–16	Nuclear-related laws were submitted to the 23rd extraordinary diet session
1955/12/19	Atomic Energy Basic Act was promulgated
1955/12/19	Atomic Energy Commission was set up in the Prime Minister's Office
1956/5/4	Special Act on the Development of Nuclear Source Material was promulgated
1956/5/4	Act on Public Corporation for Nuclear Fuel Material was promulgated
1956/5/15	Government ordinance was issued for the definition of nuclear source material
1956/5/19	STA was set up
1956/6/15	Japan Atomic Energy Agency was set up under the aegis of STA
1957/3/7	Atomic Energy Commission submitted a report for the early introduction of nuclear power plant
1957/6/10	Act on the Prevention of Radiation Hazards was promulgated
1960/3/26	Atomic Energy Commission submitted a report for institutionalizing nuclear damage compensation system
1961/6/17	Act on Nuclear Damage Compensation was promulgated
1961/6/17	Act on Nuclear Damage Compensation Contract was promulgated

more than 350 member companies, under the persuasion of Matsutaro Shoriki, who had served as the first chairman of the Japanese Atomic Energy Commission (JAEC). Almost simultaneously, the so-called "five groups in the nuclear energy industry" (see Table 3.8) were formed for research, development, and financing purposes in anticipation of future orders for nuclear power reactors.

In this way, Mitsubishi Atomic Power Industries, with a total capital of 500 million yen; Nippon Atomic Industry Group Company (Mitsui Group), with a total capital of 500 million yen; and Sumitomo Atomic Energy Industries, with a total capital of 630 million yen were founded, together with two other groups (shown in Table 3.8). In addition, Japan Atomic Power Company, with a total capital of 1 billion yen, was founded on November 1, 1957, as the main entity to receive improved Calder Hall reactors, which were the first reactors installed in Japan. Of this money held by the Japan Atomic Power Company, 42 percent was funded by nine electric power companies. The five groups in the nuclear energy industry jointly took part in designing,

Table 3.8 Composition of the Five Groups in the Nuclear Energy Industry at the Time of Formation

Name of groups	Start-up year	Member companies	Foreign technical partnership
Mitsubishi	1955	Mitsubishi Electric Co. and 26 other companies	Westinghouse
Tokyo Genshiryoku	1956	Hitachi Ltd. and 17 other companies	English Electric Group, GE
Sumitomo	1956	Sumitomo Metal Industries, Ltd. and 16 other companies	United Nuclear
Mitsui	1956	Toshiba Co. and 39 other companies	GE
Daiichi Genshiryoku	1956	Kawasaki Heavy Industries Ltd. and 27 other companies	Siemens

Source: Produced from JAIF (1965: 98–101).

manufacturing, and installing the first made-in-Japan reactor (JRR-3), the ground for which was broken on January 14, 1959.[14]

In response, the academic sector – particularly SCJ – was ultimately unable to exert effective influence during the sequence of such events. The path along which the governmental and industrial sector led and the academic sector reacted *ex post facto* is conjoined with the elements of structural disaster because of the social process by which the path was created.

Structural disaster and how nuclear energy bills are drafted

Genshiryoku Sho-hoan no Umareru made (How various nuclear energy bills are created) (1964), the type-written documents extending to over six volumes and prepared by Seijiro Sugata, who was involved in the social process to establish the nuclear energy development and utilization system as a research expert of the National Diet Library, can clarify this process. The document series began in 1956 but sat untouched by Sugata for nine years. In what follows, I refer to these documents as the "Sugata Documents."

In the process of creating the nuclear regime during the post-war period for the development and utilization of nuclear energy in which the governmental and industrial sector would lead and the academic sector would react *ex post facto*, there are two elements of structural disaster that can be observed: secrecy and quick fixes for current problems as temporary countermeasures based on convenient assumptions. First, secrecy is observed at the beginning of the process to create the nuclear regime in the post-war period, wherein the academic sector reacts *ex post facto*. It is said that Article 1 of the three principles of nuclear energy utilization of the Atomic Energy Basic Law (drafted by the governmental sector) reflects the following from SCJ (part of the academic sector) (Tezuka 1995: 88): "The Statement to Demand the Principles of Disclosure,

Democracy, and Independence in the Research and Usage of Nuclear Energy" of April 29, 1954, and issued at the 17th conference of the SCJ. As such, the principle of disclosure is supposed to have been incorporated into the law.

This principle of disclosure expressed in the statement of the SCJ directly conflicts with secrecy. Additional text of the relevant section of the SCJ's statement is as follows:

> It is our firm resolution that we shall not conduct any research related to atomic weapon of other countries, not to mention research on atomic weapon in our country. We . . . first demand that all information on the research and usage of atomic energy is completely disclosed and put forward to the public.
> (SCJ 1977: 68–69)

Conversely, the three principles of nuclear energy in the Atomic Energy Basic Law state the following:

> The research, development, and utilization of nuclear energy shall be limited to peaceful purposes, shall aim at ensuring safety, and shall be performed independently under democratic administration, and the results obtained shall be made public so as to actively contribute to international cooperation.
> (Atomic Energy Basic Law 1955: Chapter 1, Clause 2)

As such, "all information is completely disclosed" was changed to "the results obtained shall be made public." In other words, the information to be made public is limited to the results on the development and utilization of nuclear energy alone; this change enables the law to exempt the disclosure of "all information" related to the process of decision-making until the results are obtained.

Through the establishment of the Atomic Energy Basic Law, SCJ Chairman Seiji Kaya submitted on behalf of the academic sector the document "Regarding the Establishment of the Science and Technology Agency" dated October 31, 1955, and addressed to Prime Minister Ichiro Hatoyama. This statement suggested that "the administration of nuclear energy should be separated from other science and technology administration, given its delicate nature."[15] In contrast, the Keidanren (currently the Japan Business Federation) of the industrial sector unveiled a policy wherein "the main nuclear energy agency should be included in a proper form, nuclear energy headquarters for example, within the integrated science and technology authorities [that is to say, the Science and Technology Agency]" in the statement "Regarding the Manner of Establishing a Science and Technology Administration Agency" dated October 25, 1955.[16] Ultimately, the Science and Technology Agency was designated as the integrated authority permitted to handle nuclear energy matters. According to the Sugata Documents (Vol. 2: 3–52), the plan to "assign the jurisdiction . . . over science and technology administration including nuclear energy administration . . . to the Science and Technology Agency" had been made immediately after the Joint Diet Atomic Energy Committee – with Yasuhiro Nakasone as the chairman, and consisting of the Democratic, Liberal, Socialist, and Social

Democratic parties of Japan – prompted a decision-making process, in which most of Keidanren's opinions were incorporated as the main points of the bill to establish a science and technology agency (Keidanren 1978: 182–183). The Cabinet decision on the establishment of this agency for nuclear energy administration was made on February 3, 1956.

The first meeting of the Joint Diet Atomic Energy Committee was held on October 11, 1955; since then, the Committee met as often as 26 times – about once every four days – over the period of 115 days until the Cabinet decision in 1956.[17] The circumstances in which the opinions of Keidanren were mostly accepted in that process have never been made available for the public to examine; thus, the social process of the co-working of the governmental and industrial sectors remains unavailable for any public third party to examine, even about the process of determining the most basic institutional framework for installing the competent authority for the development and utilization of nuclear energy. This fact implies that secrecy as an element of structural disaster was institutionalized and deeply rooted in the process of building the nuclear regime itself in post-war Japan.

Another element of structural disaster that existed in the process of establishing the nuclear regime for the development and utilization of nuclear energy in post-war Japan was the quick fixes for current problems as temporary countermeasures based on convenient assumptions. The prevention of radiation hazards and the technical characteristics of nuclear power reactors, as prejudged in their initial introduction phase, provide fitting examples to discern this element of structural disaster in the emergent process of post-war nuclear regime.

With regard to the prevention of radiation hazards, the discussion on the outline of the Radioactive Substance Control Bill tabled at the Joint Diet Atomic Energy Committee meeting held on October 16, 1955, at the Prime Minister's Official Residence is important because it reveals the views of related ministries on the radiation hazards prevention presented there. According to the Sugata Documents, the following views were presented.[18]

The Ministry of Health and Welfare wanted to handle this problem under medical law by combining it with radiation hazard prevention that involved X-rays. The Ministry of International Trade and Industry presented their view that it could be sufficiently dealt with by the provisions for handling special hazardous materials; for example, the standards for handling high-pressure gas. The Ministry of Labor presented the view that everything, including health problems, security problems, and disposal problems related to radiation, could be handled by the Labor Standards Law. The National Personnel Authority stated that the waste generated after collecting irradiated dust needed to be processed in accordance with matters such as ore dust. The Ministry of Education ultimately wanted to be the authority to study and use the radioactive material following the accident.

We can see how each ministry was trying to include the issue of preventing radiation hazards in responsible business under their own jurisdictions and areas of specialty. In doing so, each ministry was aiming to tackle radiation hazards by envisioning practical and familiar examples such as X-rays, high-pressure gas, health issues, and ore dust. Not surprisingly, the Joint Diet Atomic Energy

Committee decided to revise the name of the bill from "The Radioactive Substance Control Bill" to "The Radiation Hazards Prevention Bill" without any substantial judgment regarding radiation hazards. As a result, the Radiation Hazards Prevention Bill was finalized as a quick fix for temporary countermeasures based on the assumptions of the practical examples that each ministry was accustomed to handle, and was enacted on June 10, 1957.

This meeting for exchanging views on institutional arrangements for preventing radiation hazards occurred when Japan had not yet had any direct experience with radiation hazards and was called "premature" by the Ministry of International Trade and Industry (Sugata Documents, Vol. 3: 103). It might be true that quick fixes for temporary countermeasures as an element of structural disaster taken to prevent radiation hazards were born of contemporary circumstances where there was no direct experience of such hazards in the science-technology-society interface. Therefore, temporary quick fixes as an element of structural disaster at this time cannot be ascribed to external circumstances alone; rather, there should remain a substantial judgment, overtly expressed or not, on the quick fix in this situation. Going further, it is better to provide an independent example displaying the contemporary judgment on the technical characteristics of nuclear power reactors soon to be introduced in Japan.

Dreams and hopes made possible by the lack of expertise

What made the quick fixes for temporary countermeasures based on convenient assumptions possible was the shared judgment that nuclear power reactors were already an established and commercialized technology; therefore, the remaining work would be to introduce the technology and to manufacture the reactors domestically. In such a situation, the prevention of radiation hazards would also be considered a normal provision associated with the transfer of such established and commercialized technology, a way of assimilating modern science and technology with which Japan had been engaging since its industrialization, which began in the mid-nineteenth century.[19]

On September 6, 1956, the JAEC finalized the first long-term plan related to the research, development, and utilization of nuclear energy and released details on two directions: one for technology introduction for early construction of a power reactor, and the other for self-reliant domestic power reactor development (Atomic Energy Long-Term Plan 1956: 7). The governmental and industrial sectors must have judged that power reactors in other countries were well-established as a commercial technology to an extent that was sufficient for them to derive the judgment that they could aim to domestically manufacture the power reactor model that was most suitable to Japan. This contemporary judgment was expressed in various different forms, including the following:[20]

> Tamaki Ipponmatsu, Director of Kansai Electric Power Company: "The waste disposal is a problem, but controlling nuclear reactors is nothing. You just press the button."

Chikara Kurata, President of Hitachi Ltd.: "The nuclear reactor itself is nothing."

Managing Director Ipponmatsu: "I would like to see 100,000-kW nuclear power generation in 10 years."

President Kurata: "By all means, please promote it, and we will cooperate as a manufacturer."

Chairman Yasuhiro Nakasone of the Joint Diet Atomic Energy Committee said: "I want to build a power reactor in Japan soon so that we can use cheap isotopes for hot springs throughout the nation to create public baths having a nuclear hot spring."[21] Ichiro Ishikawa, member of the JAEC, stated: "In short, it is the same thing as to say it is dangerous to handle high-voltage electricity when the person knows nothing about it, but it is not dangerous when the person is knowledgeable about nuclear power."[22] The subheadings of "Junengo niwa Atomu Jidai" ("The Atomic Era in a Decade"), the January 5, 1956, issue of the *Mainichi Shimbun*, were as follows:

Treating Cancer Is a Piece of Cake.
Mosquitoes and Flies Vanished from Radioactivity.
Go Around the Earth in 17 Hours by a Nuclear-Powered Aircraft.
Famine Is a Thing of the Past.

Nuclear power reactors have never reached such lofty goals and, therefore, radiation hazards had to be approached more cautiously. It was the academic sector who warned of such an approach at the time; however, as described above, in the post-war regime for nuclear energy development and utilization, the governmental and industrial sectors led and the academic sector reacted *ex post facto*.

The opportunistic statement by SCJ

The SCJ held a general meeting to discuss the JAEC's March 7, 1957 report, which finalized the direction for the early introduction of nuclear energy generation. As a follow-up, the SCJ released a set of recommendations titled "About Importing Power Reactors" dated May 6 of the same year, signed by SCJ Chairman Seiji Kaya and addressed to Koichi Uda, Director of the Science and Technology Agency.[23] Within these recommendations, the SCJ stated its opposition to the direction due to the hasty introduction of technology (the Calder Hall reactor). On November 1 of the same year, the Japan Atomic Power Company was established as the main entity for the early adoption of an improved Calder Hall reactor. From this sequence of these events, it is clear that the recommendation did not have an effective impact on the JAEC's actions or plans.

In response, Toshio Takeshita, General Manager of SCJ, submitted a quite general request titled "Regarding the Safety of Power Reactors" dated December 4, 1959, to Yoshitake Sasaki, Director of the Atomic Energy Bureau under the Science and Technology Agency.[24] However, the Japan Atomic Power Company's

Tokai power plant, which was the main entity responsible for installing the improved Calder Hall power reactor, had already signed a provisional power purchase agreement with TEPCO on March 10, 1959, more than eight months before the submission of the above-mentioned request. While there is little room for doubting the enthusiasm of the discussion among the SCJ at the time, there was a significant lack of effective influence and consistency.

Under such a governmental and industrial-sector-led nuclear regime, it is hard to say whether the academic sector represented by SCJ would have been able to achieve their objective to "make science reflected and popularized in the administration, industry, and people's lives . . . as the representative body of scientists in Japan for the people of Japan and of other nations," as set forth in Chapter 1 of Act 2 of the Science Council of Japan Law. The academic sector's role, then, seems limited to supplying human resources – rather than actually creating the nuclear regime for nuclear energy development and utilization – in order to continuously carry out research and development requested by the regime in accordance the governmental and industrial sector-created framework. In fact, nuclear-energy-related departments and graduate schools were created at universities in Japan subsequently and began supplying human resources beginning in the 1950s, only a few short years after the Science and Technology Agency was established as the only competent authority of nuclear energy administration (see Table 3.9).

The SCJ was originally expected to become the "National Diet of Scholars" for the purpose of reforming the academic sector in accordance with advice given by

Table 3.9 Nuclear Energy-Related Departments and Graduate Schools Founded in the 1950s

Year	Name of university	Quota (person)
1956	Tokai University, Faculty of Engineering Department of Nuclear Engineering	80
1957	Osaka University, Graduate School of Engineering Course of Nuclear Engineering	12 (Master course) 6 (Doctoral course)
1957	Kyoto University, Graduate School of Engineering Course of Nuclear Engineering	15 (Master course) 8 (Doctoral course)
1957	Tokyo Institute of Technology, Graduate School of Science and Engineering Course of Nuclear Engineering	8 (Master course) 8 (Doctoral course)
1958	Kyoto University, Faculty of Engineering Department of Nuclear Engineering	20
1958	Tohoku University, Graduate School of Engineering Course of Nuclear Engineering	18 (Master course) 11 (Doctoral course)

Source: Produced from STA (1974).

the General Headquarters of the Allied Forces (GHQ) to dispel the pre-modern academic structure before the war.[25] However, as mentioned above, be it pre-modern or modern, it never acquired substantial influence on the governmental and industrial sectors, as far as the process of helping to create the nuclear regime for nuclear energy development and utilization is concerned. It is true that lively discussions took place within SCJ since its Chairman, Seiji Kaya, submitted "Recommendations on the Nuclear Energy Problem" on May 1, 1954, addressed to Prime Minister Shigeru Yoshida, to express SCJ's "regret" regarding the reported nuclear energy budget.[26] The problem lies in the fact that, even though discussions were lively, they created almost no consistent or effective influence; moreover, the process of selecting SCJ members was switched from direct election to appointment by the Prime Minister in 1986.

These facts indicate that the academic sector could continue to exist – without being publicly mentioned as such by other sectors – as a pseudo opponent to the nuclear regime for nuclear energy development and utilization that has been led by the governmental and industrial sectors by playing a specific role: supplying human resources and, in exchange, receiving budget allocations and a limited power of influence. As a pseudo opponent, the academic sector (either consciously or unconsciously) harbored the possibility of reproducing a lack of effective influence due to tensions between the principle set forth in Chapter 1 of Act 2 of the Science Council of Japan Law "as the representative body of scientists in Japan" and as a stakeholder within the nuclear regime.

If this is the case, it would be difficult to expect the academic sector in Japan, as represented by SCJ, to publicly point out and correct the elements of structural disaster, such as the secrecy observed during the process of creating the nuclear regime and quick fixes for current problems as temporary countermeasures based on convenient assumptions. Therefore, in order to substantiate constructive reform without being preoccupied with ratification or denial that lacks effective influence, internally created and long-term principles for development, utilization, and disposal are necessary, to serve as foundations for the future of nuclear energy while eliminating the elements of structural disaster formed in the emerging process of the nuclear regime in post-war Japan. This is why the sociology of structural disaster is essential to conceiving positive outcomes after extreme events such as the Fukushima accident.

What, then, are the implications when it is applied to current, post-Fukushima situations? From the perspective of structural disaster, it implies that there is no agent that can escape responsibility for structural disasters, which will be illustrated with reference to the academic sector in the next section, along with focused implications of structural disaster.

The academic sector and institutionalized inaction: what comes at the end of long-standing structural disaster?

The extent to which institutionalized inaction as implied by structural disaster applies is spread across every sector. For example, when nuclear engineers faced the failure of SPEEDI (mentioned in Chapter 1), two different positions within the academic sector can be envisioned. One argues that technical experts should strive to work with and improve the technology until it is capable of making contributions that can help the general public, whom it is designed to serve, and the other argues that technical experts should properly establish the foundation for the technology's reliability by improving its simulation accuracy and determining the limits of its application.

Taking the former position, the work of technical experts does not end with creating artifacts; rather, they should stay involved throughout the entire process, from the time the artifacts are introduced and diffused in society and particularly when they experience unexpected failure. To use the example from SPEEDI, even if such a technology with perfect performance was produced, if a drawback emerged in the process of its utilization so that a warning could not be provided prior to evacuation due to an operating system failure, the experts would not be allowed to proceed with the system without taking responsibility for enacting due measures to correct the failure. In the latter position, the technical experts would, for example, need to be careful not to release the results of a simulation that did not use actual data for the initial values and call it a "prediction."

Calling the former approach "public-oriented" and the latter "expert-oriented," the workings of technology require well-coordinated relationships between the two approaches to function, particularly when coping with problems that arise in the science-technology-society interface. Specialized societies for technology experts exhibit the characteristics of professional associations when responding to public-oriented concerns and exhibit the characteristics of academic associations when responding to expert-oriented concerns. The Articles of Incorporation of the Atomic Energy Society of Japan include an equivocal objective: "advancing the science and technology related to the peaceful use of nuclear energy and radiation prioritizing the safety of the general public before anything else" (Chapter 1, Clause 3).[27] Its actual approach is determined by the appropriate balance between the characteristics and desires of professional and academic associations.

Therefore, once this balance is disturbed by, for example, a tie-in with the predetermined policy of the government, it can be expected that the society in question will transform into an institution that has interests in fund allocation from the government within the boundaries of a nuclear village. It is virtually impossible to expect this type of institutional stakeholder to serve the public interest because, according to the genealogy of institutionalized inaction, it is highly probable that such an institution exhibits no social function as either a professional association or an academic association. Instead, it can function to serve the institution's own interests, which has often become the subject of praise, as exemplified above with reference to the *yakebutori* of the National Institute for Ship Experiment after the Great Kanto Earthquake.

A similar possibility exists for academic societies in the fields of social sciences, or more generally for SCJ, which is a coalition of academic societies. As suggested in Chapter 1, if a committee that consists mostly of those who are not experts on the given problem continues to make assessments and recommendations using the Fukushima accident and related problems such as HLW disposal as points of reference, lacking valid expertise basis, this possibility would sooner or later become a reality. As indicated by the previous description and analysis of institutions working by inertia, it is possible that "good people" defined within the bounds of organizations or sectors can play a positive role within the bounds and yet still be responsible for structural disaster arising in the science-technology-society interface.

How to discern the credibility of expertise in the science-technology-society interface

Today, one can hardly live without the assistance of technical knowledge provided by relevant experts. Even if the quality of expertise deteriorates due to structural disaster (to the extent that it inconveniences the lives of the non-experts), this deterioration of quality is rarely observed by non-experts due to institutionalized secrecy implied by structural disaster. When this perspective is broadened to incorporate "lay experts," as defined in Chapter 1, into the category of non-experts, specialists in other fields could also become non-experts who are expected to undergo the influence of institutionalized secrecy implied by structural disaster. In inter-disciplinary, or trans-disciplinary, activities that cross multiple fields, the deterioration of expertise in one field is not likely to be detected by experts in other fields. Because experts in other fields are non-experts in the field in question, this is essentially the same as the situation where non-experts in a literal sense cannot detect the deterioration of expertise. If the deterioration of expertise is collectively undetected and kept away from organized skepticism, further advancement of expertise that is expected from such cross-over efforts could be stifled, and specialists in the concerned field could devote time and resources to pretending that advancement is taking place.

While this could be considered a waste of resources and time, sociologically speaking, such a waste could have a particular meaning; for example, that it was done to create belief in the advancement of a field, which could be meaningful to the agent who is expected to obtain further resources and participate in saving face. When no one has incentive to explain this state to outsiders, and, conversely, when there are incentives to avoid explaining this to outsiders, it will become institutionalized secrecy within the field.[28] In other words, expertise is sometimes credible, and at other times, not necessarily so, making it difficult to determine when to trust it and when to doubt it.

To the eyes of non-experts (including lay experts), it is natural for no criteria to be available to distinguish credible cases from others. What can be said, based on analysis of structural disaster developed in this chapter, is that expertise can be defined as something that, for a particular problem, enables us to differentiate between what appears to be and what actually is. Suppose that experts are facing a complaint about expertise originating during a critical situation for affected non-experts: When there is a self-referential way to reflexively check the quality of expertise that penetrates what appears to be apparent, then the expertise in question tends to be trustworthy. When such a self-referential way to check the quality is absent, the expertise may not necessarily be trustworthy.

Ultimately, expertise is the product of open-ended exploration without predetermined results. In contrast, work performed to justify a predetermined result is completely different in nature, so non-experts might be able to distinguish credible expertise from non-credible by examining whether or not there are anomalous elements incongruent with what appears to be apparent. When everything is too congruent and exhibits no anomalies, non-experts should be cautious in accepting its credibility. In an established field, if everything appears congruent and exhibits no anomalies, its credibility can be only perceived by experts who have specialized knowledge to detect the meaning of what they perceive. As experts in one field may be able to discriminate credible aspects from others via content, and non-experts (including experts in different fields) cannot, non-experts in this broadened sense should be cautious in assessing the quality of knowledge produced by trans-disciplinary endeavors (that is, those that crosscut different fields). Such endeavors sometimes give rise to cross-fertilization (with sometimes zero return), and in other cases give rise to "cross-futilization" such that the absence of credible expertise in one field resonates and reinforces the absence of credible expertise in other fields and eventually constitutes megaignorance. The endeavors are challenging, but the ratio of the former is usually very small and most policymakers seem to have dismissed any related risk. The risk of zero return and cross-futilization encompass not only particular individuals in academic careers associated with such endeavors but also the intellectual world as a whole, just like cross-fertilization does.

In conclusion, the following are the three main points of this chapter:

1   Institutionalized secrecy as implied by structural disaster can be generalized as a type of institutionalized inaction, which can be reconfirmed by multiple independent cases in the post-Fukushima situation. Based on this reconfirmation, institutionalized inaction can be categorized into two types: to allow stakeholders to save face in the public sphere by blurring their due responsibility; and inaction to gain something that is typically difficult to gain in a normal state through the utilization of extreme events by stakeholders.
2   Adherence to erroneous precedents and secrecy as elements of structural disaster can be traced back to the response of a national research institute following the Great Kanto Earthquake in 1923. These elements were passed down to the post-war period by institutional spin-offs triggered by the idea of a science- and technology-driven nation during the wartime mobilization of science and technology.
3   Quick fixes as temporary countermeasures as an element of structural disaster were activated through the idea of a science- and technology-driven nation as a sacred cause during the wartime mobilization of science and technology, which was further passed down to the post-war period during the formation process of nuclear villages in Japan. Based on this genealogy of long-standing structural disaster from the pre-war to the post-war period, it is probable that

at least three elements of structural disaster are still embedded in the current science-technology-society interface in the post-Fukushima situation: adherence to erroneous precedents; quick fixes for current problems as temporary countermeasures; and secrecy.

Throughout these points, the workings of institutional inertia as represented by institutionalized inaction is revealed to be a mechanism that gives rise to structural disaster. Expanded analysis of the overall mechanism at work in the dynamic process of structural disaster will be further discussed in later chapters by demonstrating the sociologically reformulated mechanism of path-dependent lock-in developed in Chapter 2, with reference to mutually independent cases within different times, places, and social contexts. While the origin of the first type of institutional inaction (for saving face by blurring due responsibility of stakeholders) has not be clarified in this chapter, it might be logical to assume that it occurred during the pre-war period, as this is the time period in which the second type originated. This possibility will be examined in the next chapter.

Referring to the trustworthiness of expertise, the next chapter will also explore if expertise with predetermined results really exists, by using an example from the not-too-distant past that presents a strong case to corroborate the possibility above. This example will provide a missing link in the historical lineage of structural disaster against the background of its genealogy.

4 Secrecy throughout war and peace
Structural disaster long before Fukushima

Chapter 4 further investigates institutionalized secrecy by examining the structural similarities between the Fukushima accident and a little-known yet serious accident in pre-war Japan from the perspective of structural disaster. In doing so, the chapter goes beyond widespread dichotomous narratives that make a clear-cut distinction between the pre-war social context of wartime mobilization of science and technology (resulting in nuclear bombing) and the post-war context of promoting science and technology for commercial use in peacetime (manifested in nuclear reactors for power generation). In particular, the chapter will probe the behavioral patterns of the agents involved in the accident that occurred immediately before WWII and was kept secret, with a comparative perspective of the Fukushima accident, which occurred more than 70 years later.

This chapter illustrates how both the pre-war accident and the Fukushima accident can be analyzed as structural disasters in a manner that is free from a hindsight narrative that is opportunistic and dichotomous. By focusing on the restriction of critical information under the name of military authority in the pre-war accident and under governmental authority in the Fukushima accident, this chapter reveals that the structural adaptation of heterogeneous agents was carried out in a path-dependent manner. The adaptation transformed structural integration into functional disintegration, which has had profound sociological implications for the post-Fukushima situation.

Structural similarities between the Fukushima accident and little-known pre-war accident: from the perspective of structural disaster

While the Fukushima accident itself was extremely shocking, the devastating failure to transmit critical information on the accident to affected people when the Japanese government faced unexpected and serious events after March 11, 2011, was perhaps the most shocking aspect of the accident overall. This failure to transmit critical information was a result of secrecy: secrecy to the people who were forced to evacuate from their birthplaces, who wanted to evacuate their children, who suffered from opportunity loss such as giving up on entering college, and others. It is impossible to enumerate individual instances of suffering and aggregate them into a single category, but suffice to say that critical information was restricted to only the insiders of the governmental sector. This situation is similar to the state of pre-war Japanese wartime mobilization, in which all information was controlled under the name of supreme military authority (TMM 2011).

While such a comparison could be viewed as merely rhetorical, this chapter argues that once patterns of behavior of the agents involved are concerned, the connection is more tangible. The pre-war Japanese military regime was oriented toward overall mobilization for war, while the post-war regime has been prohibited from mobilization for war purposes of any kind by the country's constitution. In this respect, there is a marked discrepancy between the regimes' purpose; however, similarities are evident in the patterns of behavior embedded in the regimes via the details of a hidden accident that took place just before the outbreak of WWII.

This chapter examines structural similarities in the patterns of behavior of agents involved in the Fukushima accident and those involved in the little-known but serious accident involving naval vessels that occurred immediately before WWII, with a particular focus on the subtle relationship between success and failure in the science-technology-society interface. This chapter will then contextualize the structural similarities and discuss sociological implications for affected people living in the current, post-Fukushima situation within the context of structural disaster. As such, this chapter meaningfully connects two different accidents more than 70 years apart and the social contexts in which they happened; in addition, this chapter elaborates on the sociological implications of both the similarities and differences of the two accidents.

As defined in Chapter 1, the concept of structural disaster within the science-technology-society interface provides a sociological account of the repeated occurrence of similar failures during and after extreme events (Matsumoto 2002). This chapter focuses on the interdependence of heterogeneous agents within the science-technology-society interface that give rise to institutionalized secrecy under a specific social condition. The chapter clarifies this interdependence by tracing it back to the little-known pre-war accident, which reveals an important clue to understanding the Fukushima accident from the perspective of structural disaster. To properly understand the social context of this hidden pre-war accident, it is necessary to go beyond the current social context of the post-Fukushima situation to the pre-war social context of the wartime mobilization of science and technology. Following such clarification, the current social context surrounding the Fukushima accident will be examined in relation to the little-known accident for potential future extreme events.

To approach the structural similarities between the Fukushima accident and the little-known/hidden accident that occurred before WWII from the perspective of structural disaster, two basic points should be noted: first, we need to carefully place the specifications of six nuclear reactors at the Fukushima Daiichi Nuclear Power Plant in the development trajectory of technology, which can help to clarify a dynamic aspect of structural disaster (see Table 4.1); and second, a repeated

Table 4.1 Nuclear Reactor Specifications at the Fukushima Daiichi Nuclear Power Plant

Reactor unit no.	1	2	3	4	5	6
Type of reactors	BWR	BWR	BWR	BWR	BWR	BWR
Container vessel	Mark I	Mark I	Mark I	Mark I	Mark I	Mark II
Output (×10^4 kW)	46	78.4	78.4	78.4	78.4	110
Makers	GE	GE/Toshiba	Toshiba	Hitachi	Toshiba	GE/Toshiba
Domestics (%)	56	53	91	91	93	63
Year built	1971	1974	1976	1978	1978	1979

Sources: TEPCO (2014).

occurrence of similar patterns of behavior throughout various different instances seems to suggest institutionalized secrecy.

There are two reasons for the first basic point of highlighting the development trajectory of technology to understand the dynamic aspect of structural disaster in regard to the Fukushima accident. First, each reactor at the plant had a long history of successful operation extending more than 30 years since its start in the 1970s; as such, there is a greater possibility of a more structural cause of the accident beyond blaming ad hoc errors. Second, as the ratios of domestic production indicate, the reactors at the power plant embody a turning point that shifted the country from licensed production to self-reliant production; a shift that may accompany the structural change of a system of production and operation. From these reasons, common characteristics could be seen throughout the system of production and operation of the plant's reactors, and it is possible that such characteristics are related to what is called a "common-mode failure" of the science-technology-society interface.

While the above-mentioned possibility in terms of the development trajectory of technology is one thing, the statement that such a possibility triggered a structural disaster outbreak in the science-technology-society interface is quite another. Structural similarities among the development trajectory of technology hint at the possibility that both the hidden pre-war accident and the Fukushima accident can be considered structural disaster. However, when structural disaster is broken down into its elements, specified in Chapter 1, the above may present a possible yet indirect connection to the respective elements of the disaster.

The second basic point is more directly concerned with the understanding of the Fukushima accident as structural disaster, wherein a repeated occurrence of similar patterns of behavior throughout different instances seems to suggest institutionalized secrecy. The emergency situation both during and after an extreme event such as the Fukushima accident includes the expectation of confusion and delay in transmitting information; however, the degree and range of confusion and delay went beyond a reasonable expectation from an emergency situation alone, as mentioned in Chapter 1 and Chapter 3. If the details of the Fukushima accident embody structural disaster, then institutionalized secrecy could be captured at the sector level (for example, the governmental-industrial-university complex manifested in the nuclear village). This could be a noteworthy social background against which structural similarities with the little-known pre-war accident can be scrutinized, examined, and extended through the lens of structural disaster within a broader comparative perspective.

Thus, structural disaster could be examined from a broader perspective by extracting structural similarities between the two accidents in terms of the development trajectory of technology and institutionalized inaction such as institutionalized secrecy.[1] If we can substantiate the elements of structural disaster, particularly institutionalized secrecy to understand other independent cases as structural disaster, then sociological implications from the Fukushima accident as a structural disaster can be more concretely formulated and extended to potential future extreme events. What follows is an independent substantiation of this with particular focus on institutionalized secrecy by examining the hidden accident happened long before the Fukushima accident.

Development trajectory of the Kanpon type and its pitfalls

The little-known pre-war accident that will be used in this chapter involved marine turbine developed by the Imperial Japanese Navy, which occurred in December 1937, almost two years before the outbreak of WWII. This accident can be used as an example through which to redefine the complex relationship between success and failure in the science-technology-society interface both in peacetime and in wartime. The accident was treated as top secret because of its timing, but suppression of information about it has led to a lack of consideration for the event as critical to the sociology of science and technology until now. Analysis of this accident will suggest that the development trajectory of technology can depart significantly from a unidirectional process, and more importantly, implies that the view of the science-technology-society interface must transcend a simplistic, dichotomous understanding of success or failure.

Naval turbine development

The steam turbine was patented in 1884 by British engineer C. A. Parsons, who then obtained a patent for the marine turbine 10 years later (Parsons 1894).[2] After Parsons' original invention, the marine turbine became a reliable, mature technology in the pre-war period. The hidden accident involving naval turbines that occurred immediately before WWII, however, throws doubt onto the validity of such a unidirectional view of development trajectory of technology. Since this particular trajectory is an important key to clarifying the general background of structural disaster in the realm of technology in pre-war Japan, such doubt should be confirmed with particular reference to the development trajectory of Japanese-type naval turbines by clarifying the locus of the complex relationship between success and failure.

The technology for consideration is the Kanpon type turbine, with Kanpon being the technical headquarters of the Navy. The Kanpon type was developed by the Imperial Japanese Navy around 1920 to replace imported technologies entirely for self-reliant ones. This specific naval turbine can illuminate the complex connection between success and failure involved in the development trajectory of naval turbines in pre-war Japan, because the Kanpon type was the standard turbine for Japanese naval vessels employed from 1920 to 1945. Examining its development and the little-known accident will reveal this connection.[3]

From the first adoption of the marine turbine in 1905 after intensive investigations and license contracts, the Imperial Japanese Navy accumulated experience in the domestic production of marine turbines. Throughout this process, the Navy carefully monitored and evaluated the latest developments in British, American, and other types of turbines;[4] as a result, a reduction gearing was adopted by the Navy for the first time in 1918 that contributed greatly to the total efficiency of the main turbines.[5]

However, quite unexpectedly, the introduction of reduction gearing caused one failure after another from 1918 (see Table 4.2).

Table 4.2 Geared Turbine Failures of Naval Vessels from 1918

Date	Ship name	Ship type	Specification	Turbine type
1918/10/3	Tanikaze	Destroyer	Blade Fell Out	Brown-Curtis
1918/11/30	Minekaze	Destroyer	All Blades Fell Out	Brown-Curtis (HP) Parsons (LP)
1919/2/26	Sawakaze	Destroyer	Blade Sheared & Dropped Off	Brown-Curtis (HP)
1919/4/30	Tenryu	Cruiser	Blade Sheared	Brown-Curtis
1919/11/21	Tatsuta	Cruiser	Blade Smashed	Brown-Curtis
1920/2/6	Nire	Destroyer	Blade Sheared	Brown-Curtis (HP) Parsons (LP)
1920/4	Kawakaze	Destroyer	Blade Sheared	Brown-Curtis
1920/9/28	Shimakaze	Destroyer	Blade Breakage	Brown-Curtis (HP) Parsons (LP)
1920/12/20	Kuma	Cruiser	Blade Breakage	Gihon
1922/3/18	Sumire	Destroyer	Blade Damaged	Zölly

Source: Seisan Gijutsu Kyokai (1954) and Shibuya (1970).

Note: The same naval vessels and naval vessels of the same class suffered similar failures and breakdowns many times. These repeated failures and breakdowns are omitted here. The secondary failures and breakdowns caused by the initial ones are also omitted altogether. Gihon in the table is the multiple-flow turbine designed by the predecessor of the Technical Headquarters of the Navy. Geared turbines made possible an increase of one order of magnitude in revolutions per minute, from 100–200 to 1,000–2,000, which might have affected turbines designed for 100–200 rpm.

Failures followed by a shift to self-reliance

What was most important to the Navy was the fact that all the geared turbines experiencing failures were imported foreign types, as shown in Table 4.2. The license contracts with the makers of the two leading turbines, the Curtis and Parsons types, were due to expire in June 1923 and in August 1928, respectively. Considering the failures in light of this situation, the Navy started to take official steps to develop its own type.[6] Thus, the first Kanpon type was installed in destroyers built in 1924 (see Figure 4.1) and established as the standard turbine for Japanese naval vessels.[7]

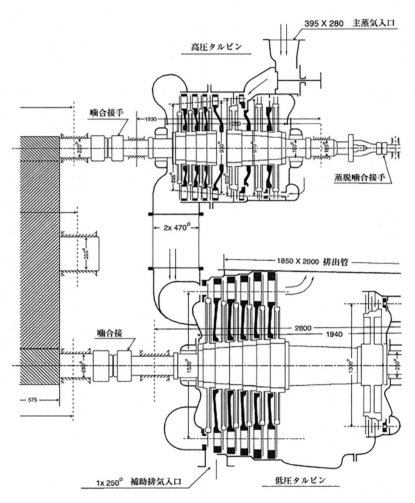

Figure 4.1 Plane View of the Kanpon Type Turbine

Source: Nippon Hakuyo Kikan Gakkai Hakuyo Kikan Chosa Kenkyu Iinkai (The Research Committee of the Marine Engineering Society of Japan), ed. n.d.

All Japanese naval vessels continued to adopt the Kanpon type until 1945 and it was regarded as a landmark that indicated the shift to self-reliant technologies. As the Shipbuilding Society of Japan wrote in its official history of naval architecture and marine engineering: "There had been no serious trouble with the turbine for more than 10 years since the early 1920s, and the Navy continued to have strong confidence in their reliability" (Shipbuilding Society of Japan 1977, Vol. 1: 668).

What follows is an important counterargument to this account, by focusing on the pitfall inherent in the development trajectory of technology that links success and failure. The detailed analysis of the little-known but serious incident of the established Kanpon type that occurred immediately before WWII will reveal how important this pitfall is for the clarification of institutionalized secrecy in the science-technology-society interface. This is because the pitfall was directly linked to the functional disintegration of the military-industrial-university complex, caused by an unbalanced institutionalized secrecy, the key factor epitomizing structural disaster in this case. The military-industrial-university complex hereafter refers to an institutional structure made up of the military sector, the industrial sector, and the academic sector as represented by universities – mutually autonomous in their behavior but expected to contribute jointly to national goals.[8]

The serious accident undisclosed: institutionalized secrecy during the wartime mobilization of science and technology

In December 1937, a newly built naval destroyer encountered an unexpected turbine blade breakage accident. Since the accident involved a standard Kanpon type turbine, it caused great alarm. A special examination committee was established in January 1938 to investigate the accident. The committee was called Rinkicho in Japanese and, therefore, this chapter will refer to the accident as the Rinkicho accident hereafter. Today, there are five publicly available books containing references to the Rinkicho accident.[9] The publication dates are different, but the authors/editors were all stakeholders of the Imperial Japanese Navy (see Table 4.3).

Table 4.3 References to the Rinkicho Accident

Year of reference	Author/editor
1952	Former Engineering Rear Admiral of the Navy
1956	Mainichi newspaper reporter (Graduate of the Naval Academy)
1969	War History Unit of the National Defense College of the Defense Agency
1977	Japan Shipbuilding Society (editor-in-chief and several members of the Editorial Committee were former technical officers of the Navy)
1981	Institute for Historical Record Compilation on the Navy

The accounts given in these references agree, for the most part, that the cause of the failure was identified soon enough to avoid serious adverse consequences. These references make up a kind of success story, though it is difficult to examine the failure more independently because little public evidence is available to corroborate these references. It appears that the accident was not made public because it occurred during wartime mobilization.

An examination of government documents from around the time of the accident can help to confirm the background of this secrecy. The government documents consulted here include the minutes of Imperial Diet sessions regarding the Navy during the 57th Imperial Diet session (held in January 1930) through the 75th Imperial Diet session (held in March 1940). The documents contain approximately 7,000 pages of Navy-related discussions. These discussions include 10 naval vessel incidents, as summarized in Table 4.4.

It is noteworthy in these discussions that the Fourth Squadron incident of September 1935, one of the most serious incidents in the history of the Imperial Japanese Navy, was made public and discussed in the Imperial Diet sessions within a year of its occurrence (on May 18, 1936).[10] The Rinkicho accident, however, occurred on December 29, 1937, and was classified and handed down informally within the Navy even though it was major incident on a par with the Fourth Squadron incident.[11]

More than two years after the Rinkicho accident, there was no mention in the Imperial Diet sessions that it was made public. Reports on the accident had already been submitted during the period from March to November 1938 (the final report was submitted on November 2); nevertheless, the Imperial Diet did not appear to have heard anything about the accident nor be aware of any measures taken to resolve or investigate its occurrence. The Rinkicho accident (like the Fourth Squadron incident) was so serious that it would likely have influenced the decision on whether to go to war with the United States and Britain.

The Fourth Squadron incident dramatically disclosed the inadequate strength and stability of the hull of standard naval vessels designed after the London naval disarmament treaty concluded in 1930.[12] Because the incident was made public and discussed in Imperial Diet sessions, there is a marked difference between the handling of the two incidents. The Director of the Naval Accounting Bureau, Harukazu Murakami, was forced to provide an answer to a question about the Fourth Squadron by Kanjiro Fukuda (Democratic Party) at the 69th Imperial Diet session held on May 18, 1936.[13] Although his answer included no information regarding the damage to human resources (all members of the crew confined within the bows of the destroyers died), it accurately stated the facts of the incident and that material damage was incurred, amounting to 2.8 million yen. Even the damage due to the collision between cruisers about five years earlier in Table 4.4 was only 180,000 yen. This answer from a naval official clearly attested that the Fourth Squadron incident was so extraordinarily serious as to oblige him to disclose this fact to the public.[14] In contrast, remedial measures for turbine problems on all naval vessels disclosed by the Rinkicho accident were expected to cost 40 million yen (Shibuya n.d.).

Table 4.4 Discussions about Naval Vessels in the Imperial Diet: January 1930–March 1940

Date	Description
February 13, 1931	Questions about the cause of the collision between the cruiser Abukuma and Kitakami. (Shinya Uchida's questions were answered by the Minister of the Navy, Abo, at the Lower House Budget Committee, the 59th Imperial Diet session)
March 2, 1931	Questions about the measures taken before and after the collision between the cruiser Abukuma and Kitakami during large-scale maneuvers in 1930 and the responsibility of the authorities. (Tanetada Tachibana's questions were answered by the Minister of the Navy, Abo, at the House of Lords Budget Committee, the 59th Imperial Diet session)
March 17, 1933	Questions about the Minister of the Navy's view on the expenditure (12,000 yen) on repairs to the destroyer Usugumo and on the fact that the destroyer struck a well-known submerged rock. (Shinya Uchida's questions were answered by the Minister of the Navy, Osumi, at the Lower House Budget Committee, the 64th Imperial Diet session)
March 2, 1935	Request for information about the results of investigation into a scraping incident involving four destroyers, apparently on training duty in Ariake Bay, reported in newspapers. (Yoshitaro Takahashi's questions were answered by the Minister of the Navy, Osumi, at the Lower House Budget Committee, the 67th Imperial Diet session)
May 18, 1936	Request for information about the seriousness of the collision between submarines I-53 and I-63 and the amount of money drawn from the reserve as a remedy. (Kanjiro Fukuda's questions were answered by the Accounting Bureau Director, Murakami, at the Lower House plenary session, the 69th Imperial Diet session)
May 18, 1936	Request for detailed information about the degree of damage to two destroyers due to violent waves in September 1935. (Kanjiro Fukuda's questions were answered by the Accounting Bureau Director, Murakami, at the Lower House plenary session, the 69th Imperial Diet session)
February 6, 1939	Brief explanation of the accident of submarine I-63. (The Minister of the Navy, Yonai, explained at the House of Lords plenary session, the 74th Imperial Diet session)
February 7, 1939	Brief explanation of the accident of submarine I-63. (The Minister of the Navy, Yonai, explained at the Lower House plenary session, the 74th Imperial Diet session)
February 25, 1939	Request for a brief explanation of the sinking of a submarine due to collision during maneuvers. (Takeo Kikuchi's questions were answered by the Director of the Bureau of Military Affairs, Inoue, at the House of Lords Budget Committee, the 74th Imperial Diet session)
February 1, 1940	Brief report on the completion of the salvage of the sunken submarine I-63. (The Minister of the Navy, Yoshida, reported at the House of Lords plenary session, the 75th Imperial Diet session)

Source: Produced from Kaigun Daijin Kanbo Rinji Chosa Ka (1984).

No detailed, open report of the Rinkicho accident, however, was ever presented at the Imperial Diet, which indicates that this accident was considered to be top secret information that never went beyond the Imperial Japanese Navy. As such, there are two important characteristics suggesting that institutionalized secrecy prevented the Rinkicho accident from being disclosed to the public: first, the accident would have influenced the decision on whether to go to war with the United States and Britain, so information on the accident could affect matters of public interest; second, the information was made top secret, and kept within the bounds of the special examination committee, and direct stakeholders. In light of the definition of institutionalized secrecy given in Chapter 1, there are two other conditions that should be met to solidly identify institutionalized secrecy: secrecy must be materialized by institutional design, and it must be considered harmful to public interests. If we can observe these conditions in the Rinkicho accident, then it can be considered "undisclosed" by institutionalized secrecy.

How can be these points be proven by evidence? This can be answered through documents owned by Ryutaro Shibuya, who was an Engineering Vice Admiral of the Navy at the time and was responsible for the turbine design of naval vessels. These documents will be referred to as the Shibuya Archives hereafter.

The hidden accident and outbreak of war with the United States and Britain: deciphering institutionalized secrecy

The Shibuya Archives consist of more than 4,000 materials on various subjects, including casualties of the atomic bomb;[15] however, this chapter discusses only materials directly concerning the Rinkicho accident. Among these, focus is placed on the special examination committee established in January 1938. The purpose of the committee was stated as follows:

> Problems were found with the turbines of Asashio-class destroyers. . . . It is necessary to work out remedial measures and study the design of the machinery involved and other related matters, so that such studies will help improvements. These research activities must be performed freely without any restrictions imposed by experience and practice in the past. The special examination committee has been established to fulfill this purpose.
>
> (The Minister of the Navy's Secretariat 1938: Military secret No. 266)

Its organization was as follows (Rinkicho Report 1938b: Top secret No. 35):

- General members who did not attend sub-committee meetings
    - Chair: Isoroku Yamamoto, Vice Admiral, Administrative Vice Minister of the Navy
    - Members: Rear Admiral Inoue, Director of the Bureau of Naval Affairs, the Ministry of the Navy; and five other members

- First sub-committee for dealing with engine design and planning
  - Leader: Shipbuilding Vice Admiral Fukuma, Director of the Fifth Department (including the turbine group), the Technical Headquarters of the Navy; and nine other members
- Second sub-committee for dealing with maximum engine power and suitable load/volume
  - Leader: Rear Admiral Mikawa, Director of the Second Department, the Naval General Staff; and eleven other members
- Third sub-committee for dealing with prior studies/experiments/systems and operations
  - Leader: Rear Admiral Iwamura, Director of the General Affairs Department, the Technical Headquarters of the Navy; and ten other members

Ignoring duplication of members belonging to different subcommittees and arranging the net members by section, the results in Table 4.5 were obtained.

The accident, as discussed, concerned the breakage of Kanpon type turbine blades. Following the history of marine turbine development in Japan since 1918, when the Navy began to adopt geared turbines, various failures had occurred with main turbines. When we classify these failures during the period from 1918 to October 1944 by location, failures involving turbine blades account for 60 percent of the total (see Table 4.6).[16]

The Imperial Japanese Navy had thus experienced many previous problems with turbine blades and had accumulated practice in handling them; accordingly, it is not surprising that the special examination committee considered the accident as merely a routine problem from the outset, based upon such history. In fact, the special examination committee drew a two-point conclusion to the problem in line with such accumulated experience: first, the accident was caused by insufficient blade strength; and second, the turbine rotor vibration made the

Table 4.5 Members of the Special Examination Committee by Section

Section	Number
Administrative Vice Minister of the Navy	1
Bureau of Naval Affairs	8
Naval General Staff	5
Technical Headquarters of the Navy	15
Naval Staff College	3
Naval Engineering School	1
Total	33

Source: Calculated based on Rinkicho Report (1938b) Top secret No. 35, Appended sheets.

Table 4.6 Naval Turbine Failures Classified by Location: 1918–1944

Location	Incidents	Percentage	Cumulative
Impulse blade and grommet	368	46.8	46.8
Reaction blade and binding strip	111	14.1	60.9
Reduction gear and claw coupling	80	10.2	71.1
Bearing and thrust bearing	66	8.4	79.5
Casing	46	5.9	85.7
Casing partition and nozzle	34	4.3	89.7
Blade wheel and spindle	22	2.8	92.5
Steam packing	20	2.5	95.0
Others	39	5.0	
Total	786	100.0	100.0

Source: Based on Seisan Gijutsu Kyokai (1954: 1–2).

Note: Reaction blade means the blade of a traditional Parsons turbine (Cf., Seisan Gijutsu Kyokai 1954: 4).

insufficient strength emerge as a problem (Rinkicho Report 1938b: Top secret No. 35). On the basis of this conclusion, a plan was developed to improve the design of the Kanpon type turbine blades and rotors for all naval vessels, changing the form of the blades to make their stress concentration lower, thereby enhancing their strength (Rinkicho Report 1938a: Top secret No. 1). The improvement of 61 naval vessels' turbines was indicated as the first step toward resolution, in accordance with the previous 66 committee-meeting reports held over a period of 10 months (Rinkicho Report 1938a: Top secret No. 1).

However, the blade breakage in the accident was significantly different from those that had occurred in the past. In impulse turbines cases, for instance, the blades were most often broken at the base where they were fixed to the turbine rotor; in contrast, one of the unique features of the Rinkicho accident was that the tip of the blade was broken off, a section that amounted to one-third of its total length.[17] Figure 4.2 shows a photograph of the locus of the breakage.

Yoshio Kubota, a naval engineering captain who was transferred to the Military Affairs Bureau in November 1938 when the special examination committee reported its conclusion, noticed this key difference in the breakage point, even though it was not considered permissible for a newcomer to the Military Affairs Bureau to object to the latest conclusion of the special committee. In addition, six months before his transfer to the bureau, the Japanese government enacted the Wartime Mobilization Law on April 1, 1938, for the purpose of "controlling and organizing human and material resources most efficiently . . . in case of war" (Clause 1). Against the background of wartime mobilization, a naval engine failure caused by small tip fragments of the main standard engine was a delicate matter for anyone to raise, as naval vessels came first in the specification of the law as "resources for wholesale mobilization" (Clause 2).[18] Despite these circumstances,

Secrecy throughout war and peace 99

Figure 4.2 Broken Part of a Blade in the Rinkicho Accident
Source: Rinkicho Report (1938a) Top secret No. 1.

Kubota strongly recommended that confirmation tests should be conducted again for naval vessels of the same type. He argued that if turbine rotor vibration was the true cause of the breakage and resulting accident, then the failure would be repeatable when the engine was run continuously at the same critical speed causing rotor vibration (nearly 6/10 to 10/10 of the full speed).[19]

The Navy finally decided to initiate continuous run tests equivalent to 10-year runs on April 1, 1939. No failures occurred. This means that the remedial measures thus far taken by the Navy functioned to adhere to erroneous precedents, causing problems to be carried over and reproduced, an element of structural disaster. This also provided the Navy with a practical rationale for canceling the overall remedial measures for all naval vessels, which were expected to require significant money and time to check for potential failures and perform necessary modifications.[20]

Upon the tests' conclusions, an order was promptly issued to postpone any modifications to the turbine blades and rotors of the Kanpon type for all naval vessels. At the same time, however, there was an urgent need to consider another possible cause for the breakage, and a study to identify the cause was restarted. The Maizuru Naval Dockyard conducted preliminary on-land tests, followed by a more thorough one at the Hiro Naval Dockyard to confirm the conditions that would recreate the failure. However, the tests were extremely difficult to carry out for two reasons. First, the complete test required the dockyards to construct from scratch a full-scale experimental apparatus for a vibration load test, which was only completed in December 1941, the month during which the war with the United States and Britain broke out. Second, the test was on such a large-scale, eventually extending to more than 35 main items, that it took far more time than expected. As a result, the schedule for identifying the cause, which was originally expected to be completed in November 1940, was extended to mid-1943.[21] Thus, it is logical to assume that all of Japan's naval vessels were operating during this time with imperfect turbines when the country went to war in 1941.

What, then, was the true cause for the accident? Previous efforts to avoid turbine vibration had been confined to one-node vibration at full speed, since multiple-node vibration below full speed had been assumed to be unworthy of attention and it was the standard of turbine design in the pre-war period.[22] The final discovery of the true cause of the Rinkicho accident drastically changed these standards. It revealed that marine turbines are susceptible to a serious vibration problem below full speed. In April 1943 the true cause was eventually identified as binodal vibration in the final report of the special examination committee – almost one and a half years after the war broke out.[23]

Only three months before the submission of the report, a theoretical study made at the Hiro Naval Dockyard supported the conclusion that the true cause was binodal vibration.[24] The results of theoretical calculation, on-land confirmation testing, and the characteristics of the actual failure matched this conclusion. The complete mechanism creating binodal vibration itself, however, was still left for further studies; even so, all results from the special examination committee that concluded in 1943 pointed to the same single cause: binodal vibration (Ono

1943).[25] Strictly in terms of the technology involved in the accident (that is, without hindsight), all the evidence suggests that the Japanese government went to war in haste in 1941, despite having an unaccounted for, highly intricate, and serious problem with the main engines of all its naval vessels. This fact was undisclosed to outsiders by institutionally legitimate procedures ranging from military secret instructions to top secret reports, as shown in Table 4.7.

Within the military-industrial-university complex, facts surrounding the accident and its cause were undisclosed by legitimately designed institutional procedures to other sectors involved.[26] The rarity of naval vessel breakdowns due to

Table 4.7 Brief List of Military Secret Instructions Issued to Deal with the Rinkicho Accident: January 1938–December 1941

Date	Military secret instructions
December 29, 1937	The accident occurred
January 19, 1938	The Minister of the Navy's Secretariat Military Secret No. 266 was issued to establish the special examination committee.
February 3, 1938	The Minister of the Navy's Secretariat Secret Instruction No. 566 was issued to examine the vibration of the main turbine blades and rotors installed in the naval vessels at the Hiro Naval Dockyard.
August 1938	The Technical Headquarters' Secret No. 15332 was issued to specify the methods of static and dynamic vibration tests on turbine blades and rotors.
November 2, 1938	Report from the Committee (Top Secret No. 35) was issued to summarize the 53 sub-committee meetings and 13 general meetings held until this date.
April 1, 1939	The Minister of the Navy's Secretariat Secret Instruction No. 1973 was issued to select a representative naval vessel from existing vessels, and to conduct long-run load tests according to the remedy implementation schedule suggested by the special examination committee's report.
February 12, 1940	The Minister of the Navy's Secretariat Secret Instruction No. 1122 was issued to begin turbine rotor load tests at the Engine Experiment Department of the Maizuru Naval Dockyard in April 1940.
May 6, 1940	The Minister of the Navy's Secretariat Secret Instruction No. 3185 was issued to postpone modifications to the main turbines of existing naval vessels.
June 20, 1941	The Minister of the Navy's Secretariat Secret Instruction No. 5389 was issued to postpone the completion of turbine rotor load tests to March 1943, postpone modifications to the main turbines of naval vessels, and make the final decision by consulting the results of on-land tests by the end of June 1943.
December 8, 1941	War with the United States and Britain declared.

Source: Murata (n.d.)

turbine troubles during the war is a matter of hindsight; thus, the Rinkicho accident strongly suggests that such practical results alone during wartime (and possibly in peacetime as well) do not prove the essential soundness of the development trajectory of technology, nor that of the science-technology-society interface and national decision-making along the trajectory.

Sociological implications for the Fukushima accident: beyond dichotomous understanding of success or failure

The sociological implications of the Rinkicho accident, which happened approximately 70 years earlier than the Fukushima accident, are closely related to the reasons why it is considered a little-known structural disaster, as it was much more serious and complex than expected and therefore kept undisclosed to outsiders by institutionalized secrecy. As such, the development trajectory of technology beyond a simplistic dichotomy of success or failure throughout wartime and peacetime must be reconsidered. According to a standard view of its technological history, Japan proceeded toward self-reliance with the establishment of the Kanpon type turbine in the 1920s, after improvements were made to deal with various problems and failure incidents. In short, a successful self-reliant phase followed subsequent to improvements after various failures.

This trajectory toward self-reliance is credited with enabling Japan to go to war in 1941. According to the analysis of the Rinkicho accident given in this chapter, however, the trajectory becomes more complex than a conventional "success story" would suggests, since there was a serious but little-known missing phase – one of "self-reliant failure" that the Navy was unable to completely solve before the outbreak of the war. Considering this with the similarities in terms of technological trajectory, such that the reactors of the Fukushima Daiichi Nuclear Power Plant embody the turning point leading from licensed production to self-reliant production, the Fukushima accident could also be considered a self-reliant failure. Because no one is able to inspect the inside of nuclear reactors, there is, unfortunately, no way to confirm this by evidence; accordingly, this remains a hypothesis to be tested in the future. Regardless, the accident contains hints of self-reliant failure, and so there is the possibility that structural disaster is related to the design, manufacture, testing, and operational systems during the shift from licensed production to self-reliant production.

Recognition of binodal turbine blade vibration as the true cause of the Rinkicho accident was beyond the standard knowledge of a turbine designer at that time; as such, this accident is a little-known failure because this type of problem could not have been recognized as obvious until the post-war period. In fact, avoiding turbine blade vibration caused by various resonances is one of the most critical topics for research on turbine design in the post-war period.[27] The Imperial Japanese Navy eventually managed to detect the true cause, but not until after serious technological and organizational errors of the Rinkicho accident remained undisclosed to outsiders by legitimate procedures such as institutionalized secrecy. Indeed, a complete solution was not found for years after the detection of the true cause.[28] In short, the problem was detected in the pre-war period, but its final solution was not discovered until after the war.[29]

Far beyond the simplistic dichotomy of success or failure throughout wartime and peacetime, this hidden and little-known accident, an important snapshot of a serious failure of Japan's self-reliant pre-war technology, provides evidence of the functional disintegration of the relationship network linking the military and other sectors. As such, the incident enables an examination of a military problem-finding and investigation techniques, and pioneering but partial diagnosis without a well-informed problem-solving process across the governmental, industrial, and academic sectors. This was the end state of the military-industrial-university complex in the pre-war period, in which a pitfall was present within the success story of technological development, from which the post-war industrial reconstruction in Japan started.

This will provide an important guideline for characterizing and understanding the Fukushima accident beyond a dichotomy of success or failure, a discussion that has been previously neglected in the sociology of science and technology, particularly in sociological studies on extreme events such as the Fukushima accident. The occurrence of the Rinkicho accident after a long history of successful technological development seems to be structurally similar to the Fukushima accident, which also happened after a long period of successful operation of nuclear reactors. Both are closely associated with the myth of safety. The crux of this structural similarity is that a pitfall is present within the success of both technologies, be it a long-term successful operation of naval turbines or that of nuclear reactors. From the viewpoint of structural disaster, there is an important sociological implication to be drawn from this similarity: when the governmental, industrial, and academic sectors are optimized in accordance with a particular type of new technology after having assimilated its domestic production, the failure of that technology necessitates structural reform of the entire science-technology-society interface because it encompasses the governmental, industrial, and academic sectors and their interaction. Since the optimization in the governmental, industrial, and academic sectors in accordance with a particular type of technology means an intensified and complicated interdependence of heterogeneous sectors, the failure of the technology has the potential to cause aggravation across all of those heterogeneous sectors. This state corresponds to an element of structural disaster wherein the complexity of a system and the interdependence of its units can aggravate problems.

Another sociological implication that could be obtained from the little-known Rinkicho accident pertains to its social context, as the accident was harmful not only to the stakeholders of the military sector but also to the general public. When evidence for such an argument is confirmed, the undisclosed state of the Rinkicho accident can be considered institutionalized secrecy as implied by structural disaster. As defined in Chapter 1, institutionalized secrecy denotes a legitimate way to keep public knowledge within the bounds of insiders through institutional designs, often to the detriment of the general public. Previous arguments have shown that the response of the Imperial Japanese Navy to the unexpected Rinkicho accident legitimately kept knowledge within the bound of insiders through institutional designs, such as a series of top secret reports, but how was this pattern of behavior detrimental to the general public?

The social context of the Rinkicho accident is an important consideration here. The social context involves wartime mobilization of science and technology, which was authorized by the Wartime Mobilization Law in 1938 and the Research Mobilization Ordinance in the following year. This legal foundation gave rise to the structural interdependence of the military-industrial-university complex under the control of the military sector, one of the unique features of the wartime mobilization of science and technology. The military sector controlled the overall mobilization, under which the industrial and academic sectors had to obey orders. Contrary to the cooperation of heterogeneous sectors on an equal footing through full information sharing, this cooperation was associated with the secretive attitude of the military toward outsiders. According to Hidetsugu Yagi, who became the president of the Board of Technology in 1944 (the central governmental authority specially set up for the wartime mobilization of science and technology) the military "treated civilian scientists as if they were foreigners."[30] Even at the central governmental authority, which was specifically set up to integrate wartime mobilization efforts of science and technology, cooperation, not to speak of coordination, with the military sector was thus very limited and the military-industrial-university complex began to lose its overall integration. Particularly in terms of the relationship between the military and other sectors, functional disintegration was exacerbated.

The social context of the wartime mobilization of science and technology reveals that, within the military-industrial-university complex in this mobilization, industrial, academic, and even governmental sectors were perceived by the military sector as outsiders to which critical information should be restricted; as a result, the performance of other sectors was hampered, as eventually was the performance of the social system as a whole. Within the context of such deterioration of the social system's performance, the Rinkicho accident was hidden to the Imperial Diet and therefore the Japanese government, not to speak of the general public, decided to go to war with the United States and Britain without knowing the crucial impact that the accident could have had on that decision. Considering all of the above, we can observe the four required conditions of institutionalized secrecy as defined in Chapter 1. Therefore, in this sense, the Rinkicho accident can be considered a kind of structural disaster.

This functional disintegration of the relationships linking the military and other sectors due to institutionalized secrecy occurred during a time when the structural integration of the complex was institutionally being reinforced by the Wartime Mobilization Law and the Research Mobilization Ordinance. This coupling of structural integration and functional disintegration through institutionalized secrecy provides grounds for establishing sociological implications of structural disaster not only in the context of pre-war Japan but in the current context of the post-Fukushima situation. Ultimately, if the Fukushima accident is a structural disaster accompanying institutionalized secrecy, it would have similar characteristics to the coupling of structural integration with functional disintegration.

SPEEDI revisited: from the perspective of structural integration and functional disintegration

From such a perspective, the undisclosed results of SPEEDI resulting from institutionalized secrecy discussed in Chapter 1 exemplify the coupling of structural integration with functional disintegration in the current context. Chapter 1 explained that the Guideline for Monitoring Environmental Radiation stipulated details on the utilization of SPEEDI at the time of the Fukushima accident as the institutional design yielding institutionalized secrecy. Probing the impetus of such a design, it is clear that structural integration existed within relating laws for nuclear disasters more than 10 years before the Fukushima accident.

The Guideline for Monitoring Environmental Radiation was originally made by the Nuclear Safety Commission in 1984.[31] In 2008, previously separated stipulations for ordinary and emergency situations were integrated, from which the detailed stipulation for the utilization of SPEEDI was embodied. The legal basis for this guideline originates in the Act on Special Measures Concerning Nuclear Emergency Preparedness that was ordained in 1999 and came into force in 2000, then amended in 2006. The objective of the act was "to strengthen the counter-measures against nuclear disasters so that the lives, bodies, and goods of the general public may be protected from the disasters" (Clause 1). Based on this act, in 2010, the Meeting of Related Ministries and Agencies to Control Nuclear Disaster Crisis resulted in the creation of the Manual to Cope with Nuclear Disasters, a manual that institutionalized the channels through which the results outputted from SPEEDI were circulated through its network system. In other words, monitoring data from nuclear power stations, weather reports from the Japan Meteorological Agency, and local monitoring data and weather reports from the local governments were inputted in the Center for Nuclear Safety Technology, from which SPEEDI was operated. After receiving instruction from MEXT, results outputted from SPEEDI were transmitted to both the local governments and the Local Nuclear Emergency Response Headquarters, or "off-site centers," through which relevant instructions are supposed to be transmitted to local residents around nuclear power stations. The flow of information conceived by this institutional design was designed to be as follows (see Figure 4.3).[32]

In addition, the Act on Special Measures Concerning Nuclear Emergency Preparedness provides stipulations for a high degree of uncertainty involved in nuclear disasters; in particular, uncertainty in assessing the seriousness of radioactive exposure and the distribution of doses that are difficult to determine under the general category of "occurrence of disasters" under the Basic Act on Disaster Control Measures. As a result of such a high degree of uncertainty, discrepancy in the assessments of a disaster and resulting delays in taking countermeasures can be expected. Precisely to prevent such a delay from taking place, the Act on Special Measures Concerning Nuclear Emergency Preparedness prescribes the

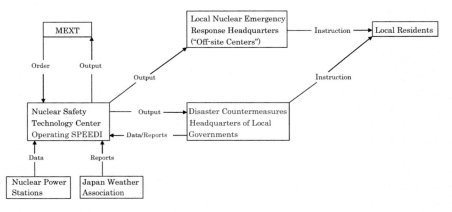

Figure 4.3 Flow of SPEEDI-Related Information
Source: Produced based on MEXT (n.d.)

Declaration of a Nuclear Emergency Situation by the prime minister. The declaration bestows a high degree of freedom on related agents to take immediate and proper measures against nuclear disasters.

Despite the structural integration of related laws and special prescriptions of this kind, in the Fukushima accident, no associated functional integration was expected from such a structural integration. It is true that a Declaration of a Nuclear Emergency Situation was made by the prime minister at 5:22 on March 12 in accordance with the act above; nevertheless, there was no transmission of the declaration from the governmental sector to residents or local governments in Namiecho and others. The original precept of the declaration, which was structurally integrated with act, was to bestow a high degree of freedom on related agents to deal with a high degree of uncertainty. However, there is no evidence showing that the declaration functioned in this intended, integrated manner because there was no release of relevant information directly to some local residents and local governments, which should have been enabled by the high degree of freedom bestowed on the related agents by the declaration at the time of the accident.

Concerning the transmission SPEEDI results, special-purpose terminal units designed for this purpose that were installed in Fukushima prefecture's Headquarters for Disaster Countermeasures were damaged by the Great East Japan Earthquake. Because of this, SPEEDI results were sent via an ordinary email server to the headquarters. According to the *ex post* investigation by the headquarters into the handling of the results sent via email, 65 out of the 86 emails conveying the results during the critical moment of the Fukushima nuclear accident (from 23:54 of March 12 to 9:45 of March 16) turned out to have been missing due to mismanagement (Headquarters for Disaster Countermeasures of the Fukushima Prefecture 2012). These emails were missing at the critical

Secrecy throughout war and peace 107

moment when evacuation was most needed for the residents around the nuclear power station, as the hydrogen explosion in Unit 1 of the nuclear power station happened at 15:36 of March 12, Unit 3 at 11:01 of March 14, and Unit 4 at 6:14 of March 15 (NAIIC 2012b; Governmental Investigation Committee 2012b; TEPCO 2012). Ultimately, SPEEDI worked, and its results were transmitted; however, they were not used (that is, they "disappeared") due to mismanagement by the local government at the critical moment of the hydrogen explosions. There is no better term to describe this situation than functional disintegration.

As to the flow of information conceived by the institutional design in the Act on Special Measures Concerning Nuclear Emergency Preparedness, there was no incoming data from nuclear power stations due to the destruction of monitoring posts by the Great East Japan Earthquake. In terms of results output by SPEEDI, its results were sent to MEXT, but the ministry did not immediately act due to institutionalized inaction, particularly institutionalized secrecy, as mentioned in Chapter 1 and Chapter 3. The original institutional design intended for the results to be sent to both off-site centers (located in Okumacho in Fukushima prefecture) and their local governments, but the special-purpose terminal units designed to receive these results had been damaged by the earthquake, such that no results arrived. As a temporary fix to respond to this situation, transmission via ordinary email was attempted but most were never received.

Even after the hydrogen explosions in Units 1, 3, and 4 of the Fukushima Daiichi Nuclear Power Plant, there was no attempt by MEXT to release the results directly to local residents around the power station. According to *ex post* inspection by MEXT (2012), for example, on the evening of March 15, they held a meeting about the SPEEDI results, but even at the time (which was immediately after the last hydrogen explosion in Unit 4), "there was no explanation about whether to make public the results of SPEEDI" nor "any concrete decision on the necessity to do so."

Thus, SPEEDI was not only working at the time of the accident but also endowed with structurally well-integrated institutional design and prescriptions to convey its results. While MEXT did not deliver the information to the local residents around the Fukushima Daiichi nuclear power station nor their local governments, during its *ex post* self-evaluation of its own behavior at the time of the accident, it concluded that its behavior "followed the manuals and other related instructions" and that its SPEEDI-related task "was carried out appropriately" as precisely stipulated by the Guideline for Monitoring Environmental Radiation prepared by the Nuclear Safety Commission (MEXT 2012: 12, 14). While, it is true that MEXT precisely followed instructions stipulated by this guideline, this is only because the goal of SPEEDI in an emergency situation is to estimate the effects of radioactive materials and radiation, as mentioned in Chapter 1.

SPEEDI's operation protocols are stipulated in accordance with the four phases of an emergency situation as follows:

1 The phase immediately after the accident
2 The phase in which emission source information is available

3   The phase in which monitoring information in an emergency situation is available
4   The phase after the end of emissions

The following are the stipulations of how to operate SPEEDI in each of the above phases:

1   "To make a monitoring plan in an emergency situation"
                                              (Nuclear Safety Commission 2008: 51)

2   "To deliver calculation figures"
                                              (Nuclear Safety Commission 2008: 51)

3   "To produce figures"
                                              (Nuclear Safety Commission 2008: 52)

4   "To contribute to the estimate of radiation exposure"
                                              (Nuclear Safety Commission 2008: 52)

As seen in the above stipulations, there the "health and safety" of the inhabitants is not considered in or included as part of the operation protocols of the guideline. As stated, the focus of these protocols is placed on estimating effects and delivering figures based on the estimations; therefore, both in goal setting and operation protocols, it is true that MEXT precisely followed instructions stipulated by this guideline. Who, then, is responsible for such devastation as was brought about by the Fukushima accident, as well as for the human and organizational errors that were deep-rooted in the nuclear village, as mentioned in Chapter 3? The answer is why institutional design matters. The concept of structural disaster enables, beyond compartmentalized description and analysis, mapping of the overall situation so that analysis can be concentrated on the matters of institutional design that have decisive power in determining the overall situation. For example, institutionalized inaction, such as institutionalized secrecy, can be seen as lacking fulfillment of relevant functions, thus breaking expectation from the structural integration of related laws and prescriptions. With the assistance of the concept of structural disaster, we can understand that structural integration encompasses the governmental, industrial, and academic sectors and that this very integration is coupled with functional disintegration of the SPEEDI network system in terms of the flow of information among the sectors, including the citizens sector.[33]

Structural disaster across pre-war/military and post-war/non-military regimes

From the perspective of structural disaster, there are two kinds of structural similarities between the Rinkicho accident and the Fukushima accident: the development trajectory of technology and institutionalized secrecy.

Regarding the structural similarity between the two accidents in the development trajectory of technology, both accidents took place within the context of wholly domestic or almost wholly domestic production of a technology, during which there was successful operation of domestically produced technologies extending more than 10 to 30 years. In that particular sense, both accidents could be categorized as the failure of self-reliant technologies.

The other structural similarity bears on the similarity between the two accidents in terms of institutionalized secrecy, where its four conditions can be validated in both the Fukushima accident mentioned in Chapter 1 and Chapter 3 and in the Rinkicho accident mentioned in this chapter. Situating institutionalized secrecy in the Rinkicho accident within the contemporary social context of the wartime mobilization of science and technology, the coupling of structural integration and functional disintegration is evident in the contemporary military-industrial-university complex. Therefore, if the structural similarity still applies after taking into account the different social contexts of today, it follows that the coupling of structural integration and functional disintegration should also reside in the current governmental-industrial-university complex behind the Fukushima accident.

There are, of course, also notable differences between the two accidents, such as in the way an element of structural disaster came to be detected and corrected, as represented in adherence to erroneous precedents that causes problems to be carried forward and reproduced. In the Rinkicho accident, the conclusion reached by the final report of the special examination committee and authorized by the Imperial Japanese Navy was dynamically canceled by carefully observed facts regardless of the rank of those who pointed out these discrepancies and the past experience accumulated within the organization. Such a dynamic reconsideration of alternative possibilities that could have upset the face-saving of the members of the special examination committee actually triggered the restart of the examination and led to a drastically different conclusion.

In contrast, there has been no sign of a public showing of such work toward a dynamic correction to the adherence to erroneous precedents as seen in the Fukushima accident. Looking at the inside stories of TEPCO, the Nuclear and Industrial Safety Agency (NISA), and other governmental bodies that have been disclosed as being actors within the situation, there is the possibility of mutual "cover-ups" within and/or between those organizations, though the possibility of the dynamic correction of the adherence to erroneous precedents might still be left open. This difference is noteworthy because, even with the working of such a dynamic correction of the element of structural disaster enabling consideration of alternative possibilities and restarting of examination, the timing of the realization of the true cause of the Rinkicho accident was too late for Japan to reconsider the soundness of national decision-making before going to war in 1941.

When considering together the similarities between the Rinkicho accident and the Fukushima accident as structural disasters in terms of institutionalized secrecy and the difference as to whether the dynamic correction of adherence to erroneous precedents could work, there is the possibility that the elements of structural disaster embedded in the Fukushima accident will continue in a path-dependent manner. In such a case, the science-technology-society interface surrounding the Fukushima accident is likely unable to tolerate another impact from a serious and unexpected event, such as a second earthquake and tsunami and/or decontamination difficulty around some critical reactor areas and/or their abrupt uncontrollability.

One of the most important sociological implications of the Fukushima accident as structural disaster can be obtained from the scrutiny of the naval turbine accident that occurred immediately before WWII: How to avoid the worst-case scenario. To do so, the seemingly structurally robust but functionally disintegrated science-technology-society interface should be changed, because of the presence of institutionalized secrecy and other elements of structural disaster.[34] As long as functional disintegration of the science-technology-society interface continues to exist and operates behind the institutionally legitimate façade of structural integration, a similar dangerous weakness, in a possibly larger-scale social context, could arise. Ultimately, the functional disintegration through structural interdependence, accompanied by institutionalized secrecy and the suppression of negative information, could give rise to structural disaster in the future extreme events.

This chapter has shown that, as far as structural disaster is concerned, there is no demarcation between the pre-war social context – such as the wartime mobilization of science and technology resulting in nuclear bombing – and the post-war one of promoting science and technology in peacetime manifested in nuclear reactors. In fact, there are structural similarities between the pre-war naval turbine accident and the post-war Fukushima accident in four different terms of structural disaster: adherence to erroneous precedents that causes problems to be carried forward and reproduced; institutionalized secrecy; the coexistence of structural integration and functional disintegration of the science-technology-society interface; and the interdependence of success and failure among the interdependence of the units of a system. The third point is a novel insight that was obtained from the analyses of the behavioral patterns of the agents involved in the pre-war accident with a comparative perspective using the Fukushima accident.

Structural integration coupled with functional disintegration in the science-technology-society interface has a telling sociological implication because, based on the analysis of the hidden pre-war accident, such a coupling eventually was the result of institutionalized secrecy as implied by structural disaster. Hence, if the Fukushima accident is a structural disaster, there is the possibility that structural integration coupled with functional disintegration will occur again as the end state of the accident in the future. Although what the end state actually means in the post-Fukushima situation depends on further investigation, it could mean that the connection between structural disaster and its end state cut through completely different social contexts.

By focusing on structural integration coupled with functional disintegration through the lens of structural disaster, it is evident that while there are opposite social contexts among the two accidents (wartime versus peacetime), structural disaster in peacetime as seen by the Fukushima accident does not guarantee that the end state of the accident will be peaceful, as opposed to the outbreak of war after the Rinkicho accident.

This chapter's key insights penetrate the dichotomous distinction between pre-war/military and post-war/peaceful regimes and thereby provide an important frame of reference from which to view unfolding events and/or states ensuing from structural disaster, freed from a narrative-in-hindsight that relies on the dichotomous distinction between wartime and peacetime. Once presupposed ways of thinking about wartime versus peacetime are liberated, the need to change the status quo via the will of the people who suffered from the event such as the Fukushima accident is clear, for the purpose of instituting a significant structural remedy. The remedy should extend beyond countermeasures that only temporarily patch over present troubles and serve to save face of responsible agents who are or are willing to be unaware of structural continuity running through pre-war/military and post-war/peaceful regimes.

5 A structural disaster in environmentally friendly oceanic energy development

The hidden link between renewable energy and stratospheric ozone depletion

This chapter explores the possibility that structural disaster can occur within the renewable energy regime as well as in the nuclear energy one, with particular reference to renewable energy's technological development process. To examine this phenomenon, an oceanic energy development project is examined for structural disaster that can underlie renewable energy technology development by focusing on the hidden link between the complex social process of the project and stratospheric ozone depletion, which is one of the most invisible global environmental problems. Renewable energy technology is often perceived to be the opposite of nuclear energy; however, this chapter will delineate the elements of structural disaster running throughout renewable energy technology development and the Fukushima nuclear accident, using the "Sunshine" project for the case study, which developed renewable energy technology from the 1970s through the early 1990s, by which time the nuclear village had established itself firmly in Japanese society.

Particular attention is given to the complex relationship between ocean thermal energy conversion (OTEC) technology and irreversible global environmental change, such as stratospheric ozone depletion.[1] This chapter reveals that the development of this supposedly environmentally friendly energy technology had the unintended consequence of potentially aggravating global environmental problems, and then explains the discrepancy between its intended purposes and actual consequences by analyzing the Sunshine project's "blind spots" that were activated by a path-dependent social mechanism. The complex relationship between the development of renewable energy technology and irreversible environmental change can thus be regarded as constituting a process that can be considered a kind of structural disaster in situations with a high degree of uncertainty hard-to-detect *ex ante*, a process that makes it difficult to address future avoidances by a precautionary principle alone. Sociological implications are also discussed with reference to allocating responsibility for problems arising from this high degree of uncertainty exemplified by dual underdetermination.

Social background of "new energy" technology development in Japan: the origin of the Sunshine project

The war that broke out in the Middle East on October 6, 1973, dramatically reduced the global supply of crude oil, driving up prices and causing an oil

Structural disaster in energy development 113

crisis, which was keenly felt in Japan. The Sunshine project was announced the following year as Japan's first national project for the development of "new energy" technology.[2] This long-term project, planned in anticipation of supply and demand increases for energy predicted for the year 2000, sought to develop a new, clean source of energy that would avoid the environmental problems common to earlier energy technologies. The *Official Gazette* stated its aim as: "Development of a new technology to produce clean energy by the year 2000 through various medium-term research projects of several years each, and to satisfy a great percentage of the energy demand for several decades in the future."[3]

Clean energy technology is one of the main ways to cope with resource problems while considering the overall environment, and can be seen in "new energy" technologies such as super-efficient gas turbines, liquid coal, heat pumps, HDR (hot dry rock) and sunlight electricity production, fuel cells, wind turbines, biomass, and nuclear fusion. These technologies can make use of both renewable and non-renewable energy sources, and some have already been put into effect or are deemed feasible for the near future, while others have not yet been deemed feasible. Including all of the ideas that have been proposed but soon dropped would result in a very long list.

One characteristic common to all of the new energy technologies is that they are intended to supplement and/or replace energy technologies that rely on fossil fuels, particularly oil. Taking into account the geopolitical situation of Japan, with its nearly total reliance on imported oil and its lack of domestic gas or coal reserves, the development of new energy technology is a crucial substitute (the only other available major energy source being nuclear fission).

According to the Special Law for the Promotion of the Utilization of New Energy enacted in 1997, new energy is defined as "power obtainable from the production and utilization of oil-substitute energy and electricity which could be particularly contributory to decreasing the degree of oil-dependence, and therefore requires aid continuously, but is still not in widespread use due to insufficient economy."[4] This definition originates from the Law for the Development and Promotion of Oil-substitute Energy (Law No. 71) on May 30, 1980. Thus, in Japan new energy long meant, almost exclusively, substitutes for oil. The first national project to develop such technology was the Sunshine project.

The social shaping of the Sunshine project from its inception was characterized by a conscious effort to create links between the governmental, industrial, and academic sectors. The Ministry of International Trade and Industry (MITI; currently METI), national test and research institutes, universities, and private corporations spearheaded the basic research underlying the project. MITI – particularly its Agency of Industrial Technology (AIT, currently the National Institute of Advanced Industrial Science and Technology) – worked closely with the test and research institutes that it governed and those with which it had a client-trustee relationship, such as universities and private corporations. In applied and developmental research, private corporations as well as MITI and the New Energy Development Organization (NEDO) took the lead. To satisfy the need for a single, unified research organization for development and application, MITI and NEDO established a link in 1980, a step that had been expected

114 *Structural disaster in energy development*

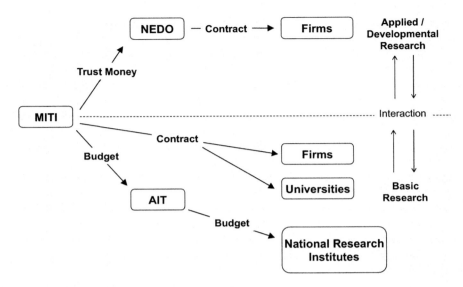

Figure 5.1 Social Shaping of the Sunshine Project
Source: Produced based on The Sunshine Project Ten-Year Anniversary Committee of AIT (1984).

since the start of the Sunshine project.[5] MITI controlled the expenditure of funds (investment, trust, and supply money, grants, subsidies) and supervised the organization's work, while NEDO's role focused on its trust-based relationships with private corporations. All agents concerned were expected to provide mutual feedback between basic and applied/developmental research. The Sunshine Project Promotion Headquarters, established within the AIT, controlled all project teams and project ideas were selected and evaluated by the New Energy Development Subcommittee of the Industrial Technology Council, an advisory organ for MITI. The overall social shaping of the project is shown in Figure 5.1.

The project's budget increased 16-fold during the first 10 years, as shown in Figure 5.2.[6] This increase resulted from the Special Account Law for Promoting Power Development and the Special Account Law for Coal, Oil, and Oil-Substitute Energies, which came into effect in May 1980.

A special account has its own source of revenue independent of the general account, with a specific purpose that is given priority by the government, which typically results in a higher degree of freedom in the execution of the budget than under the general account. From a budgetary viewpoint, the Sunshine project was an independent, long-term, large-scale project distinct from MITI's other projects.[7]

The project covered five main energy areas – solar, geothermal, coal, hydrogen, and wind and ocean – and was planned to advance through the following phases:

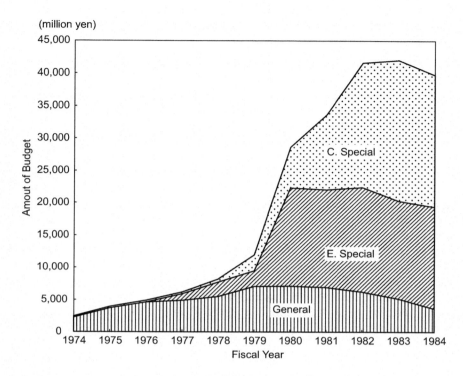

Figure 5.2 Budgetary Evolution for the Sunshine Project: 1974–1984

Source: The Sunshine Project Ten-Year Anniversary Committee of AIT (1984: 12).

Note: General, E. Special, C. Special in the table mean General Account, Electricity Special Account, Coal Special Account respectively.

basic research; conceptual design; development of component technology; and construction and operation of pilot, practical, and commercial plants.

Each phase within the five areas could be examined for its eventual contribution to the originally conceived purpose; for example, the construction and full-scale operation of OTEC commercial plants to solve resource problems. This chapter, however, argues that the Sunshine project should be evaluated via completely different standards that are independent of any evaluation of individual contributions to the given purpose of the overall project. This is because an independent, large-scale, long-term technological development project such as this one requires an analysis of its connections to global environmental assessments, which, in turn, will define structural disaster with respect to renewable energy technology development. Such projects tend to produce an unanticipated degree of complexity that necessitates global environmental assessment due to the elements of structural disaster embedded in their social process. The origin of ocean energy development within the Sunshine project will substantiate this approach.

Ocean energy development and global environmental assessment: the complex case of ocean thermal energy conversion (OTEC)

The ocean energy development project used as a case study here consisted of the following five sub-projects: (1) wave-activated power generation; (2) OTEC; (3) tidal power generation; (4) ocean current power generation; and (5) ocean density power generation. The development of OTEC merits particular attention to the relationship between renewable energy technology development and global environmental problems because its analysis can lead to pinpointing where the global environmental assessment was significant in relation to unexpected structural disaster within the social process involved in renewable energy technology development. Another reason for this particular focus is that, in the mid-1970s, OTEC was assumed to be greatly superior to the other four ocean energy development sub-projects noted above in terms of resource availability, output stability, and cost. Consequently, OTEC appeared the most promising and attracted the most attention at the time.[8] OTEC is based on the simple principle of converting the thermal difference between warm surface water and cold subsurface water into electrical energy.

Three mutually independent statements from three different sectors simultaneously called for the swift development of OTEC during the 1970s and deserve particular attention: ones from the academic sector, the industrial sector, and the governmental sector, respectively. Haruo Uehara, who was a professor at Saga University and one of the best known proponents of OTEC, published a paper in 1977 titled "Current Status and Technological Aspects of OTEC" in *Machinery Studies* (*Kikai no Kenkyu*). At the outset of the paper, he states the following:

> For the human being, energy is one of the most important concerns. At present, Japan relies on oil imports for most of its energy needs. Considering the geographical location of Japan, we should make the utmost effort to exploit the energy resources of the sea. The thermal energy of the ocean can produce electric power.
>
> (Uehara 1977)

According to Uehara, "The power available within the 200 sea mile area around Japan is about ten billion kW if produced at current technological efficiency. This is about ten times the energy (one billion kW) that Japan will require in the year 2000" (Uehara 1977). It is clear that he considered OTEC a guaranteed fix for resource problems. The next year, Hiroshi Kamogawa, Chairman of the Committee on OTEC of the Sunshine project at the AIT, published an article titled "OTEC for Solving Resource Problems" in *Monthly Report of the Federation of Economic Organizations* (*Keidanren Geppo*). He stated:

> OTEC has the potential to satisfy energy demand, the demand for sea food resources, and contribute to increased output of industrial raw materials

including uranium . . . . We hope that the Japanese government will pay most attention to OTEC at the national level and promote its development immediately.

(Kamogawa 1978)

During that same year, an even brighter and more concrete picture of the prospects for OTEC was depicted by a report from the Marine Science and Technology Center of the Science and Technology Agency (STA). The report stated:

We can expect a maximum output of 100MWe–400MWe per single OTEC plant. It is estimated that, with proper design and a viable commercial plant, OTEC will enable Japan, the US, and European countries to produce electricity in the 1990s at broadly the same moderate cost as today.[9]

(Kaiyo Kagaku Gijutsu Senta 1978: 68)

French physicist Jacques A. d'Arsonval (1851–1940) hit upon the idea for OTEC at the end of the nineteenth century,[10] proposed tapping the thermal energy of the ocean. There are two ways to apply the idea practically. One is a closed-cycle (CC) system, where the working fluid circulates, and the other is an open-cycle (OC) system, in which it does not. CC was proposed by d'Arsonval himself, and OC was invented by French industrial chemist Georges Claude (1870–1960), a former student of d'Arsonval and well-known for his successful production of synthetic ammonia. The earliest trial of OTEC used an OC system constructed by Claude in Cuba in 1928, which proved a disappointing failure.[11] CC became the focus of full-scale OTEC research after J. H. Anderson and J. H. Anderson, Jr., of the United States obtained a patent for the CC system in 1967.[12]

The pioneering research and development of OTEC was carried out mainly by scientists in France and the United States, and in the 1980s, efforts were made to carry out OTEC development in various other parts of the world such as the United Kingdom, the Netherlands, and Sweden, among other nations.[13]

In Japan, a feasibility study of the CC system was undertaken right after the start of the Sunshine project in 1974. The OTEC system (which will be referred to as only CC hereafter, except where otherwise indicated) consisted of the following three sub-systems: 1. circulating warm water, 2. circulating cold water, and 3. circulating a working fluid (see Figure 5.3). Japan had constructed three pilot plants by 1988.

Under the accelerating development plan drafted by the Sunshine project team, an OTEC pilot plant with an output capacity of about 1,000 kW was to be constructed by 1991.[14] By 2016, however, not only was no commercial plant in operation, but no further working OTEC plant has been constructed since the initial three pilot plants.[15] In this case, what is more important than an assessment of how far a target was reached is an assessment of the way the initial technology selection was made, because the selection of OTEC technology had an important relationship to global environmental problems, and this relationship eventually

118 *Structural disaster in energy development*

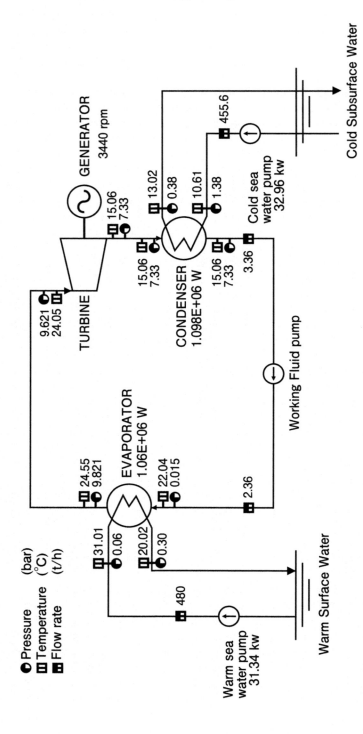

Figure 5.3 The Concept of OTEC
Source: Japanese Association for the Promotion of Industrial Technology (1987: 45).

NO.	RT	AREA		CONC
1	0.14	9,877	AIR	1.077
2	0.25	7,17,292	R12	85.111
3	0.60	1,16,401	R21	13.812
TOTAL		8,42,770		100.000

Figure 5.4 Results of Quantitative Analysis of a Working Fluid for OTEC
Source: Japanese Association for the Promotion of Industrial Technology (1987: 6).

gave way to structural disaster that underlay the social process in which renewable energy technology was developed.

The critical issue with making OTEC sustainable and/or feasible is how to use the small decrease in heat between warm and cold seawater. The average water temperature is about 28° C at the surface and about 7° C in the subsurface. Thus, the temperature difference is only about 20 degrees, compared to the several hundred degrees used in typical thermal power generation methods. To generate power from this small heat drop, the efficiency of the heat cycle must be enhanced. Since the surface water temperature is only about 28° C, using water as the working fluid is of no use in OTEC. This critical problem was solved during the basic research stage of the Sunshine project by using a working fluid for OTEC that contained chlorofluorocarbon (CFC) compounds, specifically CFC 12 and CFC 21 (see Appendix B). Figure 5.4 shows the results of a quantitative analysis of the compound fluid.

As shown in the figures, in the working fluid, CFCs accounted for about 99 percent of the fluid, with CFC 12 alone accounting for about 85 percent.[16] Unfortunately, CFC 12 is considered as the chemical most likely to be responsible for the depletion of the stratospheric ozone layer, which seems contradictory to the purpose of the Sunshine project, which was to develop a clean energy source that would not damage the environment. This invites the following question: Why was this ozone-depleting substance adopted as the principal component of the working fluid for OTEC in the Sunshine project? According to MITI, there were three reasons: (1) high thermal conductivity; (2) low boiling point (29.8° C for CFC 12); and (3) easy handling and availability (because of high chemical stability due to the C-F combination).[17]

The first proposal to employ CFCs as the working fluid for OTEC dates back to the start of the Sunshine project in 1974. In that year, a conceptual design for a 1.5-MW OTEC plant was produced as a feasibility study, and the design proposal stated:

> Two plans are proposed, and details are given of the performance and the specified designs of these plans. One plan employs a design combining the steam cycle of existing power plants with a working fluid having a low boiling point, such as a CFC, circulated by means of pumped water. The other plan performs heat exchange by connecting the two cycles directly.[18]
> (Showa 59 Nendo Sunshine Keikaku Seika
> Hokokusho Gaiyoshu 1985: 25)

120 *Structural disaster in energy development*

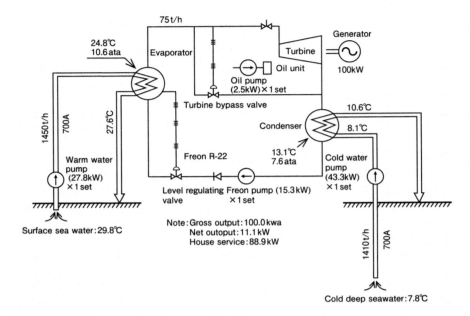

Figure 5.5 The Concept of the First Working OTEC Pilot Plant
Source: ECOR (Engineering Committee on Ocean Resources), Japan Marine Science and Technology Association (Japan National Committee for ECOR) (1989: 83).

From then on, CFCs were an important candidate for the working fluid for OTEC, along with others such as NH_3, CH_3, CH_2, $_2CH_3$, and C_3H_8. The first successfully working pilot plant, constructed in the Republic of Nauru by TEPCO, with funds from the Official Development Assistance of the Japanese Government and the AIT of MITI, used CFCs in its working fluid (see Figure 5.5).

For this working pilot plant, CFC 22 was singled out to make use of the heat drop created between the warm surface water and colder subsurface water; for this purpose, a new CFC turbine was developed that was described as being "the vanguard of energy-saving." Test experiments, which started in 1981, provided important data on the working of the turbine.[19] A continuous run test was carried out for 10 days using the working pilot plant. The report of the experiments evaluated their results as follows:

> We find that OTEC is a stable means of electricity supply. Various test experiments of the dynamic characteristics of OTEC in terms of the rotation control, start, stop, and load fluctuation, and so forth have been undertaken,

and all of them demonstrate that OTEC has sufficient stability for a generating system.

(ECOR [Engineering Committee on Ocean Resources],
Japan Marine Science and Technology Association
[Japan National Committee for ECOR] 1989: 85)

Thus, on the one hand, CFCs were considered to be the optimal technological choice for enhancing the efficiency of the OTEC heat cycle; on the other hand, they were a suspected ozone-depleting substance. Admittedly, in the case of the CC system, where the working fluid circulates only within the system, it might seem unlikely that the fluid could escape under ordinary running conditions (for example, in a refrigerator, which is a very similar system, fluid escapes during ordinary operation are unusual). In the case of OTEC, however, the problem is that a large number of plants are dispersed throughout a wide area of open sea. According to an estimate made by Hiroshi Kamogawa, a plant with an output of 100,000 kW would require at least a 20 sq. km sea area, assuming constant efficiency in extracting heat from the sea (Kamogawa 1978).

In order to get maximum heat from warm surface seawater, Japan would have to locate OTEC plants in its southern sea areas as close as possible to the Tropic of Cancer. Entirely out of coincidence, on July 1, 1977, Japan set a 200 nautical mile economic limit and extended the range of its territorial waters from 3 to 12 nautical miles from the coast. Accordingly, the above-mentioned initial development plan drafted by the Sunshine project team meant that one OTEC plant should occupy every 20 sq. km area throughout the large sea area, up to as much as 200 nautical miles from the coast of southern Japan. In fact, a special map showing the potential output of total OTEC plants per year was produced on a latitude 1° × longitude 1° basis, with particular emphasis on "more advantageous" southern sea areas, according to which potential power output within 200 nautical miles was estimated at 1.06×10^2 GWh per year (ECOR [Engineering Committee on Ocean Resources], Japan Marine Science and Technology Association [Japan National Committee for ECOR] 1989: note 23, 63).

This is, however, an area that experiences many seasonal typhoons, caused by the active evaporation of seawater. It is also a main artery of sea transportation, where many ships come and go; in fact, this area coincides with a designated sea patrol area in which the Maritime Safety Agency is required constantly to deploy patrol boats due to frequent shipwrecks caused by traffic density of sea transportation and fishery vessels as well as due to sea and weather conditions (Japan Coast Guard 1979: Appended Materials No. 24). Furthermore, preventing the plants from drifting by continuously correcting for complex influences from tidal currents posed another serious issue.

Based on all of these conditions, the possibility that CFCs would escape on a large-scale due to plant damage by natural disasters or accidents/collisions is likely. By the same token, a researcher at the Marine Energy Section of the

122 *Structural disaster in energy development*

Table 5.1 Sea Wreck Statistics in the Expected Sea Areas for OTEC Siting: 1976–1980

Year	Number between 12 and 200 sea miles from the coast	Total number
1976	298	2,665
1977	269	2,369
1978	299	2,357
1979	236	2,145
1980	231	2,386

Source: Calculated based on Japan Coast Guard (1976–1980).

Electro-Technical Laboratory of the AIT of MITI himself realized this, recommending the following in 1981:

> The ocean is a place for biological resources and transportation, and so forth as well as for energy development. Since the ocean is equally important for such a variety of different purposes, it should be kept in mind that energy plants to be placed in the ocean cannot be feasible until coexistence between these different purposes is secured.[20]
>
> (Kajikawa 1981)

In fact, contemporary statistics on shipwrecks reveal that the number of ships that have called for rescue due to typhoons and accidents in this area (within the range from 12 to 200 nautical miles from the coast) was more than 10 percent of the total number of shipwrecks in all sea areas around Japan (see Table 5.1).[21]

In short, why was a working fluid selected that is optimal from a thermal energy conversion standpoint for technology within an OTEC plant but detrimental just outside such a plant? The next section provides an answer by examining the background of the complex relationship between OTEC and global environmental problems, which should lead one step further to revealing structural disaster in the social process of renewable energy technology development.

Subtler aspects of the complex relationship between OTEC and the global environment: an unexpected path revealing structural disaster

It could be supposed that the above technological choice was made only at the basic research stage, with no intention to use CFCs as an actual working fluid; however, Table 5.2 confirms that this was not the case.

The table lists the patents using CFCs as a working fluid for OTEC, as pertaining to the OTEC heat cycle and power generation system. Seven patents using CFCs were applied for and published, and numbered consecutively in order of the date of application in the table. Six out of these seven patents were applied for

Table 5.2 Patents related to OTEC

Date of Application	Laid-open Number	Applicant	Title of Patent	CFCs Used
5/22/1984	60-245686	A. G.	Compound Working Fluid	R11, R12, R22, R114, R115
6/1/1984	60-255884	A. G.	Compound Working Fluid	R22, R133
6/1/1984	60-255885	A. G.	Compound Working Fluid for Rankin Cycle	R12, R124, R115
6/12/1984	61-285	Sa. E. Tokyo Sa. E.	Compound Working Fluid for Heat Cycle	R21, R22
7/24/1984	61-31488	A. G.	Compound Working Fluid	R11, R134
7/31/1984	60-37855	A. G.	Compound Working Fluid	R12, R123b
7/31/1984	61-37856	A. G.	Compound Working Fluid	R22, R123

Source: Produced from Showa 61 Nendo Sunshine Keikaku Itaku Chosa Kenkyu Seika Hokokusho: Tokkyo Joho Chosa Kenkyu, Kaiyo Ondosa Hatsuden (Report of Results of the Research by the Sunshine Project for 1986-1987: OTEC Patents), Nihon Sangyo Gijutsu Shinko Kyokai, March, 1987.

Note: The first figure of the Laid-open Number indicates the year of the Japanese regional calendar in which the patent was made public: 60 is 1985, 61 is 1986. The first patent in the table uses one of the CFCs put in the column or a combination. The applicant abbreviations used in the table are as follows: A. G., Asahi Glass Manufacturing Co., Ltd.; Sa. E, Sanyo Electrical Engineering Co., Ltd.; Tokyo Sa. E., Tokyo Sanyo Electrical Engineering Co., Ltd.

and published by Asahi Glass Manufacturing Co., Ltd., the leader in production capacity among the few CFC manufacturers in Japan at the time (see Table 5.3). (The production capability of the company rose from 40 thousand tons in 1980 to 91.2 thousand tons in 1990.)[22]

Asahi Glass was a latecomer to CFC manufacturing. During the period of high economic growth in the 1960s, the company decided to enter this field for the following reasons:

> More and more uses are being found for carbon fluoride as a coolant, spraying agent, and polyurethane foaming agent. In addition, high-purity natural gas is available at low cost from our mining area in Chiba. To make effective use of this natural gas supply and electrolytic chlorine obtained from caustic soda conversion, we should manufacture CFCs.[23]
>
> (Provisional Company History Compilation Section of Asahi Glass Manufacturing Co., Ltd., 1967: 449)

Table 5.3 Production Capacity of CFC Manufacturers in Japan: 1980–1990 (thousand tons)

Fiscal Year Manufacturers	1980	1981	1982	1983	1984	1985	1986	1987	1988	1989	1990
A. G.	40	60	60	60	60	67.5	79.2	79.2	91.2	91.2	91.2
D. I.	36	55	55	65	65	65	75	75	85	85	90
M. C.	26	26	26	26	26	26	30	64	64	64	64
S. E.	12	12	12	12	12	12	12	12	12	12	12

Source: Produced from The News Agency on Heavy and Chemical Industries (1980–1990).
Note: A. G.: Asahi Glass Manufacturing Co., Ltd. D. I.: Daikin Industry Co., Ltd. M. C.: Mitsui Fluoro-Chemical Co., Ltd. (Mitsui Du Pont Fluoro-Chemical Co., Ltd. since August 1984) S. E.: Showa Electric Industry Co., Ltd. Since the capacity of the Asahi Glass was expressed in monthly terms from 1985, the figures from 1985 on are calculated from the monthly production capacity. Since the above source simply mentions that Central Glass Co. Ltd. started CFCs production in 1987 without data, the figure for the company is omitted here.

Following this strategy, Asahi Glass built a CFC plant with a monthly production capacity of 500 tons within its factory in Chiba Prefecture and the plant started manufacturing CFCs in April 1964, with full production by 1967.[24]

The one remaining patent was applied for and published by Sanyo Electric Co., Ltd., a refrigerator manufacturer, for which CFCs had been used as a coolant since the 1960s. Particularly after the mid-1970s, with the introduction of more strict regulation of gas under high-pressure, the conversion from ammonia to CFCs both for domestic and industrial use was promoted by various policy measures. By the time the ozone depletion problem was recognized as being serious, CFCs had almost completely overtaken ammonia in the coolant market in Japan.[25]

Thus, it was a CFC manufacturer and a manufacturer using CFCs in its end products that selected the substance as the working fluid for OTEC. This means that, during the technology selection process for OTEC in the Sunshine project – which began with the environmentally conscious aim of developing a clean source of energy – manufacturers wanted to use compounds that were familiar to them as the working fluid for OTEC, compounds that contained CFCs, specifically CFC 12 and CFC 21. A similar phenomenon can be observed in the process of technological spin-off from one field to another; however, an intrinsic problem can be seen when viewing the timing of the technological selection for OTEC. As the patent application dates in Table 5.2 show, all occur during the period from May to July 1984, the same time period during which the first observation of an ozone hole was reported.

Shigeru Chubachi, a scientist of the Japan Meteorological Agency, reported stratospheric ozone densities observed between February 1982 and January 1983 when he was working at the Showa station in Antarctica. What he expected to observe was seasonal fluctuation of the stratospheric ozone density in Antarctica

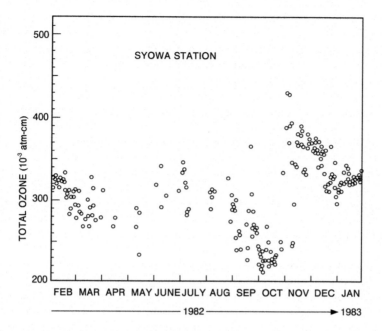

Figure 5.6 The First Evidence of an Ozone Hole
Source: Chubachi (1984a).

(Chubachi 1984a); however, the results he obtained were the first evidence of the existence of an ozone hole (see Figure 5.6). Chubachi's paper on the subject was submitted to the English journal of the National Polar Research Institute in March 1984 and published in December of the same year.

On the theoretical side, M. J. Molina and F. S. Rowland predicted the depletion of the ozone layer in their paper published in 1974. They argued that CFCs released into the air would reach the stratosphere without having been decomposed in the troposphere. In the stratosphere, sunlight would cause a free radical reaction and decompose the ozone quickly into O_2 and chlorine monoxide. Their provisional estimate of the results based on the total amount of CFCs produced up to that time and the rate of increase of their production were included in their paper's final remarks:

> It seems quite clear that the atmosphere has only a finite capacity for absorbing Cl [chlorine] atoms produced in the stratosphere, and important consequences may result. . . . A lengthy period (of the order of calculated atmospheric lifetimes) may thus be required for natural moderation, even if the amount of Cl introduced into the stratosphere is reduced in the future.
>
> (Molina and Rowland 1974: 812)

Despite these sensational predictions by Molina and Rowland (which later earned them the 1995 Noble Prize in Chemistry), computer simulations were unable to predict the existence of an ozone hole, long after the paper's publication. In this situation, Chubachi's paper is considered the first observational study that supported the theory of Molina and Rowland. As mentioned, all patents using CFCs as a working fluid for OTEC were applied for during May to July 1984, the same year in which Chubachi's paper was published (that December).

This sequence of events strongly suggests that the agents who recommended using CFCs as a working fluid for OTEC in the Sunshine project lacked the relevant perspective for connecting a new energy technology aimed at solving resource problems with stratospheric ozone depletion.[26] Under Japanese law, a patent must be published 18 months after application, which means that the publication of Chubachi's observation predated the public announcement of all seven patents (published in 1985 and 1986). While these patents were not accompanied by a request for immediate examination, it might seem odd that patents using CFCs were published after stratospheric ozone depletion had been observed.

In the scientific community at the time, however, Chubachi's observation was ignored long after its publication and even after he presented his detailed observational data at the International Ozone Symposium held in Greece three months before putting them in print (Chubachi 1984b). At the symposium, his was the only presentation on the ozone layer above Antarctica, and no other participant showed any interest in the topic. According to him, all he was able to do was to hand out two-dozen preprints of his work, and comments from within the Meteorological Agency before his presentation at the symposium reflected a general skepticism about the observation, and he was advised to recheck the data.[27] It was not until 1987, when *Nimbus 7*, a United States meteorological satellite, independently observed extremely low stratospheric ozone density above Antarctica, that Chubachi became known as one of the discoverers of the ozone hole. Thus, it took nearly three years for the significance of his observation to be recognized, during which interval (1985 and 1986) all seven patents using CFCs for OTEC were published.[28]

This sequence of events indicates that "common sense" expectations of the scientific community delayed the acceptance of the ozone hole as well as of the global environmental problems it indicated. Although Chubachi's data were published in English, the absence of any corroboration from other scientists around the world may also have hindered acceptance of his evidence.

Corroboration did appear five months later, on May 15, 1985, when J. C. Farman and other members of the United Kingdom's Antarctic observation team reported similar results in an article published in *Nature* (Farman, Gardiner, and Shanklin 1985).[29] This article later became known in Europe and the United States as the first report of an actual ozone hole,[30] reporting not only the discovery of the hole, but also rejecting theories that attributed the hole to natural phenomena such as atmospheric motion, instead suggesting the possibility of chemical reactions resulting from artificial influences, such as the release of CFCs into the atmosphere.[31] These observational data further supported Molina and Rowland's forecast in 1974. As such, although Farman's team had not heard of Chubachi's article, they effectively corroborated his data, which was supported by independent observation by *Nimbus 7*. This corroboration ultimately caused the global environmental problem to be recognized as a social problem.[32]

Feedback-for-learning channels inactivated

In contrast to these developments in Europe and the United States, there existed a curious situation in contemporary Japan with regard to the ozone layer and environmental protection. The Environment Agency (currently the Ministry of the Environment) added an item titled "CFC gas problem" to its *White Paper on the Environment* in 1981 and called for public attention to this problem every year through 1989. The item thus appeared for the first time in Japan three years before the 1984 application for patents using CFCs as a working fluid for OTEC, and five years before the publication of those patents. The agency stated the following about the ozone problem in their 1981 white paper:

1 CFC gases, such as CFCs 11 and 12, used in aerosol and coolant products, are chemically very stable. If the gases are released into the environment, they will reach the ozone layer without being decomposed and destroy the layer. As a result, the amount of ultraviolet rays reaching the earth's surface will increase, causing skin cancers and climate changes. If the ozone layer is depleted, serious problems on a global scale will occur. Early preventive measures are required to prevent these effects.
2 Outside Japan, the US and several other countries have legal restrictions on the release of CFC gases. The European Community decided to ban the release of CFCs into the atmosphere in March 1980.
3 This problem requires a full scientific analysis. In Japan, the Environment Agency and the Meteorological Agency have been conducting a continuous program of scientific research to investigate the problem and will encourage further research in cooperation with the ministries and agencies concerned.[33]

The white paper also references the forecast made by Molina and Rowland in its assertion about taking preventive action to avoid serious future problems. It also listed the positive actions taken by other countries and, in its conclusion, explained the necessity of taking action beyond the boundaries of individual ministries and agencies. Given the prior recognition of the problem and even recommendations of appropriate guidelines for addressing and reversing it, why then were the CFC-based patents approved and published? One possible explanation might be that the Sunshine project produced the patents under the support of MITI, whose programs were completely outside the authority of the Environment Agency.

However, the white paper stressed the "cooperation with the ministries and agencies concerned"; in fact, the CFCs Problem Liaison Council was organized in September 1980 as a joint undertaking of the Environment Agency, MITI, the Ministry of Foreign Affairs, the Ministry of Welfare, and the Meteorological Agency. Moreover, the Chief of the Chemical Products Division of the Basic Industries Bureau of MITI stated the following in 1988:

> In view of the importance of the CFC problem for ozone layer protection, MITI has been tackling the problem since it was first realized. By administrative guidance, the ministry has frozen the production of CFCs 11 and 12 since May 1980 and is attempting to reduce the use of CFCs 11 and 12 in aerosol products.
>
> (Komiya 1988)

Furthermore, in the Sunshine project, the new energy technology development policy of MITI was drafted in a way that was closely coupled with environmental protection policy. The *Official Gazette* stated as early as 1973 that "environmental protection is now a matter of top national priority. It must be a foremost principle that energy should be supplied and consumed within the bounds of environmental capacity."[34] Thus, despite relevant governmental authorities' realization of the possibility of stratospheric ozone depletion by CFCs, the CFC-based patents were approved and published in connection with a new energy technology development project that was aimed at seeking clean energy.

This suggests that, during the 1980s when this new energy technology development project started, patents using CFCs as a working fluid were applied for and published, and there were at least two possible channels in Japan through which feedback-for-learning might have occurred. First, the Environment Agency and MITI planned political guidelines and issued administrative instructions based on their realization that CFCs could be ozone-depleting; in tandem, Japan could have instituted a feedback-for-learning channel that would have reassessed the already initiated new energy technology development project in light of the information about CFCs, and would have amended the individual programs. Second, when Chubachi reported the ozone hole, CFCs could have come under increased suspicion and scrutiny as ozone-depleting substances, which would have enabled Japan to institute another feedback-for-learning channel to reassess the OTEC development project based on this observation and would have amended the individual programs.

In reality, however, neither channel was implemented at the time. Japan's administrative organizations of the governmental, industrial, and academic sectors did not include reflexive assessment and reassessment channels, and so they were not able to take appropriate action to pursue the development of new energy technologies while simultaneously seeking to relieve global environmental problems. This failure occurred despite the availability of information on the relationship between technological development and environmental policy since the very beginning of the Sunshine project. This strongly suggests that at least two elements of structural disaster have played a crucial role in perpetuating the given policy trajectory initiated by the significant initial investment from the special account of national revenue: first, that adherence to erroneous precedents causes problems to be carried over and reproduced, as manifested in the dismissal of the two feedback-for-learning channels; second, that quick fixes for current problems can lead to further such fixes for temporary countermeasures, as manifested in the selection of CFCs familiar to CFC manufacturers/users during the selection process for OTEC technology and through the fact that the fixture was not changed even after the discovery of an ozone hole.

Ironically, Hiroshi Kamogawa, the aforementioned Chairman of the Committee on OTEC in the Sunshine project, pointed out a possible relationship between OTEC and environmental change in the same article that urged immediate promotion of OTEC development as a way to solve resource issues. According to Kamogawa, there are two ways that OTEC could affect the environment: first, cold and warm wastewater from OTEC could affect marine ecological systems; second, the complex behavior of cold wastewater around the warmer surface seawater could alter evaporation velocity, which could lead to local changes in the ocean state around OTEC plants and changes in the troposphere's climate (Kamogawa 1978). As mentioned, these possibilities were not reflected in Japan's OTEC development policy at the time; furthermore, expanded global effects were not included in Kamogawa's consideration of ecological consequences, such as the possibility of ecological effects on large areas of the ocean and on the stratosphere.

What, then, enabled the project to run continuously while ignoring feedback-for-learning channels? This question leads to an important clue for clarifying the social context and implications of the Sunshine project from the perspective of structural disaster.

Reversible technological development and irreversible environmental change: decision-making process exhibiting structural disaster

To consider the social process that enabled the OTEC development project to run continuously without recourse for feedback-for-learning, there are two major social contexts associated with the time period in which the Sunshine project, and particularly OTEC development, took place. One is relevant to the overall process of OTEC development, from its inception in 1974 to its stagnation and fade-out in the early-1990s, and the other is relevant to the later revival of OTEC development, starting at around the time the Sunshine project ended in 1992.

From 1974 to the early-1990s, OTEC development was occurring at the same time as the Middle East War of October 1973, which triggered a global oil crisis. However, even though the Sunshine project was initiated in July 1974, the call for this new energy technology development in Japan was not in response to the oil crisis.

On May 18, 1973, a meeting among officials in charge of the future development plan for the AIT in MITI resulted in the creation of a new energy development section within the AIT (five months before the oil crisis). The newly established section became the headquarters of the Sunshine project when it started about five months later. In an independent development, on August 18, 1973, still about two months before the oil crisis, MITI submitted the following enquiry to the Special Commission on Industrial Technology:

> What kind of new industrial technology should be developed to enhance the well-being of the nation and to promote international collaboration in accordance with socio-economic needs, and how? In particular, how should the development of energy technologies be designed to avoid an energy crisis in the future and contribute to environmental protection?
> (Enquiry No. 1 from MITI to the Special Commission on Industrial Technology)

There appeared to be awareness in the contemporary industrial sector as well that the strongly oil-dependent energy policy had come to a turning point.[35] In fact, in January 1973, the Federation of Economic Organizations (Keidanren) made an official call to break away from an over-dependence on oil;[36] in other words, the policy measures taken for new energy technology development emerged from the endogenous initiatives of both the governmental and industrial sectors, rather than from external events such as the oil crisis.

The early creation of institutional settings in which such initiatives could be directed and materialized was another social context associated with the start-up of OTEC development. A fitting example of these initiatives was the drastic reorganization of the Electrical Testing Laboratory of the AIT – one of the oldest national research institutes in Japan, originating in the Telegraph Laboratory set up in 1873 – into the Electro-Technical Laboratory in 1970 to expand research activities beyond the practical business of testing and developing standards (activities in which the laboratory had long specialized).

The advent of attempts since the 1960s to produce electricity by various new technologies such as nuclear fission, magneto-hydro-dynamics (MHD), and thermoelectromotive force necessitated the laboratory's upgrade so that its research function could keep abreast of new technologies for the production of electricity. By 1970, the major practical tasks of testing and standards had been transferred to external organizations such as the Japan Electrical Appliances Testing Institute and the Japan Electrical Instruments Testing Institute. As part of the Electrical Testing Laboratory's reorganization in 1970, its Electricity Supply Division and Instruments Division were integrated into the Energy Section, where OTEC development was carried out after the start of the Sunshine project.[37]

Thus, independent of the oil crisis, the governmental and industrial sectors aimed to break away from long-standing oil-dependent energy policies (a "pull" factor) and to initiate a concomitant reorganization of research settings that created room for new energy development (a "push" factor). These were the social mechanisms at work in the process of starting up OTEC development in the Sunshine project.

Structural disaster in energy development 131

In the case of the CC type of OTEC that was developed in the Sunshine project, the key "high technology" was a system that enabled the generating system's efficiency to be enhanced, and the key technology for commercialization was a system that enabled large-scale and efficient transmission of electricity from the OTEC ocean plant to the mainland of Japan. R&D of the high technology element began in 1974, when the conceptual design of a 1.5-MW OTEC plant was drawn up in a feasibility study for the Sunshine project, and the R&D of the technology for commercialization began in 1977, when a conceptual design for a transmission system was created to estimate the cost of transmitting 80 MW over a distance of 20 km.[38] On the high technology side, the development of a new working fluid to enhance heat cycle efficiency and new chemicals to prevent biofouling of the condenser followed, and on the technology for commercialization side, the possibility of using microwave transmission and a new system to transform energy into chemicals such as H_2, NH_3, and CH_4 was investigated.

Despite these efforts, however, there was no breakthrough with either form of technology and the OTEC development unit was downsized after the Sunshine project came to an end in 1992. The Electro-Technical Laboratory, which provided the locus of OTEC development in the start-up stage of the project, announced its decision to withdraw from OTEC development in 1997 after the publication of a final, short report (Takazawa et al. 1997)[39] that stated its main reason for the decision was difficulty in finding sites where OTEC could achieve economy comparable to that of existing generating systems. The OTEC Research Association, one of the short-lived (1988–1994) research groups surrounding OTEC, described the situation as follows:

> Based on comprehensive R&D we have carried out up to now in relation to technologies for the generating system, cold water intake, multi-purpose utilization, and so on and a survey for site selection around the Southern Pacific, we find it difficult to implement a construction plan for OTEC plants that would enable sufficient economy.[40]
>
> (OTEC Research Association 1994: 26)

This reveals that OTEC development stagnated and faded out not because of the possibility that it could cause adverse effects globally or on large areas of the ocean or stratospheric ozone layer, but because it failed to achieve sufficient economy to recover the huge initial cost of construction. Notwithstanding the fact that the move toward new energy development in Japan originated from governmental and industrial sectors' initiatives, and that OTEC development once symbolized endogenous initiatives for such development, now there is no national OTEC development, as prescribed by the New Energy Promotion Law enacted in 1997. In fact, ocean energy development as a whole is absent from the target of Japan's new energy technology development strategy projected for 2030; rather, the target is focused on solar thermal power, wind turbines, biomass, heat pumps, natural gas co-generation, fuel cells, and electric vehicles. The new Sunshine

132 *Structural disaster in energy development*

project started in 1993 and aimed for the development of solar power, geothermal power, and wind power, with no OTEC or other ocean energy.[41]

OTEC, however, has not entirely disappeared; in fact, there was a noticeable resurgence of OTEC that began around the end of the initial Sunshine project in 1992. The most direct indicator of the trend is the 18 OTEC-related patents granted since 1990 (Table 5.4).

Table 5.4 OTEC-Related Patents Granted since 1990

1. "Condenser and the way of condensation for the OC type OTEC," applied for by the Director of the AIT of MITI on April 9, 1992, No. 4-116963
2. "OTEC appliances," applied for by the Toshiba Electrical Co. on June 8, 1992, No. 4-147063
3. "Thermoelectric appliances for the environmental protection," applied for by N. Sawada on November 7, 1992, No. 4-339422
4. "OTEC generators," applied for by S. Konno on December 24, 1992, No. 4-94440
5. "Thermoelectric appliances for the environmental protection," applied for by N. Sawada on February 17, 1993, No. 5-67293
6. "The utilization of deep subsurface water," applied for by the Mitsui Shipbuilding Co. on August 23, 1993, No. 5-207540
7. "OTEC apparatus," applied for by the Chancellor of Saga University on September 22, 1993, No. 5-236432
8. "The system for the purification of water," applied for by the Nakamura Electrical Co. on March 9, 1994, No. 6-66567
9. "A generating system," applied for by the Mitsubishi Heavy Industry Co. on April 11, 1994, No. 6-72043
10. "Heat transmission pipe," applied for by the Matsushita Reiki Co. on May 19, 1994, No. 6-105437
11. "The deep subsurface water intake," applied for by the Taiyo Plant Co. on June 21, 1994, No. 6-173075
12. "The energy conversion apparatus," applied for by the Chancellor of Saga University on September 20, 1994, No. 6-224918
13. "Fluid transfer device," applied for by the Hitachi Electrical Co. & the Chubu Electrical Co. on June 29, 1995, No. 7-163360
14. "OTEC system," applied for by the OTEC Development Co. on June 7, 1996, No. 9-501395
15. "The method of fresh water production by the OC type OTEC," applied for by the President of the AIT of MITI on November 27, 1996, No. 8-316533
16. "The best mix system of natural energy," applied for by the Nihon Steel Co. on September 18, 1997, No. 9-253438
17. "The intake pipe of deep subsurface water," applied for by K. Daifuku on February 25, 1998, No. 11-241788
18. "The pumping of deep subsurface water, etc.," applied for by the Trio Marine Tech Co. on November 13, 2000, No. 2000-345226

Source: Produced from the data-base provided by the Patent Office of MITI.

Two important points are seen from the above list of patents. First, various component technologies of the CC type developed during the Sunshine project serve a range of objectives in fields unrelated to the production of electricity, such as the purification and production of water, heat exchange, transportation of fluids, and the utilization of deep subsurface water. The other important point is the shift from the CC type to the OC type, as seen in patents 1 and 15 in the table. In contrast to the CC type of OTEC developed in the Sunshine project, which could potentially affect large areas of the ocean and stratosphere by a working fluid, OC circulates seawater alone so that the technology can avoid such potential damage. Achieving sufficient economy for the commercial production of electricity is a problem with both CC and OC, though OC has more severe technical obstacles, such as the need to create a vacuum of one-twentieth of atmospheric pressure and developing a large-scale and efficient turbine, among others.[42]

As far as the utilization of OTEC technology is concerned, these two points are positive aspects of the resurgence of OTEC development around 1993. What is noteworthy in both points, however, is the fact that there is a decisive transformation of the purpose that OTEC was designed to serve, as shown in the vast range of objectives of OTEC-related patents in Table 5.4, wherein none serve the originally conceived purpose of OTEC as a way to solve massive energy resource problems.

Individual aims of the two OC-related patents in Table 5.4 (Patents 1 and 15) demonstrate this point; for example, Patent 1 states the following:

> Medium-sized OC OTEC is feasible and still worthy of pursuing not only because of its medium scale production of electricity but also because of its valuable byproducts such as fresh water for drinking and industrial use. The practical use of OC is particularly promising as a means to the provision of electricity for remote islands and/or the provision of fresh water.[43]

Patent 15 likewise states that "the patent aims at the provision of a more efficient apparatus for and method of fresh water production by OC OTEC which has the advantageous capability of producing fresh water as well as electricity."[44]

In short, it is through the reversal of the means – end relationship in OTEC development that its resurgence during the 1990s becomes viable and promising. While in its original context OTEC was expected to be a means to a given end, in the later context, various elementary technologies and the switch to OC have created brighter prospects for OTEC by finding ends that are well-suited to the new means.

In general, it is possible to make an independent, large-scale, long-term technological development project of any kind into a success story by removing the originally conceived purpose and allowing space for a new one that the technology can serve, even at a later time. If such a development project is to be evaluated in terms other than global environmental assessment, careful evaluation based on whether the project can consistently achieve its original purpose is the first element to consider, unless a change in context removes the original purpose from long-term relevance. In the case of OTEC development there is nothing to suggest that a change in context after the mid-1970s removed the resource problems stemming from the geopolitical condition of Japan. Nevertheless, the later context surrounding new energy development in Japan tends to blur the originally conceived purpose. The all-party group draft plan of the Promotion Law for the Production of Electricity by Natural Energy in 2002 epitomizes the situation through its stated purpose:

> We need to build a society that contributes to a sustainable development enabled by economic growth with less environmental load. For that purpose it is necessary to stop global warming by controlling the emission of the gases contributing to the greenhouse effect and through the effective use of renewable energy resources. And measures taken for the promotion of electricity production making use of natural energy can meet both requirements simultaneously.[45]

While initiatives for pursuing new energy technology development were the focus of the Sunshine project, careful consideration of the global environment is now prominent in this new draft plan; for example, there is no description of technological development for the solution of resource problems, and the fact that the contribution of new energy to Japan's total primary energy supply is only slightly above one percent (as of 1998) should illustrate that the law is intended to reduce CO_2 emissions, not to replace oil as an energy resource (a resource that accounts for more than 50 percent of Japan's total primary energy supply).[46] A request on November 17, 2000, for the early passage of the Promotion Law for the Production of Electricity by Natural Energy clearly states that the intention of the law is "to fulfill the public pledge made in the Kyoto Protocol."[47] In fact, the share of renewable energy in both primary energy supply and R&D budget since the 1970s has surprisingly remained almost unchanged in Japan.[48]

This reveals that resource problems have not yet been solved in the way the Sunshine project originally intended, but a formal assessment of the success or failure of such projects has little meaning in sociological terms. In this particular case, OTEC development was able to continue after the initial project's conception, as the changing context surrounding energy development fueled and refueled its momentum despite its failure to appropriately solve resource problems. This process is epitomized by the transformation of the originally conceived purpose and the reversal of the means – end relationship when OTEC was revived in the 1990s. Technological development, in this case, adapted itself to changing circumstances, where such adaptation was a continuous process of legitimizing the development in relation to the circumstances, first with the image of the "guaranteed fix" for solving resource problems, and then later with the "clean" image of the technology in relation to global environmental problems. New energy technology, particularly renewable energy technology in Japan such as OTEC, has provided a symbol well-suited to such contexts of legitimization. Consequently, independent, large-scale, long-term technological development projects such as OTEC tend to run continuously, once started, as if through their own momentum.

As mentioned, the potential aggravation of stratospheric ozone depletion by OTEC was due to two elements of structural disaster within the process of its development in the 1980s: adherence to erroneous precedents that causes problems to be carried over and reproduce, as manifested in the dismissal of the two feedback-for-learning channels; and quick fixes for current problems that lead to further such fixes for temporary countermeasures, as manifested in the selection of CFCs familiar to CFC manufacturers/users during the selection process for OTEC technology. Apart from these elements of structural disaster, the self-guided momentum of independent, large-scale, long-term technological development projects such as OTEC development suggests the dynamic mechanism of structural disaster that corresponds to path-dependency generated by belief effect that can enable a continuous legitimization of the pre-given project, via the images of "sure fix" or "clean" solution to global environmental problems.

Structural disaster, the precautionary principle, and "mild freezing"

Insights obtained from examining the intricate relationship between OTEC development in the Sunshine project as one of the most promised renewable energy technology developments in the 1970s and stratospheric ozone depletion can be summarized in four points from the viewpoint of structural disaster:

1 The Sunshine project, which was set up to solve resource problems through environmentally friendly initiatives, produced, and published patents for OTEC using CFCs as the working fluid, even after the discovery of an ozone hole and their relationship with stratospheric ozone depletion.
2 This outcome cannot simply be considered a failure of policy, since the relevant ministries and agencies had duly issued a preventive guideline to deal with such depletion.
3 This case strongly suggests a hidden link between the development of new technologies and global environmental problems due to incomplete information at the time of assessment and/or decision-making. The development of a new energy technology intended to solve resource problems resulted in damage to the stratospheric ozone, an unforeseen effect by the decision-makers at the time of inception, yet was ignored when it became evident. Herein lies structural disaster in the sense that adherence to erroneous precedents causes problems to be carried over and reproduced. In addition, OTEC-related patents continued to be granted and made public even after OTEC's failure in solving resource problems, which was the originally conceived purpose of the technology.

4   In this situation, a built-in mechanism is needed to evaluate large-scale, independent, long-term technological development projects through reflexive feedback-for-learning channels. This mechanism should be free from the network of agents' interests who originally shaped the project because the function of the mechanism would be to prevent the fueling and re-fueling of the projects' momentum, made possible by transforming its originally conceived purpose in accordance with changing circumstances. If the fueling and re-fueling of the projects' momentum is materialized by transforming the original purpose and eventually canceling it, structural disaster would occur in a path-dependent manner in terms of enacting quick fixes for current problems that lead to further such fixes for temporary counter-measures.

These conclusions are based on an in-depth analysis of only one case and therefore do not exhaust the sociological implications obtainable from structural disaster in the area of renewable energy technology as a whole. The conclusions derived from the analysis of this single case do, however, contain implications worthy of discussion regarding the dynamics of the science-technology-society interface.

What is particularly important is the tangible need for an appropriate social framework within which a feedback-for-learning channel for early detection of the interconnection of completely different problems, rather than employing "easy" but unsatisfactory fixes. To design such a social framework, it is necessary to determine how to allocate social responsibility for unanticipated consequences arising from large-scale, long-term, and financially independent technological development projects such as OTEC in the Sunshine project.

The sociology of science and technology has worked to uncover the complexity of the science-technology-society interface that accompanies uncertainty, including both type-one and type-two underdetermination. The precautionary principle (or taking preventive measures before scientific evidence of actual harm is available) is one candidate for dealing with such uncertainty, as exemplified by the Vienna Agreement in 1985 and the Montreal Protocol in 1987, which both implemented this principle in an effort to take preventive measures against stratospheric ozone depletion.[49] However, preventive measures taken in connection with the Sunshine project in Japan reveal a reverse sequence of events.

Several proposals were actually made for preventive policy implementation and related legislation was passed; for example, in a move toward legal restriction of CFC production by the government, the Central Council for Environmental Pollution Control within the Environment Agency submitted a report titled "Basic System for Ozone Layer Protection." At the same time, the Ozone Layer Protection Section of the Chemical Product Council in MITI also submitted a report titled "Legal Restrictions on Chemical Production and Notes on Their Application in Japan." Based on these reports, the Japanese Diet passed into law the Specific Substances Restriction Law for Ozone Layer Protection in order to restrict the manufacture of designated CFCs and other related substances. The reports were made public in February 1988, the law passed in May of the same year, and restrictions took effect in July 1989. All of this, however, occurred after patents using CFCs as the working fluid for OTEC had been granted and published, and so at least until that time, the problem had been unnoticed or ignored.[50] If unnoticed, this sequence of events suggests the existence of structural disaster in that the complexity of a system and the interdependence of its units aggravate problems; if ignored, the sequence suggests the existence of structural disaster in that secrecy developed across different sectors and blurred the locus of agents responsible and/or in that adherence to erroneous precedents causes problems to be carried over and reproduced.

In addition, after the end of the Sunshine project in 1992, patents resulting from OTEC development continued to be granted and published but were given an environmentally friendly look by changing the proposed type of OTEC from CC to OC, and reversing the means–ends relationship in OTEC development. This *ad hoc* transformation of the means–ends relationship could have a belief effect in the path-dependent process leading to structural disaster in renewable energy technology, as such transformation and "rebranding" invites belief in environmental consideration while distracting from the complex relation of the global environmental problems to the resource problems that OTEC originally intended to solve. Global warming, another global environmental problem, necessitates constraints on the use of fossil fuels, which in turn should deepen the past and current resource problems. Due to this intricate interrelation, if the belief effect arises that makes it difficult to have a straightforward awareness of the complex relationship between global environmental problems and resource problems, both would be aggravated by the complexity of a system and the interdependence of its units. This is what an element of structural disaster implies: when belief effect works in this manner within the complex science-technology-society interface, it is difficult to problematize the potential vulnerability of renewable energy regime to structural disaster. This idea will be detailed further in the next chapter.

When the entire structure of problems is not available – or when it is available but ignored, or is extremely difficult to see clearly due to the complex process embodying structural disaster in the science-technology-society interface – the precautionary principle does not work; in addition, the allocation of responsibility for events arising in a situation of strong uncertainty, including type-one and type-two underdetermination, remains unresolved. In such a situation, it is better to follow the principle of "mild freezing" (or low or zero growth rate) in the development of a new technology. According to this principle, the budget for investment in the technology's development should sustain a low or zero growth rate while an investigation is made and parties concerned determine the necessary degree of caution based on this investigation. In other words, mild freezing enables the parties concerned to change a particular path-dependent technological trajectory to another one when necessary, to make up for the precautionary principle.[51] Under mild freezing, the allocation of responsibility is made by examining whether undesirable problems resulted from a particular technological trajectory, working from within the sphere of technology development. This is in contrast to the precautionary principle, which works from the outside through regulation. In cases where the use of technology is strongly contingent on a complex science-technology-society interface – so that initial decisions made in good faith are likely to generate irreversible environmental change in a path-dependent manner in conjunction with structural disaster – such a combination of mild freezing from within and regulations based on the precautionary principle from without will be crucial for the common good in the science-technology-society interface.

6 Structural disaster and the wind power regime
Myth creation, myth destruction, and relevant outsiders

This chapter uses wind power technology – another example of renewable energy technologies (which are categorically assumed to be the opposite of nuclear power technologies) – to illustrate the generating mechanism of structural disaster and suggests ways to break from a path-dependent track of structural disaster. The chapter examines the disorganized process of the initial development and diffusion of wind turbines in Japan, which began in the 1970s, to illustrate the path-dependent trajectory of renewable energy technologies and extends the sociological implications of structural disaster. Particular attention is paid to the social process of the technology, in which an early move toward domestic development and diffusion was eventually changed to an alternative trajectory that promoted wind turbine diffusion by a technology import, and the trajectory was "locked-in." The sociologically reformulated path-dependent mechanism of structural disaster given in Chapter 2 is applied to this social process, revealing that there is no difference between the nuclear power regime and the wind power regime in Japan in terms of the sociological path-dependent mechanism inherent in their social processes.

In addition, this chapter explores ways in which to break such a path-dependent social process; in particular, it uses significant borderline cases involving heterogeneous agents to investigate the unique roles played by relevant outsiders who were excluded from the closed inner circle of governmental, industrial, and academic sectors in wind power development and distribution. Against the background of this sociological, path-dependent mechanism, the chapter analyzes the behavior patterns of these outsiders, as they played an important role in breaking the path-dependent trajectory of technology development and diffusion. While these outsiders were marginal in terms of access to the expertise and social decision-making processes privy to the closed inner circle of governmental, industrial, and academic sectors in the process of wind turbine development and diffusion, it is this characteristic that enabled them to be immune to various myths shared by the closed inner circle and virtually counteracting them. Accordingly, relevant outsiders could also be instrumental in neutralizing various myths that have settled in both the nuclear and wind power regimes from the perspective of structural disaster; for example, the myth of nuclear power as a harbinger of sustainability linked to the myth of its being high-tech and safe that had long emboldened national pride (Hecht 1998), as well as the myth of the infeasibility of wind turbines in Japan.

If the generating mechanism of structural disaster, using the general logic of sociologically reformulated path-dependency regarding wind turbine development and diffusion, can be specified, then the occurrence of structural disaster is independent of whether nuclear power or wind power technology is selected. If this mechanism works within the social process of wind turbine development and diffusion as well as in that of nuclear power, then an independent and firm basis can be obtained to assert that structural disaster can emerge regardless of whether the involved technology is nuclear power reactors or renewable energy technologies such as wind turbines.

As was clarified in Chapter 2, the application of sociologically reformulated path-dependency means that even if certain agents are attuned to maximizing benefits at a given time and are rational in that particular sense, non-rational "lock-in" could occur due to past path selection within this type of technology. This path selection is, theoretically, affected by factors such as the network effect, belief effect, and the initial divergence of technology. What, then, are the empirical details of the network effect, belief effect, and initial divergence of technology? In addition, in what sense can a process leading to lock-in be interpreted as a generating mechanism of structural disaster with reference to Japan's wind power regime?[1] And in what sense can a role played by a relevant outsider be interpreted as contributing to the break from structural disaster? The answers to these questions will be given in this chapter.

The connection between structural disaster and path-dependency: select perspectives from important cases

The framework of path-dependency has provided a conceptual tool for clarifying the fixed trajectory of technological development in nuclear power technology, such as light water reactors (LWR) (Cowan 1990; Arthur 2009).[2] More generally, prior works have shown problems inherent in the pre-existing dominant energy technologies such as nuclear or fossil fuels (Vergragt 2012) or a centralized electricity-supplying system (Vleuten and Raven 2006) by appealing to the concept of lock-in and by also showing a way out of it by referencing emerging energy technologies such as renewables.[3] Few attempts have been made, however, to specify the structural similarities between seemingly opposite technologies such as nuclear and renewable energy technologies. Nuclear technology is not the only energy technology to which the concept of lock-in can be used in clarifying the fixed trajectory of technology development. The fixed trajectory here means that: (1) the development trajectory of technologies is locked-in without any rational consideration of other alternatives, thereby virtually precluding any chance of their introduction later; (2) the social decision-making process involved is closed to outsiders.

This chapter investigates the ways in which novel development paths that were different from the pre-existing track were created, as well as the ways in which the path-dependent track of wind turbine technology development and diffusion was formed in Japan, focusing on the relationship between the above-mentioned two aspects involved in the fixed trajectory of technological development. Based on these investigations, the chapter argues that the path-dependent social process leading to lock-in can be regarded as a generating mechanism of structural disaster, and suggests a possible divergent path.

Tracing back to two original versions of path-dependency (David 1985; Arthur 1989), a common theme running through both is that an outcome in favor of a single dominant technology does not necessarily guarantee optimum technology selection. Some "chance elements" (David 1985) or "random events" (Arthur 1989) in the technology selection process can give rise to a single dominant technology regardless of its performance. This highlights the pitfalls of the so-called "Whig interpretation of history" – wherein the world always progresses, and this progress is inevitable – in describing, analyzing, and speculating on technological development (nuclear or renewable) with hindsight.

To substantiate such theoretical insights in individual cases, however, it is critical to examine the basic assumptions of the theory of path-dependency as clarified in Chapter 2. To reconfirm the assumptions, both versions of path-dependency equally assume that agents adopt technologies based on expected returns, as determined by current market forces represented by the accumulation of prior adoption and preference. If preference-laid agents are sensitive to technologies' returns at a given time, then path-dependency could be derived from chance events under certain conditions. Since this is the basic structure of inference within the theoretical framework of path-dependency, there are two ways to substantiate the theoretical framework in individual cases: (1) the presence of agents who are sensitive to technologies' returns in the market during the process of technological adoption, then path-dependency can be tested by *ex post* assessment of whether or not the technology adopted is the "wrong system" (David 1985) or "inferior" (Arthur 1989) in terms of performance; (2) if such rational agents are not present, then path-dependency should be reformulated based on a new model of social action. In the latter case, the interaction between agents and surrounding situations will lead toward understanding the sociological implications of path-dependency, as mentioned in Chapter 2. Which way to follow depends upon what kind of agents are present.

From such a sociological perspective, the social process of introducing wind turbines in Japan cuts across the sphere applying to rational agents and the sphere that does not apply in that the behavior of agents in the introduction of wind turbines is based upon the agents' sensitivity to technologies' returns in the market and their responsiveness to various sociological factors coming from outside the market as well. These sociological factors will be specified in the following sections. Another factor that makes it difficult to understand the development trajectory of technologies solely in terms of rational agents who are sensitive to technologies' returns in the market pertains to the nature of technologies that produce different degrees of accessibility to the social decision-making process regarding the technologies. For example, when Arthur (1989) introduced the term "increasing returns" in his effort to formulate path-dependency, the technologies he focused on were science-based technologies, such as nuclear reactors, which were only made possible by advances in nuclear physics and nuclear chemistry in the twentieth century. In contrast, David (1985) introduced the term "economies of scale" with reference to nineteenth-century technologies such as the mechanical typewriter, the existence of which was not dependent on advanced sciences. As organized research and development (R&D) became more institutionalized within industrial society (Hughes 1983; Smith and Wise 1989), science-based technologies gradually began to replace those developed on less systematic bases, so that technological development started to become increasingly autonomous.

As a result, access to the social decision-making process involved in the introduction of science-based technologies by non-expert outsiders became much more difficult than for previous "common sense" technologies. Wind turbines, which first appeared for use in agriculture in Denmark in the late nineteenth century and were improved through the process of trial and error with the aid of aerodynamics, can be considered "in-between" the two contrastive types of technology mentioned above.[4] In addition, the social decision-making processes regarding wind turbine siting straddles both centralized and decentralized methods: it is centralized because it relates to national policies for the promotion of renewable energy technologies that are strategically oriented to objectives such as self-sustained energy supply, low-carbon society, and others; but it is decentralized because of its heavy reliance on local demand, management, maintenance, repair, and ownership.[5]

Thus, based on sociologically reformulated path-dependency, the case of wind power generation carries new sociological implications for understanding the generating mechanism of structural disaster as a path-dependent process. First, it crosscuts the two contrastive types of agents, rational, and non-rational, and since a particular accumulation of choice by rational agents leads to non-rational outcomes in the path-dependent process, the case is suitable for scrutinizing the nature of the process. Second, it can aid in detecting the interaction between agents and surrounding social decision-making within the process. Third, it is considered a borderline case because it falls between science-based technologies and less systematic ones, each corresponding to a contrastive degree of accessibility to the social decision-making process to the non-expert outsider, as well as to centralized and decentralized ways of decision-making. A close examination of important cases taking place during the initial phase of wind turbine introduction in Japan will provide fresh sociological insights into a fixed trajectory generating structural disaster, as well as a new path that diverges from it.[6]

Sociological path-dependency and the other side of the wind power regime: resolutions discordant with the realization of public interest

The success or failure of wind turbines is often equated with whether numerical targets for the adoption of wind power generation are achieved within a given time period. The viewpoint of sociological path-dependency, however, expands this scope in such a way that enables the identification of the mechanism by which a structural disaster could arise; in the case of wind turbines, from the interactions between agents and surrounding situations in the science-technology-society interface. Based on this framework, the analysis of wind turbines' initial development and diffusion in Japan will disclose a unique mechanism in which the resolution of the problem does not lead to the realization of public interest. By exploring the reasons for and the sociological implication of this state, structural disaster will be shown to be a type of lock-in state.

Discrepancies hiding in the development trajectory of wind turbines

The development of wind turbines in Japan dates back to the Sunshine project (see Chapter 5), which was launched in 1974. The project was Japan's first large-scale, long-term project aimed at developing renewable energy technology to solve resource problems. According to the accelerated promotion plan for the Sunshine project prepared by the AIT, a 100-kW pilot plant of wind turbines was to be constructed between 1981 and 1982 and then scaled up to a 1,000-kW pilot plant between 1984 and 1985, followed by the construction of a 10,000-kW demonstration plant between 1987 and 1989, and finally a 100,000-kW commercial plant between 1992 and 1993 (AIT 1980: 6).

In this way, the governmental sector had drafted the blueprint for an uninterrupted, long-term plan leading to commercialization over a period of 10 years; however, none of the Sunshine project's attempts to develop a domestic wind turbine have yet been commercialized. What underpins Japan's wind power generation today is instead heavily reliant on European wind turbines. For example, having established market dominance in the 1990s through a technology development method that emphasized small-scale trial and error – quite different from the model of focused breakthrough development driven by large-scale R&D used in the United States – Denmark currently occupies a leading position in the global wind turbine market.[7] In other words, there is a profound discrepancy between the Sunshine project's attempt to launch wind power generation via domestic development of Japan's own wind turbines and the current attempt to spread wind power generation by importing turbines from abroad.

Wind power generation in Japan exhibits a discrepancy between the initial path aimed at independent development of a self-reliant technology through a government-led project (the Sunshine project) and a post-Sunshine path aimed at bringing an imported technology into the market. The answer to the question of why there is such a discrepancy will illustrate why structural disaster could be a type of lock-in state, and why a resolution to the problem does not necessarily lead to public interest.

Table 6.1 reveals that Japan lags behind other countries in terms of wind power generation capacity, despite the early initiative of the Sunshine project.

Table 6.1 Wind Power Generation Capacity in Select Countries (2016)

Ranking	Country	Cumulative capacity (MW)
1	China	168,690
2	USA	82,184
3	Germany	50,018
4	India	28,700
5	Spain	23,074
6	UK	14,543
7	France	12,066
8	Canada	11,900
9	Brazil	10,740
10	Italy	9,257
11	Sweden	6,520
12	Turkey	6,081
13	Poland	5,782
14	Portugal	5,316
15	Denmark	5,228
16	Netherlands	4,328
17	Australia	4,327
18	Mexico	3,527
19	Japan	3,234

Source: Produced from Global Wind Energy Council (2017).

According to the New Energy and Industrial Technology Development Organization (NEDO) (2008) and Agency for Natural Resources and Energy (2016), the percentage of gross primary energy supply generated from renewable energy technologies (including wind power generation) in Japan has hovered between 1 percent and 4 percent since the early 1970s (when the Sunshine project began). For example, the actual level in 2014 was 4.4 percent and in 1971, 1.1 percent).

The overall results from the wind turbine development initiative launched through the Sunshine project by the Ministry of International Trade and Industry (MITI, the current Ministry of Economy, Trade and Industry, METI), in 1974 remain unreleased in the public sphere and, therefore, are unclear to this date. On account of such ambiguity of the outcomes of the first large-scale national project for the development of wind turbines, Japan is currently attempting to expand wind power generation while having a relatively poor accumulation of proprietary wind turbine-related technologies. Considering this in regard to the sociological path-dependency theory reformulated in Chapter 2, the current agents concerned are susceptible to both network and belief effects when selecting a technology. Conversely, when there is accumulation of relevant technological knowledge prior to selecting types of a technology, it is possible to compare technological performance of the different types via independent criteria; however, when the accumulated base of technological knowledge is poor, it is difficult to evaluate the relative performance of different types of technology because independent criteria are absent. Under such circumstances, it is possible that a technology with relatively inferior technological performance will be chosen within the local context of users due to the interaction between the agents concerned and the contingent situations surrounding the interaction, which is epitomized by positive feedback as envisaged by the sociological path-dependent theory. If so, the lock-in, in which the market-dominant technology is not necessarily optimal within the social context of users, could occur through the effects of network and belief; namely, undermining public interest. This is all theoretical, so what was the state of affairs in reality?

How the myth of infeasible wind power generation began

Around the time of an early wind resources survey conducted under the aegis of the Sunshine project, a myth began that deemed wind power generation to be difficult to implement due to Japan's unique wind conditions. This myth, despite having little evidence, led major manufacturers involved in early wind turbine development in Japan to withdrawal from self-reliant technology development, which contributed to the stagnation of wind power generation in subsequent stages. Here, the myth refers to a belief – albeit without clear evidence – that continuously affected the decision-making and behavior of various agents involved in wind power generation, such as MITI, electric power companies, and wind turbine manufacturers.

In 1974, the Sunshine project commissioned TEPCO and Ishikawajima-Harima Heavy Industries (IHI) to develop wind power generation capabilities. In response, a wind conditions survey was initiated by TEPCO in 1979 on Miyakejima Island, which is about 175 km away from Tokyo. In 1983, TEPCO began onsite testing of IHI's 100-kW wind turbine, which was 28 meters tall and had a blade length of 12.5 meters. Judging from the official report, released with results from a test run using this pilot unit, the company determined that there was merit in using this empirical data to continue improving the technology. In other words, there was nothing to suggest that they were withdrawing from wind turbine development.[8] TEPCO continued its test trial operations from 1985 to 1986 by importing a wind turbine manufactured by HMZ in Belgium that was 22.6 meters in height with a maximum output of 150 kW. This imported wind turbine, however, would frequently stop as the rotation speed increased, and this generated a perception that the suitability of imported wind turbines to local wind conditions specific to Japan was debatable. In 1989, this wind turbine was removed from use following damage by a typhoon.[9]

Another origin of the myth was a study conducted by the Science and Technology Agency (STA, the current Ministry of Education, Culture, Sports, Science and Technology) between 1984 and 1986 (STA 1987), which covered Tachikawa-machi (currently Shonai-machi), a small town in the Tohoku region. Strong winds that caused large fires and cold weather had afflicted the town for many years, and the study aimed to investigate the potential for small-scale wind power generation by making use of this particular local weather condition.

The test wind turbines were 15 meters in height with an output of 5 kW and would often stop rotating. The Empirical Study Report on the System for Integrated Use of Regional Energy prepared by the STA Resources Survey Institute (1987) stated that "during the entire operation period between fiscal years 1983 and 1985, the total energy generated was 18,907 kW. During the period of 811 days in total, the number of days the wind power generation system was operated normally was 549 (68 percent) for Unit 1 and 380 (47 percent) for Unit 2." As a result, the test wind turbine gave the town residents the impression that wind power generation had failed because wind conditions were poor. It also supported previous literature that discussed the difficulty of identifying a suitable location for wind power generation in Japan. For example, *Futopia Keikaku* (Windtopia Project) was another STA attempt in Kanazawa City of Ishikawa Prefecture, Annaka City of Gunma Prefecture, and the Chita district of Aichi Prefecture geared toward "using small wind turbines with high potential for commercialization at present and conducting an empirical study over the period 1978 to 1980 on technologies that can effectively utilize wind energy" (STA 1980: 1). The project report stated that "there are factors, such as wind conditions, that are not necessarily deemed optimal for the installation site this time" (STA 1980: 134, et passim).

As such, the situation was overly generalized, resulting in the myth that wind power generation would be infeasible in Japan because wind conditions are poor. According to one of the entrepreneurs of wind power generation in Tachikawa-machi: "Wind blows but the wind turbine stops. Such a situation was often seen and there arose a voice 'What is going on here.' After this, town officials tended to think that the failure of wind power generation is something ordinary."[10] In fact, in 1997, the Mayor of Tachikawa-machi stated the following: "Starting around this time [the time of project implementation by STA], the view that there are various uniqueness with wind conditions in Japan, such as not blowing all the time, the wind fluctuating and changing direction incessantly and unsuitable for wind power generation, became established as something shared" (Tatebayashi 1997).[11]

While it is true that the wind turbines in Tachikawa-machi often failed to run, the causes for failure were mechanical in nature within the wind turbines themselves, rather than the external wind conditions (see Table 6.2). There has been no empirical evidence directly indicating that the wind conditions were the cause of the failure.

Thus, neither TEPCO nor STA had any evidence to show that the introduction of the wind turbine and capture of its generated power were difficult due to wind conditions; on the contrary, at the time, the Special Committee for Energy Measures of the National Diet presented such an estimate that wind power generation "could possibly generate around 10 percent of the total energy used in our country" and indicated that the wind turbines required to do so "could be developed if we have funds, location, and opportunity" (according to the 94th National Diet Energy Measure Special Committee Meeting, minute item 4).

In addition, according to Dr. Yukimaru Shimizu, one of the pioneers of wind turbine development, the winds noted on the national wind condition map

Table 6.2 List of Wind Turbine Failures by Cause

Date	Situation	Cause
January 1983	Began test run	
April 1984	Abnormal noise generated during low rotation of Units 1 and 2	Failed hub bearing
June 1984	Pitch control failure of Unit 2	Leaked control oil
July 1984	Insufficient increase in rotation for Unit 1	Deteriorated gear for the control oil pump
October 1984	Interrupted rotation of Unit 2	Deteriorated gear for the control oil pump
	Blade broken by crosswind during a repair of Unit 2	Broken body due to material fatigue
November 1984	Repaired Units 1 and 2 by bringing them into a factory	Damaged blades, etc.
January 1985	Pitch control failure of Unit 2	Leaked control oil
April 1985	Unable to generate power despite normal rotation speed of Unit 1	Disconnected excitation circuit
October 1985	Pitch control failure of Unit 2	Damaged gear for control oil pump
January 1986	Unable to generate power despite normal rotation speed of Unit 1	Burned-out exciter coil

Source: STA Resources Survey Institute (1987: 85).

prepared at the time were underestimated against wind turbine potential capacity, in terms of parameters such as average wind speed in the inland area.[12] Surprisingly, even estimates for wind power generation potential calculated based on this understated wind condition map were not reflected in the national renewable energy policy. This is because the national target for wind power generation was set much lower than these estimates; for example, when the first target for wind power generation was approved at a cabinet meeting in 1994, the minimum level of potential generation capacity estimated by NEDO and based on the results of the Sunshine project was 1,400,000 kW (NEDO 1994), while the 2010 target stated by the General Outline for Introducing New Energy was a mere 150,000 kW (Cabinet Meeting for the Promotion of the Integrated Energy Policies 1994).

This negative outlook on the potential for wind power generation was perpetuated by subsequent policies. According to the supply target for oil-alternative energy sources, the target for wind power generation capacity in 2010 was doubled in 1998, from its 150,000 kW in 1994 to 300,000 kW (Cabinet Meeting for the Goal of Oil-substitute Energy Supply 1998); however, it remained at a level much lower than NEDO's estimated potentiality of wind power generation. In the same year, a mid-term report by the Supply and Demand Subcommittee of the Advisory Committee for Natural Resources and Energy stated that "it is difficult to expect a large amount of energy supply due to limited areas for siting wind turbines" (Agency for Natural Resources and Energy 1998: 142).

A similar tendency can be observed in the process of goal setting; for example, policymakers were forced to take the 1998 doubled target for additional energy generation and revise it again in 2001, at the New Energy Subcommittee of the Advisory Committee for Natural Resources and Energy, increasing the 2010 target for additional energy generation to 3,000,000 kW. During this process, opinions were submitted arguing that Japan ought to significantly increase the potential amount of additional generation on the grounds of increasing wind turbine size and the possibility of offshore wind power generation. As evidenced from materials ranging from the first meeting minutes (dated January 31), the fifth meeting minutes (dated May 11), and handouts for the Advisory Committee for National Resources and Energy New Energy Subcommittee meeting (held in 2001), to the report by the Advisory Committee for Natural Resources and Energy (2002), however, the majority held cautious attitudes toward increasing the target amount – though they did not show any clear basis on which to refute the above-mentioned opinions submitted. Such understated policy targets, cautious decision-making, and modest promotion strategies are converse to the process of introducing nuclear power, where it has been traditional to set bold goals and strive earnestly toward their realization.[13]

The above facts strongly suggest that the Sunshine project – the first official endeavor to promote wind power generation in Japan – attempted to develop wind turbines in tandem with a myth that wind power generation would be difficult in Japan due to its unique local wind conditions. This reveals that the belief effect, acting on this myth and coupled with network effects, led to stagnation in the early stages of wind turbine development by domestic makers. Extending this possibility to the extreme, structural disaster can be seen as a kind of lock-in state where almost all domestic makers withdrew from the development of their own wind turbines, thereby making it extremely difficult for any remaining domestic makers to enter or compete in the domestic market. In such an extreme, the solution to achieving widespread introduction of wind turbines in the domestic market did not lead to the accumulation of a technological base on which the development of self-reliant wind turbines could be improved to suit local wind conditions. If the widespread introduction of wind turbines in the domestic market, then, does not improve the suitability of the wind turbines to the local wind conditions, the state is far from securing a continuous, stable, and well-balanced energy mix in the public interest. The key to understanding this extreme in a sociological sense is the fact that there was only one wind turbine manufacturer that had nothing to do with perpetuating the wind conditions myth.

One manufacturer indifferent to and immune from the infeasibility myth

Ever since constructing a 40-kW pilot wind turbine in 1980 (Sugano and Tsushima 1983), Mitsubishi Heavy Industries (MHI) had been making efforts to consistently develop wind turbines amid the stagnation in the early development phase of wind power generation in Japan. To use the term defined in Chapter 2, there was an initial divergence in the early stage that was created through domestic technology development by MHI in addition to imported wind turbines, a divergence that continued in the 1990s and beyond. It was a daring, economically risky behavior to continue to develop wind turbines domestically amid the initial stagnation of wind power generation when there remained almost no market.

From the viewpoint of MHI, it was because the company had calculated that the potential for wind power generation would increase once it matured as a commercialized technology through continuous development;[14] in fact, after delivering a 300-kW commercial wind turbine for the Kyushu Electric Power Company in 1982, a year before the TEPCO-IHI test trial was launched under the aegis of the Sunshine project, MHI continued to develop new commercial wind turbines to suit the wind conditions specific to Japan. According to *Mitsubishi Heavy Industries Technical Review*, they were "designing a wind turbine that is highly reliable even under the locally unique Japanese wind conditions with severe wind speed fluctuation" (Takatsuka et al. 2000). In reality, however, although they had the domestic market in mind and focused on the development of commercial wind turbines to suit Japan's wind conditions, such as incessant wind speed change as represented by the development of gearless automatic transmission wind turbines (Osada et al. 2001), most orders came from overseas. As a result, after starting to export in the late 1980s, in 2004 MHI was among the top 10 companies in terms of sales in the global market (see Table 6.3).

This is not a success story of a manufacturer whose exceptional efforts paid off, enabling it to introduce and spread wind turbines suited to Japan's local wind conditions; on the contrary, MHI found it extremely difficult to enter

Table 6.3 Sales of Major Wind Turbine Manufacturers Worldwide (2004)

Manufacturer	Country of origin	Sales amount (MW)	Sales share (%)
VESTAS	Denmark	2,781	34.1
GAMESA	Spain	1,476	18.1
ENERCON	Germany	1,288	15.8
GE WIND	America	921	11.3
SIEMENS	Denmark	506	6.2
SUZLON	India	318	3.9
REPOWER	Germany	277	3.4
ECOTECNIA	Spain	212	2.6
MHI	Japan	212	2.6
NORDEX	Germany	188	2.3
Others		334	4.1

Source: BTM Consult ApS, "International Wind Energy Development," March 2005 (Copyright: NEDO).

the domestic market after imported turbines gained dominance. Its sales in the domestic market were quite unsuccessful compared with those in the global market; for example, the company's actual domestic deliveries between 2009 and 2010 (323 MW) remained at a level less than one-tenth of its international deliveries (3,484 MW). Similarly, MHI's website indicates that overseas sales accounted for 88.9 percent of total sales (MHI 2008). This is all the more telling when we look at the fact that MHI was the only domestic manufacturer that had independently accumulated experience in developing and manufacturing wind turbines to meet Japan's local wind conditions.[15]

Looking at national level statistical data, the domestic wind turbine market has been dominated mostly by imported wind turbines even after 1997, when the Act on Special Measures for the Promotion of New Energy Use was enacted, and 1998, when the "wind power rush" is said to have begun following the announcement of a buy-back price for wind power (see Table 6.4).

These facts indicate that domestically developed self-reliant technologies were neither effectively introduced nor distributed, even when an industrial sector manufacturer that was unaffected by the myth of wind conditions was able to demonstrate exceptional performance on the global market and was also able to bring its domestically developed technology to its home market. This also suggests that there was accompanying, intervening network effect, wherein once a trend toward imported technology emerged in the domestic market against the background of the myth of infeasibility of wind power generation due to local wind conditions, that trend was reinforced by domestic manufacturers that almost wholly withdrew from technology development, making it virtually impossible for domestically developed technology to enter the home market later. What is most noteworthy is not the absence of domestic technology development but its very presence along with imported ones, where the network effect seems to have worked thoroughly and blocked the entrance of newcomers with technological capability into the domestic market.

Structural disaster as a result of lock-in: following a precedent leading to non-rationality

The above reveals that there were at least three different kinds of factors – the belief effect, network effect, and initial divergence – that led to a lock-in state during the initial stage of wind power generation in Japan. According to the sociologically reformulated path-dependency theory presented in Chapter 2, in the lock-in state, it is possible that a technology that is not the most suitable can dominate the market, preventing more suitable technologies from entering. Such a state seems to have been realized in this current case: imported wind turbines virtually dominated the domestic market, overwhelming domestic wind turbines developed to adapt to Japan's local wind conditions. Such a situation can be regarded as close to a lock-in state because the three conditions causing the state have been met. The belief effect in this case reveals itself in the fact that the circumstances of the Sunshine project – promoted wind power generation attempts

Table 6.4 Number of Wind Turbines Introduced by Imported versus Domestic Units (cumulative)

	1998	1999	2000	2001	2002	2003	2004	2005	2006	2007	2008	2009	2010	2011	2012	2013	2014	2015	2016
Imported units	70	134	194	370	501	639	748	792	989	1,082	1,179	1,259	1,348	1,351	1,371	1,375	1,409	1,466	1,502
Domestic units	48	56	57	57	69	97	167	261	318	319	343	409	461	496	519	540	607	632	701
% of Domestic units	41	30	23	13	12	13	18	25	24	23	23	25	26	27	28	28	30	30	32

Source: www.nedo.go.jp/library/fuuryoku/pdf/06_kaigai_kokusan_kisuu_suii.pdf (ascertained on August 17, 2017, in Japanese).

Note: The percentage of domestic units is the rounded off ratio of the number of domestic units to the sum of domestic and imported units.

created a myth that wind power generation was infeasible due to Japan's unique wind conditions, a myth that became a leading cause of the country's wind power generation stagnation from the beginning. In addition, the network effect manifested in the almost uniform behavior patterns of domestic wind turbine manufacturers, such as withdrawing from independent technological development. Finally, initial divergence can be seen in the coexistence of imported and domestically developed wind turbines from MHI.

If imported wind turbines overwhelm domestic wind turbines in the local market due to lock-in, then the innovative behavior of the only domestic manufacturer that continued to develop wind turbines to suit local wind conditions can be considered as "unleveraged" to benefit public interest, such as the supply of public goods and service suitable for society as a whole.[16] Energy technologies designed to consistently supply stable electricity to a social system – be it nuclear or renewable – profoundly pertain to public interest, much like waste disposal technologies. Under the current wind turbine situation in Japan, which demands increasing unit output capacity, it is worth considering (from the viewpoint of public interest) the possibility that domestic wind turbines have equivalent performance to the imported wind turbines occupying a dominant position in the domestic market; alternatively, the imported wind turbines may be inferior due to their lack of consideration for local conditions specific to Japan. This implies that a one-dimensional evaluation based on the criterion of "superiority in the market determines success" could deviate from an appropriate technology selection, given that wind turbines are public goods that are dependent on regional characteristics, such as local land use, industrial base, ecosystem, and climatic conditions.

As far as the development and diffusion of wind turbines in Japan is concerned, adherence to erroneous precedents as an element of structural disaster can be interpreted as an outcome of a path-dependent social process leading to lock-in. Based on this interpretation of a generating mechanism of structural disaster, the social decision-making process leading to lock-in could be seen as related to structural disaster, such that an erroneous precedent is followed and the problem is perpetuated. Domestic and imported technologies' market shares are the aggregated result of the behavior of agents involved, so when the domestically developed technology designed to adapt to Japan's unique local wind conditions is forced out of the market, this could be interpreted as being a result of a carryover problem by the behavior of the governmental and industrial sectors. For example, the governmental sector mistakenly followed a precedent of understated goal setting regarding wind power generation policy, and the industrial sector followed a precedent of withdrawing from self-reliant wind turbine development, due in part to belief and/or network effect.

Setback of the self-denial mechanism

Incorporating social decision-making related to energy technologies in a more broad perspective, it is important to distinguish between formal processes and informal ones.[17] Formal processes are those in which the governmental sector virtually controls the entire process based on laws and regulations, such as nuclear power plant siting, the Sunshine project, and the wind resources survey. Informal processes refer to those in which subjective information, like the unsubstantiated myth that wind power generation is infeasible due to poor wind conditions in Japan, influences the social decision-making process and its outcomes.

This distinction is important because informal process influences are driven by myth and originate in a lack of transparency in formal processes, such as not making public the real assessments or results of the initial wind turbine development carried out under the aegis of the Sunshine project. This complicated relationship between the two processes involved in social decision-making on wind power generation can be expressed as a kind of self-denial mechanism, in which the particular characteristics of the formal process (such as the lack of transparency) reduce the substantial importance of the formal process itself, thereby increasing informal processes' influence.

The scope of application of this self-denial mechanism goes well beyond the development and diffusion of wind turbines; for example, the siting process of nuclear power stations in Japan had followed this mechanism long before the Fukushima nuclear accident.[18] The self-denial mechanism lacks transparency in the institutionalized processes and invites the informal influence of myths that, in turn, negate the institutionalized processes as a whole, which is similar to the working of institutionalized secrecy implied by structural disaster. When this is perpetuated, most likely for social reasons such as the face-saving of the governmental sector in charge of large-scale national projects on energy technologies, it is also similar to adherence to erroneous precedents as an element of structural disaster. Thus, the self-denial mechanism could be regarded as another mechanism that gives rise to structural disaster, in parallel with the sociologically reformulated mechanism of path-dependency.

Once this mechanism is activated, it would be difficult to escape from receiving its effects without external intervention, primarily because belief and network effects work both in the formal and informal processes of the social decision-making process, just as in the process of sociological path-dependency. As will be detailed below, one of the key criteria enabling the avoidance of this mechanism is whether it is possible to find relevant outsiders who actively participate in the process.[19]

Recapitulating what is mentioned above, we have now a couple of mechanisms that are thought to lead to structural disaster. How, then, can we get away from these mechanisms after getting into structural disaster? Japan's subsequent stages of wind turbine development provide three strategic cases for answering this question, placing the focus on the process through which the fixed trajectory of technology development and diffusion was disrupted for the first time by relevant outsiders, each case showing significant deviation from the fixed trajectory. Within the wind power regime, "outsiders" refers to agents external to the governmental, industrial, and academic sectors involved in the promotion of wind power generation (Matsumoto and Nishide 2004).

Relevant outsiders breaking the myth of wind power generation infeasibility: the case of M Project

To illustrate the role of relevant outsiders breaking the myth of wind power generation's infeasibility within a wider sociological perspective, M Project, one of the Japan's pioneering cases of wind turbine generation, epitomized the initial breakthrough of wind turbine introduction by relevant outsiders. M City is a commuter town located 10 minutes by train from the capital city of Fukui Prefecture facing the Sea of Japan with a population of about 70,000. In 1993, a 100-kW wind turbine (imported from Denmark) was installed in one of the city's parks. The aim was to supply electricity to a hotel nearby as well as sell excess electricity. The wind turbine operated at 50 percent capacity, and although the contract with the hotel was canceled due to the fluctuations in the amount of electrical power supplied, a total income of about 2,000,000 yen per year was gained from Hokuriku Electric Power Company (HEPCO).

Relevant outsiders were the impetus of this project, and they were able to destroy the long-standing myth that wind turbines generation would be infeasible in Japan because of unfavorable wind conditions.[20] In this case, insiders were agents under the top-down control of MITI, the authorized governmental body in charge of wind power generation as a national project and the first relevant outsider was the M City mayor who wanted a landmark monument to symbolize a new image for the city and, ideally, bring it comparable fame to that of the prefecture's capital city. The mayor decided on wind power generation for the theme of this landmark (along with the construction of a new city hall) after reading a newspaper article on neighboring town Osawano-machi's wind turbine, which was not for power generation but only for symbolic purpose. Since this was also a time during which the general public was becoming aware of environmental problems such as global warming, the mayor thought that a wind turbine could symbolize environmentally friendly energy sources in their home city. The wind turbine he planned to construct was for both power generation and symbolic purposes, in contrast to Osawano-machi's. To secure the initial cost he applied for a MITI subsidy to study the feasibility of commercial power generation using local energy sources. The application was successful, and as a result, a committee for the feasibility study of wind power generation in M City was formed in 1991.

The second relevant outsider was this feasibility committee, which was chaired by a professor from a local technology institute who was also the director of the Japan Wind Energy Society (which was then the only association comprised of wind turbine experts in Japan). The committee included assorted agents from MITI, the Ministry of Construction, the prefectural office, HEPCO, universities, and influential companies around the city. The inclusion of MITI officials in the committee did not indicate MITI's direct control of the committee; rather, this simply reflected a common custom of Japan, wherein government officials are keen to attend any meeting sponsored by the government in order to supervise the use of its subsidies. There was no shared knowledge within the committee at the time regarding details of wind turbines other than the realization that wind power generation had yet-unknown characteristics. The image of wind turbines was mirrored by the environmentally conscious development of local areas. The committee recommended wind turbines as a local energy source, and the recommendation was welcomed by the city congress.

The third relevant outsider was "Mr. K," who founded the Ecology Corporation, the first company in Japan to import wind turbines manufactured in other countries. He was employed by a Japanese oil company immediately after graduating university and, after quitting that job, became manager of a company owned by his mother. After the executive board of this company fired him due to his failure at the business, he set up a consultancy company in 1989 during the period of Japan's "bubble" economy. This situation enabled him to extend his business ventures to importing furniture from abroad, creating a partnership with manufacturers, such as a Japanese agency dealing with Swedish wooden furniture, which in turn directed his attention to Denmark to create a further business partnership. In 1991, he went to Denmark on business and was impressed by the wind turbines at an industrial exhibition. After returning to Japan, he collected information on wind turbines and found that Japan had no concrete prospects for wind power generation at the time. Most domestic manufacturers felt that the Japanese wind turbine market held few opportunities because of the dubious results obtained from the Sunshine project. Knowing little about the details of wind turbines, he nonetheless expected that wind turbine businesses could be a niche and went on to form the Ecology Corporation in 1991, which became the only agent to import Micon wind turbines to M City from Denmark.

In deconstructing the social processes of the initial phase of introducing wind turbines to M City into roles played by relevant outsiders, the myth of wind turbine generation's infeasibility was broken by these three different relevant outsiders (see Table 6.5).[21]

In contrast to a widespread view of the government-led siting processes of nuclear power stations, in this case, it was not MITI's subsidy that played a crucial role in dispelling the myth that discouraged wind power generation in Japan, as the mayor knew nothing about the myth when he first got the idea of building a wind turbine. In addition, Mr. K regarded MITI as the primary obstacle

Table 6.5 Relevant Outsiders Who Proved the Feasibility of Wind Turbines in Japan

Relevant outsiders	Motives	Expertise in wind turbines	Purpose
Mayor of M City	Development of the local area	None	Generation, symbolic purposes
Feasibility Committee	Development of the local area	Limited	Generation, symbolic purposes
Mr. K	Business success, energy security	None	Generation

to the promotion of wind power generation. In contrast to the stereotype of a government-led introduction of new technologies that have poor marketability in their early stages, the role played by relevant outsiders in the introduction of wind power generation was remarkable in that neither the mayor nor Mr. K were aware of the widely held views of the poor prospects for the Japanese wind turbine market in advance. In particular, the selection of a Danish wind turbine could be traced back to Mr. K's previous dealings with Danish wooden furniture; according to Mr. K, he decided to get into the wind turbine business precisely because of his lack of experience in the business. Thus, most of the relevant outsiders in this case were able to obtain the advantage of being outsiders because this position enabled them to embark on the construction of wind turbines irrespective of the myth of infeasibility of wind power generation.

Relevant outsiders creating a path to exporting domestically produced wind turbines: the case of N Project

N Project is a different case in that the project encouraged outsiders to break the current track of wind power generation by imported wind turbines by creating a new path to exporting domestically produced wind turbines. N Project was initiated by 11 toy component makers in Fukui Prefecture who were primarily subcontractors of major toy companies that manufactured jungle gyms and slides. The project started in 1994 through an association aimed at the collaborative work of small-scale companies willing to produce something new outside of the toy-production business. While initially they had been unable to find a suitable new product, a breakthrough came at a time when "Mr. N," a member of the project and a subcontractor for toy makers, talked with "Mr. M," a painter/sculptor who had once made a metal sculpture with the technical assistance of Mr. N. The prefecture was and is known as a stronghold of nuclear power stations, as 15 of them are sited in the prefecture.[22] To change this image, Mr. M proposed a small wind turbine as a symbolic counter and also because, at that time, there was a lack of serious effort to produce small-scale wind turbines in Japan, and he regarded this situation as a niche.

This idea was welcomed by the members of N Project and R&D started in 1995, followed by Mr. M reaching out to contact wind turbine experts. What they tried to produce was a small-scale wind turbine generator that was also able to serve as a symbolic monument for natural energy sources. One of the most technically critical, "reverse-salient" (Hughes 1983) questions for this small-scale wind turbine was how it would operate during very slight wind (2 meters/second). During a discussion about N Project between Mr. N and one of his golf mates, who was a magnet maker, the idea was posed to use magnets to help rotate the wind turbine during very slight wind conditions. The idea was successful and N Project completed its first small-scale wind turbine within five years of beginning R&D.

Thus, there were two relevant outsiders in the R&D stage of N Project: Mr. M, who conceived the original project idea, and Mr. N, who found a solution to the reverse salient technical question in materializing the small-scale wind turbine. Neither of them had any connection with MITI, nor was there direct top-down control of MITI. In addition, there were no wind turbine development, design, or production specialists working on the project.

A relevant outsider in the post-R&D stage was one of Mr. M's friends, "Mr. S," who was then working at a university in the prefecture and specialized in African studies. Based on his knowledge about Africa, he became responsible for the project's strategy for selling the small-scale wind turbines on that continent, based on Mr. M's idea for this type of export. Mr. S's commitment to the project coincided with one governmental agency's decision to promote the introduction of wind turbines within universities and hospitals in Africa. Such government-aided projects for developing countries had often failed in the past, mainly because people in the recipient countries cannot afford to keep operating technologies that were transferred from developed countries. When wind turbines needed maintenance, for example, the local people were unable to repair them due to the expense. Mr. S had obtained his Ph.D. in African studies from a national university, which was then carrying out a joint national project with the governmental agency in question; as such, he proposed the use of small-scale wind turbines produced by N Project for the joint national project to export wind turbines to Africa.

His strategy emphasized the image of an energy-saving society and an African community that had no formal monetary system.[23] Anti-nuclear sentiment was also one of the motives for his strategy. The proposal by Mr. S was accepted by the joint national project and N Project was able to export small-scale wind turbines to Africa that had been developed by the project. In 2001, wind turbines were installed by the project in two sites there. The relevant outsiders in this case are listed below (see Table 6.6).[24]

Success of small makers' associations in technological development and the export of their products are considered exceptional cases rather than the norm. In addition to the relevant outsiders' roles mentioned above, N Project's success might also be due to a complementary factor. That is to say, the project was not necessarily oriented toward pay-off maximization; for example, the cost of the project exceeded the government subsidy, requiring additional private

Table 6.6 Relevant Outsiders in Creating a New Path to Exporting Domestically Produced Wind Turbines to Africa

Relevant outsiders	Motives	Expertise in wind turbines	Purpose
Mr. N	Self-sustaining business	None	Increased spread through mass production
Mr. M	Self-sustaining business, anti-nuclear	None	Symbolic purposes, social reform
Mr. S	Energy-saving, anti-nuclear	None	Social reform

investment by the active members of the project, who were willing to engage in a self-sustaining economy. N Project is facing the dilemma of whether or not to proceed with mass-production of small-scale wind turbines to promote further market expansion, or to continue to produce the turbines for small communities.[25] In either situation, the manufacturing of small-scale products based on local industries coupled with loose regional networks of relevant outsiders created a unique path that led to the domestic production of wind turbines and their export to developing countries.

Relevant outsiders after a mega-disaster: the case of Hokudan-machi

For a case on the demand side (rather than supply), the behaviors of unexpected users as relevant outsiders can be seen in the case of Hokudan-machi (currently Awaji-shi), where their incentives come from outside the market, providing a window into investigating sociological factors. This case involves Hokudan-machi, where the Great Hanshin-Awaji earthquake in 1995 triggered a move to the adoption of domestically produced wind turbines.

Hokudan-machi is a town on Awajishima Island, which is 30 minutes by ship from Akashi City, one of the major cities that suffered from the Great Hanshin-Awaji earthquake. Damage by this earthquake was one of the most severe in Japan in the years since WWII, whose seismic center was a dislocation in Hokudan-machi.[26] After the earthquake, a group of geologists called for the preservation of the dislocation, which was granted by the government to serve as a monument of the natural disaster. In addition, Hokudan-machi planned to build a memorial park on the dislocation as well, following advice from the town headman.

> The next day of the earthquake, the town headman saw the dislocation and thought "the earth is split." While he was deeply shocked, he hit upon an idea to use it for local area development. He was encouraged by the scholars and others who were concerned with the preservation of the dislocation for the future generations and he promoted the plan to build the museum. Since more than 90 percent of the houses were damaged in the town, however, there arose oppositions from the residents such that they did not want to remember. Then the headman persuaded them by referring to Hiroshima, "If there were not A-bomb Dome, the memory of radiation exposure would have been more weathered."
>
> (Asahi Shimbun, June 4, 1998)

Against such a background, in April 1998, the Nojima Fault Preservation Museum was established as the central facility in the memorial park, which was named "Phoenix Park," developed by Hyogo Prefecture and Hokudan-machi. This facility aimed to preserve the dislocation as the seismic center of the earthquake and was built there to represent the enormous suffering from the earthquake and to encourage people's interest in the relationship between the earthquake and the dislocation.[27]

The town estimated the number of visitors to the facility to be 300,000 per year; in reality, 2,800,000 visitors came in the first year. The benefit from the visitor fees and associated sales in the park provided the town with a significant source of revenue. In addition, more than 100 residents, primarily older people, were employed in various associated facilities within the park. In the first year, the total benefit amounted to about 800 million yen, compared to revenue coming from the taxes of Hokudan-machi, which was around 900 million yen. As such, the facilities in the park constituted an important stream of revenue for the town.

Visitors began to decrease in the years following its initial opening and the park did not see many return visitors either, likely due to its purpose as a monument to a natural disaster. In terms of economic calculation, this decrease in visitors should have discouraged additional development of the area; however, the same town headman came up with the idea to build a wind turbine as a symbol of the park, the idea that originated during a trip to Europe where he happened to see a wind park.

The administration of the town, however, responded negatively to the idea because they saw it as a poor prospect for bringing back visitors. This was a time before the Kyoto Protocol, when wind turbines were so unpopular in Japan that most people (including those within the town's administration) regarded investments in the construction of wind turbines as too risky. A clue to changing the situation in the town came up almost by chance. Mr. Miyamoto, the planning and development chief of the town happened to come across information regarding the efforts of a neighboring town to use wind turbines to attract visitors.[28] This unexpected information coming from an adjacent local area changed his mind about using the technology for this purpose and he began to investigate the construction of wind turbines for planning the development of the town.

The administration of the town then planned to install a wind turbine in Phoenix Park, but the Communist Party opposed its introduction, arguing that the town should not spend more money on the memorial park but rather provide financial support for individual residents suffering from the earthquake who needed help to recover. Facing such opposition, the town's administration held meetings to explain the plan's benefits for the inhabitants around the proposed site of the turbine and to gain their consent. These meetings, or seminars, had been quite common and widely used in the social acceptance processes of new technologies, including nuclear power stations in Japan. The responses of the inhabitants in this case, however, were quite unusual in that there was little resistance to the idea among them; rather, even inhabitants who lived far enough away from the proposed site, with little chance to experience any side effects of the wind turbine location, also requested similar seminars to be held in their areas for explanation about this technology as well. As a result, more than 10 different areas of the town saw seminars held to this effect.[29] The town administration successfully persuaded all inhabitants to accept the wind turbine location through this type of participatory decision-making. Based on such activities, the town assembly passed the plan.

The wind turbine location was thus decided but the town faced another problem: technology selection. The town solicited presentations by different wind turbine manufacturers but could not decide which to purchase on a technical basis, primarily because the main purpose of the turbine at this location was to be symbolic – for recovery of the town from the earthquake with a hope to bring back visitors, rather than for usable power generation. The cardinal condition to be met for such symbolic use should be the continuous rotation of turbine blades at all times. An invited speaker from Vestas, one of the most prominent wind turbine makers in Denmark, questioned the necessity for continuous blade rotation as a landmark of technology selection. European wind turbines did not rotate during weak wind conditions because the energy of wind utilized for power generation grows in proportion to the cubic speed of wind; as such, operation during weak wind conditions would be unnecessary and, thus, the blades of these turbines would not be in continuous motion.[30]

In contrast, there was an exceptional wind turbine maker in Japan, MHI, whose wind turbines had been designed to work under very weak wind conditions. As mentioned above, MHI was the only domestic maker that had been developing wind turbines to function under Japan's unique wind conditions. The company had done well in the global market but was a latecomer in the domestic market. Wind turbines designed by MHI were a good match for the symbolic use of the turbine intended by the town because of their capability of continuous rotation under weak wind conditions.

In addition to their technical performance to rotate consistently despite low wind levels, the symbolic use of the wind turbine also required that maintenance could be carried out quickly when necessary. MHI assured the town that it had a higher capability of quick and stable maintenance; for example, MHI's staff could arrive within 24 hours and components for any type of turbine would be easily available to them, as compared to maintenance guarantees from foreign makers, for which it was uncertain whether their agencies in Japan would be able to replace components consistently and quickly. Considering these requirements for technical performance and maintenance capability, the town eventually decided to build a 600-kW MHI wind turbine in 2002 in the memorial park. The wind turbine was also used to provide electricity to the facilities in the park and sold surplus electricity to the local area.[31]

Contrary to its intended purpose to bring back visitors to the memorial park via its symbolic use to illustrate the fertility of nature as against destructive forces such as earthquakes, visitor numbers continued to decrease. The electricity produced by the turbine used in park facilities, however, resulted in significant cost savings amounting to eight million yen in fiscal 2002. Thus, its intended purpose in a post-disaster local context outside of the market resulted in the realization of electricity production by domestically produced wind turbines.[32] In this case, relevant outsiders are all heterogeneous agents in Hokudan-machi.

Fair public participation based on local knowledge: relevant outsiders versus choreographed outsiders

Of course, the above should be considered singular cases for the purpose of examining the roles of relevant outsiders rather than as a generalization regarding the success of wind power generation. In the first two cases, a relevant outsider created new paths leading to wind power generation amidst the long-standing tendency toward nuclear power stations, and in the last case, relevant outsiders who had had little to do with the market unexpectedly created the opportunity to introduce wind power generation around the seismic center of the Great Hanshin-Awaji Earthquake. What is common among these three independent cases is the role played by relevant outsiders in changing a fixed trajectory with adherence to erroneous precedents to a new path, a change that was triggered by influences outside the market.[33] This change in a fixed trajectory, supported by adherence to erroneous precedents, can be viewed as a change by relevant outsiders within the more general context of public participation in technology selection.

It is important, however, in a more general context of public participation, to distinguish between relevant and irrelevant outsiders; for example, a relevant outsider in one situation could become a choreographed outsider in another, merely by agreeing to provide their "stamp of approval" to the given path of the existing technology. Such a choreographed outsider would continue to play a role in legitimizing particular agents and/or sectors as needed to the detriment of public interest. For example, in the process of technology development and diffusion, a choreographed outsider could, under the disguise of reflecting public opinion, reiterate that the influence of certain stakeholders is legitimate. In order to avoid the mechanism leading to structural disaster in the process of social decision-making on public issues within the science-technology-society interface, and to maintain a proper quality of the process, identifying criteria for distinguishing relevant outsiders from choreographed outsiders is crucial for people in the citizen sector.

The demarcation between relevant and choreographed outsiders varies depending on the situation; however, there is one situation in which that demarcation is critical. Since the mechanism generating structural disaster in the science-technology-society interface is rarely recognized in a straightforward manner, making a decision without being aware of this demarcation could undermine public interest through complex interactions between heterogeneous agents having particular interests, including compromise among stakeholders. Such complex interactions tend to be kept away from public attention, so it is therefore vital to highlight the generating mechanism of structural disaster and publicly secure the visibility of such a generating mechanism in the eyes of ordinary people within the citizen sector who could be the first to suffer from the structural disaster.

If the generating mechanism becomes visible, can structural disaster be prevented? My answer is "no," because there could be another mechanism that enables people to tolerate a process that would lead to structural disaster. As suggested in Chapter 3, a significant role causing and perpetuating structural disaster can be played by "good people" who make positive contributions to organizations and/or sectors, who occasionally deviate from the realization of public interest. In this context, it becomes necessary to reconsider in more detail the mechanism of following the steps of an erroneous precedent under a locally agreeable equilibrium, both from the perspective of those who are or become good people and from the perspective of those who stand to benefit.

Needless to say, it is virtually impossible to break down the generating mechanism into the individual behaviors of each agent and observe them directly; however, we can return to historical cases in order to analyze how the aforementioned mechanism generating structural disaster looks from the perspective of and roles held by those who became good people and from those who stood to gain something. Such an analysis could provide a valuable clue to understanding, sociologically, how the mechanism triggering, generating, maintaining, and institutionalizing structural disaster actually works within the context of particular social action.

The initial process of wind turbine development and diffusion is presented here as one such historical case; in particular, to reveal why it is important to differentiate the roles played by relevant outsiders as public participants in social decision-making. For example, in a case of path-dependent stagnation of wind power generation in Japan, it is meaningful to create a channel that enables relevant outsiders to participate in social decision-making processes to prevent over-influence of the network and belief effects and lock-in and to continuously monitor the current research occurring on technological development, however modest it may be, in parallel with technology import.[34] Prior studies on the structure of the development trajectories of technologies reveal that technological progress tends to be a revisionist success story using hindsight. In many cases, however, there are various alternatives, both potential and explicit, at each stage of technological development.[35]

Accordingly, unless continuous efforts are made to keep up-to-date on the technological development of wind turbines (for example, control technology related to the optimization of operation, transmission, and network systems), it will be virtually impossible to know what alternatives are available and/or the advantages and disadvantages of each alternative. Without this kind of knowledge, it would be impossible to make a selection from among the different alternatives available and eliminate negative effects due to the sociological path-dependency that accompanies network effects and belief effects. For this reason, it is essential to make alternative technological trajectories transparent. But how?

To make alternative technology trajectories transparent in the public sphere with the aim of facilitating the well-balanced selection of an appropriate technology in the science-technology-society interface, it is essential to ensure that all actors concerned are able, when necessary, to participate in proper stages of the social decision-making process. In Japan, however, public participation in such processes has been focused only on systems for selling the electricity generated by wind turbines, or green electricity schemes. In contrast, changing the fixed development trajectory of technology necessitates public participation in earlier stages, such as technology selection.

Public participation in technology selection does not necessarily mean that citizens will be directly involved in developing technologies (though there are

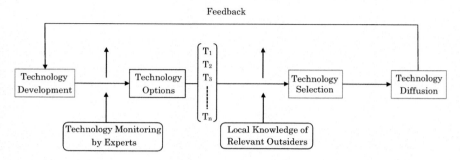

Figure 6.1 Fair Public Participation in the Selection of Technology
Note: $T_1, T_2, T_3, \ldots T_n$ indicate different types of technology.

some exceptional cases in which the public does get involved, such as with the development of tidelands), but from the perspective of structural disaster this participation helps to ensure access to channels through which relevant outsiders are able to select the type of technology to be introduced from among a number of alternative types, based on the accumulated local knowledge of the affected communities.[36] Relevant outsiders are, as defined above, expected to be instrumental in avoiding network and belief effects that could lead to a state of lock-in in the sociological path-dependent process generating structural disaster. Their participation could also provide one possible means for reducing uncertainty caused by dual underdetermination because they are expected to broaden the range of policy options by introducing alternatives in technology selection based on local knowledge. This idea of public participation by relevant outsiders in the initial technology selection process can be conceptualized as follows (see Figure 6.1).[37]

Considering that Japan's percentage of renewable energy, including wind power, remains at only 4.4 percent of its total primary energy supply as of 2014 (Agency for Natural Resources and Energy 2016), it is illogical to expect that public participation by relevant outsiders in technology selection will alter such an overall trend in the near term. The significance of this concept is quite separate from such immediate effects. Since the development and diffusion of wind turbine technology requires neither a huge budget nor large-scale revision of the existing system of electricity production and supply, and since fairly complicated problems of wind turbine design and deployment could be resolved by utilizing local knowledge and labor for repair and maintenance, public participation by relevant outsiders in wind turbine selection can be seen as a test case for their participation in singling out an appropriate type of technology and its deployment in local contexts. The significance of the concept of relevant outsiders relates to feasible ways of changing a fixed trajectory of technological development and diffusion, thereby eliminating the potentiality of structural disaster residing in a state of lock-in.

The quality of social decision-making processes

The main points made in this chapter can be summarized as follows.

1. The Sunshine project was the first large-scale, long-term national project for renewable energy development including wind turbines, but Japan's wind turbine development withdrew from national projects without any public explanation for doing so. As a result, a myth has persisted: that overall, without any evidence, it is infeasible for Japan to make power generation using wind turbines of any kind because of unfavorable wind conditions.
2. This myth prevented most domestic wind turbine manufacturers from carrying out development of the technology and accumulating technical know-how, which in turn reinforced the fixed trajectory of diffusion of this technology in Japan via imports. The myth was broken first by relevant outsiders who were external to the closed circle of governmental, industrial, and academic sectors engaging in renewable energy promotion (including the Sunshine project) and were non-experts in wind turbine development, design, or production.
3. Another type of relevant outsider was heterogeneous agents within a small town whose intended purpose for the technology – symbolic use of wind turbines in a post-disaster local context outside the market – resulted in the unintended consequence of materializing the production of electricity from the symbolic wind turbine that had been domestically manufactured. In this case, relevant outsiders played the role of breaking the fixed trajectory of technology dominated by imported wind turbines. For an unintended consequence of such a purposive social action, the production of electricity by domestically produced wind turbine resulted.
4. Analysis of the independent cases used in this chapter suggests that relevant outsiders could play a key role in altering the fixed trajectory of a technology. This can be particularly decisive at a time when a large-scale national project by a closed circle of experts and agents yields little meaningful results, wherein an assessment of the results is not made public. In such a situation, relevant outsiders' input into technology selection could be a candidate for public participation for changing the fixed trajectory that could potentially lead to structural disaster.

Thus, the path-dependent development of renewable energy technology and diffusion via imports was coupled with a closed decision-making process conducted by insiders alone. The participation of relevant outsiders' in technology selection processes could disentangle this coupling and prevent the adoption of a single fixed trajectory, as their status as outsiders enables them to be relatively free from shared belief and network effects that typically serve to maintain the fixed trajectory adhered to precedents. Based on these points, it is possible to tentatively formulate the following three criteria by which the quality of social decision-making processes can be evaluated in terms of identifying alternatives.

Since the fixed trajectory could turn into structural disaster when the precedents are erroneous, the criteria could become a preliminary device to detect the potential for structural disaster.

1. Whether or not it is possible to escape from network effects and belief effects in the initial phase of social decision-making.
2. Whether or not it is possible for relevant outsiders to take part in both the technology selection and technology diffusion stages.
3. Whether or not it is possible to make public the reasons for failure of large-scale national projects and to avoid inadequate accounts that are colored by myths from agents concerned.

The role of relevant outsiders formulated here, however, cannot be applied broadly to every situation because, as mentioned above, the demarcation between relevant and choreographed outsiders can vary depending on issues and situation-specific details. Relevant outsiders in one instance, for example, could become irrelevant by playing the role of a mediator between different stakeholders or "petit experts" (experts of nothing but impression management) to build a consensus in order to give official backing to a fixed trajectory.[38] In such cases, choreographed outsiders could rightly meet the needs of bureaucratic decision-making of the governmental sector by providing a given policy option with legitimacy. When legitimacy in such a context is achieved under the name of the will of people in the citizen sector and the stake of the governmental sector sticking to a given policy is procured in this way, this type of legitimation could lead to a techno-mass democracy, or decision-making on technology by particular stakeholders via a legitimate "social" consensus in participatory appearance. If the distinction between democracy and mass-democracy thus defined is blurred by the stereotypical dichotomy of technocratic versus participatory way of decision-making, then structural disaster could emerge in a path-dependent manner. This was manifested in the role played by Café Scientifique in the Tohoku district before the Fukushima nuclear accident, which is used as an example of institutionalized secrecy in Chapter 1. Democracy and mass-democracy are similar in their mode of representation in the public sphere but the former reflects the interests of people in the citizen sector, while the latter never reflects this interest. From the perspective of structural disaster, it should be remembered here that techno-mass democracy, as epitomized by Café Scientifique before the Fukushima accident, paved the way to the accident.

Therefore, discriminating between relevant outsiders expected to play a role for democracy and choreographed ones designed to play a role for mass-democracy will be one of the most important tasks for further sociological studies on structural disaster and beyond.

7 To understand or not to understand?
Infinite responsibility for HLW disposal, or ongoing structural disaster

Meltdown, hydrogen explosion, half-life, condenser, and dose level are technical terms in science and technology that have rushed into people's daily lives since March 11, 2011, when one of the most severe nuclear accidents in history happened in Fukushima, along with an earthquake of a once-per-one-thousand-year magnitude. This was a hybrid disaster, made up of multiple extreme events both occurring in natural environments and affecting artifacts. In such a situation, the behaviors of all actors could resemble an as-yet-unseen social experiment, for which some might argue the government was ill-prepared in handling – both the events and the social fallout – despite early warnings. Some residents attempted to make rough estimates regarding radiation dose levels in their local area, while others tried to send relief donations for the victims via their own personal means, rather than facing potential delays of the aid going through official routes. Some parents attempted to evacuate their children while they themselves remained in their local residence. There are innumerable, untold other cases that occurred within the citizen sector, and after some time had passed, these people started to seek expertise and guidance for the questions they were facing.

Against the background of such a situation, Prime Minister Abe bid for the Olympic Games to be held in Tokyo in 2020, declaring that everything in the post-Fukushima situation, including surface debris and radioactive materials underground and in the water would be "under control."[1] This chapter analyzes the nature of ongoing structural disaster by highlighting a persistent problem that will continue whether the post-Fukushima situation is under control or not. The main concern is radioactive waste, particularly High-level Radioactive Waste (HLW) disposal; as such, this chapter focuses on the role of expertise entangled with HLW disposal issues and scrutinizes the reason why such disposal could be regarded as an ongoing structural disaster, which involves an infinite term of responsibility.

Discourse in the post-Fukushima situation involves two different narratives: one emphasizes the need to enhance science and technology literacy among the citizen sector, which could lead to enhanced understanding of nuclear reactors, radioactivity, and other topics; and the other asserts the need to seek an alternative course for civilization, one that is not driven solely by the progress of science and technology. The two narratives might initially seem to represent opposing viewpoints, as the former aims to disseminate science and technology expertise while the latter fundamentally reconsiders the weight or value of expertise in science and technology on a civilizational scale. However, there is a common thread that is shared by these seemingly opposing narratives. From the viewpoint of sociology, both narratives tend assign the Fukushima accident affairs to "other people" despite the logical impossibility of doing so. In this connection, the concept of structural disaster is designed to prevent such a tendency from arising and attributes a due portion of the accident to all actors and sectors.

How to make visible and share the horizon of extreme events

In the post-Fukushima situation, inequality arose among the victims of the accident, such as inequality in payments for decontamination, in compensation due to unrealistic demarcation between contaminated and decontaminated areas, aggravated economic inequality in certain local areas, and incurable worry imposed on the elderly population, among other examples.[2] From the viewpoint of structural disaster, these are all problems for ordinary people who were personally distanced from the Fukushima accident as well as for the victims of the accident. Nevertheless, it would be very difficult for ordinary people in the citizen sector to see that the inequality affecting the victims goes far beyond recovery from the accident. The concept of structural disaster enables us to widen our perspective to command a "bird's-eye view" of such a complicated situation, in this case, using HLW disposal as an ongoing structural disaster.

It will take dozens of years for the post-Fukushima devastation to be temporarily settled; however, there is a big discrepancy between these concerns and HLW disposal, as the latter demands a much longer time frame, extending over millions of years. This discrepancy explains why HLW disposal can help to clarify how structural disaster concerns all of us. There are two strands of structural disaster that pertain to HLW disposal: one is adherence to erroneous precedents that carries problems over and reproduces them; the other is how the complexity of a system under consideration and the interdependence of its units can aggravate problems.

Associated with the above arguments are subtler issues regarding the complicated relationship between expertise and democracy. On one hand, there are many issues in which democratic decision-making by people within the citizen sector cannot proceed without expertise, such as food and energy supply, testing of new drugs, environmental protection, and nuclear safety. On the other hand, there is no *a priori* reason to believe that expertise guarantees a democratic way of decision-making. This potential tension between expertise and democracy springs from current salient conditions made up of at least three characteristics:[3]

1 Asymmetrical relationships between experts and lay people: Most people in the citizen sector depend on expertise in their daily lives; however, they are unable to judge the validity of the work done by experts.
2 Functional specificity of expertise: No one can be an expert of everything.

168 *To understand or not to understand?*

3   The resulting universal presence of the asymmetrical relationship: No actor can escape from this relationship nor the distribution of expertise within the sphere of their daily lives.

Of course, the relationship between expertise and democracy is only one aspect of HLW disposal issues. What is essential to the issues involved in HLW disposal is the accompaniment of infinite responsibility for social decision-making on these issues; in other words, any decision-making by the current generation will undeniably affect the state of future generations for an almost infinite duration of time based on the long half-life of some radionuclide. This means that a social decision made at any given time will continue to affect future generations for an almost infinite duration. However, no single actor can bear infinite responsibility, so the resulting problem is how to transform infinite responsibility into something finite that can be socially allocated, and because failure to do so will invite collective irresponsibility, it is crucial to allocate due social responsibility after the transformation, by which infinite responsibility could be better managed. Based on the sector model developed in Chapter 2, the allocation of due social responsibility according to independent analysis of the engagements of the governmental, industrial, academic, and citizen sectors in HLW disposal issues is crucial to preventing collective irresponsibility from emerging.[4] For a more robust account of this point, it is necessary to probe type-two underdetermination (mentioned in Chapter 1) with particular reference to HLW disposal.

Revealing the way to fix type-two underdetermination in HLW disposal

The production of electricity by nuclear power stations started around 1970 in Japan and, until the Fukushima accident, more than one-third of the country's total supply of electricity was produced by nuclear power. This implies that a significant amount of radioactive waste has accumulated in Japan for about 40 years. The method in which high-level radioactive waste is handled is critical when considering the large time scale, because the half-life of this waste can range from 10,000 to 100,000 years, up to 2 million years (for Neptunium-237).[5] In fact, the law for the final disposal of specific radioactive waste was issued in 2000 and the Nuclear Waste Management Organization of Japan (NUMO) was established that same year. The waste is currently being preserved in an intermediate storage space in Rokkasho village of Aomori Prefecture.[6] This handling method, however, can only continue for several dozen years due to space limitations.

How, then, should the waste be handled during the longer term, and ultimately for perhaps millions of years? This is a question that also applies to other countries supported by nuclear power generation. As a topic of focus for these countries, geological disposal has been presented as one of the most feasible options for HLW disposal. This chapter not only looks at the high degree of scientific uncertainty inherent in the interaction between sites for geological disposal and the surrounding water flow, underground microbes, dislocations, and other unknown factors,[7] but focuses on the situation where type-two underdetermination arises even if we assume that there is no type-one underdetermination springing from a scientific uncertainty in geological disposal.

Even if radioactive waste disposal in the deep underground is the most effective solution to HLW disposal and there is no scientific uncertainty involved in this option due to the interaction between the sites for disposal and the surroundings of the sites, this is not indicative of social decision-making in how to proceed with long-term (nay, virtually infinite) disposal. It is, apparently, difficult to find a meaningful way to take responsibility for the results of a particular social decision made at the current time, the results of which could continue for as long as 10,000 to 2 million years. This duration of time is one of the reasons for singling out geological disposal, as geologic strata could be effective as protective barriers against radioactive waste that needs to be contained for a very long time. Such social decision-making will reverberate for a long time beyond several human generations – and the resulting complex non-linear effects could occur in the science-technology-society interface. No singe actor can take infinite responsibility of such magnitude; therefore, the question is how to convert infinite responsibility into finite responsibility such that the settings of social decision-making fall within reasonable bounds of responsibility for the results of decision-making.

Geological disposal is not a technique that guarantees stable isolation of potentially dangerous materials from human living spheres without intervention; rather, the idea is a *sui generis* social arrangement to fix type-two underdetermination by making infinite responsibility finite with the hope that HLW disposal could be handled within the ordinary parameters of social decision-making.[8]

There are two different ways to implement a geological disposal policy based on the above idea. One way takes a multi-stage approach to determine what is regarded as socially desirable without limiting the scope of policy options to geological disposal alone. France embodied this in a 1991 law that was based on the principle that a multi-staged and open-ended process of social decision-making should be sought while allowing room for alternative policy options such as fractional partitioning, transmutation, and long-term storage. The logic behind this way is that the current knowledge of radioactive waste disposal and the criteria to evaluate social decision-making could change in the future. In Sweden as well, when the Swedish Nuclear Fuel and Waste Management Company (SKB) stated that "if available knowledge within any area is not complete, a poorer outcome than can be reasonably expected is pessimistically assumed" (SKB 2000: 100), a similar logic was expressed in a different manner. Another way employs a multi-stage approach, but what is different about this way is that it splits the entire process of policy implementation made by the current generation into three steps. The duration of the entire process extends over several hundred years, but this way allocates the largest responsibility to the current generation, which is expected to monitor any radioactive waste disposed in the deep underground and ascertain its settlement for several hundred years. Canada employs this method, according to which the third stage will start 60 years from implementation and end 300 years later. It is assumed that the isolation and containment of radioactive waste will be completed during this time.[9]

What is common among these ways is, as mentioned, a multi-stage approach. Behind this are two basic principles. First, the decision-making process should not reduce the scope of policy options available to future generations. Second, the decision-making process should, as much as possible, eliminate the "points of no return" in presenting policy options. This latter principle is typically expressed under the concept of reversibility and retrievability.[10]

According to OECD/NEA (2011: 4), the two concepts are defined as follows:

> Reversibility "describes the *ability in principle* to reverse or reconsider decision taken during the progressive implementation of a disposal system; reversal is a concrete action of overturning a decision and moving back to a previous situation."
>
> Retrievability "is the *ability in principle* to recover waste or entire waste packages once they have been emplaced in a repository; retrieval is the concrete action of removal of the waste."

Naturally, a higher degree of freedom in policy options resulting from these principles entails further type-two underdetermination. For example, France's proceeding of prescribing details relevant to law enforcement for radioactive waste disposal in the first way has no scientifically necessary foundation; rather, it strongly depends on the local context. In France, the local context would include development of social movements against initial site selection for radioactive waste disposal that was implemented from 1987 through 1989 and subsequent suspension of the siting processes in 1990. Likewise, behind the SKB's attitude to the change of knowledge and the way of social decision-making in HLW disposal, there was the Swedish local context, such as antagonism toward the results of a preliminary investigation of 10 sites carried using a boring machine during between 1977 and 1985, which resulted in the temporary suspension of radioactive waste disposal. In Canada, the 300-year period for monitoring is based on little scientifically confirmed evidence; rather, it depends on a series of social events inflated within the Canadian context – publication of the initial environmental assessment of radioactive waste disposal; suspension of the government's disposal plan due to objection from governmental review panels; and the results of interviews with more than 15,000 citizens and engineers conducted over a period of 10 years.[11]

The infinite responsibility expected from HLW disposal thus generates a need for the reduction of points of no return in social decision-making, a need that naturally expands the range of possible disposal options, thereby increasing type-two underdetermination. This increased type-two underdetermination can interact with the type-one underdetermination involved in the issue, so that the complexity and interdependence of the science-technology-society interface could become amplified and result in a difficult resolution to the problem. To put it in the context of structural disaster, the possibility that the complexity of the interface and the interdependence of its units could aggravate disposal problems. If true, HLW disposal can be said to be a kind of ongoing structural disaster. As this possibility has not been explored fully and has, therefore, received little attention, further analysis will be undertaken in this chapter.

Revealed policy underdetermination: beyond the underdetermination of expertise

The possibility that the complexity and interdependence of the system's units can aggravate problems can be seen in the case of Yucca Mountain, which was selected as a United States HLW disposal site in 2002. According to Office of Civilian Radioactive Waste Management (1998), one of the most important technical bases of the decision was that there was a low rate of groundwater recharge at the site and very little water moving through the unsaturated zone.[12] Initial estimates of the infiltration of rate of water from the surface to the repository were between less than 0.5 and up to 4.0 mm per year at 300 meters below the surface (Flint et al. 2001; Macfarlane 2003). However, geologist Allison Macfarlane, who was later nominated by President Obama on May 24, 2012, as the chairperson of the NRC, called attention to the "discovery" of the presence of the ^{36}Cl isotope in rocks at the repository level located 300 meters below the surface in the mid-1990s.[13] Because atmospheric testing of nuclear weapons had been carried out in the adjacent Nevada Test Site during the 1950s, "water traveled from the surface down through 300 m of rock in less than 50 years" (Macfarlane 2003). Estimating the velocity of the water – assuming that the strata in this case are comprised entirely of rock – infiltration rates would exceed 80 mm per year (Flint et al. 2001). This was much faster than expected, ranging from 20 times to more than 100 times faster; therefore, one of the most important grounds for singling out Yucca Mountain as an HLW disposal station appears to have been falsified. Despite this, the United States Department of Energy (DOE) did not change the decision; rather, it changed the criteria of evaluation to suit the data. In other words, the DOE ascribed more than 99 percent of site capability to engineering and only 0.1 percent to the geology of the site (Macfarlane 2003). Considering that the initial DOE assessment placed a great deal of importance on the geology of the site, this change is symptomatic enough to suggest a predetermined plan, to which the contribution of engineering can be seen through the flexible construction of assessment.[14]

If there is a rational and socially positive reason for singling out the site, other than its geology, this story would be easier to understand. On the contrary, however, according to Ishiyama (2004), the land around Yucca Mountain has adjoins residences for indigenous peoples who are considered an ethnic minority group in the United States. In particular, for the Western Shoshone people, the mountain has been a sacred object of worship; therefore, the decision to designate the area as a HLW disposal site could result in damage to such a sacred object and, in a way, deny the identity of the Western Shoshone people. In addition, the indigenous people around the mountain use the underground water for drinking.[15]

Eventually, the plan to invite HLW disposal facilities to Yucca Mountain was canceled by President Obama, resulting in the loss of 10 billion dollars expended to implement the plan. The resulting conflicts between the federal government and the indigenous people, as well as among the indigenous people themselves, would not have occurred if there had been no plan to use the site for HLW disposal.

The cancelation of the Yucca Mountain station brought issues related to temporary storage to the forefront. What is important here is that most candidates for these sites are located in places that adjoin indigenous peoples' residential areas, such as Skull Valley, which is home to the Goshute, Apache, and Yakama tribes, populations that rely on fragile financial bases for economic support. A similar tendency can be observed in HLW disposal candidate sites in Japan. For example, from the need to fix the increased type-two underdetermination, a concentration of disposal candidate sites resulted in poor areas carrying huge financial deficits, as will be detailed below. Thus, the means to reduce type-one underdetermination, such as avoiding points of no return, amplified type-two underdetermination, which in turn could potentially magnify social inequality within local societies. As far as aggravating the problem through complexity and interdependence, these are grounds on which an argument for HLW disposal as an ongoing structural disaster can be made.

Regarding HLW disposal issues in Japan, type-two underdetermination could increase going forward because there have been no cataclysmic nationwide discussions or social movements centering on the issue until now. In the situation before and after the Fukushima accident, type-two underdetermination has been fixed mainly by appealing to a series of procedural precedents, such as a long-term plan for nuclear development in Japan issued in 1994, a law for the final radioactive waste disposal issued in 2000, and a subsequent decision by the cabinet based on the law. For example, the first open-ended way mentioned above, which considers alternatives other than geological disposal, is not viable because the decision by the cabinet set the deadline for disposal at 2040, assuming that geological disposal is the best available technology.

More important than such an overt way to fix type-two underdetermination are the implicit assumptions that penetrate the entire process of policy-making, implementation, and evaluation. Concerning type-one underdetermination, there have been attempts to reveal implicit technical assumptions introduced to fix this type of underdetermination since the pioneering work on Winscale by Wynne (1982: 11–14, 1987), Yucca Mountain by Macfarlane (2003), and the atomic bomb by Eden (2004), among others. In contrast, it is extremely difficult to virtually reveal implicit assumptions that have been introduced to fix type-two underdetermination because these assumptions tend to be embedded and naturalized within day-to-day social settings in which policies are made, implemented, and evaluated.

Implicitly assumed social model in HLW disposal

Risk perception depends on a social model that assumes a shared and understood "lived experience" common within a society in which risks are framed. Therefore,

To understand or not to understand? 173

social models assumed by risk sciences in HLW disposal provide an important clue to revealing implicit assumptions introduced to fix type-two underdetermination.[16] To specify such an assumed social model with reference to HLW issues in Japan, this section details a systematic examination of papers that have appeared in *Transactions of the Atomic Energy Society of Japan*.

Transactions began in 2002 as a refereed journal that is distinct from the official journal of the Atomic Society of Japan, *ATOMOΣ*, which is published for the general public. The readers and contributors of *Transactions* include a range of specialists in nuclear-related topics, such as those specializing in risk sciences in a broad sense. By conducting keyword searches of all papers appearing in the journal denominating radioactive waste disposal and/or risk as keywords – from its inception to the issue immediately prior to the Fukushima accident in 2011 – resulted in the retrieval of 16 papers. Papers retrieved by mere mechanical or coincidental matches without relevance to risk sciences and their relation to assumed social models were removed. Ultimately, seven papers were singled out.[17] The subjects of the papers are as follows:

Table 7.1 Subjects of Papers Pertaining to Risk Sciences in *Transactions of the Atomic Energy Society of Japan*, 2002–2011

- "The Framework Which Aims at Improving Compatibility of the High-level Radioactive Waste Disposal Technology with Social Values and the Role of Risk Communication"
- "Study on the Framework of Site Selection Aimed at Enhancing the Acceptability of a High-level Radioactive Waste Disposal Facility"
- "Policy Issues on Technology Development for High-level Radioactive Waste Disposal from the Viewpoint of Intergenerational Equity: Through Analyzing the Arguments on Retrievability"
- "Intergenerational Ethics of High-level Radioactive Waste"
- "Clarification of Nuclear Risk Recognition Scheme through Dialogue Forum"
- "Risk Communication on the Sting of Radioactive Waste Management Facility"
- "Social Acceptance Process Model for Ensuring the High-level Radioactive Waste Disposal Site"

Source: Produced based on *Transactions of the Atomic Energy Society of Japan*, 2002–2011.

Although individual subjects vary from one paper to another, a strikingly similar structure of arguments can be found among them, which creates a macro-level social model. In particular, the papers assume a specific way of thinking in order to understand the social state, fix type-two underdetermination, and determine the structure of the social model in tandem with how artifacts are utilized. Such a way of thinking is shared among engineers who generally refer to the safety of nuclear power stations. The following statement is one example of this way of thinking:

> The nuclear power stations in Japan have been operating since its start in 1966 with a high degree of reliability. . . . Nevertheless, the hasty reports by

mass media of troubles and incidents having little to do with nuclear safety have been damaging the sense of security of the residents around the stations.
(Ishibashi et al. 2010)

This way of thinking can be deconstructed into the following four-step argument when applied to HLW issues:

1   Assumption: There is reliability through using science and technology to solve problems such as geological disposal of radioactive waste.
2   Observed facts: Despite this reliability, the science and technology in question could turn out to be difficult to be accepted in society, resulting in a radioactive waste disposal project that does not proceed as planned.
3   Reasoning: The cause of such difficulty could be entirely ascribed to a lack of understanding of the science and technology for geological disposal of radioactive waste among the general public.
4   Conclusion derived: Therefore, the problem could be solved by having specialists talk to the general public about the confidence that they have in the reliability of the science and technology to be used.[18]

What runs through this four-step argument is a kind of zero-sum social model that is made up of two conflicting agents: specialists and the general public. If the confidence of specialists in science and technology is not shared by the public, then opposition to a project utilizing these tools arises. If the confidence, however, is shared, consent ensues. This social model implies that public understanding of science and technology is tantamount to an attitude toward a project as either for or against; therefore, the logic of the model could be expressed by the following formalism:

$$(\text{PUS} \rightarrow \text{For P}) \vee (\overline{\text{PUS}} \rightarrow \text{Against P})$$

*PUS: Public understanding of science and technology; P: Projects

Science and technology assumed in such a social model have a specific mission predetermined by particular sectors of society, and therefore aim to achieve this mission by appealing to different kinds of criteria to judge validity, such as cost-benefit analyses, among others. In contrast to ordinary criteria used to judge validity as represented by objectivity of science and technology, such criteria are specifically designed to maximize the social use of science and technology within a particular configuration of money, information, human resources, and materials among the governmental, industrial, academic, and citizen sectors. Of course, science and technology appearing in this formalism is quite different from ordinary science and technology that is used to understand nature via the criteria of validity independent of society.[19]

This social model was drawn from a systematic examination of peer-reviewed papers, and this insight should be complemented by the analyses of the actual social conditions in which the logic is applied and utilized as an implicit assumption for the implementation of HLW disposal policy. The revelation of such implicit assumptions standing on this logic is difficult to come by in ordinary situations. An extraordinary siting process for Toyocho for a survey into the history of geological events (before the Fukushima accident) ended up as a complete failure and can provide an exceptional case for a detailed examination of a strategic research site, not only toward the analyses of the logic of the social model actually working in the implementation of policy on HLW disposal, but also for elaboration on the logic itself.

Hidden social model implicating infinite responsibility for HLW disposal: the Toyocho case

Toyocho is a small town on Shikoku Island. It is an underpopulated area with a population density of only 46 persons per square kilometer, which is one-eighth the average population density of Japan (Kochi Prefecture 2008).[20] There are three factors that make this small town extraordinary within the context of HLW disposal:

1 This was the first town in which the mayor decided to break the NIMBY-like (Not in My Backyard) patterns of behavior regarding HLW disposal.
2 This decision by the town mayor was also the first instance in which it was eventually cancelled due to inhabitants' objections and resistance to HLW disposal, calling for the resignation of the town mayor.
3 It represents one of the rare instances that reveals a typical, implicit assumption embedded and naturalized in an ordinary situation that takes for granted day-to-day social settings to fix type-two underdetermination.

For the purposes of this chapter, the third point deserves further scrutiny because it illustrates a typical way of thinking by which type-two underdetermination is fixed in the pre-Fukushima situation. This way of thinking is such that suffering from being selected as a site for HLW disposal could be accepted in exchange for a significant amount of money granted to that local area. For example, Toyocho was offered 2 billion yen of grant money by the government if they would accept a preliminary documentary survey into the history of geological events in the area. The amount of this grant almost equaled the town's entire annual budget. A brochure made by the Nuclear Waste Management Organization of Japan (NUMO) for candidates of this preliminary documentary survey illustrates the characteristics of this way of thinking by focusing on the economic effects over a period of about 60 years that can be expected during the period of construction and initial operation of the HLW disposal site. The total estimated economic effects are presented to the candidates by grouping the effects into the following categories (see Table 7.2).

Policy measures made and implemented based on this particular way of thinking have a long history of success in Japan in persuading local residents to accept the location of nuclear power stations (approximately 50 sites). In fact, almost every

Table 7.2 Economic Effects Expected from HLW Disposal Estimated by NUMO

- Order for local industries
  740 billion yen
- Side effects from branching production
  1.65 trillion yen
- Ripple effects on additional labor force
  130,000 workers
- New employment at the site and its related facilities
  17,000 workers
- Property tax
  160 billion yen

Source: NUMO (2008).

kind of public facility has been built by grants-in-aid from the government that were intensively given to targeted sites selected for nuclear power station locations, as shown in Table 3.3 in Chapter 3. By the same token, all candidates for the application of the preliminary documentary survey into the history of geological events (14 places through 2009, including Toyocho) had been so underpopulated that they suffered from heavy financial deficits prior to being sited (see Table 7.3).

Toyocho, for example, was forced to create a Scheme for a Drastic Financial Reform, which states:

> Since the town cannot expect the increase of revenue because of depopulation and progressive aging . . . the finance of the town would collapse without a drastic reform.
>
> (Toyocho n.d.: 3)

This situation gives the town a strong incentive to accept the way of thinking mentioned above, as the local economic condition that could induce residents and their local government to accept policy measures in the siting process of HLW disposal, similar to that which permeated past siting processes for nuclear power stations. The policy measures to deal with HLW disposal also employ similar social models to those embedded in the siting process of nuclear power stations. The way of thinking that backs up the policy measures relies on two assumptions:

1. The amount of money put into a target area can be commensurate to all kinds of demerits that may result from siting.
2. As such, the problem of HLW disposal siting can be solved by appropriate compensation, if the local residents are rational enough in terms of economic calculation.

In other words, the logic of the social model assumed to fix type-two underdetermination expressed above could involve these assumptions, if introduced in the

Table 7.3 Financial State of Local Governments Showing Interests in the Geological Survey for HLW Disposal

Prefecture	City/town/village	Population	Population growth (%)	Financial Power Index	Grant from Three Laws on Power Source Siting	Year
Kochi	Toyocho	2,947	−12.97	0.13	Not obtained	2010
Aomori	Higashidori-mura	7,252	−9.82	1.06	Obtained	2010
Akita	Kamikoani-mura	2,727	−12.23	0.12	Obtained	2010
Kochi	Tsuno-cho	6,407	−6.63	0.16	Not obtained	2010
Nagasaki	Tsushima-shi	34,407	−10.59	0.19	Not obtained	2010
Nagasaki	Shinkamigoto-cho	22,074	−11.84	0.27	Not obtained	2010
Kagoshima	Minamiosumi-cho	8,815	−10.93	0.17	Obtained	2010
Kagoshima	Uken-son	1,932	−5.66	0.10	Not obtained	2010

Source: Produced from http;//area-info.jpn.org/index.html (ascertained on June 25, 2010, in Japanese).

Note: Population growth is estimated for the term from 2005 to 2010. To be accurate, mergered municipalities during this period were excluded. Data excluded were Izumi-mura, Fukui (present Ono-city), Yogo-cho, Shiga (present Nagahama-city), Saga-cho, Kochi (present Kuroshio-cho), Nijo-cho, Fukuoka (present Itoshima-City), Goshoura-cho, Kumamoto (present Amakusa-city), and Kasasa-cho, Kagoshima (present Minamisatsuma-city).

actual implementation process of HLW disposal policy; therefore, the elaborated logic can be expressed by the following formalism.

$$[\text{PUS} \cdot (\text{Com} \to \text{SocAcp}) \to \text{For P}] \vee [\overline{\text{PUS}} \vee \overline{(\text{Com} \to \text{SocAcp})} \to \text{Against P}]$$

*PUS: Public understanding of science and technology; P: Projects; Com: Compensation; SocAcp: Social acceptance of demerits

This is the overall logic of the social model employed by the governmental, industrial, and academic sectors in advising and persuading local governments and citizens residing in targeted siting areas. What, then, is the social response of these local governments and citizens?

The hidden social model failed in HLW disposal: resistance in Toyocho

Policy measures materializing from the above logic completely failed due to a movement by residents in Toyocho who spoke out against the town mayor, who made public a positive response to the measures. A series of events leading from a self-nomination by the town mayor for a preliminary documentary survey into the history of geological events to the complete failure can be arranged into order as follows (all events took place in 2007):

Table 7.4 Timelines of HLW Siting Failure in Toyocho in 2007

Date	Events
1/25	The town mayor applied for a preliminary documentary survey.
2/6	The governors of the two adjacent prefectures stated their objection to the survey to the government and NUMO.
2/9	Bill requesting the resignation of the town mayor passed a special town council.
2/15	Bill opposing the survey passed one of the adjacent prefecture assemblies.
2/19	A pro-town mayor group named "How should our town be tomorrow?" was formed.
2/22	Bill opposing the survey passed another adjacent prefecture assembly.
2/27	Forum for discussion of the safety of underground disposal was held, enrolling both pro and con groups.
2/28	NUMO requested permission from METI for the survey.
3/2	The town council received the bill prohibiting the carriage of radioactive waste in the town.
3/22–23	Further discussions were held about the bill.
3/27	The council rejected the bill following the additional discussions.
3/28	METI granted permission to examine the survey plan.
4/5	The town mayor resigned.
4/6	The town mayor had a meeting with the governor of one of the adjacent prefectures.
4/12	An "Energy Support Group" meeting was held by METI in the town.
4/22	A new town mayor opposing the survey was elected by a vote of 1821 to 761 (amounting to 89.26 percent of the vote).
4/23	The new town mayor sent a paper canceling the earlier application for the survey to Agency for Natural Resources and Energy and to NUMO.
4/25	NUMO requested that METI permit a change in its business plan.
5/20	Bill for regulations that prohibit the carriage of radioactive nuclear waste passed the town council.

To understand or not to understand? 179

Voices of the citizen sector can be ordered along this series as well, based on articles in local and commercial papers and leaflets created by opposition movements (see Table 7.5).

Table 7.5 Articles in Local and Commercial Papers and Leaflets Created by Opposition Movements: 2006–2007

Date	Contents and Sources
12/27	"No fallout in Toyocho"; "The town mayor intends to apply?"; "Everything has proceeded in secret"; "Sweet but dangerous temptation: What the huge grants mean" (Rentai, 12/27, 2006)
1/25	A citizen group started a campaign to collect signatures for enacting regulation that would prohibit the carriage of radioactive waste and the construction of an underground disposal site in the prefecture. (Kochi Simbun, 1/28, 1/31, 2007)
2/1	"Support for making a direct claim for the enactment of the regulation to Prohibit the carriage of radioactive waste"; "Let's raise [our] voice against the reckless action of the town mayor" (Rentai, 2/1, Extra, 2007)
2/3	"Bill opposing the survey submitted with 2,179 signatures"; "The town mayor submitted the application form at his own discretion last year too"; "Democracy ignored"; "Evidence tells the truth, we will not be deceived" (Rentai, 2/3, 2007)
2/6	"Volunteer residents issued a joint communiqué requesting the town mayor to cancel the application for the survey"; "We cannot accept"; "Arbitrary decision overturns democracy" (Kochi Shimbun, 2/6, 2007)
2/6	"The direct claim was submitted to the election board of the town for the enactment of the regulation to prohibit the carriage of radioactive waste and the construction of facilities for its disposal, with 50 percent signatures out of the electorate." (Kochi Shimbun, 2/7, 2007)
2/6	Six anti-nuclear movement groups requested the cancelation of the application for the survey. (Kochi Shimbun, 2/8, 2007)
2/15	Three-hundred volunteer residents rallied in front of the town hall regarding the cancelation of the application for the survey. (Kochi Shimbun, 2/13, 2/14, 2007)
2/19	A group of 40 supporters of the application for the survey was established, inviting the head of the Agency for Natural Resources and Energy's PR office and several NUMO officials to hear their argument: "Since the residents of opposing groups fear radioactivity and believe that there is no halfway cancelation, the government should explain more about the safety of the disposal"; "Part of the problem is the poor understanding of the current financial state of the town by the residents." (Kochi Shinbun, 2/20, 2007)
2/27	A discussion forum was held and drew 450 supporting and opposing residents.
3/2	An opposing resident stated: "If the facilities for disposal are constructed, people will leave the town and depopulation gets worse." (Kochi Shimbun, 3/2, 2007)

(*Continued*)

180 *To understand or not to understand?*

Table 7.5 (Continued)

Date	Contents and Sources
3/24	A representative of supporters stated: "We should like to keep studying from a neutral viewpoint rather than from pro or con viewpoint." (Denki Shimbun, 3/27, 2007)
3/27	A representative of the opposition groups stated: "We have intended to cancel the construction of facilities for the disposal by the enactment of regulation but the town mayor has never accepted our request. We cannot help feeling indignation against the deed. We will seek recall as the last means to resort to." (Kochi Shimbun, 3/24, 2007)

The main issues raised by the citizen sector can be summarized into the following three items:

1 The town mayor acted on his own discretion, without consulting residents;
2 The social implications of the large grants for permitting a documentary survey; and
3 The poor understanding by the town residents of the documentary survey and implications of the carriage of radioactive waste.

Item 1 was due to shortcomings regarding the application procedure for the documentary survey, as the application was designed to be made by the discretion of town mayors without requiring permission from town councils.[21] As such, responsibility for this item belongs to the designers of the application procedure in general rather than problems specific to Toyocho case. Therefore, substantial issues perceived by the citizen sector in Toyocho with respect to the siting of HLW disposal facilities are found in items 2 and 3. Item 2 suggests that the two assumptions introduced to fix type-two underdetermination mentioned above do not work in the actual field setting of Toyocho, as represented in the following statement: "The grants to be given to local governments in question in exchange for the siting of HLW disposal are tremendously huge. This huge size of the grants tellingly attests how dangerous the siting could be." (*Rentai*, December 27, 2006)

As mentioned above, however, the grants were to be given to Toyocho for applying for a documentary survey of the history of geological events (the first of three steps in the siting process), not for accepting the siting of radioactive waste disposal facilities.[22] Despite this, the citizen sector in Toyocho suspected something dangerous due to the large grants amounting to almost the town's annual budget to be given by the government. As a result, the citizen sector opposed the governmental plan. The nature of this issue cannot be understood within the bounds of a broad public understanding of science and its variants, where the promotion of public understanding sponsored by the government has been assumed to encourage acceptance of governmental offers. Contrary to this assumption, in reality there arose a new dimension of distrust among the local residents, one that made the residents suspicious of a hidden intention and/or a hidden social model aimed at public understanding of science. Once this distrust surfaced, it encouraged the residents to form their own attitudes free from the hidden social model.

If monetary compensation commensurate with risk can solve the problem of siting, as has long been assumed, the problem could be reduced to a transaction between the governmental sector and local residents within the citizen sector. In such a situation, trust could efficiently lessen transaction costs,[23] and distrust could cause the costs to increase infinitely. Therefore, distrust is expected to result in failure of the transaction itself, which aligns with the course of events that occurred in Toyocho. In fact, the election for a new town mayor was overwhelmingly won by the candidate who opposed the geological survey (1,821 votes), against the other candidate who supported the survey (761 votes).[24]

Item 3 was raised at the inauguration ceremony of the Association for Considering Toyocho's Tomorrow, a new organization that was established to support the offer from the government. This item is comprised of two elements: how to resolve the town residents' request for the government to explain the safety of the potential facilities, and how to make the town residents understand the financial condition of the town. Either element makes sense only with the assumption that a better understanding of the safety and the financial condition will lead to a smoother promotion of the siting of HLW disposal facilities, an assumption that seems to be uniformly shared by both the governmental and the academic sectors.

Despite the failure of Toyocho, the way of thinking that combines commensuration by money with compensation is still employed to fix type-two underdetermination in HLW disposal in the post-Fukushima situation. Looking at the policy trajectory of HLW disposal in Japan, a change did occur from a solicitation policy for application of local governments for siting HLW disposal facilities to a nomination policy, which is made in a top-down manner by the central government during the period from 2013 to 2015.[25] In May 2013, the METI formed the Radioactive Waste Working Group of the Advisory Committee on Energy and Natural Resources as an expert committee to consult on the policy change and also established the Geological Disposal Technology Working Group as its "sister commission" in October of the same year. Both of these working groups published their interim reports in May 2014 (METI 2014a, 2014b). After discussions within those working groups, and METI's in-house policy decisions at ministers' meetings for final disposal held in December 2013, September 2014, and May 2015, the revised "basic policy for final disposal" was decided by the cabinet on May 22, 2015. One key point of the policy is as follows: "Clear recognition of uncertainty and the lack of public support and emphasis on trust re-building through more participatory and transparent policy and practices in the HLW final disposal program" (METI 2015).

In contrast to the outlook of this policy change on HLW disposal by METI, Sugawara and Juraku (2010) pointed out that the Japanese HLW program still had a strong tendency to trivialize the issues into a so-called "siting problem," neglecting the fact that the core of HLW management is the societal challenge of coping with unparalleled uncertainty, including type-one and type-two underdetermination and potentially infinite responsibility. The tendency closely coexists with the above-mentioned way of thinking that combines commensuration by money with compensation due to past successful experiences of nuclear power expansion in Japan, as represented by the siting of the nuclear power stations. Policy-makers have long believed that the obstacles to nuclear programs have little to do with fundamental institutional design and a basic way of thinking but rather that they are strongly related to social acceptance or political and social management of public trust and perception. One of the most important foci of social acceptance, using the example of siting of nuclear-related facilities, was the siting of the facilities itself. This tradition seems to have weakened Japanese policymakers' awareness of the link between expertise, democratic decision-making, and the quality of policy-making processes and implementation. This traditional way of thinking depends on the assumption that the management of the political atmosphere and public opinion is most important, while leaving aside the way of thinking that combines commensuration by money with compensation.[26]

Thus, the ways of thinking and assumptions introduced to fix uncertainty involved in social decision-making, particularly type-two underdetermination, seem to follow a path set by past experience and events. This "past track" has been institutionalized in power source siting laws; however, this path-dependency eventually led to the Fukushima accident, as shown in Chapter 3. Therefore, what is mentioned above regarding HLW disposal is nothing but adherence to erroneous precedents as an element of structural disaster, another argument for HLW disposal issues as an ongoing structural disaster. As far as this following of an erroneous past track as an element of structural disaster is concerned, this has not changed even with the shift in the procedure of site selection process for HLW disposal from a solicitation policy to a nomination policy, as mentioned above. To reconfirm this point, the past track pertains to social models made up of the assumptions of risk sciences, and the way of thinking and the patterns of behavior as represented in commensuration by money for compensation. There is a structural similarity between a policy trajectory of HLW disposal and the concept of ongoing structural disaster in terms of adherence to erroneous precedents.

Subtler configurations of intra-sector and inter-sector relationships

Within the sectors concerned, there arises a different kind of structure when examining the Toyocho case. Within the governmental sector here, the central government acts as a subsector, requesting local residents within the citizen sector to be tolerant of potential hazards while the local government of Toyocho as another subsector conflicts with the central government. Although there is no directly available observation of an academic subsector pertaining to the Toyocho case, except for the risk science subsector, potential subsectors could be geology, mineralogy, petrology, geophysics, geochemistry, and seismology. Within the citizen sector, there is a sharp conflict between subsectors supporting the central government's policies for HLW disposal and other subsectors opposing.

To understand or not to understand? 183

Regarding intersectoral relationships in the Toyocho case, two relationships can be observed. First, the risk science subsector of the academic sector and the citizen subsector supporting government policies share a social model, such that the permeation of public understanding activities contributes to the smooth promotion of HLW disposal. Second, NUMO as a subsector of the governmental sector and the citizen subsector opposing government policies have sharply conflicting social models as to the effects of subsidies provided by the government. The social model of the former reveals that the large subsidies from the government enable the concerned parties in the citizen sector to accept a potential hazard, whereas that of the latter regards this as too dangerous to accept.

The overall configuration of Toyocho's internal structure of respective sectors and the intersectoral relationships between the subsectors is expressed in Figure 7.1.

The sector model developed in Chapter 2 is important in understanding the overall configuration in Figure 7.1. Because the structure depicted by the sector

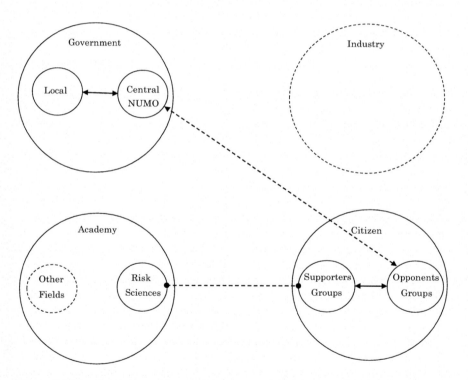

Figure 7.1 Configuration of Internal Structure within Sectors and the Intersectoral Relationships between Subsectors

Note: Double-headed arrows indicate conflicting relationships, and lines with double black circles indicate relationships that different agents share views. Solid lines indicate relationships within sectors, and dotted lines between sectors. Dotted circles indicate sectors and subsectors that are not problematized here.

model is a "snapshot" of a particular time, the configuration can change depending on the situation surrounding the sectors and actors therein. For example, NPOs and/or NGOs are usually understood in the citizen sector as being organized to fulfill the needs of inhabitants in the local areas; however, taking into account the mutually conflicting citizen subsectors that either support the central government's policies for HLW disposal or oppose them, there is a possibility that NPOs and/or NGOs organized to invite HLW disposal sites to a local area are set up in collaboration with the central government promoting related policies. For example, the HLW committee of the Nuclear Power Section of Electric Utility Branch of Advisory Committee for Natural Resources and Energy of METI set forth the following "reinforcement measures" based on the failure of the Toyocho case:

> To obtain understanding and cooperation in siting the final disposal stations, it is necessary to develop public understanding activities from the perspective of the people involved. Therefore the government and NUMO should promote grassroots public understanding activities in collaboration with NPOs and their networks in the citizen sector such as workshops in the local areas in question.
>
> (METI 2007: 8)

When the reinforcement measures are successfully materialized, a new interrelationship will emerge between NUMO as the governmental subsector and an NPO promoting HLW disposal policies of the government through public understanding activities for the citizen subsector, as shown in Figure 7.2.

The configuration of agents involved in HLW disposal can thus change from the clear-cut conflict shown in Figure 7.1 to a "double-bind harmony," as shown in Figure 7.2, where the governmental and citizen subsectors can collaborate with one another. When such a change happens, it is crucial to discern whether the collaboration of the governmental and citizen subsectors reflects the will of the people involved or simply pretends to represent this will behind a smokescreen of harmony toward a hidden yet intentional end. The nature of this problem is similar to discerning whether relevant outsiders or choreographed ones are seeking to escape from structural disaster as a lock-in state, as discussed in Chapter 6. What is questioned in both problems is the distinction between agents who play an endogenous role based on their own will and agents who play a role choreographed by other stakeholders. This distinction is particularly important in HLW disposal issues, in which infinite responsibility for future generations will evolve. For example, when there is a split of wills among the citizen subsectors, as shown in Figures 7.1 and 7.2, social decision-making can blur this distinction and hide the existence of such a split. When HLW disposal facilities are accepted by the citizen sector as a result of such social decision-making, the tolerance of acceptance is imposed on one of the subsectors without allocating due social responsibility for creating such a subsector, whose will is actually impaired by the decision. Therefore, social decision-making related to HLW disposal issues

To understand or not to understand? 185

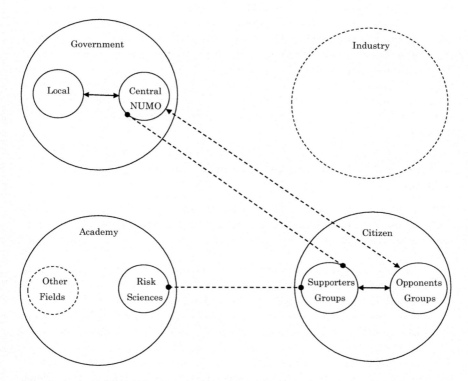

Figure 7.2 Configuration of the New Relationships between Governmental and Citizen Subsectors

Note: Double-headed arrows indicate conflicting relationships, and lines with double black circles indicate relationships that different agents share views. Solid lines indicate relationships within sectors, and dotted lines between sectors. Dotted circles indicate sectors and subsectors that are not problematized here.

requires making public the split of opinion within the citizen subsectors and, based on that design, making social arrangements to transform infinite responsibility to finite responsibility.

Speaking theoretically, fixing type-two underdetermination by simply assuming that the governmental sector advocates for HLW disposal policies and the citizen sector is opposed to them, and that the two sectors always conflict, could detract from the reality of specific situations. This is because the distribution of opinion within and between respective sectors could dynamically change, as illustrated above, beyond the dichotomous scheme of the governmental versus citizen sector. This expectation of dynamic change in the future leads to a higher degree type-two underdetermination that should be fixed by additional assumptions for policy-making and implementation. In this context, the Cabinet Office of Japan has developed authorization procedures for NPOs, organized workshops for reinforcing the infrastructure of NPOs, and, more generally, supported citizen groups' activities, mainly through subsidy measures. Thus, if something unsolvable happens in fixing type-two underdetermination, it is important to recheck the way of thinking and assumptions introduced to fix it, and replace them with new ones rather than patching over individual problems and sustaining those old ways of thinking. The need for such a structural reform of the decision-making system, rather than "piecemeal engineering," is one of the most important insights revealed by focusing on type-two underdetermination involved in HLW disposal.

Sociological implications of an ongoing structural disaster

Shifting the focus from front-end problems of nuclear power generation to back-end ones such as HLW disposal issues leads to four sociological points about an ongoing structural disaster:

1. Adherence to erroneous precedents carries over and reproduces problems, and can be seen in the way of thinking and the patterns of behavior in HLW disposal in Japan before and after the Fukushima accident. As this is one of the elements that characterize structural disaster, as shown in Chapter 1, in this sense, HLW disposal issues can be regarded as an ongoing structural disaster.

2. The complexity of the science-technology-society interface and the interdependence of its units has amplified type-two underdetermination, which in turn enlarged its intricate interaction with type-one underdetermination in HLW disposal in Japan before and after the Fukushima accident. As this is another element that characterizes structural disaster, in this sense, HLW disposal issues can be regarded as an ongoing structural disaster.

3. Conversely, what is specific to HLW disposal as an ongoing structural disaster is the emergence of infinite responsibility. As a result, to fix type-two underdetermination in HLW disposal issues, paramount importance should be given to a social arrangement that makes infinite responsibility finite and converts a social decision-making process into one in which the allocation of responsibility is logical. The complicated configurations of heterogeneous sectors and actors involved in the issues given by the sector model could be more instrumental than models that are optimized to achieve the consensus of an abstract "citizen" in serving as a common basis for allocating due social responsibilities.

4. Particularly in Japan, commensuration by money for compensation in HLW disposal has a path-dependent tendency in fixing type-two underdetermination. It is important to clarify the working mechanism of such a path-dependent tendency and find a new one toward the structural reform of social decision-making, particularly now that there are unsolved difficulties such as those manifested in the failure of the Toyocho case. In such a

situation, a complicated collaboration between the subsectors of different sectors could be formed, necessitating a prudent cross-examination to distinguish the choreographed citizen subsector (embodying the will of stakeholders) from the endogenous one as a realistic basis for social decision-making.

Policy and participation have become coupled in the current science-technology-society interface (Juraku, Suzuki, and Sakura 2007), and this coupling is closely associated with problems epitomized by "expert regress" and the "monotonically increased theory of participation" (Collins and Evans 2002). This chapter analyzes a still-perplexing situation where the problem of knowledge distribution cannot be self-contained within the sphere of knowledge, because it is inextricably related to the allocation of responsibility under type-two underdetermination, as exemplified by the siting of HLW disposal facilities. A similar situation can be found in environmental regulations and guidelines for bioethics, among others.

As such, it is pertinent to elaborate the sociological implications of the above conclusions via the arguments for users' responsibility for electricity consumption in the context of HLW disposal. The arguments for users' responsibility vindicate the responsibility of the users for HLW disposal, on the grounds that HLW is a necessary result of this use of electricity. One typical expression of these arguments can be found in a reply from METI to the nine public comments collected by the Advisory Committee for Natural Resources and Energy (2006), which were solicited between June 19, 2006, and July 18, 2006. One comment urged METI to change the "current generation" as a whole, which was supposed to be responsible for future generations regarding HLW disposal, to "those scientists, businesspersons, and politicians who have promoted nuclear power generation." To this, METI replied as follows: "Current electricity production is made mainly by hydro, thermal, and nuclear technologies, all of which require measures for environment preservation. Therefore those who use electricity are obliged to take responsibility for taking such measures."

There are two keywords that have been mobilized to maintain such arguments for users' responsibility for electricity consumption: NIMBY and responsibility for future generations. The term NIMBY is misused in this context, as it literally means a double standard of behavior, such as arguing for the safety of HLW disposal while rejecting the siting of its disposal facilities in the areas in which the arguers live.[27] Because users of electricity are simply consumers who do not necessarily overlap those who argue for the safety of HLW disposal, the usage of the term in this context is not accurate. As there is no double standard of behavior involved, the above arguments are difficult to distinguish from such households that urge the dumping of less waste and consuming fewer goods and/or services. While one might argue that the supply and consumption of electricity are public goods and/or services, the dictum of the household falls under private goods and/or services. It does not necessarily follow, then, that Japanese citizens are obliged to tolerate HLW facilities siting in exchange for consuming electricity under the Electric Utility Industry Law and other ordinances.

Even assuming that the people of Japan are obliged to accept the siting of HLW disposal facilities in areas where they reside in exchange for using electricity, it still does not guarantee that living without using electricity guarantees no responsibility for HLW disposal. Personal preference for living with or without electricity is one thing, and how to deal with HLW disposal is quite another, the latter belonging to the public sphere for which the social system as a whole should be responsible, independent of personal preference. Despite this, if there are arguments that attempt to confuse the two in the public sphere, it would be highly advisable to suspect the possibility that such arguments intend to guide someone to a predetermined way from the beginning.

Using the terminologies of the sector model, there is no difference between the governmental, industrial, academic, and citizen sectors in terms of their consumption of electricity. In contrast, a sharp difference between the sectors is inherent in the design of an electricity supply system – with the nuclear fuel cycle – made up of fossil fuels, natural gas, and nuclear energy in Japan. The governmental and industrial sectors (and the academic sector to a lesser extent) have been key players in the design of such a system, as shown in Chapter 3; however, the citizen sector has consistently played no role in such design processes, resulting in consumers not being given any resources related to or authority over the system design. To be more specific, the governmental, industrial, and academic sectors have been the stakeholders and agents concerned with technological development, production of due laws and ordinances, organizational developments, budget creation, human resources allocation, and the promotion of related industries, while the citizen sector has been consistently seen as a third party or bystanders. In this respect, there has been a sharp asymmetry between the governmental, industrial, and academic sectors and the citizen sector.

In addition, the governmental, industrial, and academic sectors have been the stakeholders requesting the citizen sector to accept the siting of HLW disposal facilities, while the citizen sector has been the only agents concerned who have been asked to accept and tolerate the siting. This reveals another asymmetry specific to HLW disposal as an ongoing structural disaster; therefore, from the viewpoint of the sector model developed in Chapter 2, the problem is that the infinite responsibility for HLW disposal is imposed on the citizen sector alone without social arrangements for making infinite responsibility finite and allocating social responsibility for disposal within social system as whole. The governmental, industrial, and academic sectors have been the direct stakeholders in designing the electricity production and supply system necessitating HLW, yet they have thus far evaded the infinite responsibility caused by HLW disposal, which reflects an unbalanced state in terms of the allocation of social responsibility.

The other key tenet to maintaining users' responsibility for electricity consumption is the responsibility for future generations, as exemplified in this statement by METI (2007: 1): "The current generation benefits from nuclear power generation in using electricity and therefore we owe the responsibility for disposing HLW produced from nuclear power generation." The similarity of logical structure here to the arguments developed by the other keyword (NIMBY, mentioned above) is evident in that the responsibility for HLW disposal is also derived from the consumption of electricity generated by nuclear power over a very long time horizon, leading from the current generation to future generations. This looks like the argument for the allocation of responsibility for HLW disposal among multiple generations, but from the viewpoint of the sector model, several modifications should be carefully made.

First, as mentioned above, since HLW disposal entails infinite responsibility and no single generation can assume infinite responsibility, the arguments are illogical without specifying the way to transform infinite responsibility into finite so that it could be socially allocated. Second, despite the necessity of devising social arrangements for transforming infinite responsibility into finite, there has been an extreme imbalance in which the citizen sector alone has been urged to accept and tolerate such "self-responsibility" for electricity consumption. This is tantamount to ignoring the responsibility inherent in the governmental, industrial, and academic sectors' design of the electricity production and supply system, which inevitably results in HLW. From the viewpoint of the sector model, it is desirable to make visible the responsibility for system design and actualize the fair allocation of social responsibility for such activity.

Prospects for moving away from ongoing structural disaster

As long as the extreme imbalance of the allocation of responsibility remains among the heterogeneous sectors, it would not be surprising to see that the agents with the least amount of resources and authority (such as the citizen sector) begin to take on the risk of accepting of HLW disposal facilities with little opportunity to raise their concerns in the public sphere. There seems to be little difference between social relationships among individuals in such a situation and in "such a war as is of every man against every man" in the "natural condition" (Hobbes 1651: 65).[28]

Considering the dual underdetermination given in Chapter 1 and elaborated upon in this chapter, it is difficult to find a unique or optimum solution to the issue of transforming infinite responsibility into finite in order to allocate fair social responsibility among heterogeneous agents within the social system as a whole regarding HLW disposal. One of the keys to breaking through this complicated situation is to make visible the connection between nuclear power generation, HLW disposal, and ensuing infinite responsibility, and make all parties aware of their connection. One way to guarantee that is to use the public space for comprehensively preserving, classifying, and updating all possible information on HLW disposal and related policies (pro or con) from all heterogeneous actors and sectors concerned. In general, a public record office dedicated to the serious issues relating to structural disaster that everyone can consult is crucial for reconciling techno-science with democracy under dual underdetermination.[29]

From the viewpoint of the sector model, the heterogeneous sectors should duly engage in setting up such a public record office to store all possible information on critical issues accompanying infinite responsibility, such as HLW disposal, to guarantee the citizen sector's awareness of the infinite responsibility that originates from any policy on this disposal. Without such a public space in which all types of information on controversial issues have been coherently accumulated, any effort to build consensus would result in a "deadlock" or an endless postponement of substantial decision-making.

When reflecting on HLW disposal issues as an ongoing structural disaster, one of the basic principles to securing the legitimacy and feasibility of policy measures should be that those agents who plan, implement, and evaluate policy measures must also accept due risk related to HLW disposal and undesirable effects from the policy measures. Specifically, it is almost impossible for any policy measures to obtain trust in the public sphere without redressing the asymmetry between the citizen sector being asked to thoroughly accept risks emanating from HLW disposal and the governmental, industrial, and academic sectors who are requesting it. Even if policy measures lacking trust in the public sphere (and, therefore, legitimacy) are carried out, it would be difficult for them to serve the public interest because measures that lack trust and legitimacy could be easily transformed as a means for gaining private interest.[30] Accordingly, if the governmental sector is willing to expend a large subsidy (such as the 2 billion yen offered to Toyo-cho) to solicit the citizen sector's acceptance of the geological survey for HLW disposal, it is advisable to abolish a means of expenditure that lacks transparency and accountability and is almost indistinguishable from bribery, and to create new social arrangements by the fund to redress the noted asymmetry.

If the governmental sector, for example, is still willing to expend such funds to solicit the targeted local governments suffering from declining populations and the resulting financial crisis to accept the siting of HLW disposal facilities and associated risk, part of the fund should be used to solicit members of the governmental, industrial, and academic sectors to live in the targeted local areas in question to monitor and manage the facilities, and make related technological development and geological surveys. This means that the asymmetry between the citizen sector and the governmental, industrial, and academic sectors in accepting HLW disposal as well as the asymmetry between the flow of money and that of human resources would be redressed. In doing so, the acceptance and tolerance of HLW disposal should be equally shared by the heterogeneous sectors within the social system as a whole, which in turn would correct the extreme imbalance in terms of the allocation of social responsibility for the problem. Such an effect would eventually take the situation one step closer to transforming infinite responsibility for HLW disposal into finite; thus, the acceptance of HLW disposal should be converted to the redevelopment of the targeted local areas, including betterment of residents' living conditions. Only with such a change can the lack of trust in policy measures and the resulting absence of legitimacy be ameliorated.

Of course, the above illustration presupposes the sector model, and there might be other possibilities for changing the nature of HLW disposal issues from an ongoing structural disaster to a problem that is not as far-reaching. As far as the problems entailing infinite responsibility are generally concerned, however, it is essential to break the chain of distrust and avoid the resulting loss of legitimacy because the existence of the chain necessitates a large amount of both human resources and money to cancel negative social outcomes from the chain by continuously carrying out directed consensus building, bilateral communication, and participatory evaluation, as well as appearance management practices as the means of temporarily patching over the problems. Understanding HLW disposal as an ongoing structural disaster suggests the need to disengage from a policy trajectory devoid of fair and balanced sharing of social responsibility for the disposal and to implement drastic structural reform across all sectors involved.

8 Conclusion
Renovating the principle of symmetry beyond a pre-established harmony between expertise, policy, and democracy

This concluding chapter integrates all of the main points discussed previously and analyzes the overall implications of the findings regarding currently under-researched but critical issues within the science-technology-society interface to provide inspiration for future research. First, the main points made in each chapter will be outlined to reveal the overall structure of arguments developed throughout the book. Second, a new consideration of the principle of symmetry will be introduced, one that provides a more realistic and fair configuration of socially responsible agents when allocating responsibility for decisions on crucial yet uncertain and complex issues such as HLW disposal. Third, acknowledging the strong uncertainties represented by dual underdetermination, this chapter presents a multiple-assumptions approach to communication between experts and the citizen sector, the provision of scientific advice for the governmental sector, and public funding for research by the academic sector. To properly carry out decision-making under such strong uncertainties in the science-technology-society interface, this multiple-assumptions approach can enable more extensive policy options to the public sphere so that those who are obliged to be engaged in decision-making can do so with a well-balanced and broad perspective – broad enough to go beyond simplistic thinking, which is the pitfall of assuming that there is a pre-established harmony between expertise, policy, and democracy along the horizon one has been accustomed to seeing.[1]

Overall structure of the arguments developed throughout the book

Chapter 1 presented new sociological frameworks for investigating extreme events by breaking through the self-reinforcing loop of risk society arguments, which is perpetuated when ad hoc interpretations of the event are made via hindsight. Three important points are made: (1) the concept of structural disaster is introduced and defined as the key to proper exploration of extreme events, detecting precursors of similar events, and contriving preventive measures; (2) through the concept of structural disaster, the nature and reach of institutionalized secrecy are illustrated with reference to the utilization of the SPEEDI, the report on HLW disposal by SCJ, and governmental decontamination policy in Japan in the post-Fukushima situation; and (3) to obtain a systematic mapping of different extreme events, a disaster matrix is presented as a heuristic device.

Based on these points, two broader sociological implications of structural disaster are drawn: (1) the explanation given by structural disaster entails counterarguments that cast doubt on cultural essentialism and any holistic explanation; (2) as this book regards structure as penetrating different dimensions throughout the disaster matrix, it follows that institutionalized secrecy, and structural integration coupled with functional disintegration can affect individual social action through a social systems in a fractal manner. Thus, an explanation given through structural disaster requires a scale-free application of the concept from social action through social system, which enables a wider variety of potential sociological implications.

Chapter 2 lays a theoretical foundation for frameworks that enables us to understand the static and dynamic aspects of structural disaster and articulate elements involved in the frameworks that are grounded on the sociology of science and technology. First, through a critical examination of the epistemological chicken dispute between SSK and ANT, epistemological, and ontological dimensions are extracted as rudimentary elements in defining the universe of discourse for examining the sociological theory of structural disaster. Six basic terminologies, ranging from individual agents to social systems, are defined to categorize the universe of discourse into four types and to specify the arguments in this book based on the units of analysis in the sociology of science and technology.

Second, as to the static aspect of structural disaster, the five-sectors model is formulated to show the importance of a multi-dimensional analysis of controversial issues in the science-technology-society interface as illustrated in extreme events, such as war and the Fukushima accident, among others. The term "multi-dimensional" in this book means overlapping and deviance between the state of the epistemological dimension and the ontological one, together with the similarities and differences among sectors. In addition, five types of actors are introduced to articulate multi-dimensionality of extreme events, in which the dilemma of knowledge commons is formulated. Regarding the dynamic aspect of structural disaster, the sociologically expanded theory of path-dependency is reformulated to show the generating mechanism and dynamic aspect of structural disaster. In particular, the social process leading to a lock-in state provides a focal point of the analysis of the dynamic aspect of the disaster as well as the process in which network effect, belief effect, and the initial divergence of technology could arise as key factors.

To integrate the static and dynamic parts of structural disaster, the book presupposes four postulates. First, the five elements of structural disaster mentioned in Chapter 1 pertain mainly to the features of the dynamic process generating structural disaster; in addition, the end state of structural disaster is not confined to the Fukushima accident alone but can include a variety of extreme events occurring across time, place, and social contexts. Second, the sector model formulated in Chapter 2 is presupposed as the background against which the dynamic processes embodying structural disaster is specified in subsequent chapters. Third, all individual agents are assumed to be stakeholders (in a broad sense), except where otherwise stated. Fourth, the focus of attention is placed on the creeping aspect within the context of structural disaster. In the creeping aspect, there are no well-defined boundaries where all actors (such as parties concerned, stakeholders, third parties, and others) gather, making it difficult to clearly delineate the problem area. With these postulates, the book's arguments intend to reconcile the broad scope of incorporating heterogeneous cases with the in-depth treatment of them systematically.

Chapter 3 examines a broader and richer perspective to trace the genealogy of structural disaster and generalize its sociological implications within a longer time span by investigating three independent cases: (1) the dual organizational structure of the Governmental Investigation Committee on the Fukushima accident; (2) METI's Report on Severe Accidents in 1992 and its connection with the framework of policy measures to deal with the post-Fukushima situation; and (3) the procedural legitimation of siting nuclear power stations based on existing power source siting laws. In doing so, the chapter generalizes institutionalized secrecy to institutionalized inaction and specifies two different types: institutionalized inaction enacting face-saving measures in the public sphere by blurring the responsibility of stakeholders, and that which develops an opportunistic utilization of extreme events by stakeholders to gain benefits that would be difficult to gain in a normal state. In either case, institutionalized inaction serves as a tool to realize a pay-off, be it saving face or material gain, at the cost of endangering public interest, including the safety of society.

Chapter 3 also discusses how adherence to erroneous precedents and secrecy as the elements of structural disaster can be traced back to the response of the contemporary National Institute for Ship Experiment to the Great Kanto Earthquake in 1923. These elements were passed down to the post-war period by institutional spin-offs triggered by the idea of a science- and technology-driven nation during the wartime mobilization of science and technology. Endless quick fixes as temporary countermeasures as an element of structural disaster were activated through the idea of a science- and technology-driven nation as a sacred cause during the wartime mobilization of science and technology, which was also passed down to the post-war period in the formation process of nuclear villages in Japan. Based on the genealogy of long-standing structural disaster from the pre-war to the post-war period, it is probable that at least three elements of structural disaster are still embedded in the current science-technology-society interface in the post-Fukushima situation: adherence to erroneous precedents; quick fixes for current problems as temporary countermeasures; and institutionalized secrecy. The workings of institutional inertia as represented by institutionalized inaction in generating structural disaster corresponds to the sociologically reformulated mechanism of path-dependent lock-in developed in Chapter 2.

Chapter 4 further investigates institutionalized secrecy by searching for the missing link between the Fukushima accident and the genealogical origin of structural disaster in the pre-war period. This chapter focuses on the patterns of behavior of the agents involved in a "hidden accident" that occurred immediately before WWII and was kept secret, with a comparative perspective of the Fukushima accident (which occurred more than 70 years later), in the wartime mobilization of science and technology in the pre-war period. Looking at the Fukushima accident from the perspective of structural disaster, it is noteworthy that critical information was restricted to government insiders despite the expected incalculable damages on the citizen sector as a result of the accident. This is reminiscent of the state of pre-war Japanese wartime mobilization, as represented in the hidden Rinkicho accident, in which all information was controlled under the name of supreme military authority. This chapter argues that the comparison between the two accidents is valid as far as the involved agents' patterns of behavior are concerned. Through the lens of structural disaster, this chapter contextualizes the possibility that functional disintegration, coupled with structural integration and institutionalized secrecy, can be detected both in the Rinkicho accident (in the wartime mobilization; referred to as the "hidden accident") and the Fukushima accident (in peacetime).

From the perspective of structural disaster, two kinds of structural similarity between the Fukushima accident and the pre-war Rinkicho accident are apparent: one relating to the development trajectory of technology and the other to institutionalized secrecy. Regarding structural similarity in terms of the development trajectory of technology, both Fukushima and the hidden pre-war accident took place within the context of wholly domestic production of a technology once produced externally or through license contracts, during which there was successful operation of domestically produced technologies extending by more than 10 to 30 years. In that particular sense, both accidents could be categorized as the failure of self-reliant technologies. The second structural similarity, in terms of institutionalized secrecy, cuts across pre-war military and post-war peaceful regimes. In both accidents discussed in Chapter 4, institutionalized secrecy was perpetuated by adherence to erroneous precedents as another element of structural disaster. Institutionalized secrecy in the pre-war Rinkicho accident is visible by observing the coupling of structural integration and functional disintegration within the contemporary military-industrial-university complex. If a structural similarity is still viable after contextualization, then the coupling of structural integration and functional disintegration could reside in the current government-industrial-university complex in the post-war situation, or that behind the Fukushima accident.

Differences between the two accidents include that adherence to erroneous precedents was eventually abandoned in the Rinkicho accident, whereas there has been no sign of such a dynamic correction of this adherence to erroneous precedents within the context of the Fukushima accident. When considering their similarities as structural disasters in terms of institutionalized secrecy and the differences in dynamic correction regarding adherence to erroneous precedents, there remains the possibility that the elements of structural disaster embedded in the Fukushima accident will continue in a path-dependent manner.

Thus, Chapter 4 implies that there is no demarcation between the pre-war social context of wartime mobilization of science and technology (resulting in nuclear bombing) and the post-war context of promoting science and technology in peacetime (manifested in nuclear reactors). In fact, the structural similarities between the Fukushima and Rinkicho accidents can be seen in four respects: adherence to erroneous precedents that causes problems to be carried over and reproduced; institutionalized secrecy; the coexistence of structural integration and functional disintegration of the science-technology-society interface; and the interdependence of success and failure among the interdependent units of the interface. In particular, when looking at the Fukushima accident as structural disaster, structural integration coupled with functional disintegration could be an end state of the disaster. This insight suggests the need for a significant structural remedy that is far beyond countermeasures that only temporarily patch over current troubles and serve to allow responsible agents to save face.

Chapter 5 examines structural disaster in renewable energy technology with particular reference to intricate relationship between OTEC development as a once-promising renewable marine energy technology and stratospheric ozone depletion. Based on this chapter's analysis, structural disaster was shown to go beyond the dichotomous distinction between nuclear power technology and renewable energy technology by using the case of the Sunshine project, which started in 1974 as an effort to solve resource problems through environmentally friendly initiatives. Despite these intentions, the project produced and published patents for OTEC using CFCs as the working fluid, even after the discovery of an ozone hole that was primarily attributed to CFC-12. However, this cannot be reduced to a simple policy failure, as the relevant ministries and agencies had duly issued a preventive guideline to deal with stratospheric ozone depletion. This case strongly suggests a hidden link between renewable energy technology development and global environmental problems due to incomplete information at the time of assessment and/or decision-making. The development of a "new energy" technology intended to solve resource problems resulted in damage to the stratospheric ozone, an unforeseen event by the decision-makers at the time of inception, yet was ignored when it became evident. In the process of granting patents using CFCs as the working fluid for OTEC after the discovery of ozone holes, the complexity of the science-technology-society interface that accompanies uncertainty (including both type-one and type-two underdetermination) had been either unnoticed or ignored. If unnoticed, this suggests the existence of structural disaster, in terms of the system's complexity and the interdependence of its units as aggravating problems; if ignored, this suggests the existence of structural disaster in that institutionalized secrecy developed across different sectors and blurred the locus of agents responsible and/or in that adherence to erroneous precedents causes problems to be carried over and reproduced.

In such a situation, it is crucial to create a built-in mechanism to evaluate large-scale, independent, long-term technological development projects through reflexive feedback-for-learning channels. This mechanism should prevent the fueling and re-fueling of the outdated projects' momentum made possible by transforming its originally intended purpose, lest structural disaster occur in a path-dependent manner in terms of enacting quick fixes for current problems that lead to further such fixes for temporary measures. What is particularly important is the need for an appropriate social framework within which a feedback-for-learning channel for early detection of the interconnection of completely different problems can work, rather than employing simplistic "quick fixes." To design such a social framework, it is necessary to determine how to allocate social responsibility for unanticipated consequences arising in the science-technology-society interface. To be specific, the principle of mild freezing (or low or zero growth rate) could result in the parties concerned changing a particular path-dependent technological trajectory to another when necessary, to supplement the precautionary principle. In cases in which the use of technology is strongly contingent on a complex science-technology-society interface – so that initial decisions made in good faith are likely to generate irreversible environmental change in a path-dependent manner in conjunction with structural disaster – the combination of mild freezing from within and precautionary principle from without is required.

Chapter 6 examines another mode of structural disaster in renewable energy technology and a way to break from a path-dependent process related to the development and diffusion of wind turbines that was initiated by the Sunshine project. Another mode concerns network effect and belief effect as triggers to sustain the path-dependent process as the dynamic aspect of structural disaster. Belief effect can be illustrated through the myth creation involved in the process, wherein Japan's wind turbine makers involved in the Sunshine project halted their wind turbine development. Two kinds of myths were involved in this situation: the first alluded to wind conditions unique to Japan; the second generalized the first myth without evidence into an almost universal statement that it would be infeasible for Japan to successfully generate power by wind turbines of any kind. These myths led to a network effect (wherein a given agent's decision-making is affected by formal and informal relationships with other agents), contributing to the obstruction of wind turbine development and accumulation of the technical know-how by most domestic wind turbine manufacturers, a hindrance that, in turn, reinforced the fixed trajectory of technology leaning toward diffusion by import alone.

The myths were broken for the first time by two types of relevant outsiders: (1) non-experts in wind turbine development, design, and production who were outside the closed circle of governmental, industrial, and academic sectors promoting renewable energy technology projects such as the Sunshine project; and (2) a small group made up of heterogeneous agents in a small town whose use of small-scale wind turbines for symbolic purposes in a post-disaster local context outside the market resulted in the viable production of electricity by these turbines as an unexpected result. In this case, relevant outsiders broke the fixed trajectory of technology dominated by imported wind turbines by adopting domestically produced wind turbines that functioned within the local context. The fixed trajectory of technology in this context corresponds to adherence to erroneous precedents as an element of structural disaster, as manifested in the fueling and re-fueling of a national project by a closed circle of experts and agents (such as the Sunshine project) with few meaningful results. As such, relevant outsiders' participation in technology selection could create a new horizon to change the fixed trajectory.

Generalizing these insights, it is possible to formulate three criteria by which the quality of the social decision-making processes can be evaluated: (1) Whether or not it is possible to escape from network and belief effects in the initial phase of social decision-making; (2) Whether or not it is possible for relevant outsiders to take part in both the technology selection and diffusion stages; (3) Whether or not it is possible to make public the reasons for national project failures and avoid inadequate explanations by the agents concerned, colored by myths.

This potential role of relevant outsiders, however, is not always useful because there can be both relevant and choreographed outsiders playing different roles. The demarcation between relevant and choreographed can vary depending on issues specific to different situations. Relevant outsiders in one instance, for example, could become irrelevant by playing the role of a mediator between different stakeholders (likely experts of nothing but impression management) to build a consensus in order to give official backing to a fixed trajectory. In such cases, choreographed outsiders could rightly meet the needs of the governmental sector by providing legitimacy to a given policy option, leading to a techno-mass democracy, or decision-making on technology by particular stakeholders via a legitimate social consensus in participatory appearance. If the distinction between democracy and mass-democracy is blurred by the stereotypical dichotomy of technocratic versus participatory way of decision-making, structural disaster could emerge in a path-dependent manner. This was manifested in the role played by Café Scientifique in the Tohoku district before the Fukushima nuclear accident, which perpetuated institutionalized secrecy (mentioned in Chapter 1). Therefore, specifying how to discriminate between relevant and choreographed outsiders in different contexts will be one of the most important tasks for further sociological studies on a new path that breaks from structural disaster.

Chapter 7 analyzes an ongoing structural disaster with reference to HLW disposal and seeks to clarify prospects for creating a new path toward the structural reform of social decision-making. HLW disposal as an ongoing structural disaster includes adherence to erroneous precedents causing problems to be carried over and reproduced, and quick fixes for current problems, leading to further fixes for temporary countermeasures. In particular, extreme imbalance of the allocation of responsibility remains among the heterogeneous sectors in HLW disposal. Leaving such imbalance, the agents with the least resources and authority, such as the citizen sector, are more likely to take on the risk of accepting HLW disposal facilities with little opportunity to raise their concerns in the public sphere.

Because infinite responsibility exists in the current science-technology-society interface with dual underdetermination, it is virtually impossible to obtain a solution without transforming infinite responsibility into finite in order to allocate fair social responsibility among heterogeneous agents within the social system as a whole regarding HLW disposal. One way to do this is to make publicly visible the connection between nuclear power generation, HLW disposal, and infinite responsibility, guaranteeing that the public space is used for comprehensively preserving, classifying, and updating all possible information on HLW disposal and related policies (pro or con) from all heterogeneous actors and sectors concerned. Such a public record office dedicated to the serious issues relating to structural disaster, which everyone can consult, is crucial for reconciling techno-science with democracy under dual underdetermination.

From the viewpoint of the sector model, all sectors should engage in the establishment of such a public record office, where all types of information on controversial issues have been accumulated. Such public goods are indispensable to guaranteeing awareness among those in the citizen sector of infinite responsibility for HLW disposal. Without such public goods, any effort to build consensus would result in a deadlock, or an endless postponing of substantial decision-making. Ultimately, it is necessary to redress the asymmetry between the citizen sector (requested to accept risk accompanying HLW disposal) and the governmental, industrial, and academic sectors (that have been requesting them to do so). For example, if the governmental sector is willing to expend a huge amount of public funds to solicit local governments' acceptance of even an early phase of the siting of HLW disposal facilities and associated risk – as they are often suffering from declining population and economic hardships – part of the fund could be used to solicit members of the governmental, industrial, and academic sectors to live in the targeted local areas to monitor and manage the facilities, and make related technological developments and geological surveys.

Thus, there is not only asymmetry between the citizen sector and the governmental, industrial, and academic sectors in accepting HLW disposal but also asymmetry between the flow of money and that of human resources from the latter to the former. Both asymmetries should be redressed; in doing so, the acceptance and tolerance of the burden expected from HLW disposal should be shared by the heterogeneous sectors within the social system as a whole, which in turn would correct the extreme imbalance in terms of the allocation of social responsibility for the problem. There is a need to disengage from any policy trajectory that is devoid of fair and well-balanced sharing of social responsibility for the ongoing structural disaster among the sectors involved and to implement drastic structural reform.

A renovated principle of symmetry

Based on the above points that are discussed in more detail in the previous chapters, this book will present a renovated principle of symmetry that details a more realistic and fair allocation of social responsibility for decisions on highly uncertain and complex issues such as HLW disposal. The scope of this renovation is twofold: first, symmetry between the governmental, industrial, academic, and citizen sectors in taking due social responsibility for decision-making on highly uncertain and complex issues and results from such decision-making; second, symmetry between the flow of money and human resources in accepting social responsibility.

To solve problems in the science-technology-society interface caused by structural disaster, trust in the institutional arrangements designed to solve these problems is particularly important in that the arrangements should be transparent in taking on due social responsibility for the results expected from such attempts. As institutional arrangements are supposed to be an embodiment of collective trust, when there is no institutional trust in such arrangements, they cannot fulfill the public role for which they were originally designed, and thus could be utilized for the benefit of private interests. This can occur for two reasons: first, when there is no renovated principle of symmetry nor well-balanced allocation of due social responsibility, sociological path-dependency coupled with institutional inertia could result in stakeholders responsible for structural disaster to continuously accept official posts that should be filled by a third party for the protection of public interest; second, when the results of structural disaster are so serious that there arises infinite responsibility for something socially decided (as exemplified by HLW disposal), there would be unanimous distrust of institutional arrangements that do not make publicly clear the due social responsibility of those who actually decided. This is because any party engaged in decision-making regarding such institutional arrangements could be the first victim when the next structural disaster happens.

It should be noted that to take social responsibility differs from the enhancement of a particular party's consciousness of social responsibility, though there are some cases in which the consciousness of social responsibility matters. For example, after hearing a vice president at TEPCO (who said nothing about the company's social responsibility for its behavior on the day of the Fukushima accident) speaking to the Parliamentary Investigation Committee, Ms. Sugako Hachisuka, who was a member of the committee and forced to evacuate from her home following the Fukushima accident, said: "Safety and the sense of safety . . . these are the very words we should be truly careful never to be tricked again" (NAIIC 2012d). Similarly, in the governmental sector, then-administrative vice-minister of METI Kazuo Matsunaga frequently responded with "I do not remember" and "I do not know" to questions from Kiyoshi Kurokawa, the chair of the committee. Kurokawa said: "It is a great pity that the administrative head of METI responsible for the Fukushima accident is so forgetful" (NAIIC 2012e). These instances reveal cases in which the consciousness of social responsibility matters to affected people at the time.

On the other hand, taking social responsibility in the context of this book concerns the essential social condition that enables any institutional arrangement to work as originally designed; namely, implementing a way to allocate due social responsibility for something socially decided that is not reliant on hindsight. Such action is critical to warranting the reliability of institutional arrangements; in particular, it is meaningful in the post-Fukushima situation to ask how it might be possible to portray a viable path that makes due social responsibility visible, and, based on this, devises institutional arrangements to avoid structural disaster. This concluding chapter will examine this idea by presenting three concrete proposals based on the previous arguments presented in this book.

Three proposals within the multiple-assumptions approach to structural disaster

Going back to the basic assumptions presupposed to analyze structural disaster in this book, two of them should be recalled here to address the three above-mentioned proposals. First, it is assumed that there are novel problems not yet seen in past situations and that have no unique solution due to dual underdetermination in the science-technology-society interface. Second, it is assumed that when facing such novel problems, it is difficult for society to have a uniform response because the behavior patterns of the governmental, industrial, academic, and citizen sectors are heterogeneous. That is to say, when problems that have no unique solution due to dual underdetermination are faced with a society made up of heterogeneous sectors, a divergence of responses is much more likely than a convergence within that society. This seemingly troublesome expectation provides important clues to the three proposals presented here.

To cope with strong uncertainties as represented by dual underdetermination in the science-technology-society interface, it is critical to make transparent the assumptions presupposed in dealing with extreme events such as the Fukushima accident. Assumptions here are quite different in nature from ideas and beliefs usually deep-rooted in value-orientation, as the term here means factors that are more instrumental because they function to specify basic, indispensable conditions to deriving possible conclusions to complex and novel problems that have strong uncertainties. This book argues that in approaching such problems, a divergence of approach is necessary to exhibit sufficiently extensive policy options so that a divergence of assumptions should be recommended. For example, when science and technology communication is approached by mediators (or interpreters/facilitators), if problems have strong uncertainties, such as dual underdetermination, so that no unique solution is expected, different kinds of interpreters or facilitators need to be secured. This is because strong uncertainties cannot be properly resolved in the science-technology-society interface without considering the opinions of those holding mutually heterogeneous conditions and deriving heterogeneous conclusions.[2] The effects of low-level radioactive exposure on the human body provide a well-known example to illustrate this point: If one assumes that there is a threshold for damage to the body by radiation, then it follows that there is no damage below this threshold; conversely, if one assumes there is no threshold, no one can deny damage at any level of exposure. Thus, in accordance with such divergent sets of assumptions and conclusions, what is communicated to society regarding a single issue can be quite different.[3]

Other similar cases that necessitate such divergent sets of assumptions and conclusions due to a lack of known unique solutions include the following: results of monitoring the diffusion of radioactive materials depending on measurement conditions; the future ratio of nuclear power generation to primary energy supply; best available energy mix; and different road maps showing prospects for the geological disposal of HLW depending on various probabilistic safety assessment models assumed for the disposal.

If only a single type of facilitator or interpreter is institutionalized in communicating these cases to society, this would unduly narrow the range of policy options to certain predetermined and limited bounds. This kind of institutionalization of the role played by a single type of facilitator or interpreter hints at the existence of a unique solution only in its limited options, while in reality there is no such unique solution. When this occurs in the science-technology-society interface, the institutionalization of a single type of facilitator or interpreter is almost equal to impression management, which would further complicate the novel problems in the interface. When there is significant room for impression management serving stakeholders, the situation hides the real stake of the agents concerned in the citizen sector, who are more likely to suffer from the problems in the first place.

To prevent this series of events from happening, this book proposes a new institutional design to promote communication in the science-technology-society interface with the least amount of reliance possible on impression management. In other words, this book proposes a transparent multiple-assumptions approach in institutionalizing facilitators or interpreters in the interface to secure divergent sets of assumptions and conclusions for problems with strong uncertainties. As society is comprised of the governmental, industrial, academic, and citizen sectors, and their behavior patterns are heterogeneous, there are two requisites for materializing this new type of institutional design: first, the divergent sets of assumptions and conclusions should be uniformly seen by each heterogeneous sector; second, all sectors should engage in and take due social responsibility for the institutional design and the results of communication activities based on the renovated principle of symmetry. Figure 8.1 shows the general conceptual configuration of this new institutional design.

The goal of this new institutional design is engagement of the governmental, industrial, academic, and citizen sectors based on the renovated principle of symmetry, where sectors supply equal amounts of human resources and a reasonable amount of monetary resources to set up a channel of interaction for different assumptions and conclusions. Equal representation of each sector is ensured in terms of the engagement of human resources while also allowing for unequal monetary contribution in the following manner. "Scientists and engineers" (shown in Figure 8.1) means a group of voluntary scientists and engineers (not necessarily professionals), and the academic sector in the figure means the overall academic community embracing all disciplines, ranging from natural sciences to social sciences and humanities. Based on the renovated principle of symmetry, the groups of voluntary scientists and engineers are equally engaged in the interaction of multiple-assumptions and conclusions without monetary contributions. Information is freely exchanged between those groups within the channel of interaction. All information that is released from this channel of interaction is circulated among all other sectors involved and then sent to the public record office of structural disaster (see Chapter 7), through which it is made public to serve social decision-making. By means of such an institutional design, the governmental, industrial, academic, and citizen sectors are expected to take due social responsibility for the design and results of communication activities in the science-technology-society interface.

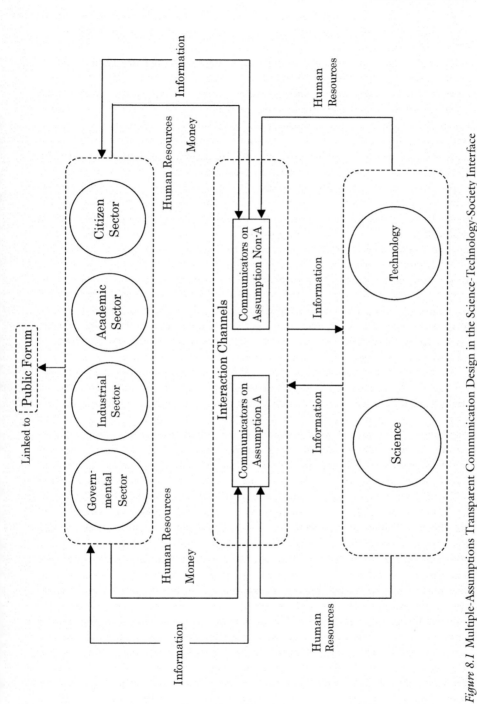

Figure 8.1 Multiple-Assumptions Transparent Communication Design in the Science-Technology-Society Interface

Note: The members of the academic sector are scholars except for scientists and engineers. Boxes with dotted lines mean that the activities within the boxes are transparent to all the members of social system.

When the output coming from the channel of interaction is changed to expert advice, a multiple-assumptions transparent expert advice design can be shown as follows in Figure 8.2.

The illustration of this institutional design is the same as that of the multiple-assumptions transparent communication design given above, except for one point: in this institutional design, all the sectors involved are expected to take social responsibility for the contents of expert advice as well as the overall institutional design. As the content of expert advice can directly influence the range of policy options, social responsibility for the contents of such advice means more direct responsibility for policy-making and implementation compared with the above multiple-assumptions transparent communication design. This does not imply, however, that all sectors involved take an equal amount of social responsibility for policy-making and implementation; rather, the governmental sector, for example, is expected to take on a larger share of responsibility in this institutional design because one of its most important functions is to make clear the distinction between social responsibility for expert advice in broadening and enriching policy options and that for final decisions on policy-making and implementation. In this multiple-assumptions transparent expert advice design, it is obvious who is responsible for working out policy options and who is responsible for the final decision in singling out and implementing one policy among other options. As long as this institutional design works as intended, it becomes transparent in the public sphere that the academic sector determines the policy options and the governmental sector singles out and implements a chosen policy.

These two designs are intended to avoid the utilization of the academic sector for the legitimation of policy-making, implementation, and evaluation by the governmental sector. When such a legitimation of the governmental sector's work by the academic sector is institutionalized, positive feedback is expected to reinforce the existing policy trajectory in a path-dependent manner; in such a situation, it is extremely difficult for those in the citizen sector, who have no expertise, to assess the validity of policy options for themselves nor realize the need to change policy trajectory when necessary to avoid or get out of structural disaster.[4]

The transparent multiple-assumptions approach can also be applied to public funding for academic research; however, such an application would need significant modifications specific to this issue. Within a public funding system for academic research, particularly for the early stages of research that explore complex and novel problems, there could be a sharp conflict in terms of basic assumptions that can lead to a mismatch between applicants and evaluators. For example, when pro-nuclear evaluators examine research proposals by anti-nuclear applicants and vice versa, it is obviously difficult to carry out a fair and presumably valid evaluation due to bias. A similar situation can also occur in transparent multiple-assumptions communication design in the science-technology-society interface mentioned above; however, there is a striking difference in the sociological implications within the different settings, in which the same approach is applied: conflicts of different assumptions in multiple-assumptions transparent communication design are simply a preference-based choice among the general

Conclusion 205

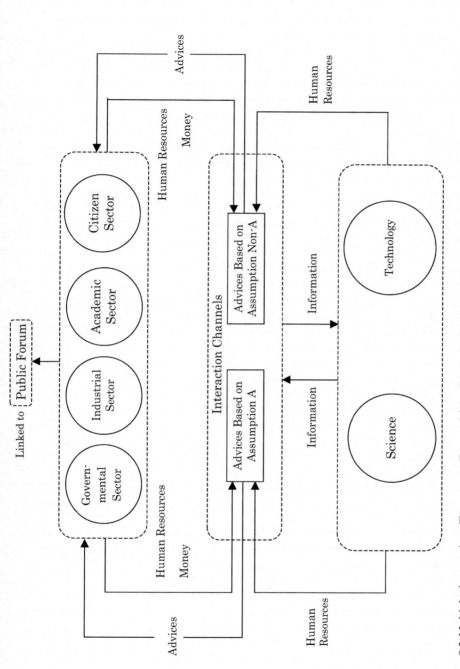

Figure 8.2 Multiple-Assumptions Transparent Expert Advice Design in the Science-Technology-Society Interface

Note: The members of the academic sector are scholars except for scientists and engineers. Boxes with dotted lines mean that the activities within the boxes are transparent to all the members of social system.

public in the citizen sector, while the same thing being applied to a public funding system for academic research pertains to validity and justification of public knowledge among experts in the academic sector. A lack of consensus implies quite different things depending on the two cases: it implies the presence of type-one underdetermination in the public funding system for academic research, and the presence of type-two underdetermination in communication design.

For this particular reason, in applying the transparent multiple-assumptions approach to a public funding system, it is necessary to create complementary institutional arrangements that are designed to differentiate multiple tracks through which the evaluation of research proposals is carried out in accordance with the contents of the aforementioned basic presupposed assumptions. For example, according to this modified institutional design, research proposals on an ideal energy mix, in terms of primary energy supply based on pro-nuclear assumptions and those based on anti-nuclear assumptions, are requested and evaluated independent of one another in the academic sector, to avoid bias regarding pro- or anti-nuclear standpoints. As a result of such an independent evaluation within each track, the best proposals are singled out independently and the results of the selected proposals' actual research are made public for "confirmation by replication" by others in the academic sector. Which research should be utilized, then, is left up to the discretion of other sectors, particularly the governmental sector regarding policy-making and implementation. In this respect, who is responsible for policy selection and implementation, based on which research, should be made transparent in the public sphere, which in turn would bring us a step closer to a more realistic, fair allocation of social responsibility for decisions made in the science-technology-society interface as well as the results from the decision.

In addition, based on an *ex post* evaluation of research results that were singled out and completed, further refinement of tracks could be sought in the next funding term; for example, new tracks with basic assumptions other than simplified pro- or anti-nuclear standpoints should be sought, because a track assuming nuclear power could cooperate with renewable energy, versus the track that assumes no nuclear power cooperation with highly efficient other sources of generation including fossil fuel, hydro power, and natural gas generation.[5] The continuous refinement and articulation of such tracks based on *ex post* evaluation of research results could work as one of the most compelling countermeasures against strong uncertainties, such as dual underdetermination (see Figure 8.3).

In particular, type-two underdetermination due to the saving of face of the agents involved and ritualized manners to fix this underdetermination deserve examination in light of drastic reform that includes refined and articulate procedures based on *ex post* evaluation. For example, despite the considerable type-two underdetermination in the current public funding system installed for allocating grants-in-aid for scientific research and evaluating the results of research conducted under the aegis of JSPS, the need for the heterogeneous agents involved to save face seems to have produced highly ritualized methods taken to fix the underdetermination. These methods contain a means to replace substantial peer reviews by relevant experts with highly formal procedures, to

Conclusion 207

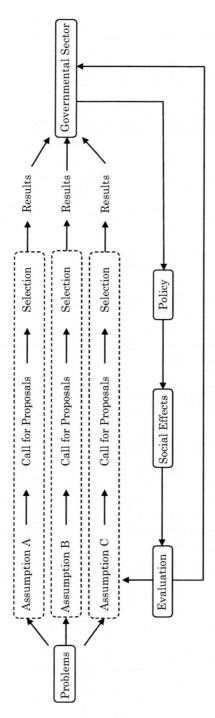

Figure 8.3 Multiple-Assumptions Transparent Design for Public Funding for Academic Research in the Science-Technology-Society Interface
Note: The number of assumptions could be modified as a result of evaluation for each term.

make up for the lack of a coherent system to search for relevant experts to evaluate research proposals across different disciplines, sub-disciplines, and problem areas in Japan's academic sector. A usual means is to replace the evaluation of the quality of academic work with the evaluation of compliance with procedural formality, as manifested in the administrative classification of disciplines, sub-disciplines, and problem areas, the classification which is often dissociated from the reality of academic activities. By this means, the more self-contained a project is in terms of paperwork, the more evaluation is conducted, and vice versa; therefore, an inherent tendency toward positive feedback ensues, which is another aspect of the above-mentioned overreliance on formality, which can hollow out substantial peer review in evaluation of research.[6] These ritualized manners are kept as institutionalized secrecy, which has functioned as a means of saving face for the heterogeneous agents involved, such as applicants and evaluators in the academic sector as well as those in the governmental sector in charge of granting public funding for academic research.

As regards the more realistic and fair allocation of social responsibility, the above-mentioned transparent multiple-assumptions approach to public funding for academic research with independent, track-based evaluation results in transparent social responsibility of evaluators in the academic sector regarding their decisions on those ultimately chosen from the applications. In the new institutional design, any actor or sector can see which evaluators (and with what basic assumptions) have singled out which applicants and with what quality of results by *ex post* evaluation. In doing so, inappropriate evaluators and less valid basic assumptions can be replaced. Thus, this institutional design could potentially renovate the quality of both the academic sector and governmental sector responsible for public funding for academic research.

A focus on drastic structural reform

The three proposals mentioned above are not presented as a means to realize "piecemeal" reform, because this could be somewhat easily transformed by external situations into an element of structural disaster as quick fixes for current problems, leading to further quick fixes for temporary countermeasures; rather, the proposals are presented as a means to realize drastic structural reform, exemplified by the following illustration. A large amount of special subsidies for power development based on siting laws in Japan were expended as compensation for the siting of nuclear power stations throughout Japan until the Fukushima accident (see Chapter 3); the same fund could be transferred into new arrangements for expenditure for opposite purposes, such as decommissioning nuclear reactors and promoting power generation by renewable energy sources in some strategically authorized zones, such as Fukushima Prefecture,[7] thus transferring the means into new arrangements for different goals, which is what is meant by drastic structural reform in this chapter. To supplement one collateral condition concerning the above-illustrated transference, there are no legal constraints on this transfer because the purpose of the laws is not confined to power development by nuclear power stations but, rather, is broad enough to include renewable energy sources, such as the siting of hydro-electric power stations.

The three proposals mentioned above aim for drastic structural reform in collaboration with the institutional design for the public record office of structural disaster proposed in Chapter 7. Even with such drastic changes, it could still be uncertain whether the total cost – including social costs – would be covered by the proposed reform. The reason for this suspicion lies in the deep-rooted nature of structural disaster, wherein facts have been dismissed and certain logic neglected up until the Fukushima accident, ranging from the dismissal of a new theory about the possibility of earthquakes around the plate boundary that was identified in the 1980s to the neglect of the logic that older types of reactors that were designed without incorporating new advances, such as those in the Fukushima Daiichi stations, should be updated (Macfarlane 2012). Even after the accident, vague countermeasures were mobilized to maintain the status quo, dismissing certain facts and paths of logic in the post-Fukushima situation, as mentioned in Chapters 1 and 3, a situation that corroborates the deep-rooted nature of structural disaster.

This is not to say that there is no need to take swift counter-action against apparent problems in the post-Fukushima situation; rather, this book argues that without carrying out drastic structural reform simultaneously while undertaking swift countermeasures, the causes of the problems will by no means disappear because of the deep-rooted nature of structural disaster. The transparent multiple-assumptions approach, as exemplified by the three proposals mentioned above, is intended to serve as only one effective means for drastic structural reform that could serve to reduce the cause of another novel and complex problem in the science-technology-society interface that could congeal in a path-dependent manner and stimulate the next structural disaster. To eliminate this possibility and ensure that those who are seriously impacted by the disaster will be able to come forward, we should trigger this drastic structural reform.

Of course, the social process solidifying novel and complex problems in the science-technology-society interface working with a sociological path-dependency at a deep-rooted level does not necessarily always bring about structural disaster. Naturally, there are other relevant conditions that make these potentials manifest as structural disaster. Roughly speaking, there are two relevant conditions yet to be discussed.

The "certainty trough" and the distribution of power in social decision-making

One of the relevant conditions concerns the necessity of the multiple-assumptions transparent approach, which can be clarified by the concept of a "certainty trough" (MacKenzie 1990: 370–372, 2001: 332–334). The concept indicates a situation in which the perception of certainty of those who are not the producers of knowledge (but who are committed to certain technologies and/or technological institutions/programs) would be significantly higher than that of the

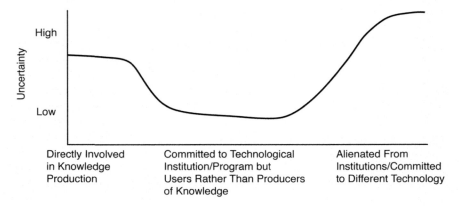

Figure 8.4 Certainty Trough
Source: MacKenzie (1990: 372, Figure 7.2), reproduced by the permission of the MIT Press.

certainty of those directly involved in knowledge production and that of those alienated from such institutions/programs (see Figure 8.4).

Those directly involved in knowledge production can be almost uniformly interpreted as experts and those alienated from technologies and/or technological institutions/programs can also be almost uniformly interpreted as non-experts. There is an intermediate category, however, in-between experts and non-experts, that could comprise those who "believe what the brochures tell them" (MacKenzie 1990: 371) or "managers without direct 'hands-on' involvement" (MacKenzie 2001: 334).[8]

This book interprets the above-mentioned intermediate category as well-informed non-experts who are authorized to get involved in relevant technologies and/or technological institutions/programs. Based on this interpretation, those who have official power to make decisions about technologies and/or technological institutions/programs fall into this category of well-informed non-experts. They range from politicians and bureaucrats within the governmental sector, who promote the introduction of certain technologies and/or technological institutions/programs, to agents of the industrial sector who actually introduce the technologies and/or manufacture them. Both experts and non-experts who have an equally high degree of perception of uncertainty are typically not those who are authorized to get involved in the social decision-making process and actually have power to decide. In terms of the distribution of power, therefore, there is a reversed configuration, as shown in Figure 8.5.

When comparing Figure 8.4 and Figure 8.5, there is a mismatch between the distribution of authorized power for decision-making in the science-technology-society interface and the distribution of perceived certainty, as shown in Figure 8.6. This reveals the possibility that agents within the governmental or industrial sector, be they concerned agents or stakeholders, who are well-informed non-experts

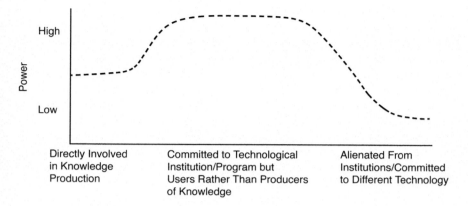

Figure 8.5 Power Distribution
Source: Produced based on MacKenzie (1990: 372, Figure 7.2).

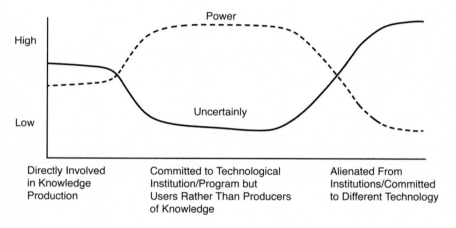

Figure 8.6 Mismatch between Power and Certainty
Source: Produced based on MacKenzie (1990: 372, Figure 7.2).

who have a strong tendency to underestimate uncertainty, can decide something important that is relatively independent of both academic sector experts and non-experts of citizen sector who are much more prudent and conservative in estimating the degree of uncertainty.

If this reasoning is correct, regarding who has the real power to decide and who has not, there is a split between the governmental and industrial sectors on the one hand and the academic and citizen sector on the other. The real problem in the science-technology-society interface, in terms of the distribution of power, resides in this split. The multiple-assumptions transparent approach, as exemplified by the three proposals in this chapter, is designed to function as an approximate solution to this divide within the social system as a whole, or by the renovated principle of symmetry enabling the academic and citizen sectors, where there is little authorized or substantial power to decide, to have opportunity to get engaged in the social decision-making process in parallel with the governmental and industrial sectors (which have such power). When this approach takes effect, the discrepancy between the distribution of power and that of perceived certainty will be leveled, allowing the unbalanced distribution of power and the perceived certainty to be redressed. With such changes, it is reasonable to expect that this approach would contribute to drastic structural reform against the mismatch between the distribution of power and that of awareness of uncertainty; however, when it is not sufficiently effective (for any number of reasons), this book conjectures that structural disaster would appear in conjunction with various conditions. Among these is circular arguments over the allocation of social responsibility in the science-technology-society interface, which is another relevant condition that results in the manifest of structural disaster when there is potential for such disaster.

Circular arguments in the science-technology-society interface

In this context, there are at least four critical conditions without which it is meaningless to ascribe responsibility to a particular agent, be it sectors or individuals. Attribution of responsibility here means that those who actually decide something socially important should be responsible for the results of that decision. While this might initially seem reasonable, the following four critical conditions solidify its logic.

First, any decision-making by agents should be mutually independent. When there is a network effect and/or belief effect (discussed in Chapter 2 and Chapter 6), there emerges a complex interaction of multiple agents within the sphere of decision-making, so that it becomes virtually impossible to particularize which part of the decision-making belongs to which agent. Second, the broadest possible options in decision-making should be presented uniformly among the agents involved. Partial disclosure of options can reveal the existence of a hidden agenda; as a result, any decision made under such a condition is considered a guided one, making it difficult to determine who is responsible for what aspects. When there is a difference in accessibility to or availability of the broadest possible options by a group or groups of people, it is also difficult to determine responsibility of a particular agent. Third, responsibility can be defined only in a fixed situation. When a situation is fluid and/or complex, leading to possible unintended social consequences of purposive individual action, it is impossible both in theory and in practice to determine who is responsible for what. In such a situation, an accurate assessment of the situation, which is made up of multiple courses of mutually entangled events, would precede the determination of responsibility. Fourth, even after confirming the existence of the above three critical conditions, there could be cases in which it is practically impossible to determine allocation of responsibility in the science-technology-society interface. In particular, when the arguments for assigning responsibility are circular in structure, allocation of responsibility cannot be determined within the interface. For example, ad hoc employment of technological determinism and social determinism (as defined in Chapter 2) can easily produce such a circular structure. Ascribing the responsibility for a social problem in the interface to the state of science and technology by technological determinism while at the same time ascribing responsibility for the state of science and technology to the state of society by social determinism brings us back to the first argument, after which a continuous circulation of arguments will follow.[9] The possibility of this kind of circular argument makes it difficult to specify and properly allocate responsibility for structural disaster because of the circular structure of the argument itself.

According to technological determinism, the state of science and technology without due effort to replace an old nuclear reactor type with the latest one is responsible for the Fukushima accident; at the same time, according to social determinism, the state of society as exemplified by the nuclear village is responsible for such a state of science and technology. This argument brings us back to another argument for ascribing responsibility for the Fukushima accident as a social problem to the state of science and technology, or a state with little attention to extreme events in designing multiple protections by technological determinism. As a result of this type of circular argument, particular agents in the governmental, industrial, and academic sectors rarely come to the forefront in specifying and allocating due responsibility. Without breaking down society into sectors and specifying particular agents of these sectors, society as a whole is assumed to play the role of consumer with only a "Yes" or "No" response to nuclear power generation.

If the citizen sector can be taken as an independent constituent of society, this assumption might provide one approximation. This book posits, however, that there are at least three other sectors in society; moreover, as suggested above, there is a divide in terms of the distribution of power between the citizen sector coupled with the academic one on the one hand, and the governmental and industrial sectors on the other. Therefore, this conceptualization of society resulting from circular arguments in the science-technology-society interface is over-simplified because it makes it extremely difficult to make visible in the public sphere due agents in the governmental and/or industrial sectors who are expected to activate a feedback-for-learning channel (see Chapter 5) when there is the potential for structural disaster. Thus, through the inactivation of early detection of and preventive measures against structural disaster, circular arguments in the science-technology-society interface could manifest as a trigger of a structural disaster.

This over-simplified conceptualization of society seems to have originated in the concept of a consumer or user saying simply "Yes" or "No" to certain technologies, which can be seen in the "communication turn" of expertise since the 1990s. This turn indicates arguments that uphold the importance of bilateral communication and dialogue-based communication in an effort to link expertise, democracy, and policy in the public sphere. In a broad sense, the communication turn is the other side of policy turn, shown in the "third-wave" arguments in the social studies of expertise (Collins and Evans 2002, 2007). In fact, the communication turn of expertise has been institutionalized among bureaucrats in the governmental sector and scientists and engineers in the academic sector to such an extent that mastering communication skills as represented by bilateral communication and dialogue-based communication assumes that society is comprised of "consumers of expertise."

Thanks to this consumer-oriented turn of expertise – which has been taken for granted in understanding the relationships between expertise, democracy, and policy in the public sphere since the 1990s – it has become extremely difficult to accurately differentiate agents concerned and stakeholders in the science-technology-society interface. Particularly in extreme events, such as the Fukushima accident, it can be inferred that there arise mismatches and conflicts between agents concerned in the citizen sector and stakeholders of the governmental and industrial sectors, and that these mismatches and conflicts will be driven to incommensurable communication. If such a situation arises, it is difficult for a third party to make a thorough and accurate observation of the situation because the term "incommensurable communication" in this context means, literally, the discarded possibility of making a holistic observation by a third party. In such a situation, particular attention should be paid to "blind spots" that could result from the functioning of communication turn under strong uncertainties, which could aggravate inequality in the distribution of burdens from extreme events. A comparative analysis of ways to forget structural disaster could systematically reveal the blind spots of communication turn. Alternative relationships between expertise, democracy, and policy for the future should be presented only after the critical examination of structural disaster and its sociological implications, including these blind spots.

Looking toward the future

One could say that this book adopts a view of the darker side of the science-technology-society interface, and this would be true; however, the arguments presented here cannot be viewed under the ordinary, dichotomous saying that there is both a bright and a dark side to everything. What this book states, rather, is that when there is structural disaster in the science-technology-society interface, there arise significant blind spots that cannot be observed by sectors and/or actors that exist within the interface. This is, once again, different from a traditional dictum of sociology where observations cannot be made in a social vacuum. This implies that structural disaster generates victims, yet they tend to be intrinsically invisible within the science-technology-society interface, as suggested above, in relation to the divide between the citizen sector and other sectors such as government and industry. According to the renovated principle of symmetry outlined in this chapter, however, there is no reason to believe that such victims are confined to the citizen sector. Any actor within any sector could become a victim of structural disaster and, due to blind spots associated with such a possible divide, it would be difficult for anyone to be confident in defining who the victims of structural disaster actually are in the science-technology-society interface.

From this viewpoint, it follows that any actor in any sector who makes an observation is inclined to predicate the validity of that observation within the bounds of his or her expertise or knowledge. In other words, actors intrinsically tend to generalize the range of the validity of their observations to the science-technology-society interface as a whole. Thinking reflexively, when there is structural disaster, it is difficult for anyone to be unaffected by blind spots and what could be considered a confusing generalization associated with the disaster. For example, one may keep producing a myth that results in erroneously expecting a unique solution based on the accumulation of many temporary and makeshift quick fixes. As long as this way of thinking and patterns of behavior continue, there can be no solution to structural disasters.

It is better, then, to have failures in theory than failures in reality, particularly when those failures could have devastating consequences. While there is resilience both in theory and reality, failures in which resilience cannot be expected are more tragic. The term "resilience" originates in both physics and psychology, with engineers referring to the term as the counter-balancing power of external forces in the context of new safety requirements in designing artifacts after the Fukushima accident. In the context of social science literature concerning extreme events such as ecological discontinuities, organizational theorists refer to organizational resilience as a feature that is built prior to the accident (Linnenluecke, Griffiths, and Winn 2012).

When one faces a crisis from an irreversible, path-dependent process leading to lock-in in the real world but is also ignorant or pretending to be ignorant of the failures, one would be subject to devastating failures in the real world without an opportunity to learn. When the science-technology-society interface is in such a state, it is possible that at the very moment when self-evaluation of the interface is completing, the interface collapses. Ways to cope with the problems before, during, and after extreme events such as the Fukushima accident and the subsequent situations after the accident remind us of this possibility.

The devastating failure in the science-technology-society interface as a whole and as explored through the lens of structural disaster in this book pertains to everyone, whether they are affiliated with science and technology or not. There are no bystanders who are not impacted by structural disaster except for those who are ignorant or pretend to be ignorant of the blind spots of their perceptions of the science-technology-society interface. In light of this logic, the three proposals mentioned in this concluding chapter should be carried out in combination with methodological agnosticism to become effective in reality when facing structural disaster. For example, they will become effective when using methodological agnosticism to sort out problems that have strong uncertainties springing from structural disaster while dealing with daily affairs in a deterministic manner. The challenge may be small for one agent, but the accumulated interaction of challenges across sectors can become deterministic, affecting the quality of the science-technology-society interface of the following generations.

Appendix A
Policy formulation and revision-related administrative documents prior to the establishment of the Agency of Technology (June 1940 to October 1941) from the Kokusaku Kenkyukai Archives

Date	Classification	Documents	Submitters
6/25/1940	Top secret	Proposal for the enlargement of technical research institutes	The Planning Agency
8/3/1940	Top secret	On the promotion of science and technology	Ministry of Commerce and Industry
8/5/1940		Tentative plan of the integrated body of industrial technology in Japan	Niki, S.
8/8/1940	Top secret	Measures for organizing the integrated scientific research institutes	The Planning Agency
8/23/1940	Top secret	Outline of establishing the new system for science and technology	The Planning Agency
8/29/1940	Top secret	An exposition of the outline of establishing the new system for science and technology	The Planning Agency
8/30/1940	Top secret	Outline of establishing the new system for science and technology	The Planning Agency
9/2/1940	Top secret	Points of measures for the outline of establishing the system for science and technology	The Planning Agency
9/3/1940	Top secret	Outline of establishing the system for science and technology	The Planning Agency
9/5/1940	Top secret	Outline of establishing the system for science and technology	The Planning Agency
9/5/1940	Top secret	Points of measures for the outline of establishing the system for science and technology	The Planning Agency
9/10/1940	Top secret	Outline of establishing the system for science and technology	The Planning Agency

(*Continued*)

Appendix A 217

Date	Classification	Documents	Submitters
n.d.	Reference	Illustration of research institutes to be transferred	
n.d.	Reference	Illustration of major research topics	
9/13/1940	Top secret	Proposal for the outline of establishing the system for science and technology	The Planning Agency
n.d.	Top secret	Proposal for the outline of the measures for the promotion of science	Ministry of Commerce and Industry
n.d.	Top secret	Questions for the outline of establishing the system for science and technology	
9/26/1940	Top secret	Proposal for the outline of establishing the system for science and technology	The Planning Agency
n.d.	Top secret	Reply to questions and opinions from the Ministry of Education	
n.d.		Agreements reached during the Cabinet meeting	
10/1/1940	Top secret	Proposal for the outline of establishing the system for science and technology	The Planning Agency
n.d.	Top secret	Outline of explanation for the jurisdiction of the integrated administrative organization	
10/3/1940	Top secret	Proposal for the outline of establishing the system for science and technology	The Planning Agency
12/6/1940	Top secret	Proposal for points of measure for the outline of establishing the new system for science and technology	The representatives of the academic sector
12/18/1940	Top secret	Proposal for the outline of establishing the system for science and technology	The Planning Agency
1/3/1941	Top secret	Proposal for the outline of establishing the system for science and technology	The Planning Agency
1/1/1941	Top secret	Proposal for the outline of establishing the system for science and technology	The Planning Agency
1/20/1941	Top secret	Proposal for the outline of establishing the system for science and technology	The Planning Agency

(*Continued*)

Date	Classification	Documents	Submitters
1/24/1941	Top secret	Illustration of mobilization system under the control of aircraft production supervisors	
1/24/1941	Top secret	Explanatory leaflet for a proposal for the outline of establishing the new system for science and technology (1)	The Planning Agency
1/24/1941	Top secret	Explanatory leaflet for a proposal for the outline of establishing the new system for science and technology (2)	The Planning Agency
1/24/1941	Top secret	Explanatory leaflet for a proposal for the outline of establishing the new system for science and technology (3)	The Planning Agency
1/24/1941	Top secret	Explanatory leaflet for a proposal for the outline of establishing the new system for science and technology (4)	The Planning Agency
1/25/1941	Top secret	Proposal for the outline of establishing the new system for science and technology	The Planning Agency
1/25/1941	Top secret	Explanation of the organization and task of the Agency of Technology	The Planning Agency
n.d.	Top secret	Explanatory leaflet of a proposal for the outline of establishing the new system for science and technology	The Planning Agency
n.d.	Top secret	Proposal for the outline of establishing the system for science and technology	
n.d.		Ordinance for the mobilization of science and technology	
n.d.		Proposal for industrial property coordination law	
n.d.		Outline of expenditure for the establishment of the Agency of Technology	
1/26/1941	Secret	Explanatory leaflet of a proposal for the outline of establishing the new system for science and technology	The Planning Agency
n.d.	Top secret	On the tasks to be transferred to the Agency of Technology	
5/8/1941	Top secret	Proposal for the outline of establishing the new system for science and technology	The Planning Agency

(*Continued*)

Appendix A 219

Date	Classification	Documents	Submitters
5/21/1941		Opinions by the Minister of Education of the new system for science and technology and reply from the Prime Minister	
5/27/1941		Outline of establishing the new system for science and technology	Cabinet meeting
5/29/1941	Top secret	Tentative plan of the organization of the patent office	
5/29/1941	Top secret	Memorandum on the tasks to be transferred to the Agency of Technology	
6/9/1941	Top secret	Outline of the organization of the patent office	
6/9/1941	Top secret	Outline of the organization of the information office	
6/11/1941	Top secret	Outline of the preparatory committee for founding the Agency of Technology	
6/12/1941	Top secret	Outline of the association for founding the Agency of Technology	
6/15/1941		Supplement for the association for founding the Agency of Technology	
6/16/1941	Top secret	Comparative list of the organization of the Agency of Technology and the outline of the new system for science and technology	
6/17/1941	Top secret	Comparative list of the organization of the Agency of Technology and the outline of the new system for science and technology	
6/17/1941	Top secret	Proposal for the outline of the science council	
n.d.	Secret	Schedule and progress of establishing the Agency of Technology	
6/17/1941	Top secret	Proposal for the outline of the organization of the Agency of Technology	
6/19/1941	Secret	Outline of the businesses of the association for founding the Board of Technology and related bodies	

(*Continued*)

220 *Appendix A*

Date	Classification	Documents	Submitters
6/20/1941		Table of chairs for the members of the association for founding the Board of Technology	
6/27/1941	Top secret	Reason for founding the integrated research institute by special laws	
8/4/1941		Proposal for the structure of the Agency of Technology	The Planning Agency
8/7/1941		Tasks to be transferred to the Agency of Technology and the integrated research institute for science and technology	
8/7/1941	Top secret	Proposal for the division of duties of the Agency of Technology	The Planning Agency
8/7/1941	Top secret	Tasks to be transferred to the Agency of Technology and the integrated research institute for science and technology	
8/7/1941	Top secret	Proposal for the outline of the organization of the Agency of Technology	The Planning Agency
8/7/1941		Proposal for the division of duties of the Agency of Technology	The Planning Agency
8/9/1941	Top secret	Explanatory leaflet of the outline of the organization of the Agency of Technology	The Planning Agency
8/12/1941		Outline of the businesses of association for founding the Agency of Technology	
8/12/1941	Top secret	Proposal for the special appointment of technical officers of the Agency of Technology	
8/12/1941	Top secret	Proposal for the social standing of army and navy officers appointed as technical officers of the Agency of Technology	
8/12/1941	Top secret	Proposal for the revision of edict no. 262	
8/12/1941	Top secret	Proposal for the revision of salary ordinance of senior officials	
8/13/1941		Outline of the first meeting of the preparatory association for founding the Agency of Technology	
8/14/1941	Top secret	Explanatory leaflet of the outline of the organization of the Agency of Technology	

(*Continued*)

Date	Classification	Documents	Submitters
8/20/1941	Top secret	Minutes from the first meeting of the preparatory association for founding the Agency of Technology	
8/21/1941	Top secret	Proposal for the outline of the Science and Technology Council	The Planning Agency
8/22/1941	Top secret	Proposal for the outline of the Imperial Research Institute	The Planning Agency
8/30/1941	Top secret	Opinions on the agenda of the preparatory association for founding the Agency of Technology	The Planning Agency
9/3/1941		Opinions on the agenda of the preparatory association for founding the Agency of Technology (full text)	The Planning Agency
9/12/1941		Proposal for supplementary provisions	
10/1/1941		Proposal for the division of duties of the Agency of Technology	The Planning Agency
10/7/1941		Proposal for the outline of the organization of the Agency of Technology	The Planning Agency
10/10/1941		Proposal for the Cabinet decision on the outline of the organization of the Agency of Technology	
n.d.		Cabinet decision on the organization of the Agency of Technology	
10/15/1941		Explanatory leaflet of the outline of the organization of the Agency of Technology	The Planning Agency

Appendix B
The results of gas chromatography analysis of a working fluid for OTEC

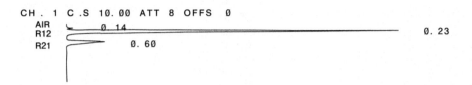

Source: Japanese Association for the Promotion of Industrial Technology (1987: 6)

Notes

Chapter 1

1 As to this distinction, also see Luhmann (1993: Chapter 6). The term "decision" is used throughout this chapter and includes decisions that were made in the participatory settings.
2 What is asserted here is not that these arguments are invalid; rather, most are valid but simply almost tautological. See Beck (2011).
3 For example, the self-reinforcing loop could proceed as follows: the cause of severe accidents could be detected only with the assistance of techno-science as an inextricable constituent of risk society.
4 The literature on social construction of technology (SCOT) is too broad to comprehensively discuss here. Current modes of thinking incorporating SCOT in a broad sense seem to have settled in the sociology of science and technology and related fields (Law 2017; Matsumoto 2017).
5 See Wynne (1996); Collins and Evans (2002); and Eden (2004) to illustrate a few in regard to extreme events.
6 To place the term "structural," as it is employed here, within earlier frames of reference has a more long-term historical orientation than the usage of the term by Martin (2009) and more locally contingent specification than that used by Tilly (1998). A sociological interpretation of path-dependent trajectory formation corresponds to what the term "structural" indicates in this chapter.
7 This state could be regarded from the viewpoint of environmental justice as it is a violation of concerned/affected people's right to know (Brown 2007: 266).
8 The estimation by SPEEDI included the effect of iodine on infant thyroiditis for one-year-olds who were in the large area around the Fukushima Daiichi Nuclear Power Plant (NISA 2012).
9 This has been reconfirmed by the results of *ex post* inverse computational simulation; see www.nisameti.go.jp/earthquake/speedi/erc/11-03121342.pdf (confirmed on June 1, 2012), and others.
10 Prime Minister Abe's words in the process of inviting the 2020 Olympics to Tokyo.
11 For related details of this situation, see Matsumoto and Juraku (2017).
12 Replacing the former NISA secretariat officials with external, independent experts could be one step toward breaking the chain of institutionalized secrecy, particularly in the context of restarting nuclear power stations that have been shut since the Fukushima accident.
13 For further details of the process in which an organizational error contributed to the accident and how the error was kept secret from outsiders, see Matsumoto (2014). Secrecy could bring about different outcomes in different social contexts.

For example, secrecy in the context of national security coupled with the assessment of enemies' bioweapon capability can "reify a technologically sophisticated adversary" (Vogel 2013: 13).
14 See Wildavsky (1995); Perry and Quarantelli (2005); and Dowty and Allen (2011) as collected works on disaster studies.
15 Café Scientifique as one type of bilateral communication between citizens and scientists originated in European endeavors in the 1990s in the context of the public understanding of science. It became popular in Japan in the 2000s.
16 The source data of what is mentioned here was confirmed on November 18, 2011, through the following Japanese portal of Café Scientifique: http://cafesci-portal.seesaa.net/
17 Also see Fortun et al. (2017).
18 See Chapter 2 for the definition of these two different aspects in more detail.
19 The work introducing network analysis into the sociology of science and technology can be traced back to Mullins (1973).
20 Since relevant factors can range from local networks and disaster experts to macro-sociological trends such as urbanization, industrialization, and others (Knowles 2011), the factors placed in the disaster matrix are selective. The criterion of selection was to specify unnoticed and/or relatively unexplored factors.
21 While a contractor, Morton Thiokol, is included in the analysis, the focus is placed on the internal organizational structure of the National Aeronautics and Space Administration (NASA) with relatively less scope for the inter-organizational dynamics among external independent partners (either private or public).
22 By ranking extreme events according to the depth of issues and relevant factors involved, the book offers examples of structural disaster in various independent cases within the context of the disaster matrix. The goal is to strike a balance between expertise and democracy in the science-technology-society interface.
23 The combination of a supposedly independent investigation committee and its secretariat, which belongs to the Cabinet Office, in organizing the Governmental Investigation Committee on the Accident at Fukushima Nuclear Power Stations of TEPCO is a good example of this (Governmental Investigation Committee 2011a). With dual institutional structure juxtaposing third parties and stakeholders in this manner, institutionalized secrecy could deepen, even in participatory decision-making regarding resilience in extreme events.
24 The terms "structure" and "function" used here have no relation to the term "structural-functionalism" used in sociology.

Chapter 2

1 The social constructionism of science and technology was once looked upon as the sociology of science and technology itself by physicists involved in the so-called "Science Wars" (Sokal and Bricmont 1998). Apart from such labeling (and against the background of social construction of technology [SCOT] arguments) some sociologists of science and technology have critically examined social constructionism (Woolgar and Pawluch 1985; Shapin 1988); as a result, a criterion for evaluating work in the sociology of science and technology gradually emerged, which required researchers to thoroughly describe specific cases to substantiate their sociological arguments and implications. As to the extension of what is regarded as having been created via social constructionism, see Hannigan (1995); Hacking (1999); and McCright and Dunlap (2003). There are two points to distinguish social constructionism in sociology that originated in studies on the social construction process of social problems (Kitsuse and Spector 1977) and

Notes 225

SCOT: first, while the former keeps the traditional dichotomy that demarcates social sciences studying the social world and natural sciences studying the nature, the latter breaks the dichotomy; second, the former is founded on the introduction of "claim making" activities, while the latter is founded on a quite different theoretical assumption: the strong program. These points of distinction form a background against which the criticism from the latter to the former was once made (see Woolgar and Pawluch 1985).

2 Callon (1986a).
3 Considering that metaphysical elements are important constituents of ANT (Latour 2005), the relative advantages of SSK and ANT for empirical investigation are arguable. In any event, the loose coupling of SSK and SCOT on the one hand and ANT on the other have formed the two major axes of the theoretical development in the field. The substantiation of these theoretical frameworks by in-depth analysis has been a requirement to vindicate both frameworks' capability. Analyses of SSK, SCOT, and ANT as major axes of the theoretical development are based on Matsumoto (2017).
4 Words within the brackets are supplemented by the present writer.
5 For caution's sake, it is also better in this connection to state that "interest theory" in this context means a spotty connection between a particular scientific belief and a particular state of society within a specific context on a case-by-case basis, as manifested in causality in the strong program. It differs from causal explanation by universal law and initial conditions; for example, the connection between a particular scientific belief and a particular state of society that is specified in one case cannot be applied to another without modifications. Therefore, interest theory makes no claims that a single interest will correspond to a single causal connection, as the connotation was already denied by SSK (Yearley 1982).
6 Ontological dimension as defined here relates to infrastructure studies, one of the origins of which can be traced back to historical materialism by Karl Marx and also with ontological turn in science and technology studies. In fact, the definition of the dimension given here has little connection with either concept, in philosophical terms. The basic idea that provides such a definition here is that ontological dimension is distinct from the epistemological one, as accommodated in the early stage of science and technology studies when its theoretical foundation is sought, as exemplified through the analysis of the epistemological chicken dispute. Conversely, the basic idea of either is a rediscovery of the risk of positionism, though some illustrations have interesting implications. Regarding the infrastructure studies in science and technology studies, see Edwards, Jackson, Bowker, and Knobel (2007) and Rowland and Passoth (2015); regarding ontological turn in science and technology studies, see Woolgar and Lezaun (2013).
7 There is no logical reason to believe that technological and social determinisms are contradictory with each other. Looking at ad hoc employment of respective determinisms in omnifarious documents turning up in the science-technology-society interface, it is more plausible that both determinisms have been co-working with each other depending on circumstances.
8 See Sohn-Rethel (1970).
9 See Merton (1970).
10 There are two extensions of the meaning of the term "reward" compared with the ordinary usage in the sociology of science. First, the meaning of reward here is not restricted to honorific reward, but extended to incorporate resources including money, information, human resources, and goods. Second, institutions and/or organizations here are not restricted to the scientific community but include any kind of institution or organization in the social system (other than the scientific community).

11 Beyond the boundary of a single organization, this level of analysis deserves explicit formulation in various problem areas other than the sociology of science and technology. In environmental sociology, for example, whether the unit of production is affiliated within the subcontracting system could be related to the emission rate of pollutants. See Grant II, Jones, and Bergesen (2002).
12 This way of defining sector originates in the understanding of the division of labor based on *spezifizierung* by Weber ([1921–1922]1976: S. 62–66).
13 When the theory of public goods was first formulated by Olson (1965), one of the core problems was how to make the goods sustainable through collective action while avoiding the issue of "free-riders." The formulation presupposed various strong assumptions, and arguments appearing after the classical formulation, as represented by the tragedy of the commons (Hardin 1968), have tended to keep presupposing unrealistic assumptions, such that there is no communication between users, and that such users chase the short-term maximization of pay-off (Hess and Ostrom 2007: 11). The arguments developed in this book do not presuppose these assumptions.
14 For one of the earliest attempts to describe and analyze scientific knowledge by the concept of public knowledge, see Ziman (1968).
15 Since technological knowledge is often patented for exclusive use, it might be regarded as club goods. To be accurate, then, the arguments developed in the following chapters should be applied to public and quasi-public goods including club goods and common-pool resources. There is the possibility that a pro-patent strategy could deter innovative behavior (see Heller and Eisenberg 1998). Relatedly, there is a structural similarity in reasoning with the tragedy of the anti-commons (see Heller 1998). If we assume first order condition, it has been shown that the tragedy of commons and that of anti-commons are symmetrically derived (see Buchanan and Yoon 2000).
16 Regarding this, see The Royal Society's ad hoc group (1985); Shortland (1988); Durant, Evans, and Thomas (1989); Raichvarg and Jacques (1991); and Durant (1992).
17 The question illustrated here is a real item on a questionnaire (see Miller 1992).
18 For various attempts to make a critical examination of the substantial quality of participatory methods in the science-technology-society interface, see Irwin (2006); Lin (2006); Rothstein (2007); Kerr, Cunningham-Burley, and Tutton (2007); and Evans and Plows (2007).
19 It is not until employing this kind of *ex post* narrative with hindsight that we are able to talk about something one-dimensional regarding the development trajectory of technology; in this case, the trajectory leading to creating requirements for the maximization of velocity compatible with that for the maximization of range (see Dosi 1988 as to illustration of the performance of aircrafts by this criterion).
20 In Chapter 6, to illustrate this mechanism, I use the process of developing and diffusing renewable energy technologies – wind turbines, in particular – in Japan and explain the generating mechanism that led to structural disaster. This means that the generating mechanism of structural disaster presented in this book is arranged to be independent of the question of whether to select nuclear power technology or renewable energy technology. If the generating mechanism of structural disaster is shown to also work within the social process of wind turbine development and diffusion, then it can be argued that structural disaster can emerge regardless of the type of technology.
21 For example, see David (1994) and Aoki (2001). The range of application of path-dependency theory extends over diffusion process of new products, industrial location, decision-making process of business enterprises, standards setting, and historical change other than technological development and institutional change.

See Arthur (1994); Magnusson and Ottosson (1997); Mahoney (2000); and Puffert (2002).
22 See Arthur (1989). To be accurate, it is assumed here that there is a natural preference for A or B according to the type of agents (Arthur 1989). For the sake of making clear the logic of the theory by simplification, this assumption is not wholly applicable. For a sociological study that questioned the assumption by showing the context-dependency of preference itself, see Espeland (1998).
23 Technically speaking, the basic structure of the original theoretical framework of path-dependency (based from Arthur [1989, 1994]) is outlined as follows. The dynamics of path-dependency can be formulated by equations of path-dependency, which can be classified into three main types: (a) the equation of stochastic process based on a model of agents involved; (b) master equation; (c) Fokker-Planck equation. In Type (a), solutions fall on fixed points. Type (b) enables a clear intuitive understanding of the phenomenon, while Type (c) allows for approximate solutions. Essentially, (a) and (b) are different expressions of the path-dependent mechanism, while (c) is mathematically derived from (b), so that what (a), (b), and (c) imply is mutually translatable.
24 Only with this kind of prerequisite assuming rational individual agents and a contingent situation surrounding the agents is it possible to talk about the one-dimensional development trajectory of technology. See, for a classical formulation, Dosi (1988).
25 Regarding initial cost effect, see Shapiro and Verian (1998); learning effect, see Ruttan (2000); network effect, see Bonaccorsi and Rossi (2003); and belief effect, see Arthur (1989) as pioneering arguments.
26 Incorporating interaction among agents and the surrounding situations into the sociologically reformulated path-dependency framework thus means introducing network and belief effects into the framework. One way to do this is the explicit introduction of rational expectation as expressed by the following formula: $\Gamma(\Omega) \equiv \Omega$ (Arthur 1989: Appendix). This corresponds to what is termed a "self-fulfilling prophecy" in sociology. The resulting dynamics of macrostructure are likely to be path-dependent since the dynamics represent a more amplified movement toward a "lock-in" state as envisaged by Arthur: "We now have a rational expectation equilibrium if the actual adoption process that result from agents acting on these beliefs turns out to have conditional probabilities that are identical to the believed process. . . . In general, expectation may interact with self-reinforcing mechanisms to further destabilize an already unstable situation. Little work has been done here yet, but it appears that the presence of dynamic, rational expectations leads more easily to monopoly outcomes." (1994: 128) In sociology, the theoretical investigation of network effect through simulation has attracted some attention in studying the mechanism of collective behavior. See, for example, Granovetter (1978); Oliver, Marwell, and Teixeira (1985); Oliver, Marwell, and Teixeira (1988); and Macy (1991).
27 As to other theoretical attempts to explain the dynamic development trajectory of technology, see Nelson and Winter (1982); Basalla (1988); Freeman and Soete (1990); Rosenberg (1994); and Ziman (2000), most of whom rely on metaphor and analogy of evolution. This reliance on metaphor and analogy of evolution seems to detract due attention from an effort to specify the detailed sociological mechanism that should work in the science-technology-society interface. This is why these studies in evolutionary economics (in a broad sense), as well as Arthur (2009), are outside the range of consideration for this chapter.
28 As to the situation of prior studies in regard to the relationships between in-depth case analyses and width of coverage enabled by conceptual tools, see Buchanan (1991); Law (1991); Scranton (1991); and Edgerton (1993).

228 Notes

29 This statement is reminiscent of the discrepancy between the commonplace way of investigation in social sciences and a crisis in the real world, a discrepancy that seems to resonate with some reflexive attempts to renovate sociology. See, for example, Lynd (1939) and Burawoy (2005).

Chapter 3

1 The governmental-industrial-university complex of nuclear power, which functions to blur the conflicts of interest between the promotion and regulation of nuclear power generation (as mentioned in Chapter 1) indicates what is called a nuclear village throughout the book.
2 As will be detailed in Chapter 4, a little-known and serious accident in pre-war Japan had a similar effect on national decision-making long before the Fukushima accident because saving the face of a particular village (not a nuclear village) endangered national safety. As will be shown, if institutionalized inaction of either type – as implied by structural disaster – repeats even after having such a pre-war experience, there is the possibility that structural disaster has been reproduced by following erroneous precedents (itself an element of structural disaster). This way of recursive reproduction might be one of the most serious sociological implications of structural disaster.
3 According to the Interim Report of the Governmental Investigation Committee (2012a), there were 456 interviewees who were involved in the accident. For the final report of the Committee, see Governmental Investigation Committee (2012b).
4 Quotations are from the rule ordained by the cabinet in setting up the Governmental Investigation Committee of May 31, 2011.
5 As of April 30, 2017, all reactors at the Ohi nuclear station have been stopped for periodic inspection, according to KEPCO (Kansai Electric Power Company)'s website (www.kepco.co.jp/corporate/pr/2017/0501_2j.html, confirmed on May 15, 2017). This move triggered subsequent applications for restarting by many nuclear power stations, of which 10 have been permitted by the newly established Nuclear Regulation Authority, according to the Federation of Electric Power Companies of Japan's website (www.fepc.or.jp/theme/re-operation/, confirmed on May 15, 2017).
6 One way that enables us to escape from taking responsibility for all of these is to make these facts secret to keep them away from the eyes of "lay experts" who were invited to participate in the decision-making process on whether to restart the Ohi nuclear reactors No. 3 and No. 4, and argued for self-responsibility. If that way is chosen, however, there immediately arises another question related to secrecy; for example, who is responsible for such decision-making in circumstances where there is no regulatory system to manage the "double-check" system installed within the same ministry (METI)? Even if one is successful in diverting people's attention from the question, another more fundamental question arises: How can one validate the decision to restart the reactors after the Fukushima accident despite the fact that the decision predated the submission of the final report of the Parliamentary Investigation Committee on the accident? Likewise, the chain of secrecy could continue further.
7 Regarding the process of creating the Agency of Technology in the wartime mobilization of science and technology, see Sawai (1991) and Yamazaki (1994).
8 For the details of the National Mobilization Law and its historical background in the wartime mobilization science and technology, see Ishikawa (1975–1987).
9 The linear model was first discussed by Price and Bass (1969). Many instances deviating from this model have been found since the mid-1980s, but this is a different topic to be considered separately.

10 Moreover, despite the structural disaster in the form of the Fukushima accident, a national debate that goes beyond "it is good to promote and understand science and technology in any case" does not often take place.
11 Aikawa then cooperated in carrying out tasks such as liaising between the Greater East Asia Co-Prosperity Sphere and the Japanese heavy industry sector, the Greater East Asia Co-Prosperity Sphere and the Japanese light industry sector, and the Greater East Asia Co-Prosperity Sphere and the Japanese technology sector, making rapid technological progress and expanding production capacity for the integrated technology structure in Greater East Asia, thus building up this region (Kokusaku Kenkyukai 1945: 109–114).
12 Regarding the shift of interest in nuclear bombs in pre-war Japan to interest in nuclear reactors in post-war Japan, see Yamazaki (2011). Considering that there was an endogenous collaboration between the Japanese academic sector and the Atomic Bomb Casualty Commission (ABCC) on devastation caused by atomic bombing (Lindee 1994; Sasamoto 1995), there could be structural disaster involved in the process; however, there is no room for such an investigation in this book.
13 For the earliest move regarding the budget administration of researches for nuclear power generation by MITI, see MITI (1954: 187–188).
14 The above description is based on JAIF (1965); Japan Atomic Power Co. (1989); and *Monthly Report of Atomic Energy Commission* (1957).
15 This document is kept by the SCJ.
16 Bracketed words were added by the present writer.
17 The above description is based on the Sugata Documents, Vol. 2: 3–52, Vol. 6: 143–263.
18 The relevant part of the document consulted here is Sugata Documents, Vol. 1 (Diary and Memorandum on the Drafting and Debating Processes of Nuclear-related Laws, in Japanese): 19–24.
19 To be accurate, there were also cases in which cutting-edge technologies that were not yet pre-established or commercialized were almost simultaneously assimilated through well-structured social process of technology transfer on the basis trial and error, occasionally far bolder than expected from the stereotypical understanding of technology transfer (see Matsumoto 2006). Therefore, this social process should not be hastily identified with cases simply representing "latecomer advantages."
20 "Zadan-kai: Nihonkeizai no Yume o Kataru" (Roundtable: Discussion on Dream for Japanese Economy, Parts I and II), *Asahi Shimbun*, January 4, 1956.
21 "Honsha Zadan-kai: Genshiryoku Heiwa Riyo no Yume" (Roundtable: Dream for Peaceful Use of Nuclear Power), *Yomiuri Shimbun*, January 1, 1956.
22 "Honsha Zadan-kai: Genshiryoku Iinkai Hossoku ni Atatte" (Roundtable: Upon the Establishment of the Japanese Atomic Energy Commission, Part II), *Yomiuri Shimbun*, January 6, 1956.
23 This document is kept by the SCJ.
24 This document is kept by the SCJ.
25 A kind of feudalistic control of the academic sector by senior scholars of prestigious universities and organizations such as the Imperial Academy of Japan (Teikoku Gakushiin), JSPS (Nihon Gakujutsu Shinkokai), and National Research Council (Gakujutsu Kenkyu Kaigi) was one of the important targets for GHQ to destroy. In reality, however, the influence of persistent human networks of these senior scholars still remains. To be accurate, there was an endogenous movement for the reform by the Committee on the Reorganization of the Academic Sector (Gakujutsu Taisei Sasshin Iinkai) in parallel with an advice by Dr. Harry C. Kelly, Deputy Director of Science and Technology Department of Economic and

Science Section of GHQ at the time. Regarding the former, see, for example, Hata (1998). As to the latter, see, for example, GHQ/SCAP (1951).
26 This document is kept by the SCJ.
27 After the Fukushima accident, the objective was changed in 2013 from "advancing the science and technology related to the peaceful use of nuclear energy" (Chapter 1, Clause 3) to the current contents stated here. See RIST (2017).
28 For further details of the above arguments, see Matsumoto (2002, 2012).

Chapter 4

1 One of the problem areas related to institutional inaction is broad studies on organizational errors because they were created in the context of technological failures. See Vaughan (1996); Macfarlane (2003); Eden (2004); and see Jobin (2013) regarding the Fukushima accident. For a pioneering study referring to the dynamic aspect of technological trajectory in the history of technological change, see Constant II (1980).
2 For the procession of events before 1884, see Scaife (1991).
3 Few studies exist on the innate connection between success and failure of the science-technology-society interface from the sociological point of view.
4 The British type originated in Parsons and the American type in Curtis turbines, respectively. The first demonstration of the Parsons turbine at the Naval Review in 1897 caused a sensation; see Legett (2011). With respect to the Curtis turbine, see Somerscale (1992). For detailed descriptions and analyses of the Navy's dual strategies outlined here, see Matsumoto (2006: 54–63). For a more general background of the relationship between the Navy and private companies, see Matsumoto (2006: 74–78).
5 To maximize thermodynamic efficiency and to minimize the loss of thrust caused by cavitation, reduction gearing that decreases the number of revolutions per minute started to be employed after the introduction of steam turbines to marine propulsion.
6 In February 1921, a turbine conference was organized by the director of the Military Affairs Bureau of the Navy to drastically reconsider the design, production method, materials, and operation method of geared turbines. As a result, the configurations, materials, strength, and installation of the turbines' blades were all improved. In addition, in August 1922, the Yokosuka arsenal of the Navy undertook an experiment on the critical speed of turbine rotors in accordance with the Military Secret No. 1148 directive in order to determine the normal tolerance of turbine rotors in terms of revolutions per minute. The above descriptions are based on Shibuya (1970) and Murata (n.d.).
7 For expanded detail of this first Kanpon type turbine, see Matsumoto (2006: 50–80) and Nippon Hakuyo Kikan Gakkai Hakuyo Kikan Chosa Kenkyu Iinkai (n.d.).
8 There is no implication here that the complex was designed in Japan by the "rich nation, strong army" policy in a top-down manner; rather the complex in Japan had an endogenous origin. See Matsumoto (2006: 50–80). As for the "rich nation, strong army" policy, see Samuels (1994). The endogenous origin of the complex might also be detected in Britain, as shown by the connection between physics and engineering in the life of Lord Kelvin; see Smith and Wise (1989). For a study on the complex with reference to American science and technology, see Leslie (1993).
9 In 1952, seven years after WWII ended, the first reference appeared in Sendo (1952) under the leadership of Michizo Sendo, who was an Engineering Rear Admiral of the Navy. Four years later, the second reference appeared in Ito

(1956), who was a Mainichi newspaper reporter and also a graduate of the Naval Academy. The third reference, in 1969 from the War History Unit of the National Defense College of the Defense Agency (1969), provides the most authentic history of the failure among the five books. Eight years later, the fourth reference appeared in The Shipbuilding Society of Japan (1977). The editor-in-chief was a former engineering officer of the Navy, and the editorial committee of the society also included several other engineering officers of the Navy. Of the five books, this reference provides the most detailed description of the technical aspects of the failure. In 1981, the last reference appeared (Institute for the Compilation of Historical Records Relating to the Imperial Japanese Navy 1981), based on newly discovered primary source materials.

10 The *Tomozuru* incident of March 11, 1934, was the first major one for the Imperial Japanese Navy. Only a year and a half after this, a more serious incident occurred on September 26, 1935 – the Fourth Squadron incident.

11 Based on interviews by the present writer with Dr. Seikan Ishigai (on September 4, 1987, and June 2, 1993) and with Dr. Yasuo Takeda (on September 25, 1996, and March 19, 1997).

12 The purpose of this treaty was to restrict the total displacement of all types of auxiliary warships other than battleships and battle cruisers, while that of the Washington Naval Treaty of 1922 (a disarmament treaty) was to restrict the total displacement of battleships and battle cruisers. This London treaty obliged the Imperial Japanese Navy to produce a new idea in hull design that enabled heavy weapons to be installed within a small hull, though this was proved to be achieved at the expense of the strength and stability of the hull, as the incident dramatically showed.

13 "When the Fourth Squadron was conducting maneuvers in the sea area to the east of Japan, they encountered a furious typhoon. They were attacked by very rare high waves. Two destroyers were tossed about tremendously. As a result, their bows were damaged. The damage to the engines and armament was considerable – two million yen for the ship and 800 thousand yen for its armament, a total of 2.8 million yen" (Kaigun Daijin Kanbo Rinji Chosa Ka 1984: 86).

14 The damage due to the collision between cruisers *Abukuma* and *Kitakami* in terms of contemporary currency is based on the above-mentioned answer by the Navy minister, Kiyotane Abo, to a question by Viscount Tanetada Tachibana made on March 2, 1931, during the 59th Imperial Diet Session. Kaigun Daijin Kanbo Rinji Chosa Ka (1984: 831).

15 When Japan was defeated in 1945, most military organizations were ordered to burn documents they had kept. Many documents of the Imperial Navy were burned before the General Headquarters of the U. S. Occupation Forces ordered the government to submit documents regarding the war. Ex-managers and ex-directors of the Imperial Japanese Navy then held meetings and decided to undertake a research project to collect, examine, and preserve any surviving technical documents. The Shibuya Archives were the result of this project and came into the hands of Ryutaro Shibuya. The description of the background of the Shibuya Archives is based on Shibuya Bunko Chosa Iinkai, Shibuya Bunko Mokuroku (Catalogue of the Shibuya Archives), March 1995, Commentary.

16 This classification assumes that if a problem at one location produces another problem at another location, the latter problem is not counted separately, but is considered part of the former.

17 The breakage as described in the record written at that time is as follows: "Moving blades and the rivets on the tip of the 2nd and 3rd stages of the intermediate-pressure turbines were broken. . . . The break in every moving blade was located at 40 to 70 mm from the tip" (Rinkicho Report 1938a: Top secret No. 1).

18 Ishikawa (1982: 412). The author was in charge of drafting the national mobilization plan at the Cabinet Planning Board (Kikaku In) in the pre-war period. For the Navy, war preparation updates started in August 1940. See Sanbo Honbu (1967: 93–94). Sugiyama was the Chief of the General Staff at that time.
19 Records of an interview with Yoshio Kubota made by the Seisan Gijutsu Kyokai (Association for Production Technology) on March 19, 1955; Kubota (1981).
20 These original remedial measures are kept in the Shibuya Archives.
21 The descriptions here are based on Kaigun Kansei Honbu Dai 5 Bu (1943). This is the final report of the special examination committee.
22 In general, such was the standard of turbine design in the pre-war period Sezawa (1932); Pigott (1937); *Mechanical Engineering* (1940), et al.
23 According to this report, "binodal vibration occurs when the product of the number of nozzles and the revolution of blades . . . equals the frequency of the blades at binodal vibration" (Kaigun Kansei Honbu Dai 5 Bu 1943). This means that a forced vibration caused by steam pulsation and a specific binodal frequency of blades resonate with each other, as a result of which binodal vibration occurs.
24 It proved that even if uniform vertical and horizontal sections were assumed for the purpose of simplification, binodal vibration could produce maximum stress at places less than three-fifths of the distance from the tip of a blade, which matched the place of the actual breakage in the failures (Engineering Lieutenant Nozaki 1943).
25 Shigeru Mori, a contemporary Navy engineer who graduated from the Department of Physics of the Imperial University of Tokyo, seems to have tried to construct an analytical model to identify the mechanism, the details of which are not currently available; see Mori (1969). When other circumstantial evidence is examined, such as the fact that the blade breakage was limited to a relatively small number of turbines of particular newly built destroyers, it was still plausible that the strength of particular blades was related to the cause of the failure. The Navy therefore revised its design directive to ensure a significant increase (from 0.4 to 1.5 mm) in the thickness of turbine blades just after the submission of the final report of the committee in April 1943. The original design directive had been issued on May 1, 1931, the documents of which are collected in the Shibuya Archives. In interpreting this circumstantial evidence, there were possibly two closely associated aspects in the failure: one is a universal aspect leading to the detection of binodal vibration; and the other is a more local aspect possibly due to the testing and quality control of the strength of the particular broken blades. Whatever weight may be given to each aspect in the analysis of the failure, however, as the date of the final report indicates, it was only after April 1943 that both aspects were finally noticed. By then, about a year and a half had already passed since the outbreak of the war with the United States and Britain in 1941. The author is indebted to Dr. Ryoichiro Araki for technical advice.
26 Even within the military sector, there was a strong sectionalism between the Army and the Navy throughout the wartime mobilization of science and technology. For example, according to Hidetsugu Yagi, who became the president of the Board of Technology in 1944, "The Army and the Navy never collaborated with each other. They thought it was much better losing the war than collaborating with each other" (GHQ/SCAP 1945b).
27 Cf., Andrew and Duncan (1956); Luck and Kell (1956); Leist (1957); Wahl (1957); and Visser (1960); as well as an article on the QE2's turbine reported that a similar failure occurred even in 1969 (Report on *QE2* turbines 1969).
28 The same type of turbine blade breakage still occurred in the same class of destroyer more than one year after the final report of the special examination

committee had been submitted, where around "one-third of the blade from the tip" experienced breakage on July 21, 1944, an incident even less known than the Rinkicho accident (Seisan Gijutsu Kyokai 1954: 158–159). Also see Matsumoto (1999).

29 Post-war industrial development, and the development of the steam turbine for commercial purposes, began with a careful re-examination of the binodal vibration problem left unsolved by the pre-war/wartime military sector. For example, in 1953, Kawasaki Heavy Industries Ltd. invited three technical advisers to help develop an independent turbine technology for the future: Yoshitada Amari (ex-Engineering Rear Admiral of the Navy), and Kanji Toshima and Shoichi Yasugi (both ex-Engineering Captains of the Navy). They were all in the Technical Headquarters of the Imperial Japanese Navy at some stage of their pre-war careers and were also concerned with the Rinkicho accident. Every detail of pre-war turbine failures including the Rinkicho accident was inputted into an IBM computer and re-analyzed, from which the company obtained an exact normal tolerance for the strength of turbine blades and a design to avoid binodal vibration, based on Takeda (1955) and a letter from Yasuo Takeda to Kanji Toshima (n.d.). For a detailed description and analysis of the Rinkicho accident, see Matsumoto (2006: 159–172).

30 The statements by Yagi are based on GHQ/SCAP (1945b). These are Yagi's words on September 11, 1945, when interrogated by General Headquarters of U.S. Army Forces, Pacific Scientific and Technical Advisory Section. He also invented the pioneering Yagi antenna, a crucial component technology of radars.

31 In 1992, the utilization of SPEEDI was also included in the Guideline for the Disaster Measures of Nuclear-related Facilities that was ordained by the Nuclear Safety Commission.

32 Apart from SPEEDI, METI developed and operated ERSS (Emergency Response Support System) to monitor the state of nuclear power stations, the output of which includes the estimate of source terms in an emergency situation. The output from ERSS was supposed to be sent to SPEEDI, but in the Fukushima accident, this communication/transmission did not occur.

33 Similar coupling of structural integration with functional disintegration might happen in other independent cases. For example, as mentioned in Chapter 1, functional disintegration of the network of relationships linking the government, TEPCO officials, and the relevant reactor designers might be taking place just at the time the strong structural integration of the governmental-industrial-university complex was institutionally reinforced by the seemingly well-organized ordinances and laws revolving around the "double-check" system within a single ministry in the past and that between two ministries now (METI and the Ministry of the Environment), ministry-bounded in either case.

34 As to institutionalized secrecy, it should be recalled here as noted in Chapter 1 that there had been virtually no *Café Scientifique* on anything nuclear including the risk of nuclear power stations out of 253 carried out in the Tohoku district, including in the Fukushima prefecture before the Fukushima Daiichi accident. This implies that various activities intended to facilitate well-balanced links between science, technology, and society in reality did nothing proactive regarding the communication of the negative aspect of nuclear power plants and therefore played no role in early warning against extreme events such as the Fukushima accident. Therefore, the change of this type of communication activities that celebrate a particular artifact without communicating their negative aspects in public is required. For a provisional proposal to carry out such a change, see Chapter 8.

234 Notes

Chapter 5

1 One of the most noteworthy characteristics of global environmental problems is irreversible environmental change, such that once the environment has suffered from human influence in a particular way, it is extremely difficult for it to revert to its earlier state within a short period, such as an individual human's lifespan. A classical definition of irreversibility in social sciences can be found in Arrow and Fisher (1974). Despite the fact that studies of science and technology from a social impact perspective have expanded into broad problem areas, detailed analyses of global environmental problems by sociologists of science and technology are rare. For case studies of emerging global environmental problems that concern the formation of scientific disciplines, their dynamics, and relationships with policy, see Hart and Victor (1993) and Van der Sluijs, van Eijndhoven, Shackley, and Wynne (1998). For policy-oriented studies on global environmental problems and risk management, which are centered on various global environmental problems, including production and disposal of new chemicals, see Jasanoff (1985); Clarke (1989); Lowe and Ward (1998); and Miller and Edwards (2001). For literature on environmentalism, environmental philosophy, ecology, and various agents and pressure groups in environmental social movements, see Nelkin (1971); Cramer (1987); Elliot and Gare (1983); Milbrath (1984); Moore (1987); and Yearley (1996).

2 This does not mean that the project resulted from the oil crisis, because on August 18, 1973, about two months before the crisis, the MITI had already inquired to an advisory organ of the ministry (Industrial Technology Council) about how to advance the development of new energy technologies to help prevent an energy crisis and ensure environmental protection. In addition, it was on May 18, 1973, about five months before the crisis, that the ministry's Agency of Industrial Technology decided to call for the establishment of a department for the development of new energy. This department became the Sunshine Project Promotion Headquarters when the project was started in July 1974. Apart from this early background of the project within the ministry, before the oil crisis, the industrial sector increasingly called for a change to oil-dependent energy policies. This resulted in a request for a revision of the policy in January 1973 by the Federation of the Economic Agency (Keidanren). See *Keidanren Geppo* 21(1), 1973: 16–17. Thus, the Sunshine project should be understood as a product of two different factors: a demand for the development of new energy technologies from within the governmental and industrial sectors and also the crisis, an external factor, accelerating the move to answer these varied concerns.

3 Supplement to *Official Gazette* No. 14066 (November 14, 1973): 10.

4 Quoted from the Clause 2 of Law No. 37 enacted on April 18, 1997.

5 The foregoing descriptions are based on The Sunshine Project Ten-Year Anniversary Committee of AIT (1984: 16). At first, the organization was expected to control new energy development projects, but it gradually came to be a coordinating organization.

6 Even after adjustment is made for the increase in the wholesale price index during the period, the budget increase is still more than tenfold. Wholesale price index here is based on Keizai Kikakucho (Research Bureau of the Economic Planning Agency) (ed.), Keizai Yoran (Economic catalog).

7 For the development of energy efficient technologies, the Moonlight project was started in 1978 within MITI's ordinary large-scale projects sector. For the context of this technology development, see Watson (1997: Chapter 8)

8 In 1977, OTEC fell under the Sunshine project's category of integrated research (sogo kenkyu) for the first time. From 1979, OTEC led development of new energy technology, which itself began to take priority within that project category.

See Industrial Technology Council, Shin Enerugi Gijutsu Kaihatsu no Susumekata ni tsuite (A report on how to advance the development of new energy technology). January, 1974; *Annual Report of MITI*, 1977: 235; *Annual Report of MITI*, 1979: 240.
9 Kaiyo Kagaku Gijutsu Senta (Research Center for Marine Science and Technology) belonged to the Science and Technology Agency.
10 Jacques A. d'Arsonval is best known for his invention of the galvanometer.
11 See Claude (1930). As for the intricate relationship between different aspects of his career, see Blondel (1985).
12 J. H. Anderson & J. H. Anderson, Jr., US Patent 3312054, "Sea water power plant," filed 27 September, 1966, Serial No. 600287, *Official Gazette*, US Patent Office, 837, 1–2, 4 April, 1967.
13 Science Application International Corporation and Meridian Corporation under Contract No. DE-AC01-86CE30844 for DOE, Compendium of International Ocean Energy Activities, Draft (December 1988).
14 Sunshine Keikaku (Sunshine project), a brochure issued by the AIT in March 1987.
15 The Electro-Technical Laboratory of the AIT, which was in charge of the development of component technology of OTEC, withdrew from OTEC-related research in March 1997. In September 1994, the OTEC-related Study Group (set up on February 1, 1988 independently of the Sunshine project) also dissolved.
16 Showa 61 Nendo Sunshine Keikaku Kenkyu Kaihatsu no Gaikyo (The outline of R&D of the Sunshine project for fiscal 1986). Nihon Sangyo Gijutsu Shinko Kyokai, 1987: 6.
17 Ibid., 2. Interpolation within brackets by the present writer.
18 This feasibility study was carried out within the category of Sogo Kenkyu (comprehensive research).
19 The passage within parentheses in the text is quoted from *Chiiki Reidanbo* 6, a brochure for promoting the sales of new technologies issued on December 15, 1975.
20 Unfortunately, this realization was not reflected in Japan's national policies of the day as mentioned later.
21 Statistics before 1976 classified the number within the range from 100 to 500 sea miles altogether. Due to this, the table only shows suitable data from 1976 to 1980, during which the estimate of the required sea area for OTEC appeared.
22 The News Agency on Heavy and Chemical Industries (1980–1990).
23 Fluorine derivatives were also planned to be manufactured.
24 CFC 11 and CFC 12 were manufactured at that time. The company also started manufacturing CFC 22 in October 1966.
25 Shigeyasu Nakanishi, "Reibai Mondai to Reinetsu Hassei no Koritsu nitsuite (On problems caused by coolant and its efficiency)", *Nihon Kikai Gakkai Gijutsu to Shakai Bumon Koen Ronbunshu*, No. 99-64. November 21, 1999: 15–18.
26 We may interpret this as a type of unanticipated consequence of action, which here means that both advantageous and disadvantageous consequences were not anticipated at the time of decision-making by those agents concerned within the science-technology-society interface. For a classical formulation of an unanticipated consequence of action in sociology, see Merton (1936), which contains nothing that particularly excludes nature and artifacts.
27 Based on an interview with S. Chubachi on May 15, 1997.
28 The first monitor map of an ozone hole produced from observations made by TOMS (Total Ozone Mapping Spectrometre) of *Nimbus 7* was made public on August 28, 1986. See Stolarski et al. (1986). *Nimbus 7* adopted a measurement program designed to reject such an extraordinary ozone density value as one below 180 DU (or Dobson units), if it were detected, so that it was inherently

impossible to obtain observation data below that level. See Gribbin (1988). One DU corresponds to the amount in a 1/100 mm ozone layer when the amount of total ozone is measured at a pressure of 1 atmosphere and 0° C. It was only after the program had been revised that the overall quantity of stratospheric ozone above Antarctica was found to have decreased about 20–40 percent on average in September and October 1979 to the same period in 1985 (R. S. Stolarski et al. 1986).

29 According to this article, the stratospheric ozone layer above Antarctica showed strange behavior from 1957 to 1984, which overturned the results of the conventional computer simulation. The article states: "Recent attempts to consolidate assessments of the effect of human activities on stratospheric ozone (O_3) using one-dimensional models for 30°N have suggested that perturbations of total O_3 will remain small for at least the next decade. Results from such models are often accepted by default as global estimates. The inadequacy of this approach is here made evident by observations that the spring values of total O_3 in Antarctica have now fallen considerably" (Farman, Gardiner, and Shanklin 1985: 207).

30 As mentioned, S. Chubachi actually reported the same observation results about six months earlier.

31 It stated that "the circulation in the lower stratosphere is apparently unchanged, and possible chemical causes must be considered," and ended with the following remark: "An intensive program of trace-species measurements on the polar-night boundary could . . . improve considerably the prediction of effects on the ozone layer of future halocarbon releases" (Farman, Gardiner, and Shanklin 1985: 210).

32 In fact, it greatly accelerated the movement to the total ban on release of CFCs, which had already begun to slow down with the installation of the Reagan administration in the United States.

33 White Paper on the Environment by the Environment Agency (Kankyo Hakusho) (1981: 163). (The subtitle of this white paper is "Seeking Total Environmental Preservation".) In September 1980, the director of the Environment Agency organized a meeting on global environmental problems. According to the 6th report of this meeting, titled "A Report of the Select Committee on the Environment and International Trade (Kankyo to boeki ni kansuru tokubetsu iinkai hokoku)" issued in April 1995, the term "global environmental problems" is used to refer to two different sub-problems: one is global scale environmental problems, such as global warming and stratospheric ozone depletion, the other is environmental problems extending beyond borders, such as acid rain. This book uses the term to refer only to the former, since the two are different in the mechanisms through which they become social problems and in the means for their solution.

34 Supplement to *Official Gazette*, No. 14066 (November 14, 1973): 10.

35 "Tenki ni Tatsu Enerugi Seisaku" (Energy Policy Facing Turning Point), *Keidanren Geppo* 1970. 18(10): 28–41; "Okina Magarikado o Mukaeta Enerugi Mondai" (Energy Problem Facing a Big Turning Point), *Keidanren Geppo* 1970. 20(5): 14–31, et al.

36 "Sekiyu o Chushin tosuru Enerugi Seisaku nikansuru Yobo" (The Call for Breaking Away from the Strongly Oil-Dependent Energy Policy), *Keidanren Geppo* 1973. 21(1): 16–17.

37 The description of the reorganization of the Electrical Testing Laboratory into the Electro-Technical Laboratory is based on The Sunshine Project Ten-Year Anniversary Committee of the AIT (1984), note 5.

38 Showa 59 Nendo Sunshine Keikaku Seika Hokokusho Gaiyoshu (Sogo Kenkyu) (The outline of R&D of the Sunshine project for fiscal 1984). Nihon Sangyo Gijutsu Shinko Kyokai, 1985: 25–26.

39 As will be explained in greater detail later, this sort of fade-out of a technological development is not problematized according to the criteria of success or failure; rather, the criteria have been providing a framework for R&D management. See, for example, Morris and Hough (1987).
40 Economy here included economy to be achieved around the equator.
41 The above description is based on The Agency for Natural Resources and Energies, Enerugi Gijutsu Senryaku Sakutei nikansuru Chosa Kenkyu (Report on the Strategic Policy of New Energy Technology Development), 2000: 14–15.
42 For a difficulty of this kind, see Avery and Wu (1994: 210–267).
43 Patents Record issued by the Patent Office of MITI, (A) 5-288481, "Opun saikuru kaiyo onndosa hatsuden yono gyoshukusochi narabini gyoshukuhoho" ("Condenser and method of condensation for the OC type OTEC"): 2.
44 Patents Record issued by the Patent Office of MITI, (A) 10-159709, "Opun saikuru kaiyo ondosa hatsuden yono tansuiseizo sochi narabini tansuiseizo hoho" ("The method of fresh water production by the OC type OTEC"): 1.
45 See www.jca.apc.org/~gen/houann.htm (confirmed on March 13, 2002).
46 The contribution of new energy to Japan's total primary energy supply is from Agency for Natural Resources and Energy, ed. Sogo Enerugi Tokei (Energy Statistics). In 2001, the category of new energy in the statistics practice was revised, resulting in a doubling of the new energy figures, but the detail criteria of the revision have not been publicly clarified.
47 Green Energy Law Network, November 17, 2000 (in Japanese).
48 See Agency for Natural Resources and Energy, ed. Sogo Enerugi Tokei (Energy Statistics); IEA, Energy Technology R & D Statistics, 1974–1995.
49 Cases that embody the principle include The Third Declaration on the North Sea (1990), Rio Agenda 21 Principle 15 (1992), and Wingspread Statement (1998). As for international politics in the protection of the ozone layer, see Benedick (1991). Extensive case histories of the precautionary principle can be found in Harremoës et al. (2002). According to M. MacGarvin, early warning in fisheries dates back to the fourteenth century (Harremoës et al. 2002: 24). For studies on the practical application of the principle, see McIntyre and Mosedale (1997), and Raffensperger and Tickner (1999).
50 For a general view of the Japanese scientific community on the ozone hole before this restriction by law took effect, see Kokuritsu Kyokuchi Kenkyujo, *Nankyoku no Kagaku, 3 Kisho* (Antarctic Science, 3 Climate). Tokyo: Kokonshoin, 1988: 134–158.
51 The term "trajectories" here broadly indicates the patterns of change specific to a certain area of science and technology. Apart from classical diffusion studies of technology (such as Ogburn 1946), there are two contexts in which the term is used. One is neo-Schumpeterian innovation studies, in which the term is broadly understood to mean technological change accompanied by economic effects within a certain sector. The other is studies of path-dependency, in which the term is more specifically understood as a stochastic process indicating a divergence of dominant technologies from an optimum pathway. What the extension of the term employed here shares with these two different contexts is the incalculable and/or unanticipated nature of change by the involved parties at a given time. For a sociological study on the failure of a technology trajectory in this sense, see Matsumoto (1999). For an example from neo-Schumpeterian innovation studies, see Dosi (2000). For other references related to use of the term in this context, see Nelson and Winter (1982); Freeman and Soete (1990); and Rosenberg (1994). Studies on path-dependency originate in the pioneering studies by David (1985) and Arthur (1989). For later developments relating to these two research traditions, see Ziman (2000). Works that coincide with these two research traditions can be found in Hughes (1983) and Basalla (1988).

Chapter 6

1 As mentioned in Chapter 1, this question is based on the understanding that a particular type of social mechanism could be regarded as a disaster in that genuine social action could unintendedly result, through a complex interaction between agents and contingent situations, in devastating outcomes to a social system. Attention to social mechanism in recent sociological literature is usually tied up with realizing the limitation peculiar to "variable approach" in sociology, where "one should always be aware that statistical analysis, particularly [when] it is based on implausible assumptions or on ad hoc statistical models with numerous independent variables, can establish 'artifacts' rather than 'facts,' thus hindering us rather than helping us to arrive at appropriate answers" (Hedström 2005: 23, n. 11). Also see the treatise on the "black box problem" regarding variable approach in sociology by Goldthorpe (2007: 52–60).

2 The usage of the framework can be found in other technologies such as epidemic disease control strategies (Cowan and Philip 1996) and, more broadly speaking, in institutional dynamics such as the emergence, change, inertial continuance, and demise of institutions (David 1994). However, as far as the original theoretical foundation is concerned, there seems to have been two hitherto unnoticed shortcomings in the application of the framework to the development trajectory of individual technologies as mentioned in Chapter 2. First, there is a gap between the logic of the framework to derive lock-in from its theoretical foundation and the actual accounts given of individual cases. Second, there has been a lack of attempts to scrutinize the similarities and differences between the framework to derive lock-in and profoundly related frameworks of the sociology of science and technology such as SCOT, the lack of which seems to have delayed the sociological development of the concept of lock-in.

3 Hitherto unnoticed shortcomings mentioned in note 2 can also be seen in these studies.

4 Path-dependency could appear and lead to a state wherein what is predominant in the market is not necessarily the most suitable. This tendency corresponds to the "increasing return" case in the original formulation by Brian Arthur (1989).

5 The contrast between the ownership of big government and/or big firms of nuclear power and that of local government, communities, and/or citizens' homes of wind power is a topic that this book cannot afford to treat but deserves separate consideration. As to a social context of the latter, see Hess (2009: 161–183).

6 Moreover, since a wind turbine is a technology that is strongly dependent on local contexts, the success or failure of wind turbine technologies is not simply determined by advantage in the market. The consideration of these local contexts and residents' local knowledge should be considered important elements of well-balanced criteria to evaluate the social decision-making in introducing wind turbine technologies into society.

7 The rankings made by Bloomberg New Energy Finance are based on the new-build market share of onshore wind turbine manufacturers in 2016 (https://about.bnef.com/blog/vestas-reclaims-top-spot-annual-ranking-wind-turbine-makers/ (confirmed on July 14, 2017). As to the contrastive ways in which wind turbines are developed in Denmark versus the United States, see Est (2000) and Garud and Kanøe (2003).

8 As to the wind conditions survey, see Iwamura (1981); for a technical report on the results of the test trial by engineers of TEPCO, see Mori (1986a); for a technical report on the results of the test trial by engineers of IHI, see Turbine Plants Engineering Department, Products Development Center (1983).

9 In the initial stage of this test trial, it was reported that "the wind turbine of HMZ . . . is considered to have some elements unsuitable to the local wind conditions of

Japan" (Mori 1986b). A similar outlook on the issue of suitability has been independently confirmed by interviews with "Mr. I" of a TEPCO-associated company (made on February 10, 2005, in his company), and with "Mr. N" of TEPCO (made on February 10, 2005, in Tokyo).
10 I. Maeda, *Furyokuhatsuden Bijinesu Saizensen* (The Forefront of the Wind Power Generation Business). Tokyo: Futabasha, 1999: 40. The author, Mr. Maeda, was at that time the PR Manager of Tachikawa Wind Power Generation Ltd. This view was preserved subsequently so that even a 2001 report by the Environment Agency (currently the Ministry of the Environment) stated that "a wind power survey was carried out without promising results, which suggested a gloomy future of wind power generation" (Ministry of the Environment 2001: 41).
11 Expressions within parenthesis have been supplemented by the present writer.
12 Based on an interview with Dr. Yukimaru Shimizu (made on February 26, 2005, in Tokyo).
13 The situation becomes all the more strange because, around that time, wind power seems to have attracted worldwide attention as a new energy source, as portrayed by the advent of such a report that aimed to achieve 12 percent of the world's electricity from wind power by 2020 (European Wind Energy Association and Greenpeace 2005). There is certainly a possibility that the monotonic increase of nuclear power in terms of primary energy supply since the 1970s prevented wind power generation from being materialized in Japan but there is little available evidence to this effect. Regarding the possibility that withdrawal from nuclear power generation associated with an anti-nuclear culture led to the relative commercial success of wind power generation, see Simmie, Sternberg, and Carpenter (2014).
14 Based on an interview with "Mr. Y", an engineer of MHI (made on December 5, 2003, in Tokyo).
15 Sales promotion for the introduction of wind turbines into the domestic market by MHI is supposed to have been relatively weak in terms of cutting expenditures for maintenance, repairs, and other labor-intensive services for installed wind turbines.
16 Ever since the original formulation of the theory of public goods by Olson (1965), the provision of public goods through the market mechanism is difficult due to the scarcity of goods and associated factors; therefore, the supplementary mechanism is required to encourage the provision and protect their diminishment by "free-riders."
17 In organizational theory, there is a distinction between "organization" and "institution" (Selznick 1996), which is similar to the distinction between "formal" and "informal." On the other hand, there are few attempts to make an analytical distinction of that kind as to social decision-making by heterogeneous agents who are mutually interacting beyond organizational bounds in the public sphere.
18 Regarding the analysis of the siting process for nuclear power stations in Japan, see Pickett (2000) and Juraku and Suzuki (2007). For work on the subject within a comparative perspective, see Aldrich (2010).
19 As will be spelled out later in this chapter, the distinction between substantial participation of relevant outsiders and procedural participation of choreographed outsiders should be carefully made. This is because one of the most influential streams in the current science-technology-society interface is the "participatory turn" of the interface. In fact, the importance of bilateral communication and dialogue-based communication has been institutionalized so that mastering communication skills for participation within the interface has become a form of basic literacy for bureaucrats in the governmental sector and scientists and engineers in the academic sector. Thus, the participatory turn seems to indicate the other side of the "policy turn" in the third wave of science and technology studies (Collins and Evans 2002). Since there could be incommensurable communication between agents

concerned in the citizen sector and stakeholders in the governmental, industrial, and academic sectors, particular attention should be paid to distribution inequalities regarding the tolerance of burdens caused by extreme events, inequalities that could be aggravated by the functioning of participatory turn as an unintended and collective consequence due to hyper-uncertainties and complexity embraced in structural disaster. Critical comparative analysis of insensibility in facing extreme events (and in forgetting them) will enable us to elucidate the blind spots of participatory turn and possible ways to go beyond them. For studies relating to the blind spots, see Lin (2006); Irwin (2006); Kerr, Cunningham-Burley, and Tutton (2007); Evans and Plows (2007); and Rothstein (2007).

20 Considering that multiple learning processes among heterogeneous agents have served as the infrastructure of wind turbine development in Denmark (Karnøe and Garud 2012), a country from which Japan has long imported wind turbines, it is surprising that such a myth had been upheld for so long under the top-down control of a governmental sector. This is another reason for arguing the structural similarity between nuclear and wind power regimes from the perspective of structural disaster because carrying over problems by following erroneous precedents as an element of the disaster seems to dominate both regimes.

21 The description of M Project in this section is based on interviews with Mr. K (made on July 26, 2004, at his office); Mr. T, who worked for a different company in the wind power generation business (made on July 28, 2004, at his office); with Mr. I of M City (made on March 7, 2003 at city hall); with Mr. S of M City (made on April 21, 2003, at city hall); and with Mr. M of M City (made on April 21, 2003, at city hall).

22 All of them stopped operation after the Fukushima nuclear accident, though some show a move to restarting.

23 Of course, among the current agrarian African communities there are some elements of market economy that go beyond autarchy and barter. See Sugimura (2004: 222–244).

24 The description of N Project in this section is based on interviews with Mr. S (made on September 1, 2003, at his office and on February 26, 2005, in Tokyo), and with Mr. N and Mr. M (made on July 18, 2003, at the office of Mr. N).

25 With hindsight, the former way turns out to be taken.

26 After the earthquake, the town opposed the recovery policy put forth by the administration. The issue was whether to construct a wider road, making traffic of ambulances and fire engines easier, which, in turn, would contribute to the safety of the residents; however, the residents were expected to forfeit part of their own lands for the construction. The reason for the conflict and opposition was that Hokudan-machi was the most aged area in the island, so the old residents did not find merits from the road. On this occasion, the Communist Party increased its influence on the residents by arguing against the plan.

27 Regarding the Phoenix Park, see www.nojima-danso.co.jp/ (confirmed on July 15, 2017).

28 Based on an interview with Mr. Miyamoto (made on April 12, 2004, at the town office of Hokudan-machi).

29 Based on an interview with Mr. M of Hokudan-machi (made on April 12, 2004, in Hokudan-machi). This request, made by inhabitants who lived far away from the site with little chance to be negatively impacted by side effects from the wind turbine's construction or location, reminds us of the possibility that the sense of equity and fairness is the determinant of the attitudes of those involved in the siting process of wind turbines (Wolsink 2007).

30 European wind turbine makers were then proceeding to the stage of scaling up their output per unit site by large-scale wind farms. As far as average output by

Notes 241

wind turbines per one private company engaging in wind power generation is concerned, a similar trend can be seen in Japan as well, since 1999. See Sugie and Baba (2004: Figure 7 and Figure 8).

31 As the background of selection of MHI, there were some cases where imported turbines caused problems. The advice by consultant Hashimoto on the trustworthiness of MHI as a firm and the future prospect of its technology led the administration to choose it for the project. Hashimoto was a member of Japan Wind Energy Association and lived on the island, working for survey and design firm Akitsu Chiken Consultants. He was interested in wind power generation and giving information about NEDO's subsidies for wind power generation to the neighboring towns.

32 The description in this paragraph is based on an interview with Mr. M of Hokudan-machi (made on April 12, 2004, in Hokudan-machi).

33 Apart from the focused interviews mentioned in the earlier notes, the following additional interviews were made to obtain the general background information surrounding the M Project and N Project: interviews with Mr. T, Mr. N, and Mr. F of the Ishikawa Prefectural Office (made on July 17, 2003, at the Ishikawa Prefectural Office), and with Mr. J of Japanese Society for Preservation of Birds (made on August 11, 2003, at his home).

34 Reflecting on the introduction of new technologies since the days of Meiji Japan, national projects have tended to accept technology as given or something to be introduced from abroad and then improved upon domestically. As far as the internal aspect of these national projects is concerned, the maximization of spill-over effects such as job creation for special interest groups as represented by nuclear village have virtually been providing a foundational basis of the projects. As a result, a conscious effort to select the most appropriate technology has tended to be neglected, and the absence of such deliberate examination and selection of the different types of technologies has been a persistent blind spot. Contrary to the popular understanding of technological trajectory in Japan, there was an endogenous social mechanism which enabled the country to make a deliberate examination and selection of the different types of technologies in the pre-war period. See Matsumoto (2006).

35 In fact, the initial stages of technological development correspond to the initial divergence of technology defined in Chapter 2.

36 The importance of local knowledge has long been pointed out in the post-disaster management and recovery context, ranging from fallout estimation after nuclear accidents (Wynne 1982, 1987, 1996) to the management of flood disasters such as Elbe River floods (Central Europe) and floods caused by Hurricane Katrina in the United States (Weichselgartner and Brévière 2011). Since the reduction of noise annoyance around the wind turbine sites could probably be made "at the expense of maximum energy yield" (Berg 2013), this is all the more important in the location of wind turbines.

37 The dimension of locality of this conceptual design could be further modified in accordance with the fields of action of "alternative pathways" (Hess 2007: 173).

38 See Kiba (2003) for the role of "petit experts" in Japan.

Chapter 7

1 Abe's talk was given at the 125th International Olympic Committee Session held on September 7, 2013, in Buenos Aires.

2 As far as the decontamination model project by Japan Atomic Energy Agency is concerned, there arises a criticism by engineers who were engaged with the project in Fukushima regarding the lack of preparedness of the project, ranging from a

lack of participation by local inhabitants to a lack of realistic strategy by simplistically assuming that there is no recovery before overall decontamination (see Nakayama 2016). Although this chapter cannot address the continuous effects of low-level doses on the health conditions of the people in Fukushima, it might be worth considering the possibility that this unrealistic strategy is related to the skewed process of budget allocation suggested by Petryna (2013: Preface to 2013 edition).

3 In addition, there has been abundant literature accumulated in sociology on the relationship between expertise and society. Among other things, a hot dispute has emerged over the nature of expertise and its relation to democracy triggered by the "third wave" arguments posed by Collins and Evans (2002). Regarding these third wave arguments, the basic standpoint of this book is that they posed a crucial question about the nature of expertise and its relation to politics, but its answer is too narrowly framed to fully draw meaningful sociological implications in analyzing a subtle situation revolving around extreme events, as exemplified in Fukushima. On this standpoint, this book points to a path going beyond the third wave arguments and develops a new framework to analyze extreme events with particular reference to HLW disposal in the post-Fukushima situation in Japan. First, the book focuses on a theoretical challenge to STS revealed by the third wave dispute and suggests an alternative, based on the disputes, to approach the challenge. To devise this alternative, the book clarifies the dual underdetermination in Chapter 1 and exemplifies it in reference to the decision-making process of HLW disposal in this chapter. This way of investigation into expertise and responsibility in light of extreme events is different from other ways, including those suggested by both Collins and Evans and their critics. Regarding another important question posed by Collins and Evans (2002) that is framed as the problem of the "monotonically increasing" theory of participation, there have appeared many prior studies: see Matsumoto (2002); Irwin (2006); Lin (2006); Evans and Plows (2007); Kerr, Cunningham-Burley, and Tutton (2007); and Rothstein (2007). For a reflexive work on radioactive waste disposal issues focusing on procedural politics of analytic-deliberative practices that would eventually undermine public trust, credibility, and legitimacy, see Chilvers and Burgess (2008).

4 One of the significant reasons for pressing the importance of "independent description and analysis" in this context of allocating social responsibility is shown in the policy failure of the low-level radioactive waste (LLRW) disposal issues such that the battle of social construction of reality between proponents and opponents of LLRW policy has given birth to a deadlock: "It is difficult to find players who are more interested in finding real solutions to an important problem than in marketing their particular socially constructed version of 'reality.'" (Albrecht and Amey 1999).

5 See Muraoka (1995).

6 As of 2016, a nuclear fuel reprocessing plant is also under construction in the village. It is suggested that the siting of this reprocessing plant was the second choice of the government after the cancelation of the plan to site the plant on the remote island of Tokunoshima. See Kashimoto (2016).

7 Because it takes an extraordinarily long time – beyond the span of a few generations – to obtain empirical evidence to prove anything about the interaction, it is usual to appeal to estimation by simulation, which is different from insights based on empirical evidence. Due to this difference, there is a considerably higher degree of type-one underdetermination in HLW disposal. Technical reports laying the foundation of the current disposal policies in Japan have officially acknowledged this difference: see JNC (Japan Nuclear Cycle Development Institute, currently Japan Atomic Energy Agency) (1999a, 1999b, 1999c, 1999d). Risk sciences

Notes 243

mobilized for safety assessments of HLW disposal share similar characteristics because the systems for their studies are too complex to approximate without a variety of assumptions in simulation. See JNC (1999e), as well as Umeki (1990) and Nagasaki et al. (1995). There is also a type-one underdetermination in LLRW disposal, in which a particular type of uncertainty tends to be singled out from other types. See Bedsworth, Lowenthal, and Kastenberg (2004).

8 Apart from HLW disposal, the usage of geological strata for energy resources requires a social arrangement to fix type-two underdetermination as well as, or more than, science and technology to fix type-one. See Bleicher and Gross (2016).

9 The above descriptions are based on JAIF (n.d.). For the current state of affairs in France see ANDRA (2016); in Sweden see Swedish Radiation Safety Authority (2016); in Canada see NWMO (2016). Monitoring is usually understood as a supplementary method to geological disposal. Regarding the strategy of Swedish Nuclear Management Company (SKB), see Lidskog and Sundqvist (2004) as well as Dawson and Darst (2006). I thank Mr. Hidenari Akasaka of JAIF for his helpful comments.

10 In France, reversibility was explicitly stipulated in law in 2006 (Loi no 2006-739). To be accurate, in Sweden, according to E. Setzman of SKB, there is currently no legislation or other provision "prescribing that it should be possible to retrieve spent nuclear fuel. However, SKB cannot exclude situations whereby the issue of retrieving material from a repository may have to be addressed" (OECD/NEA 2012: 113). When Yucca Mountain was decided as a site for a radioactive waste repository in the United States, a similar idea seems to have been one of the grounds for the decision. See NRC (2001, 2003).

11 The above descriptions are based on JAIF (2008). As to the worldwide phase development of HLW disposal as socioeconomic and political issues as well as technical ones for social sciences, see Solomon, Andrén, and Strandberg (2010).

12 The unsaturated zone indicates the region above the water table about 300 meters below the surface. For a cross-section of Yucca Mountain in the vicinity of the repository, see Craig (1999: Figure 4).

13 With respect to the observed elevated value for ^{36}Cl in the subsurface, see Long and Ewing (2004: Figure 4).

14 It is possible to see the challenge that social sciences are facing now, as noted by Bloomfield and Vurdubakis (2005): "Under the terms of the Yucca Mountain project, many philosophical traditional dilemmas and oppositions . . . are encountered not just as 'abstract theory' or 'mere talk' divorced from the material world but rather situated concrete *practical* problems." What distinguishes the arguments developed here from this recognition in a general sense consists in considering the possibility that the same Yucca Mountain project could aid in reformulating the foundation of the current social sciences, including sociology, due to the infinite responsibility coming out of HLW disposal issues.

15 The possibility of this kind of environmental racism has been one of the significant issues of environmental justice (see White 1998). Regarding more recent issues of environmental justice regarding radioactive waste policy, see Huang, Gray, and Bell (2013).

16 This kind of social model has been conceptualized as "typification by commonsense constructs" by Schutz (1962a: 15–19). In this particular sense, it is observed that the egalitarian social model tends to be coupled with a skeptical attitude toward nuclear energy and a hierarchical one tends to be coupled with a positive attitude toward it. Even in risk assessments done by specialists, a similar coupling of risk perception with assumed social models has been observed (Slovic 2000: 390–412).

17 The details of each paper are as follows: Shuichi Sakamoto and Kenji Kanda, "Koreberu Hoshasei Haikibutsu no Shobungijutsu no Shakaitekigosei Kojo notameno

Wakugumi to Risuku Komyunikeishon no Arikata" (The Framework Which Aims at Improving Compatibility of the High-Level Radioactive Waste Disposal Technology with Social Values and the Role of Risk Communication), *Transactions of the Atomic Energy Society of Japan* 2002. 1(2): 228–241; Shuichi Sakamoto and Kenji Kanda, "Koreberu Hoshasei Haikibutsu Shobunchi Sentei no Shakaijuyosei o Takamerutameno Kadai nikansuru Kosatsu" (Study on the Framework of Site Selection Aimed at Enhancing the Acceptability of a High-Level Radioactive Waste Disposal Facility), *Transactions of the Atomic Energy Society of Japan* 2002. 1(3): 270–281; Shuichi Sakamoto and Kenji Kanda, "Sedaikan no Kohei no Kantenkarano Koreberu Hoshasei Haikibutsu Shobungijutsu no Kaihatsuriyo nikansuru Seisakutekikadai" (Policy Issues on Technology Development for High-Level Radioactive Waste Disposal from the Viewpoint of Intergenerational Equity: Through Analyzing the Arguments on Retrievability), *Transactions of the Atomic Energy Society of Japan* 2002. 1(3): 303–311; Kunihiko Takeda, Akiko Nasu, and Yoshihiro Maruyama, "Koreberu Haikibutsu no Sedaikanrinri karano Kosatsu" (Intergenerational Ethics of High Level Radioactive Waste), *Transactions of the Atomic Energy Society of Japan* 2003. 2(1): 1–8; Ekou Yagi, Makoto Takahashi, and Masaharu Kitamura, "Taiwa Foramu Jissen niyoru Genshiryoku Risuku Ninchikozo no Kaimei" (Clarification of Nuclear Risk Recognition Scheme through Dialogue Forum), *Transactions of the Atomic Energy Society of Japan* 2007. 6(2): 126–140; Minoru Okoshi, Hiroyuki Torii, and Yasuhiko Fujii, "Hoshasei Haikibutsu Kanrishisetsu no Ricchi niokeru Risukukomyunikeishon" (Risk Communication on the Siting of Radioactive Waste Management Facility), *Transactions of the Atomic Energy Society of Japan* 2007. 6(4): 421–433; Ryutaro Wada, Satoru Tanaka, and Shinya Nagasaki, "Koreberu Hoshasei Haikibutsu Shobunjo no Ricchi Kakuho nimuketa Shakaijuyo Purosesumoderu" (Social Acceptance Process Model for Ensuring the High-Level Radioactive Waste Disposal Site), *Transactions of the Atomic Energy Society of Japan* 2009. 8(1): 19–33.
18 In this kind of social model there seems to be a tendency to equate specialists' confidence in science and technology with the general public's trust in science and technology, a tendency that is sociologically disputable. As the validity of this social model is not at issue here, I state the contents of the model as it stands.
19 Regarding the numerical tools, including cost-benefit analyses, usually employed to display the social use of science and technology rather than the innate validity that they could create, see Porter (1995: 148–189). In more general terminology, costs, and benefits have been widely used in assessing new energy technologies such as biofuels (see Carolan 2009).
20 The average population density of Japan is based on the Census of Japan (2005).
21 It is quite telling that such a large subsidy is arranged to be expended by the completion of a one-page A4 sheet application form, evincing a sharp contrast to a lot of "red tape" involved in ordinary procedures to fund public activities, including basic research conducted at universities.
22 NUMO (2007: 1–2).
23 In the context of game theory, the concept of trust has been extended to interpret it as the tolerance of betrayal; for example, such an extended interpretation of trust can lead to a coordinated solution in social dilemma (see Yamaguchi 2006).
24 Regarding the process of this social conflict within Toyocho, see Sugawara and Juraku (2010).
25 METI begins to call this new top-down policy a policy that can present "scientifically promising sites" by the government. See, for example, Uno (2017).
26 Regarding the analysis of this part, also see Matsumoto and Juraku (2017).
27 For NIMBY-related politics in regard to the siting process of nuclear power stations and other facilities, see Aldrich (2010).

Notes 245

28 Reference work with the original text by Thomas Hobbes was done here with the assistance of the McMaster University Archive of the History of Economic Thought, prepared by Rod Hay (https://socserv2.socsci.mcmaster.ca/econ/ugcm/3ll3/hobbes/Leviathan.pdf#search=%27Leviathan+hobbes%27). As an early work of the sociology of science and technology on the controversy between Thomas Hobbes and Robert Boyle that influenced the subsequent thoughts of the field, see Shapin and Schaffer (1985).
29 Matsumoto (2002: 264–266).
30 There have been innumerable cases that prove this as well as other cases showing that this lack of trust can become associated with the absence of a personal sense of responsibility for HLW disposal (see Ramana 2009). When the United States' government proposed to site an HLW disposal repository in Yucca Mountain, it was statistically shown as a statewide sample that the compensation payment had no relation to supporting or opposing the proposal but rather that the level of trust did (Flynn, Burns, Mertz, and Slovic 1992).

Chapter 8

1 By using a disaster matrix to rank extreme events according to the depth of problems and relevant factors involved, this book could show the potential for structural disaster in various independent cases with the hope of striking a subtle balance between expertise and democracy in the science-technology-society interface.
2 Regarding type-one and type-two underdetermination in HLW disposal, see Macfarlane (2003).
3 To be accurate, the fact that current expertise cannot always provide unique solutions to problems with strong uncertainties is one thing; the statement that everyone can be an expert in his or her own right is quite another. Care should be taken to avoid mistaking the former for the latter to ensure healthy relationships between expertise, policy, and democracy – see, for example, Kiba (2003).
4 This need should be realized even when there is no structural disaster at the current time because risk of highly uncertain and complex events could be aggravated by the lack of well-balanced and divergent policy options, which in turn could invite future structural disaster.
5 Although there is no reason to be limited to binary options, for the sake of simplicity, a further refinement of tracks in the next funding term is illustrated in a binary mode here. The track that assumes no nuclear power combined with a highly efficient combination of multiple sources of generation, including fossil fuels, hydro power, and natural gas generation, was actually a core element of the Moonlight project between 1978 and 1993 in Japan. Conversely, the track that assumes nuclear power combined with renewable energy corresponds to the Basic Energy Plan decided at the cabinet meeting of the Abe regime in April 2014. From the viewpoint of the best energy mix, as understood as one of the policy options for a national energy plan, both this track and the Plan are too rough in that they lack appropriate weight given to different energy sources.
6 The reversal of the means-ends relationship intervenes here, which is similar to the reversal of the means (indicators)–ends (academic excellence) relationships in the context of academic ranking – see, for example, Espeland and Sauder (2007); Espeland and Vannebo (2007); and Sauder and Espeland (2009). Regarding the university setting, the formulation of this problem likely originates in Veblen (1918). As to the overreliance on formality, one can look at what kind of formality is required in the first step by JSPS through the following website: www.jsps.go.jp/english/e-grants/index.html (confirmed on November 22, 2017). The system of public funding by JSPS for academic research is in the midst of reform since 2016,

but the reform seems to have nothing to do with the problems of ritualized methods mentioned here.
7 The focus on strategically authorized zones such as Fukushima Prefecture is based on the assumption that there is an accumulative disadvantage and, in particular, an increasing inequality in environmentally hazardous places. Though there is little crucial evidence to determine the validity of this assumption, some preliminary results are available – see, for example, Schultz and Elliott (2013) and Elliott and Frickel (2015).
8 The quote from MacKenzie (1990) is originally based on the author's interview with Dr. James Schlesinger, which took place on September 22, 1986, in Washington, DC.
9 A circular structure of this kind entails a well-known fallacy, as pointed out by Karl Popper when he stated: "Everything is deducible from an inconsistent set of premises" (Popper 1959: 91, n. 2).

Bibliography

Manuscripts and unpublished materials

Headquarters for Disaster Countermeasures of the Fukushima Prefecture. 2012. Fukushima Daiichi Genshiryokuhatsudennsho Hassei Toshono Denshi mail niyoru SPEEDI Shinsankekka no Toriatsukaijokyo no Kakuninkekka (The report of the confirmation of the handling of the results of SPEEDI transmitted by emails at the time of the accident of the Fukushima Daiichi Nuclear Power Station), April 20.

Kaigun Kansei Honbu Dai 5 Bu. 1943. Rinji Kikan Chosa Iinkai Hokoku ni kansuru Shu Tabin Kaizo narabini Jikken Kenkyu ni kansuru Hokoku (Report on the remedy and the experimental research of the main turbines in connection with the Rinkicho report), Bessatsu, April 1.

Kokusaku Kenkyukai Archives (University of Tokyo Library).

Murata, S. n.d. Asashio Gata Shu Tabin no Jiko (An accident of the main turbines of the Asashio-class), Manuscript.

Nippon Hakuyo Kikan Gakkai Hakuyo Kikan Chosa Kenkyu Iinkai (The Research Committee of the Marine Engineering Society of Japan), ed. n.d. Nippon Hakuyo Kikan Shi Joki Tabin Hen Soko (An unpublished manuscript of the history of marine engineering in Japan: The steam turbine), Appended tables.

Parsons, Charles. 1894. Improvements in mechanism for propelling and controlling steam vessels, Patent Record No.394 A.D.1894 (Tyne & Wear Archives Service, Newcastle upon Tyne).

Pickett, Susan E. 2000. "Integrating Technology and Democracy: Nuclear Energy Decision Making in Japan", Doctoral Thesis submitted to the University of Tokyo, Department of Quantum Engineering and System Science.

Rinkicho Report. 1938a. Top secret No. 1, Issued on February 18 through Top secret No. 27, Issued on October 13.

Rinkicho Report. 1938b. Top secret No. 35. Issued on November 2.

Shibuya Archives (Kobe University Library).

Sugata Documents. 1964. 6 vols.

Watson, W. James. 1997. "Constructing Success in the Electric Power Industry: Combined Cycle Gas Turbines and Fluidised Beds", D. Phil Thesis in Science and Technology Policy, the Energy Programme, SPRU, University of Sussex.

Other references

Abe, Kiyoshi. 2015. "Ulrich Beck and Japan", *TCS Public Domain*, January 23. www.theoryculturesociety.org/ulrich-beck-and-japan/ (confirmed on May 2, 2016).

Advisory Committee for Natural Resources and Energy, the Demand Subcommittee. 2002. Kongo no Enerugi Seisaku ni Tsuite (Report on the future energy policy).
Advisory Committee for Natural Resources and Energy, the Nuclear Safety and Radioactive Waste Subcommittee. 2006. Hoshasei Haikibutsu no Chisoshobun nikakawaru Anzenkisei Seido no Arikata nitsuite (On the design of the regulatory measures for geological disposal of radioactive waste).
Agency for Natural Resources and Energy. 1998. 21 Seiki Chikyukankyo Jidai no Enerugi Senryaku (Energy policies with global environmental consciousness in the 21st century).
Agency for Natural Resources and Energy. 2016. Enerugi Hakusho (White paper on energy).
Ahn, Joonhong. 2013. "The Resilience of HLW Disposal and the Role of Nuclear Fuel Cycle", Paper presented at the Japan Nuclear Energy Agency, October 21.
Ahn, Joonhong, C. Carson, M. Jensen, et al., eds. 2014. *Reflections on the Fukushima Daiichi Nuclear Accident*. Heidelberg: Springer.
AIT (Agency of Industrial Technology). 1980. Introduction (in Japanese).
Albrecht, Stan L. and Robert G. Amey. 1999. "Myth-Making, Moral Communities, and Policy Failure in Solving the Radioactive Waste Problem", *Society and Natural Resources* 12(8): 741–761.
Aldrich, Daniel P. 2010. *Site Fights: Divisive Facilities and Civil Society in Japan and the West*. Ithaca, NY: Cornell University Press.
Allison, Paul D. and John A. Stewart. 1974. "Productivity Differences among Scientists: Evidence for Accumulative Advantage", *American Sociological Review* 39(4): 596–606.
ANDRA (Agence Nationale pour la Gestion des Dechets Radioactifs). 2016. www.andra.fr/international/ (confirmed on September 24, 2016).
Andrews, F. and J. P. Duncan. 1956. "Turbine Blade Vibration: Method of Measurement and Equipment Developed by Brush", *Engineering* 17: 202–208.
Aoki, Masao. 2001. *Toward a Comparative Institutional Analysis*. Cambridge, MA: The MIT Press.
Arrow, Kenneth J. and Anthony C. Fisher. 1974. "Environmental Preservation, Uncertainty, and Irreversibility", *Quarterly Journal of Economics* 88(2): 312–319.
Arthur, Brian. 1989. "Competing Technologies, Increasing Returns, and Lock-in by Historical Events", *Economic Journal* 99(394): 116–131.
Arthur, Brian. 1994. *Increasing Returns and Path Dependence in the Economy*. Ann Arbor, MI: The University of Michigan Press.
Arthur, Brian. 2009. *The Nature of Technology: What It Is and How It Evolves*. New York: Free Press.
Atomic Energy Long-Term Plan (Genshiryoku Choki Keikaku). 1956. (in Japanese).
Atomic Energy Society of Japan. 2009. http://www.aesj.or.jp/awards/2008/2008-119-120.pdf (confirmed on March 21, 2013, in Japanese).
Atomic Energy Society of Japan. 2014. *Fukushima Daiichi Genshiryokuhatsudennsho Jiko sono Zenbo to Asunimuketa Teigen: Gakkaijimocho Saishuhokokusho* (All about the Fukushima Nuclear Accident for the Future: Final Report). Tokyo: Maruzen.
Avery, W. H. and C. Wu. 1994. *Renewable Energy from the Ocean: A Guide to OTEC*. Oxford: Oxford University Press.
Baba, Shuichi. 1971. "1930 Nendai to Nihon Chishikijin (Japanese Intellectuals in the 1930s)", *Kikan Shakaishiso* 1: 4–47.

Balogh, Brian. 1991. *Chain Reaction: Expert Debate and Public Participation in American Commercial Nuclear Power, 1945–1975.* Cambridge: Cambridge University Press.
Bank of Japan. 1966. *Meiji Iko Honpo Shuyo Keizaitokei* (The Economic Statistics of Japan since the Meiji Period). Tokyo: Bank of Japan.
Barnes, B. 1982. "The Science-Technology Relationship: A Model and a Query", *Social Studies of Science* 12(2): 166–172.
Basalla, G. 1988. *The Evolution of Technology.* Cambridge: Cambridge University Press.
Beck, Ulrich. (1986)1992. *Risikogesellschaft: Auf dem Weg in eine andere Moderne.* Frankfurt am Main: Suhrkamp. Translated by Mark Ritter, *Risk Society: Toward a New Modernity.* London: Sage.
Beck, Ulrich. 1987. "The Anthropological Shock: Chernobyl and the Contours of the Risk Society", *Berkeley Journal of Sociology* 32: 153–165.
Beck, Ulrich. 2011. "Kono Kikai ni (On This Occasion)", in U. Beck, M. Suzuki, and M. Ito, eds. *Risukuka suru Nihonshakai* (Japanese Society on Its Way to Risk Society). Tokyo: Iwanami Shoten, pp. 1–12.
Bedsworth, L. W., M. D. Lowenthal, and W. E. Kastenberg. 2004. "Uncertainty and Regulation: The Rhetoric of Risk in the California Low-Level Radioactive Waste Debate", *Science, Technology and Human Values* 29(3): 406–427.
Benedick, Richard E. 1991. *Ozone Diplomacy: New Directions Safeguarding the Planet.* Cambridge, MA: Harvard University Press.
Berg, Frits van den. 2013. "Wind Turbine Noise: An Overview of Acoustic Performance and Effects on Residents", Proceeding of Acoustics: Victor Harbor, November 17–20, pp. 1–7.
Bergek, Anna and Ksenia Onufrey. 2014. "Is One Path Enough? Multiple Paths and Path Interaction as an Extension of Path Dependency Theory", *Industrial and Corporate Change* 23(5): 1261–1297.
Bernal, J. D. 1939. *The Social Function of Science.* London: Routledge & Kegan Paul.
Bertsch, Kenneth A. and Linda S. Shaw. 1984. *The Nuclear Weapons Industry.* Washington, DC: Investor Responsibility Research Center.
Bijker, Wiebe E. 1995. *Of Bicycles, Bakelites, and Bulbs: Toward a Theory of Sociotechnical Change.* Cambridge, MA: The MIT Press.
Bijker, Wiebe E., Thomas P. Hughes, and Trevor Pinch, eds. 1987. *The Social Construction of Technological Systems: New Direction in the Sociology and History of Technology.* Cambridge, MA: The MIT Press.
Bleicher, Alena and Matthias Gross. 2016. "Geothermal Heat Pumps and the Vagaries of Subterranean Geology: Energy Independence at a Household Level as a Real World Experiment", *Renewable and Sustainable Energy Review* 64: 279–288.
Blondel, Christine. 1985. "Industrial Science as a 'Show': A Case-Study of George Claude", in Terry Shinn and Richard Whitley, eds. *Expository Science: Forms and Functions of Popularisation, Sociology of the Sciences Yearbook,* Vol. 9. Dordrecht: D. Reidel, pp. 249–258.
Bloomfield, Brian P. and Theo Vurdubakis. 2005. "The Secret of Yucca Mountain: Reflections on an Object in Extremis", *Environment and Planning D* 23: 735–756.
Bloor, David. 1976. *Knowledge and Social Imagery.* London: Routledge & Kegan Paul.
Boltanski, Luc and Ève Chiapello. 1999. *Le nouvel esprit du capitalisme.* Paris: Gallimard.

Boltanski, Luc and Laurent Thévenot. 1991. *De la justification: les économie de la grandeur*. Paris: Gallimard.
Bonaccorsi, A. and C. Rossi. 2003. "Why Open Source Software Can Succeed", *Research Policy* 32: 1243–1258.
Bowden, Gary. 2011. "Disaster as System Accident: A Socio-Ecological Framework", in Rachel A. Dowty and Barbara L. Allen, eds. *Dynamics of Disaster: Lessons on Risk, Response and Recovery*. London: Earthscan, pp. 47–60.
Bowker, Geoffrey C. and Susan Leigh Star. 1999. *Sorting Things Out: Classification and Its Consequences*. Cambridge, MA: The MIT Press.
Brinkley, Douglas. 2007. *The Great Deluge: Hurricane Katrina, New Orleans, and the Mississippi Gulf Coast*. New York: Harper.
Brown, Phil. 2007. *Toxic Exposures: Contested Illnesses and the Environmental Health Movements*. New York: Columbia University Press.
Buchanan, J. M. and Y. J. Yoon. 2000. "Symmetric Tragedies: Commons and Anticommons", *Journal of Law and Economics* 43(1): 1–13.
Buchanan, R. A. 1991. "Theory and Narrative in the History of Technology", *Technology and Culture* 32(2): 365–376.
Burawoy, M. 2005. "For Public Sociology", *American Sociological Review* 70(1): 4–28.
Bush, Vannevar. 1946. *Endless Horizons*. Washington, DC: Public Affairs Press.
Cabinet Meeting for the Goal of Oil-Substitute Energy Supply. 1998. (in Japanese).
Cabinet Meeting for the Promotion of the Integrated Energy Policies. 1994. Sin Enerugi Donyu Taiko (The fundamental principles for the introduction of new energy).
Callon, Michel. 1986a. "Éléments pour une sociologie de la traduction: la domestication des coquilles Saint-Jaques et des marins-pêcheurs dans la baie de Saint-Brieuc", *L'Année sociologique* 36: 169–208.
Callon, Michel. 1986b. "The Sociology of an Actor-Network: The Case of Electric Vehicle", in Michel Callon, J. Law, and A. Rip, eds. *Mapping the Dynamics of Science and Technology*. Basingstoke: Palgrave Macmillan, pp. 19–34.
Callon, Michel and Bruno Latour. 1992. "Don't Throw the Baby Out with the Bath School!: A Reply to Collins and Yearley", in A. Pickering, ed. *Science as Practice and Culture*. Chicago: The University of Chicago Press, pp. 343–368.
Carolan, Michael S. 2009. "The Cost and Benefits of Biofuels: A Review of Recent Peer-Reviewed Research and a Sociological Look Ahead", *Environmental Practice* 11: 17–24.
Census of Japan. 2005. http://www.stat.go.jp/data/kokusei/2005/youkei/02.htm (in Japanese).
Chilvers, Jason and Jacquelin Burgess. 2008. "Power Relations: The Politics of Risk and Procedure in Nuclear Waste Governance", *Environment and Planning A* 40: 1881–1900.
Chomsky, Noam. 1975. *The Logical Structure of Linguistic Theory*. New York: Plenum Press.
Chubachi, Shigeru. 1984a. "Preliminary Result of Ozone Observations at Syowa Station from February 1982 to January 1983", *Memoirs of National Institute of Polar Research* Special Issue 34: 13–19.
Chubachi, Shigeru. 1984b. "A Special Ozone Observation at Syowa Station, Antarctica from February to January 1983", Proceedings of the Quadrennial Ozone Symposium, September 3–7, Halkidiki, Greece, pp. 285–289.

Bibliography 251

Clarke, Lee. 1989. *Acceptable Risk? Making Decisions in a Toxic Environment*. Berkeley, CA: The University of California Press.
Clarke, Lee. 1999. *Mission Improbable: Using Fantasy Documents to Tame Disaster*. Chicago, IL: The University of Chicago Press.
Clarke, Lee. 2008. "Possibilistic Thinking: A New Conceptual Tool for Thinking about Extreme Events", *Social Research* 75(3): 669–690.
Claude, George. 1930. "Power from the Tropical Seas", *Mechanical Engineering* 52(12): 1039–1044.
Collins, Harry. 2011. "The Third Wave of Science Studies: The Development and Politics", *Japanese Journal for Science, Technology and Society* 20: 81–106.
Collins, Harry and Rob Evans. 2002. "The Third Wave of Science Studies: Studies of Expertise and Experience", *Social Studies of Science* 32(2): 235–296.
Collins, Harry and Rob Evans. 2007. *Rethinking Expertise*. Chicago, IL: The University of Chicago Press.
Collins, Harry, Rob Evans, and Martine Weinel. 2017. "Interactional Expertise", in Ulrike Felt, Fouché Rayvon, Clark Miller, and Laurel Smith-Doerr, eds. *Handbook of Science and Technology Studies*, 4th ed. Cambridge, MA: The MIT Press, pp. 765–792.
Collins, Harry and Steven Yearley. 1992a. "Epistemological Chicken", in A. Pickering, ed. *Science as Practice and Culture*. Chicago: The University of Chicago Press, pp. 301–326.
Collins, Harry and Steven Yearley. 1992b. "Journey into Space", in A. Pickering, ed. *Science as Practice and Culture*. Chicago, IL: The University of Chicago Press, pp. 369–389.
Congressional Research Service. 2011. Japan-Us Relations: Issues for Congress, June 8.
Connelly, Matthew. 2008. *Fatal Misconception: The Struggle to Control World Population*. Cambridge, MA: Harvard University Press.
Constant II, Edward. 1980. *The Origins of the Turbojet Revolution*. Baltimore, MD: Johns Hopkins University Press.
Cowan, Robin. 1990. "Nuclear Power Reactors: A Study in Technological Lock-in", *Journal of Economic History* 50: 541–556.
Cowan, Robin and Philip Gunby. 1996. "Sprayed to Death: Path Dependence, Lock-in and Pest Control Strategies", *Economic Journal* 106: 521–542.
Craig, Paul. 1999. "High-Level Nuclear Waste: The Status of Yucca Mountain", *Annual Review of Energy and Environment* 24: 461–486.
Cramer, Jacqueline. 1987. *Mission-Orientation in Ecology: The Case of Dutch Fresh-Water Ecology*. Amsterdam: Rodopi.
David, Paul A. 1985. "Clio and the Economics of QWERTY", *American Economic Review* 75(2): 332–337.
David, Paul A. 1994. "Why Are Institutions the 'Carriers of History'?: Path Dependence and the Evolution of Conventions, Organizations and Institutions", *Structural Change and Economic Dynamics* 5(2): 205–220.
David, Paul A. 2001. "Path Dependence, Its Critics, and the Quest for 'Historical Economics'", in P. Garrouste, S. Ioannides, and European Association for Evolutionary Political Economy, eds. *Evolution and Path Dependence in Economic Ideas: Past and Present*. Cheltenham: Edward Elgar, pp. 15–40.
Dawson, Jane I. and Robert G. Darst. 2006. "Meeting the Challenge of Permanent Nuclear Waste Disposal in an Expanding Europe: Transparency, Trust and Democracy", *Environmental Politics* 15(4): 610–627.

Djelie, Marie-Laure and S. Quack. 2007. "Overcoming Path Dependency: Path Generation in Open Systems", *Theory and Society* 36(2): 161–186.
Dolsak, Nives and Elinor Ostrom, eds. 2003. *Commons in the New Millennium: Challenges and Adaption.* Cambridge, MA: The MIT Press.
Dosi, Giovanni. 1988. "Sources, Procedures, and Microeconomic Effects of Innovation", *Journal of Economic Literature* 26(3): 1120–1171.
Dosi, Giovanni. 2000. *Innovation, Organization and Economic Dynamics.* Cheltenham: Edward Elgar.
Downer, John. 2014. "Disowning Fukushima: Managing the Credibility of Nuclear Reliability Assessment in the Wake of Disaster", *Regulation and Governance* 8(3): 287–309.
Dowty, Rachel A. and Barbara L. Allen. 2011. *Dynamics of Disaster: Lessons on Risk, Response and Recovery.* London: Earthscan.
Durant, John. 1992. "Editorial", *Public Understanding of Science* 1: 1–5.
Durant, John, G. A. Evans, and G. P. Thomas. 1989. "The Public Understanding of Science", *Nature* 340: 11–14.
ECOR (Engineering Committee on Ocean Resources), Japan Marine Science and Technology Association (Japan National Committee for ECOR). 1989. Ocean Energy Systems: Report of ECOR International Working Group, February.
Eden, Lynne. 2004. *Whole World on Fire: Organizations, Knowledge, and Nuclear Weapons Devastation.* Ithaca, NY: Cornell University Press.
Edgerton, David. 1993. "Tilting at Paper Tigers", *British Journal for the History of Science* 26: 67–75.
Edwards, Paul N. 2010. *A Vast Machine: Computer Models, Climate Data, and the Politics of Global Warming.* Cambridge, MA: The MIT Press.
Edwards, Paul N., Steven J. Jackson, Geoffrey C. Bowker, and Cory Knobel. 2007. Understanding Infrastructure: Dynamics, Tensions, and Design, Report of a Workshop on History and Theory of Infrastructure (NSF Grant 0630263).
Elliot, Robert and Arran Gare, eds. 1983. *Environmental Philosophy: A Collection of Readings.* Milton Keynes: Open University Press.
Elliott, James R. and Scott Frickel. 2015. "Urbanization as Socio-Environmental Succession: The Case of Hazardous Industrial Site Accumulation", *American Journal of Sociology* 120(6): 1736–1777.
Engineering Lieutenant Nozaki. 1943. Tabin Yoku no Shindo ni kansuru Kenkyu (A theoretical study on turbine blade vibration), January 15.
Espeland, Wendy Nelson. 1998. *The Struggle for Water: Politics, Rationality, and Identity in the American Southwest.* Chicago, IL: The University of Chicago Press.
Espeland, Wendy Nelson and Michael Sauder. 2007. "Rankings and Reactivity: How Public Measures Recreate Social Worlds", *American Journal of Sociology* 113(1): 1–40.
Espeland, Wendy Nelson and Berit Irene Vannebo. 2007. "Accountability, Quantification, and Law", *Annual Review of Law and Social Science* 3: 21–43.
Est, R. van. 2000. *Winds of Change: A Comparative Study of the Politics of Wind Energy Innovation in California and Denmark.* Utrecht: International Books.
European Wind Energy Association and Greenpeace. 2005. Wind Force 12: A Blueprint to Achieve 12% of the World's Electricity from Wind Power by 2020.
Evans, Rob and A. Plows. 2007. "Listening without Prejudice?: Re-Discovering the Value of the Disinterested Citizen", *Social Studies of Science* 37(6): 827–853.

Farman, J. C., B. G. Gardiner, and J. D. Shanklin. 1985. "Large Losses of Total Ozone in Antarctica Reveal Seasonal ClOx/NOx Interaction", *Nature* 315: 207–210.

Flint, Alan, Lorraine Flint, Guddmundur Bodvarsson, Edward Kwicklis, and June Fabryka-Martin. 2001. "Evolution of the Conceptual Model of Unsaturated Zone Hydrology at Yucca Mountain, Nevada", *Journal of Hydrology* 247(1): 1–30.

Flynn, James, William Burns, C. K. Mertz, and Paul Slovic. 1992. "Trust as a Determinant of Opposition to a High-Level Radioactive Waste Repository: Analysis of a Structural Model", *Risk Analysis* 12(3): 417–429.

Fortun, Kim. 2001. *Advocacy after Bhopal: Environmentalism, Disaster, New Global Orders*. Chicago, IL: The University of Chicago Press.

Fortun, Kim, Scott Gabriel Knowles, Vivian Choi, Paul Jobin, Miwao Matsumoto, Pedro de la Torre III, Max Liboiron, and L. F. Murillo. 2017. "Researching Disaster from a STS Perspective", in Ulrike Felt, Rayvon Fouché, Clark Miller, and Laurel Smith-Doerr, eds. *The Handbook of Science and Technology Studies*, 4th ed. Cambridge, MA: The MIT Press, pp. 1003–1028.

Freeman, Christopher and L. Soete, eds. 1990. *New Explorations in the Economics of Technical Change*. London: Pinter.

Frickel, Scott and Kelly Moore, eds. 2006. *The New Political Sociology of Science: Institutions, Networks, and Power*. Madison, WI: The University of Wisconsin Press.

Garud, Raghu and Peter Kanøe. 2003. "Bricolage versus Breakthrough: Distributed and Embedded Agency in Technology Entrepreneurship", *Research Policy* 32: 277–300.

Geels, Frank W. 2004. "From Sectoral Systems of Innovation to Socio-Technical Systems: Insights about Dynamics and Change from Sociology and Institutional Theory", *Research Policy* 33: 897–920.

GHQ/SCAP. 1945a. Records Box No. 9090 NRS-06247, Report on Scientific Intelligence Survey in Japan, Vol. 1.

GHQ/SCAP. 1945b. Records Box No. 8354 ESS (1)-00727), Report on Scientific Intelligence Survey in Japan, Vol. 3, Appendix 3-A-1.

GHQ/SCAP. 1951. Records Box No. 7339, ESS(B)11589-(B)11632, Science Reorganization-Research Restoration Council, 1947 to JSC No. 5.

Global Wind Energy Council. 2017. http://www.gwec.net/wp-content/uploads/vip/GWEC_PRstats2016_EN_WEB.pdf#search=%27wind+power+world+by+country+statistics%27 (confirmed on August 17, 2017).

Goldthorpe, John H. 2007. *On Sociology, Vol. 1: Critique and Program*. Stanford, CA: Stanford University Press.

Gould, Roger V. 1991. "Multiple Networks and Mobilization in the Paris Commune, 1871", *American Sociological Review* 56(6): 716–729.

The Governmental Investigation Committee on the Accident at Fukushima Nuclear Power Stations of Tokyo Electric Power Company. 2011a. The Draft of Interim Report, Materials (in Japanese).

The Governmental Investigation Committee on the Accident at Fukushima Nuclear Power Stations of Tokyo Electric Power Company. 2011b. The Agreement of the Methods of Hearing of the Governmental Investigation Committee: July 8 (in Japanese).

The Governmental Investigation Committee on the Accident at Fukushima Nuclear Power Stations of Tokyo Electric Power Company. 2012a. The Interim Report (in Japanese).

The Governmental Investigation Committee on the Accident at Fukushima Nuclear Power Stations of Tokyo Electric Power Company. 2012b. The Final Report (in Japanese).

Granovetter, Mark. 1978. "Threshold Models of Collective Behavior", *American Journal of Sociology* 83(6): 1420–1443.

Grant II, D. S., A. W. Jones, and A. J. Bergesen. 2002. "Organizational Size and Pollution: The Case of the U.S. Chemical Industry", *American Sociological Review* 67(3): 389–407.

Gribbin, J. 1988. *The Hole in the Sky: Man's Threat to the Ozone Layer*. London: Corgi Books.

Gusterson, Hugh. 1996. *Nuclear Rites: A Weapons Laboratory at the End of the Cold War*. Berkeley, CA: The University of California Press.

Hacking, Ian. 1999. *The Social Construction of What?* Cambridge, MA: Harvard University Press.

Hannigan, John A. 1995. *Environmental Sociology: A Social Constructionist Perspective*. London: Routledge.

Hardin, G. 1968. "The Tragedy of the Commons", *Science* 162: 1243–1248.

Harremoës, Poul, David Gee, Malcolm MacGarvin, Andy Stirling, Jane Keys, Brian Wynne, and Sofia Vaz, eds. 2002. *The Precautionary Principle in the 20th Century*. London: Earthscan.

Hart, David M. and David G. Victor. 1993. "Scientific Elites and the Making of US Policy for Climate Change Research, 1957–74", *Social Studies of Science* 23(4): 643–680.

Hashimoto, Takehiko. 1994. "Obei niokeru Furyokuhatsuden Gijutsu (Wind power generation technology in U.S. and Europe)", NEDO Report on Technological Inheritance, pp. 93–118.

Hata, Takashi. 1998. *Gakujutsu Taisei Sasshin Iinkai Kankei Shiryo Mokuroku* (The Catalogue of Materials of the Committee on the Reorganization of the Academic Sector). Hiroshima: Research Institute for Higher Education of the Hiroshima University.

Hecht, Gabrielle. 1998. *The Radiance of France: Nuclear Power and National Security after World War II*. Cambridge, MA: The MIT Press.

Hecht, Gabrielle. 2012. *Being Nuclear: Africans and the Global Uranium Trade*. Cambridge, MA: The MIT Press.

Hedström, Peter. 2005. *Dissecting the Social: On the Principles of Analytical Sociology*. Cambridge: Cambridge University Press.

Heilbron, Johan. 2011. "Practical Foundations of Theorizing in Sociology", in Charles Camic, et al., eds. *Social Knowledge in the Making*. Chicago: The University of Chicago Press, pp. 181–205.

Heller, M. A. 1998. "The Tragedy of the Anticommons: Property in the Transition from Marx to Markets", *Harvard Law Review* 111(3): 621–688.

Heller, M. A. and R. S. Eisenberg. 1998. "Can Patent Deter Innovation?: The Anticommons in Biomedical Research", *Science* 280: 698–701.

Hess, Charlotte and Elinor Ostrom, eds. 2007. *Understanding Knowledge as a Commons: From Theory to Practice*. Cambridge, MA: The MIT Press.

Hess, David J. 2007. *Alternative Pathways in Science and Industry: Activism, Innovation, and the Environment in an Era of Globalization*. Cambridge, MA: The MIT Press.

Hess, David J. 2009. *Localist Movements in a Global Economy: Sustainability, Justice, and Urban Development in the United States*. Cambridge, MA: The MIT Press.

Hilgartner, S. and C. L. Bosk. 1988. "The Rise and Fall of Social Problems: A Public Arena Model", *American Journal of Sociology* 94(1): 53–78.
Hiroshige, Tetsu. 1973. *Kagaku no Shakaishi, Kindai Nihon no Kagaku Taisei* (The Social History of Science: Scientific Institutions in Modern Japan). Tokyo: Chuokoronsha.
The History of Science Society of Japan. 1964. *Nihon Kagakugijutsushi Taikei* (The Compendium of the History of Science and Technology in Japan), Vol. 5. Tokyo: Daiichi Hoki.
Hobbes, Thomas. 1651. "Leviathan: Or, the Matter, Form, and Power of a Commonwealth", in William Molesworth, ed. 1839–1845. *The English Works of Thomas Hobbes of Malmesbury*, 11 vols. London: John Bohn.
Huang, Gillan Chi-Lun, Tim Gray, and Derek Bell. 2013. "Environmental Justice of Nuclear Waste Policy in Taiwan: Taipower, Government, and Local Community", *Environment, Development and Sustainability* 15(6): 1555–1571.
Hughes, Thomas P. 1983. *Networks of Power: Electrification in Western Society, 1880–1930*. Baltimore, MD: Johns Hopkins University Press.
Hughes, Thomas P. 1986. "The Seamless Web: Technology, Science, Etcetera, Etcetera", *Social Studies of Science* 16(2): 281–292.
The Institute for the Compilation of Historical Records Relating to the Imperial Japanese Navy. 1981. *Kaigun* (The Navy).
Irwin, Alan. 2006. "The Politics of Talk: Coming to Term with the 'New' Scientific Governance", *Social Studies of Science* 36(2): 299–320.
Ishibashi, A., D. Karikawa, M. Takahashi, T. Wakabayashi, and M. Kitamura. 2010. "Genshiryoku Hatsudenbunya niokeru Anzenishiki Kojo notameno Crew Resource Management Gainen ni motozuku Kunrenshuho (Training Method for Enhancement of Safety Attitude in Nuclear Power Plant Based on Crew Resource Management)", *Transactions of the Atomic Energy Society of Japan* 9(4): 384–395.
Ishikawa, Junkichi. 1975–1987. *Kokka Sodoin Shi* (The History of Wartime Mobilization), 13 vols. Tokyo: Kokka Sodoin Shi Kankokai.
Ishiyama, Tokuko. 2004. *Amerika Senjuminzoku to Kaku Haikibutsu* (Indigenous Peoples of the U. S. and Nuclear Waste). Tokyo: Akashi Shoten.
Ito, M. 1956. *Dai Kaigun o Omou* (On the Imperial Japanese Navy). Tokyo.
Iwamura, Hisashi. 1981. "Furyoku Hatsuden (Wind Power Generation)", *Karyoku Genshiryokuhatsuden* 32(10): 150–158.
Jacobs, E. N., K. E. Ward, and R. M. Pinkerton. 1933. "The Characteristics of 78 Related Airfoil Sections from Tests in the Variable-Density Wind Tunnel", Report No. 460, NACA.
JAIF (Japan Atomic Industrial Forum). 1965. *Genshiryoku Kaihatsu 10 Nenshi* (The Ten Years History of Nuclear Development). Tokyo.
JAIF. 2008. Kaigai Dokochosa Saishu Hokokusho (The final report of the world trends of HLW disposal).
JAIF. n.d. Materials Circulated at Study Group of HLW Disposal (in Japanese).
Japan Atomic Power Co. 1989. *Nihon Genshiryokuhatsuden 30 Nenshi* (The Thirtieth History of Japan Atomic Power Co.). Tokyo.
Japan Coast Guard. 1976–1980. Kaijo Hoan Hakusho (White paper).
Japanese Association for the Promotion of Industrial Technology. 1987. *Showa 61 Nendo Sunshine Keikaku Kenkyu Kaihatsu no Gaikyo, Sogo Kenkyu* (The Outline of R & D of the 'Sunshine' Project for Fiscal 1986). Tokyo: Nihon Sangyo Gijutsu Shinko Kyokai, April.

Jasanoff, Sheila. 1985. *Controlling Chemicals: The Politics of Regulation in Europe and the U. S.* Ithaca, NY: Cornell University Press.

JNC (Japan Nuclear Cycle Development Institute). 1999a. Wagakuni okeru HLW Shobun no Gijutsuteki Sinraisei (Technological reliability of HLW disposal in Japan: General report), JNC TN1400 99-020.

JNC. 1999b. Wagakuni okeru HLW Shobun no Gijutsuteki Sinraisei Chikyu Kankyo (Technological reliability of HLW disposal in Japan: The environment of the earth), JNC TN1400 99-021.

JNC. 1999c. Wagakuni okeru HLW Shobun no Gijutsuteki Sinraisei Kogaku Gijutsu (Technological reliability of HLW disposal in Japan: Engineering), JNC TN1400 99-022.

JNC. 1999d. Wagakuni okeru HLW Shobun no Gijutsuteki Sinraisei Chiso Shobun Sisutemu no Anzensei Hyoka (Technological reliability of HLW disposal in Japan: Safety assessment), JNC TN1400 99-023.

JNC. 1999e. HLW Mondai no Kaiketsu ni mukete Chisoshobun Kenkyu Kaihatsu (For the solution of HLW disposal: R&D on geological disposal).

Jobin, Paul. 2013. "Radiation Protection after 3.11: Conflicts of Interpretation and Challenges to Current Standards Based on the Experience of Nuclear Plant Workers", Paper presented at Forum on the 2011 Fukushima/East Japan Disaster, May 13, Berkeley.

Jones, Bryan D. 2001. *Politics and Architecture of Choice: Bounded Rationality and Governance*. Chicago, IL: The University of Chicago Press.

JSPS (Japan Society for the Promotion of Science). 1993. The 149th Committee on High-Tech and Global Environment, Gunjigijutsu kara Minseigijutsu heno Tenkan (The spin-off from military technology to commercial technology).

JSPS. 1996. The 149th Committee on High-Tech and Global Environment, Gunjigijutsu kara Minseigijutsu heno Tenkan II (The spin-off from military technology to commercial technology II).

Juraku, Kohta. 2013. "The Failure of Japan's 'Successful' Nuclear Program: Structural Problems Revealed by the Fukushima Daiichi Nuclear Accident", in R. Hindmarsh, ed. *Nuclear Disaster at Fukushima Daiichi: Social, Political and Environmental Issues*. Abingdon: Routledge, pp. 41–56.

Juraku, Kohta and T. Suzuki. 2007. "Genshiryokuk no Fukyu niokeru Shakai Ishikettei Purosesu (Social Decision-Making Process in the Diffusion of Nuclear Power: The Case of Siting in Maki-Machi and Hokkaido)", in T. Suzuki, et al., eds. *Enerugi Gijutsu no Shakai Ishhikettei* (Social Decision-Making on Energy Technologies). Tokyo: Nihon Hyoron Sha.

Juraku, Kohta, T. Suzuki, and O. Sakura. 2007. "Social Decision-Making Processes in Local Contexts: A STS Case Study on Nuclear Power Plant Siting in Japan", *East Asian Science, Technology and Society* 1: 53–75.

Kaigun Daijin Kanbo Rinji Chosa Ka (Temporary Research Section, the Minister of the Imperial Japanese Navy's Secretariat), ed. 1984. *Teikoku Gikai Kaigun Kankei Giji Sokki Roku* (Minutes of Imperial Diet Sessions Regarding Navy-Related Subjects), Bekkan 1, 2. Reprinted ed., Vol. 3, Part 1. Tokyo: Hara Shobo.

Kaiyo Kagaku Gijutsu Senta (Research Center for Marine Science and Technology). 1978. Wagakuni no Kaiyo Kaihatsu Vijon to Kaiyo Kagaku Gijutsu Kadai nikansuru Chosa Hokokusho (Report on the ocean development program and the targets for marine science and technology). Tokyo: Kaiyo Kagaku Gijutsu Senta.

Kajikawa, Takenobu. 1981. "Kaiyo Ondosa Hatsuden-nodosa Hatsuden (OTEC and Energy Conversion Using Salinity Gradient)", *Oyo Butsuri* 50(4): 415–423.
Kamogawa, Hiroshi. 1978. "Shigen Mondai Kaiketsu notameno Kaiyo Ondosa Hatsuden (OTEC for Solving Resource Problems)", *Keidanren Geppo* 26(5): 76–82.
Karnøe, Peter and Raghu Garud. 2012. "Path Creation: Co-Creation of Heterogeneous Resources in the Emergence of the Danish Wind Turbine Cluster", *European Planning Studies* 20(5): 733–752.
Kashimoto, Yoshikazu. 2016. "Kakunenryo Saishori Mondai no Perspective: Tokunoshima Ricchikeikaku to sono Hantai Undo (The Perspective of the Nuclear Fuel Reprocessing Problem in Japan: The Construction Plan for a Nuclear Fuel Reprocessing Plant on Tokunoshima Island and the Residents' Resistance)", *Japanese Journal for Science, Technology and Society* 25: 77–106.
Kawamura, Minato. 1996. *Daitoa Minzokugaku no Kyojitsu* (The Reality and Surface of Folklore in the Greater East Asia). Tokyo: Kodansha.
Keidanren. 1978. *Keidanren 30 Nenshi* (The 30th Years History of the Federation of Economic Organizations). Tokyo.
Kerr, A., S. Cunningham-Burley, and R. Tutton. 2007. "Shifting Subject Positions: Experts and Lay People in Public Dialogue", *Social Studies of Science* 37(3): 385–411.
Kiba, Takao. 2003. *Chishikishakai no Yukue: Petit Senmonka Shokogun o Koete* (The Prospect of Knowledge Society: Beyond Petit Expert Syndrome). Tokyo: Nihon Keizai Hyoronsha.
Kitsuse, J. I. and M. Spector. 1977. *Constructing Social Problems*. San Francisco, CA: Cummings.
Knowles, Scott Gabriel. 2011. *The Disaster Experts: Mastering Risk in Modern America*. Philadelphia, PA: University of Pennsylvania Press.
Kochi Prefecture. 2008. http://www.pref.kochi.jp/~toukei/ (confirmed on November 14, in Japanese).
Koestler, Arthur. 1960. *The Watershed: A Biography of Johannes Kepler*. New York: Doubleday.
Kokusaku Kenkyukai. 1945. *Daitoa Kyoeiken Gijutsu Taisei-ron* (The Socio-Technical System of the Greater East Asia Co-Prosperity Sphere). Tokyo: Nihonhyoronsha.
Komiya, Y. 1988. "Furon Kisei Mondai to Nihon no Taio (CFC Control Problem and Actions Taken by Japan)", *Kogai to Taisaku* 24(3): 45–53.
Kotake, Munio. 1941. *Kagakusha no Shinkyo* (A State of Mind of a Scientist). Tokyo: Unebishobo.
Krimsky, Sheldon and Alonzo Plough. 1988. *Environmental Hazards: Communicating Risks as a Social Process*. London: Auburn House.
Kubota, Y. 1981. *85 Nen no Kaiso* (Reminiscences of 85 Years). For private distribution. Tokyo.
Kuchinskaya, Olga. 2014. *The Politics of Invisibility: Public Knowledge about Radiation Health Effects after Chernobyl*. Cambridge, MA: The MIT Press.
Kuhn, Thomas S. 1962. *The Structure of Scientific Revolutions*. Chicago, IL: The University of Chicago Press.
Latour, Bruno. (1984)1988. *Les Microbes: Guerre et paix, suivi de irréductions*. Paris: Editions A. M. Métailié. Translated by Alan Sheridan and John Law, *The Pasteurization of France*. Cambridge, MA: Harvard University Press.
Latour, Bruno. 1991. *Nous n'avons jamais été modernes: Essai d'anthropologie symétrique*. Paris: La Découverte.

Latour, Bruno. (1993)1996. *ARAMIS ou l'amour des techniques*. Paris: La Découverte. Translated by C. Porter, *ARAMIS or the Love of Technology*. Cambridge, MA: Harvard University Press.
Latour, Bruno. 2005. *Reassembling the Social: An Introduction to Actor-Network-Theory*. Oxford: Oxford University Press.
Law, John. 1991. "Theory and Narrative in the History of Technology: Response", *Technology and Culture* 32(2): 377–384.
Law, John. 2002. *Aircraft Stories: Decentering the Object in Technoscience*. Durham, NC: Duke University Press.
Law, John. 2017. "STS as Method", in Ulrike Felt, Rayvon Fouché, Clark Miller, and Laurel Smith-Doerr, eds. *Handbook of Science and Technology Studies*, 4th ed. Cambridge, MA: The MIT Press, pp. 31–57.
Legett, D. 2011. "Spectacles and Witnessing: Constructing Readings of Charles Parsons's Marine Turbine", *Technology and Culture* 52(2): 287–309.
Lehtonen, Markku. 2010. "Risk, Hazards and Crisis in Public Policy", *Policy Studies Organization* 1(4): 139–179.
Leigh Star, Susan. 1989. "The Structure of Ill-Structured Solutions: Boundary Objects and Heterogeneous Distributed Problem Solving", in Les Gasser and Michael N. Huhns, eds. *Distributed Artificial Intelligence*, Vol. 2. London: Pitman.
Leist, K. 1957. "An Experimental Arrangement for the Measurement of the Pressure Distribution on High-Speed Rotating Blade Rows", *Transactions of the American Society of the Mechanical Engineers* April: 617–626.
Leslie, Stuart W. 1993. *The Cold War and American Science: The Military-Industrial-Academic Complex at MIT and Stanford*. New York: Columbia University Press.
Lévi-Strauss, Claude. 1958. *Anthropologie Structurale*. Paris: Plon.
Library of Congress. 2012. "Fukushima Daiichi Genpatsujiko to Yottsuno Jikochosaiinkai (The Fukushima Nuclear Accident and Four Investigation Committees)", *Issue Brief* 756: 1–20.
Lidskog, Rolf and Göran Sundqvist. 2004. "On the Right Track?: Technology, Geology and Society in Swedish Nuclear Waste Management", *Journal of Risk Research* 7(2): 251–268.
Liebowitz, Stan J. and S. E. Margolis. 1990. "The Fable of the Keys", *Journal of Law and Economics* 33(1): 1–25.
Liebowitz, Stan J. and S. E. Margolis, eds. 2014. *Path-Dependence and Lock-in*. Cheltenham: Edward Elgar.
Lin, K. 2006. "Inequalities, Knowledge and Public Deliberation: Three Consensus Conferences in Taiwan", Proceeding of EASTS Conference, pp. 1–28.
Lindee, Susan. 1994. *Suffering Made Real: American Science and the Survivors at Hiroshima*. Chicago, IL: The University of Chicago Press.
Linnenluecke, Martina, Andrew Griffiths, and Monika Winn. 2012. "Extreme Weather Events and the Critical Importance of Adaptation and Organizational Resilience in Responding to Impacts", *Business Strategy and the Environment* 21: 17–32.
Long, Jane C. S. and Rodney C. Ewing. 2004. "Yucca Mountain: Earth-Science Issues at a Geologic Repository for High-Level Nuclear Waste", *Annual Review of Earth and Planetary Science* 32: 363–401.
Lowe, P. and S. Ward, eds. 1998. *British Environmental Policy and Europe: Politics and Policy in Transition*. London: Routledge.
Luck, G. A. and B. C. Kell. 1956. "Measuring Turbine Blade Vibrations: Development of Barium Titanate Transducers", *Engineering* 31: 271–273.

Luhmann, Niklas. (1991)1993. *Soziologie des Risikos*. Berlin: Walter des Gruyter. Translated by R. Barrett, *Risk: A Sociological Theory*. Berlin: Walter des Gruyter.
Lynd, Robert. 1939. *Knowledge for What?: The Place of Social Science in American Culture*. Princeton, NJ: Princeton University Press.
Macfarlane, Allison. 2003. "Underlying Yucca Mountain: The Interplay of Geology and Policy in Nuclear Waste Disposal", *Social Studies of Science* 33(5): 783–807.
Macfarlane, Allison. 2012. "The Nuclear Fuel Cycle and the Problem of Prediction", *Japanese Journal for Science, Technology and Society* 21: 69–85.
Mack, P. E. 1990. *Viewing the Earth: The Social Construction of the Landsat Satellite System*. Cambridge, MA: The MIT Press.
MacKenzie, Donald. 1978. "Statistical Theory and Social Interests: A Case Study", *Social Studies of Science* 8(1): 35–83.
MacKenzie, Donald. 1981. *Statistics in Britain: 1865–1930*. Edinburgh: Edinburgh University Press.
MacKenzie, Donald. 1990. *Inventing Accuracy: A Historical Sociology of Nuclear Missile Guidance*. Cambridge, MA: The MIT Press.
MacKenzie, Donald. 2001. *Mechanizing Proof*. Cambridge, MA: The MIT Press.
Macy, M. 1991. "Chains of Cooperation: Threshold Effects in Collective Action", *American Sociological Review* 56(6): 730–747.
Magnusson, L. and J. Ottosson, eds. 1997. *Evolutionary Economics and Path Dependence*. Cheltenham: Edward Elgar.
Mahoney, J. 2000. "Path Dependence in Historical Sociology", *Theory and Society* 29(4): 507–548.
March, James and Herbert Simon. 1993. *Organizations*, 2nd ed. Hoboken, NJ: John Wiley & Sons.
Martin, John Levi. 2009. *Social Structures*. Princeton: Princeton University Press.
Masco, Joseph. 2006. *The Nuclear Borderlands: The Manhattan Project in Post-Cold War New Mexico*. Princeton, NJ: Princeton University Press.
Matsumoto, Miwao. (1998)2016. *Kagaku Gijutsu Shakaigaku no Riron* (A Sociological Theory of the Science-Technology-Society Interface). Tokyo: Bokutakusha.
Matsumoto, Miwao. 1999. "A Hidden Pitfall in the Path of Prewar Japanese Military Technology", *Transactions of the Newcomen Society for the History of Engineering and Technology* 71(2): 305–325.
Matsumoto, Miwao. (2002)2012. *Chi no Shippai to Shakai* (The Failure of the Science-Technology-Society Interface). Tokyo: Iwanami Shoten.
Matsumoto, Miwao. 2005. "The Uncertain But Crucial Relationship between a 'New Energy' Technology and Global Environmental Problems", *Social Studies of Science* 35(4): 623–651.
Matsumoto, Miwao. 2006. *Technology Gatekeepers for War and Peace*. Basingstoke: Palgrave Macmillan.
Matsumoto, Miwao. 2009. *Tekunosaiensu risk to Shakaigaku* (The Social Risks of Techno-science). Tokyo: The University of Tokyo Press.
Matsumoto, Miwao. 2010. "Theoretical Challenges for the Current Sociology of Science and Technology: A Prospect for its Future Development", *East Asian Science, Technology & Society: An International Journal* 4(1): 129–136.
Matsumoto, Miwao. 2012. *Kozo Sai* (Structural Disaster). Tokyo: Iwanami Shoten.
Matsumoto, Miwao. 2013. "'Structural Disaster' Long before Fukushima: A Hidden Accident", *Development and Society* 42(2): 165–190.

Matsumoto, Miwao. 2014. "The 'Structural Disaster' of the Science-Technology-Society Interface: From a Comparative Perspective with a Prewar Accident", in J. Ahn, C. Carson, et al., eds. *Reflections on the Fukushima Daiichi Nuclear Accident*. Heidelberg: Springer, pp. 189–214.

Matsumoto, Miwao. 2017. "The Sociology of Science and Technology", in Kathleen Korgen, ed. *Cambridge Handbook of Sociology*, Vol. 2. Cambridge: Cambridge University Press, pp. 166–177.

Matsumoto, Miwao and Kohta Juraku. 2017. "'Structural Disaster' beyond Fukushima: Messages from the Sociology of Science and Technology", in K. Chou, ed. *Energy Transition in East Asia: A Social Science Perspective*. Abingdon: Routledge, pp. 145–159.

Matsumoto, Miwao and Takuo Nishide. 2004. "The Path-Dependency of Renewable Energy Technology and the Role of Relevant Outsiders", Proceedings of International Workshop on Social Decision Making Process for Energy Technology Introduction, pp. 19–31.

McCright, Aaron M. and Riley E. Dunlap. 2003. "Defeating Kyoto: The Conservative Movement's Impact on U.S. Climate Change Policy", *Social Problems* 50(3): 348–373.

McIntyre, Owen and Thomas Mosedale. 1997. "The Precautionary Principle as a Norm of Customary International Law", *Journal of Environmental Law* 9(2): 221–241.

Mechanical Engineering. 1940. "Turbine-Blade Fatigue Testing", 62(12): 919–921.

Merton, Robert K. 1936. "The Unanticipated Consequences of Social Action", *American Sociological Review* 1: 894–904.

Merton, Robert K. 1957. *Social Theory and Social Structure: Toward the Codification of Theory and Research*, revised ed. New York: Free Press.

Merton, Robert K. 1970. *Science, Technology and Society in Seventeenth Century England*. New York: Howard Fertig, originally published in 1938 in *Osiris* 4(2): 360–632.

METI (Ministry of Economy, Trade and Industry). 1992. Accident management no Kongo no Susumekata nitsuite (Procedures to implement counter-measures against accidents), July.

METI. 2008a. http://www.shigen-energy.jp/atom/note/095096.htm (confirmed on March 14, 2009, in Japanese).

METI. 2008b. Agency of Natural Resources and Energy, Dengen Ricchi Seido no Gaiyo (The outline of the siting of power sources), March.

METI. 2014a. Hosha-sei Haiki-butsu WG Chukan Torimatome (Interim report of radioactive waste working group), May 2014.

METI. 2014b. Saishin-no Chiken-ni Motozuku Chiso-shobun Gujutsu-no Saihyoka: Chishitsu-kankyo Tokusei oyobi Chishitsu-kankyo-no Choki Antei-sei nitsuite (Reevaluation of geological disposal technology based on the latest scientific knowledge: On the characteristics of geological environment and long-term stability of geological environment), May.

METI. 2015. Basic Policy on the Final Disposal of Designated Radioactive Wastes was Revised: The Government of Japan will Play a Proactive Role in Resolving the Issue of Designated Radioactive Wastes, Press Release on May 22, 2015. www.meti.go.jp/english/press/2015/0522_01.html.

METI. 2016. http://www.enecho.meti.go.jp/topics/pamphlet/dengen_pamphlet.pdf (confirmed on September 25, 2016, in Japanese).

METI, HLW Committee of Nuclear Power Section of Electric Utility Branch of Advisory Committee for Natural Resources and Energy. 2007. Hoshaseihaikibutsu

Shoiinkaihokokusho Chukantorimatomean, Saishushobunjigyo o Suishinsurutameno Torikumi no Kyokasaku nitsuite (The draft of the interim report of HLW committee: The reinforcement measures for the siting of the final HLW disposal stations), September 12.
MEXT (Ministry of Education, Culture, Sports, Science and Technology). 2012. Higashinihonndaishinsai karano Fukkyu Fukko nikansuru Monbukagakusho no Torikumi nitsuiteno Kenshokekka no Matome (Inspections into the measures taken by MEXT for recovery from the Great East Japan Earthquake, second report), July 27.
MEXT. n.d. Genshiryoku Kankyo Bosai Nettowaku Genshiryoku Bosai Joho (Environment protection and nuclear disaster prevention network and information).
MHI (Mitsubishi Heavy Industries, Ltd). 2008. www.mhi.co.jp/power/wind/supplier/index.html (confirmed on December 21, in Japanese).
Milbrath, Lester W. 1984. *Environmentalists: Vanguard for a New Society*. Albany, NY: State University of New York Press.
Mileti, Dennis S. 1999. *Disasters by Design: A Reassessment of Natural Hazards in the United States*. Washington, DC: Joseph Henry Press.
Miller, Clark A. and Paul N. Edwards, eds. 2001. *Changing the Atmosphere: Expert Knowledge and Environmental Governance*. Cambridge, MA: The MIT Press.
Miller, J. D. 1992. "The Origins and Consequences of Scientific Literacy in Industrial Societies", Paper presented to the International Conference on the Public Understanding of Science and Technology, October 6, Tokyo.
Ministry of the Environment. 2001. Chikyukankyo Sogokenkyusuishinhi Shuryo Hokokuso (The final report of the global environmental research funded by Ministry of the Environment, 2000–2001).
Ministry of the Environment. 2012. Josen Tokubetsuchiiki niokeru Josen no Hoshin: Josen Roadmap no Kohyo nitsuite (The decontamination policy in the designated areas for the clearance of evacuation: The roadmap of decontamination), January 26.
Ministry of Internal Affairs and Communications. 2014. http://law.e-gov.go.jp/htmldata/H07/H07HO130.html (confirmed on February 20, 2017, in Japanese).
The Minister of the Navy's Secretariat. 1938. Military secret No. 266. Issued on January 19.
MITI (Ministry of International Trade and Industry). 1954. Annual Report of MITI (in Japanese).
Molina, M. J. and F. S. Rowland. 1974. "Stratospheric Sink for Chlorofluoromethanes: Chlorine Atomic-Catalyzed Destruction of Ozone", *Nature* 249: 810–812.
Monthly Report of Atomic Energy Commission. 1957. 2(9): 16–18 (in Japanese).
Moore, N. W. 1987. *The Bird of Time: The Science and Politics of Nature Conservation*. Cambridge: Cambridge University Press.
Mori, Sadao. 1986a. "Furyokuhatsuden to sono Unten Seigyo (Wind Power Generation and the Control of Operation)", *Denkigakkai Zasshi* 106(9): 879–886.
Mori, Sadao. 1986b. "Jisshoshikenchu no Miyakejima no Furyokuhatsuden nitsuite (On the Test Trial of Wind Power Generation in the Miyakejima Island)", *Doryoku* 36(174): 18–24.
Mori, Shigeru. 1969. "Waga Seishun (My Youth)", *Shizuoka Newspaper*, August 29, August 30, September 1.
Morris, Peter W. G. and George H. Hough. 1987. *The Anatomy of Major Projects: A Study of the Reality of Project Management*. Oxford: Major Projects Association, Templeton College, University of Oxford.

Mullins, N. C. 1973. *Theories and Theory Groups in Contemporary American Sociology*. New York: Harper & Row.

Muraoka, Susumu. 1995. "Ko Rebel Hoshasei Haikibutsu (HLW)", *Transactions of the Atomic Energy Society of Japan* 37(11): 989–990.

Murphy, Raymond. 2009. *Leadership in Disaster: Learning for a Future with Global Climate Change*. Montreal & Kingston: McGill-Queen's University Press.

Nagasaki, Shinya, Hideo Kimura, Joonhong Ahn, Shigenobu Hirusawa, and Toru Murano. 1995. "Chisoshobun no Kadai (The Problems of HLW Disposal)", *Transactions of the Atomic Energy Society of Japan* 37(11): 1010–1016.

NAIIC (National Diet of Japan Fukushima Nuclear Accident Independent Investigation Commission). 2012a. Report, Executive Summary.

NAIIC. 2012b. Report (in Japanese).

NAIIC. 2012c. The Minutes of the 2nd Meeting of January 16 (in Japanese).

NAIIC. 2012d. The Minutes of the 6th Meeting of March 14 (in Japanese).

NAIIC. 2012e. The Minutes of the 13th Meeting of May 16 (in Japanese).

Nakanishi, Tomoko, et al., eds. 2013. *Agricultural Implications of the Fukushima Nuclear Accident*. Heidelberg: Springer.

Nakanishi, Tomoko and Keitaro Tanoi, eds. 2016. *Agricultural Implications of the Fukushima Nuclear Accident: The First Three Years*. Heidelberg: Springer.

Nakayama, Shinichi. 2016. Materials Given at the the Joonhong Ahn Memorial Symposium on Back End Sciences, The University of Tokyo, June 25, 2016 (in Japanese).

National Institute for Ship Experiment. 1956. *Senkei Shikenjo Kinenshi* (The Commemorative History of the National Institute for Ship Experiment). Tokyo.

NEDO (New Energy and Industrial Technology Development Organization). 1994. www.nedo.go.jp/kankobutsu/foreigninfo/html9908/08229.html (confirmed on March 13, 2006, in Japanese).

NEDO. 2008. Furyoku Hatsuden Donyu Gaidobukku (The guidebook for the introduction of wind power generation).

NEDO. 2012. www.nedo.go.jp/library/fuuryoku/state/1-03.html (confirmed on June 1, in Japanese).

Nelkin, Dorothy. 1971. *Nuclear Power and Its Critics: The Cayuga Lake Controversy*. Ithaca, NY: Cornell University Press.

Nelson, Richard and Sidney G. Winter. 1982. *An Evolutionary Theory of Economic Change*. Cambridge, MA: Harvard University Press.

NISA (Nuclear and Industrial Safety Agency). 2011. Plan to Implement Overall Assessment and Evaluation of the Safety of All the Existing Nuclear Power Plants Devised on the Accident of the Fukushima Daiichi Power Station, July 21 (in Japanese).

NISA. 2012. http://www.nisa.meti.go.jp/earthquake/speedi/erc/speedirerc index.html (confirmed on July 12, 2012, in Japanese).

NRC (Nuclear Regulatory Commission), Committee on Disposition of High-Level Radioactive Waste through Geological Isolation, Board on Radioactive Waste Management, Disposition of High-Level Waste and Spent Nuclear Fuel. 2001. The Continuing Societal and Technical Challenges.

NRC, Committee on Principles and Operation: Strategies for Staged Repository Systems. 2003. One Step at a Time: The Staged Development of Geologic Repositories for High-Level Radioactive Waste.

Nuclear Safety Commission. 2008. Kankyo Hoshasen Monitoring Shishin (The guideline for monitoring radiation in the environment, revised in April 2010).

NUMO (Nuclear Waste Management Organization of Japan). 2007. Kochiken Toyocho Bunkenchosa Keikakuksho (The plan of the documentary survey of the history of geological events in Toyocho in Kochi Prefecture).
NUMO. 2008. http://www.numo.or.jp/new_koubo/pdf/kyo-010.pdf (confirmed on August 7, 2009, in Japanese).
NWMO (The Nuclear Waste Management Organization). 2016. www.nwmo.ca/en/Canadas-Plan/Canadas-Used-Nuclear-Fuel/Regulatory-Oversight (confirmed on September 24, 2016).
OECD/NEA. 2011. Reversibility and Retrievability (R & R) for the Deep Disposal of High-Level Radioactive Waste and Spent Fuel: Final Report of the NEA R & R Project (2007–2011).
OECD/NEA. 2012. Reversibility and Retrievability in Planning for Geological Disposal of Radioactive Waste: Proceedings of the "R&R" International Conference and Dialogue. No. 6993.
Office of Civilian Radioactive Waste Management. 1998. "Volume 1: Introduction and Site Characteristics", in *Viability Assessment of a Repository at Yucca Mountain: DOE/RW-0508*, December. Washington, DC: Department of Energy.
Ogburn, William F. 1946. *The Social Effects of Aviation*. Boston, MA: Houghton Mifflin.
Oliver, Pamela, Gerald Marwell, and Ruy Teixeira. 1985. "A Theory of Critical Mass, I: Interdependence, Group Heterogeneity, and the Production of Collective Action", *American Journal of Sociology* 91(3): 522–556.
Oliver, Pamela, Gerald Marwell, and Ruy Teixeira. 1988. "The Paradox of Group Size in Collective Action: A Theory of Critical Mass, II", *American Sociological Review* 53(1): 1–8.
Olson, Mancur. 1965. *The Logic of Collective Action*. Cambridge, MA: Harvard University Press.
Ono, Kansei. 1943. Tabin Yoku no Kyosei Shindo ni kansuru Kinji Keisan (An approximate calculation on the forced vibration of turbine blades). Engine Laboratory, Department of Sciences, Naval Technical Research Institute, August.
Osada, Isamu, et al. 2001. "Giyaresu Kahensoku Furyokuhatsudensochi no Kaihatsu (The Development of Gearless Automatic Transmission Wind Turbines)", *Mitsubishi Heavy Industries Technical Review* 38(2): 100–103.
Ostrom, Elinor. 1990. *Governing the Commons: The Evolution of Institutions for Collective Action*. Cambridge: Cambridge University Press.
OTEC Research Association. 1994. Katsudo Keika Hokokusho (Report of our activities). September.
Owen-Smith, J. 2003. "From Separate Systems to a Hybrid Order: Accumulative Advantage across Public and Private Science at Research One Universities", *Research Policy* 32(6): 1081–1104.
Oyodo, Shoichi. 1989. *Miyamoto Takenosuke to Kagakugijutsu Gyosei* (Takenosuke Miyamoto and the Admistration of Science and Technology). Tokyo: Tokai University Press.
Perin, Constance. 2005. *Shouldering Risks: The Culture of Control in the Nuclear Power Industry*. Princeton, NJ: Princeton University Press.
Perrow, Charles. 1984. *Normal Accidents: Living with High Risk Technologies*. New York: Basic Books.
Perrow, Charles. 1999. *Normal Accidents: Living with High Risk Technologies: With a New Afterword and a Postscript on the Y2K Problem*. Princeton, NJ: Princeton University Press.

Perrow, Charles. 2007. *The Next Catastrophe: Reducing Our Vulnerabilities to Natural, Industrial, and Terrorist Disasters*. Princeton, NJ: Princeton University Press.

Perry, Nick. 1977. "A Comparative Analysis of 'Paradigm' Proliferation", *British Journal of Sociology* 28(1): 38–50.

Perry, Ronald W. and E. L. Quarantelli. 2005. *What Is a Disaster? New Answers to Old Questions*. International Research Committee on Disasters.

Petryna, Adriana. 2013. *Life Exposed: Biological Citizens after Chernobyl, with a New Introduction by the Author*. Princeton, NJ: Princeton University Press.

Pickering, Andrew. 1984. *Constructing Quarks: A Sociological History of Particle Physics*. Chicago, IL: The University of Chicago Press.

Pickering, Andrew. 1992. *Science as Practice and Culture*. Chicago, IL: The University of Chicago Press.

Pigott, S. J. 1937. "Some Special Features of the S.S. Queen Mary", *Engineering* 143: 387–390.

Pinch, Trevor and Frank Trocco. 2004. *Analog Days: The Invention and Impact of the Moog Synthesizer*. Cambridge, MA: Harvard University Press.

Poincaré, Henri. 1902. *La Science et L'hypothèse*. Paris: Flammarion.

Popper, Karl R. 1959. *The Logic of Scientific Discovery*. New York: Basic Books.

Porter, T. M. 1995. *Trust in Numbers: The Pursuit of Objectivity in Science and Public Life*. Princeton, IL: Princeton University Press.

Price, J. and L. W. Bass. 1969. "Scientific Research and the Innovative Process", *Science* 164: 802–806.

Prime Minister's Office. n.d. Ohi Genshiryoku Hatsudensho 3, 4 goki no Saikido nitsuite (On the restarting of the reactor No. 3 and No. 4 at the Ohi nuclear power station). http://www.kantei.go.jp/jp/headline/genshiryoku.htm (confirmed on October 5, 2017).

Proctor, Robert N. and Londa L. Schiebinger, eds. 2008. *Agnotology: The Making and Unmaking of Ignorance*. Stanford, CA: Stanford University Press.

Provisional Company History Compilation Section of Asahi Glass Manufacturing Co., Ltd., ed. 1967. *Asahi Garasu Shashi* (The history of Asahi Glass Manufacturing Co., Ltd). Tokyo: for private distribution,

Puffert, D. J. 2002. "Path Dependence in Special Networks", *Explorations in Economic History* 39: 282–314.

Quine, W. V. O. 1951. "Two Dogmas of Empiricism", *The Philosophical Review* 60: 20–43.

Raffensperger, C. and J. Tickner, eds. 1999. *Protecting Public Health and Environment: Implementing the Precautionary Principle*. Washington, DC: Island Press.

Raichvarg, D. and J. Jacques. 1991. *Savants et ignorants: une histoire de la vulgarisation des sciences*. Paris: Seuil.

Ramana, M. V. 2009. "Nuclear Power: Economic, Safety, Health, and Environmental Issues of Near-Term Technologies", *Annual Review of Environment and Resources* 34: 127–152.

Report on *QE2* Turbines. 1969. *Shipbuilding and Machinery Review* March 13: 24–25.

RIST (Research Organization for Information Science and Technology). 2017. www.rist.or.jp/atomica/data/dat_detail.php?Title_Key=13-02-02-04 (confirmed on February 27, 2017, in Japanese).

Rosenberg, Nathan. 1994. *Exploring the Black Box: Technology, Economics, and History*. Cambridge: Cambridge University Press.

Rothstein, Henry. 2007. "Talking Shops or Talking Turkey? Institutionalizing Consumer Representation in Risk Regulation", *Science, Technology and Human Values* 32(5): 582–607.
Rowland, Nicholas J. and Jan-Hendrik Passoth. 2015. "Review Essay: Infrastructure and the State in Science and Technology Studies", *Social Studies of Science* 45(1): 137–145.
The Royal Society's ad hoc group. 1985. *The Public Understanding of Science*. London: The Royal Society.
Russell, S. 1986. "The Social Construction of Artefacts: Response to Pinch and Bijker", *Social Studies of Science* 16(2): 331–346.
Ruttan, W. V. 2000. *Technology, Growth, and Development*. Oxford: Oxford University Press.
Samuels, Richard J. 1994. *Rich Nation, Strong Army: National Security and Technological Transformation of Japan*. Ithaca, NY: Cornell University Press.
Sanbo Honbu, ed. 1967. *Sugiyama Memo* (Sugiyama Memorandum). Reprinted, Vol. 1. Tokyo: Hara Shobo.
Sasamoto, Yukio. 1995. *Beigun Senryoka no Genbakuchosa: Genbaku Kagaikoku ninatta Nihon* (Atomic Bombing Casualty in the U. S. Occupation Period: Japan as a Proprietor of Atomic Bombing). Tokyo: Shinkansha.
Sauder, M. and W. N. Espeland. 2009. "The Discipline of Rankings: Tight Coupling and Organizational Change", *American Sociological Review* 74(1): 63–82.
Saussure, F. de. 1916. *Cour de linguistique générale*, 1er éd. Lausanne: Payot.
Sawai, Minoru. 1991. "Kagakugijutsu Shintaisei Koso to Gijutsuin no Tanjo (The Blueprint for the New Regime of Science and Technology and the Establishment of Agency of Technology)", *Osaka Daigaku Keizaigaku* 41(2&3): 367–395.
Sawai, Minoru. 2012. *Kindai Nihon no Kenkyu Kaihatsu Taisei* (Research and Development System in Modern Japan). Nagoya: Nagoya University Press.
Scaife, W. G. 1991. "Charles Parsons' Experiments with Rocket Torpedoes: The Precursors of the Steam Turbine", *Transactions of the Newcomen Society for the Study of the History of Engineering and Technology* 60: 17–29.
Schelling, T. C. 1978. *Micromotives and Macrobehavior*. New York: W. W. Norton.
Schmid, Sonja D. 2015. *Producing Power: The Pre-Chernobyl History of the Soviet Nuclear Industry*. Cambridge, MA: The MIT Press.
Schreyögg, George and Jörg Sydow, eds. 2010. *The Hidden Dynamics of Path Dependence: Institutions and Organizations*. Basingstoke: Palgrave Macmillan.
Schultz, Jessica and James R. Elliott. 2013. "Natural Disasters and Local Demographic Change in the United States", *Population and Environment* 34(3): 293–312.
Schutz, Alfred. 1962a. "Common-Sense and Scientific Interpretation of Human Action", in Maurice Natanson, ed. *Alfred Schutz, Collected Papers, Vol. I: The Problem of Social Reality*. The Hague: Martinus Nijhoff, pp. 3–47.
Schutz, Alfred. 1962b. "The World of Scientific Theory", in Maurice Natanson, ed. *Alfred Schutz, Collected Papers, Vol. I: The Problem of Social Reality*. The Hague: Martinus Nijhoff, pp. 245–259.
SCJ (Science Council of Japan). 1977. *Nihon Gakujutsukaigi 25 Nenshi* (The 25th Years History of the Science Council of Japan). Tokyo.
SCJ. 2012. Ko Reberu Hoshaseihaikibutsu no Shobun nitsuite (On high level radioactive waste disposal), September 11.
SCJ. 2015. http://www.scj.go.jp/en/index.html (confirmed on December 26, in Japanese).
Scranton, P. 1991. "Theory and Narrative in the History of Technology: Comment", *Technology and Culture* 32(2): 385–393.

Seisan, Gijutsu Kyokai, ed. 1954. *Kyu Kaigun Kantei Joki Tabin Kosho Kiroku* (Record of the Problems and Failures of Naval Turbines of the Imperial Japanese Navy). Tokyo: Seisan Gijutsu Kyokai (for private distribution).

Selznick, Philip. 1996. "Institutionalism 'Old' and 'New'", *Administrative Science Quarterly* 41(2): 270–277.

Sendo, Michizo, ed. 1952. *Zosen Gijutsu no Zenbo* (A Conspectus of Warship Construction Technology). Tokyo.

Sezawa, K. 1932. "Vibrations of a Group of Turbine Blades", *Zosen Kyokai Kaiho* 50: 197–206.

Shapin, Steven. 1988. "Following Scientists around", *Social Studies of Science* 18(3): 533–550.

Shapin, Steven and Simon Schaffer. 1985. *Leviathan and the Air-Pump: Hobbes, Boyle and the Experimental Life*. Princeton, NJ: Princeton University Press.

Shapiro, Carl and Hal R. Verian. 1998. *Information Rules: A Strategic Guide to the Network Economy*. Brighton, MA: Harvard Business School Press.

Shibuya, Ryutaro. 1970. *Kyu Kaigun Gijutsu Shiryo* (Technical Materials of the Imperial Japanese Navy), Vol. 1. Tokyo: Association for Production Technologies (for private distribution).

Shibuya, Ryutaro. n.d. Jugo Zuihitsu (Essays). sono 4.

The Shipbuilding Society of Japan, ed. 1977. *Showa Zosen Shi* (The History of Shipbuilding in the Showa Period), 2 vols., Tokyo: Hara Shobo.

Shortland, M. 1988. "Advocating Science: Literacy and Public Understanding", *Impact of Science on Society* 38(4): 305–316.

Showa 59 Nendo Sunshine Keikaku Seika Hokokusho Gaiyoshu (The outline of R&D of the Sunshine project for fiscal 1984). 1985. Nihon Sangyo Gijutsu Shinko Kyokai.

Simmel, Georg. (1908)1950. *Soziologie: Untersuchung über die Formen der Vergesellschaftung.* Translated by Kurt H. Wolff, *The Sociology of Georg Simmel.* Glencoe, IL: Free Press.

Simmie, James, Rolf Sternberg, and Juliet Carpenter. 2014. "New Technological Path Creation: Evidence from the British and German Wind Energy Industries", *Journal of Evolutionary Economics* 24(4): 875–904.

SKB (Swedish Nuclear Fuel and Waste Management Company). 2000. Integrated Account of Method, Site Selection and Programme Prior to the Site Investigation Phase, Technical Report TR-01-03.

Slovic, Paul. 2000. "Trust, Emotion, Sex, Politics and Science: Surveying the Risk-Assessment Battlefield", in P. Slovic, ed. *The Perception of Risk*. London: Earthscan, pp. 390–412.

Smith, Crosbie and Norton Wise. 1989. *Energy and Empire: A Biographical Study of Lord Kelvin*. Cambridge: Cambridge University Press.

Sohn-Rethel, A. 1970. *Geistige und köperliche Arbeit: Zur Theorie der gesellschaftlichen Synthesis*. Frankfurt am Main: Suhrkamp.

Sokal, Alan and J. Bricmont. 1998. *Fashionable Nonsense: Postmodern Intellectuals' Abuse of Science*. New York: Brockman.

Solomon, Barry D., Mats Andrén, and Urban Strandberg. 2010. "Three Decades of Social Science Research on High-Level Nuclear Waste: Achievements and Future Challenges", *Risk, Hazards and Crisis in Public Policy* 1(4): 13–47.

Somerscale, E. F. C. 1992. "The Vertical Curtis Steam Turbine", *Transactions of the Newcomen Society for the Study of the History of Engineering and Technology* 63: 1–52.

STA (Science and Technology Agency). 1974. *Genshiryoku Pokettobukku* (The Pocket Book on Nuclear Power). Tokyo.
STA. 1980. Kaze Enerugi no Yukoriyo Gijutsu nikansuru Chosa Hokoku: *Futopia Keikaku* Chosa Hokoku (Survey report on the efficient utilization technology of wind energy).
STA, Resources Survey Institute. 1987. Chiiki Enerugi Sogo Riyo Shisutemu Jissho Chosa Hokoku (Empirical research report on the system for integrated use of regional energy).
Stallings, R. A. 1995. *Promoting Risk: Constructing the Earthquake Threat*. NY: Aldine de Gruyter.
Steinberg, Ted. 2000. *Acts of God: The Unnatural History of Natural Disaster in America*. Oxford: Oxford University Press.
Stolarski, R. S., A. J. Krueger, M. R. Schoeberl, R. D. McPeters, P. A. Newman, and J. C. Alpert. 1986. "Nimbus 7 Satellite Measurements of the Springtime Antarctica Ozone Decrease", *Nature* 322: 808–811.
Suchman, Lucy. 1987. *Plans and Situated Action*. Cambridge: Cambridge University Press.
Sugano, Hiroshi and Ken Tsushima. 1983. "Furyokuhatudensochi no Genjo to Mira (The Current Status and Future Prospect of Wind Turbines)", *Kikai no Kenkyu* 35(2): 9–13.
Sugawara, Shinetsu and Kohta Juraku. 2010. "Ko-level Housya-sei Haiki-butsu Saisyu Shobun-jo no Ricchi Process o meguru Kagaku-gijutsu-shakai-gaku-teki Kousatsu: Gen-patsu Ricchi Mondai kara-no 'Kyoukun' to Seido-sekkei no 'Shippai' (A Sociology of Science and Technology Study on the Siting Process of High-Level Radioactive Waste Disposal Plant: 'Lessons' from Nuclear Power Siting and 'Failure' of Institutional Design)", *Japanese Journal for Science, Technology and Society* 19: 25–51.
Sugie, Shuhei and Kenshi Baba. 2004. "Trends in New Energy Introduction in Japan", Proceedings of International Workshop on Social Decision Making Process for Energy Technology Introduction, pp. 12–18.
Sugimura, Kazuhiko. 2004. *Afurika Nomin no Keizai* (Economy in African Farmers). Kyoto: Sekaishisosha.
The Sunshine Project Ten-Year Anniversary Committee of AIT, ed. under supervision of the Sunshine Project Promotion Headquarters of the AIT, MITI. 1984. *Sunshine Keikaku 10 Nen no Ayumi* (The Ten-Year History of the Sunshine Project). Tokyo: The Sunshine Project Ten-Year Commemorative Business Promotion Group/The Japan Industrial Technology Association.
Swedish Radiation Safety Authority. 2016. Consultation Response on the License Application under the Environmental Code from the Swedish Nuclear Fuel and Waste Management Company (SKB) for a System for Management of Final Disposal of Spent Nuclear Fuel. Document No.: SSM2016-546-5.
Takata, Yasuma. 1926. *Shakai Kankei no Kenkyu* (Study on Social Relations). Tokyo: Iwanami Shoten.
Takatsuka, Hiroshi, et al. 2000. "1 MW Furyokuhatsudensochi no Kaihatsu (The Development of Wind Turbines with the Output of 1 MW)", *Mitsubishi Heavy Industries Technical Review* 37(1): 22–25.
Takazawa, Hiroyuki, et al. 1997. "Kanshoiki niokeru Takinokata Kaiyo Ondosa Enerugi Riyo Shisutemu no Kenkyu (Study on Multi-Function OTEC Utilization System for Coral Reef Area)", *Bulletin of the Electro-Technical Laboratory* 61(9): 11–16.

Takeda, Yasuo. 1955. Kawaju wa Kanpon Shiki Tabin o Doshite Toraetaka (How did the Kawasaki Heavy Industries Ltd. assimilate the points of the Kanpon Type turbine? Kawasaki Tabin Sekkei Shiryo (Kawasaki Turbine Design Materials)), Dai 2 Bu, October.

Tatebayashi, Shigeki, et al. 1997. "Zadan-kai Mirai o Tsukuru Eko-enerugi: Tokushu Jichitai Eko-enerugi Seisaku (Round Table Eco-Energy for Creating Future: Feature Article on Eco-Energy Policy of Local Governments)", *Monthly Jichiken* 9(8): 18–29.

Tateishi, Yuji. 2016. "The Health Effects of Radiation Exposure from the Fukushima Daiichi Nuclear Disaster in Japan: How Should We Discuss Uncertainty in the Context of Environmental Issues?", Paper presented at the Franco-Japanese Workshop on "Structural Disaster", March 30, Tokyo.

TEPCO (Tokyo Electric Power Company). 2012. Fukushima Genshiryoku Jiko Chosa Hokokusho (The report of the investigation into the Fukushima nuclear accident), June 20.

TEPCO. 2014. http://www.tepco.co.jp/nu/f1-np/intro/outline/outline-j.html (confirmed on June 9, in Japanese).

Tezuka, Akira. 1995. *Nihon no Kagaku Seisaku* (Science Policy in Japan). Tokyo: Yushodo.

The News Agency on Heavy and Chemical Industries, ed. 1980–1990. *Nihon no Jukagaku Kogyo* (Petrochemical Industry in Japan). Tokyo.

Tilly, Charles. 1998. *Durable Inequality*. Berkeley, CA: The University of California Press.

TMM. 2011. No. 1119, June 25 sent by No Nukes Plaza Tokyo (in Japanese).

Toyocho. n.d. Shuchu Kaikaku Plan (The scheme for a drastic financial reform).

Turbine Plants Engineering Department, Products Development Center. 1983. "Ogata Furyokuhatsuden Shisutemu no Kaihatsu (The Development of Large-Scale Wind Power Generation System)", *The Technical Report of IHI* 23(6): 543–547.

Uehara, Haruo. 1977. "Kaiyo Ondosa Hatsuden no Genjo to Gijutsuteki Kadai (Current Status and Technological Aspects of OTEC)", *Kikai no Kenkyu* 29(9): 1025–1031.

Umeki, Hiroyuki. 1990. "Iko Shinario no Tokucho (The Characteristics of State Transition Scenarios)", *Transactions of the Atomic Energy Society of Japan* 32(11): 1052–1055.

Uno, Yuya. 2017. Ko-reberu Haikibutsu no Saishushobun nitsuite (On the final disposal of HLW).

Van der Sluijs, Jeroen, Josée van Eijndhoven, Simon Shackley, and Brian Wynne. 1998. "Anchoring Devices in Science for Policy: The Case of Consensus around Climate Sensitivity", *Social Studies of Science* 28(2): 291–323.

Vaughan, Diane. 1996. *The Challenger Launch Decision: Risky Technology, Culture, and Deviance at NASA*. Chicago, IL: The University of Chicago Press.

Veblen, Thorstein. 1918. *The Higher Learning in America: A Memorandum on the Conduct of Universities by Businessmen*. New York: Sagamore.

Vergragt, Philip. 2012. "Carbon Capture and Storage: Sustainable Solution or Reinforced Carbon Lock-in?", in Geert Verbong and Derk Loorbach, eds. *Governing the Energy Transition: Reality, Illusion or Necessity?* Abingdon: Routledge, pp. 101–124.

Vincenti, Walter G. 1990. *What Engineers Know and How They Know It: Analytical Studies from Aeronautical Studies*. Baltimore, MD: Johns Hopkins University Press.

Visser, N. J. 1960. "Turbine Blade Vibration", *VMF Review* 2: 61–62.

Vleuten, Erik van der and Rob Raven. 2006. "Lock-in and Change: Distributed Generation in Denmark in a Long-Term Perspective", *Energy Policy* 34: 3739–3748.
Vogel, Kathleen M. 2013. *Phantom Menace or Looming Danger? A New Framework for Assessing Bioweapon Threats*. Baltimore, MD: Johns Hopkins University Press.
Wahl, A. M. 1957. "Stress Distribution in Rotating Disks Subjected to Creep at Elevated Temperature", *Journal of Applied Mechanics* June: 299–305.
Walker, Samuel. 2004. *Three Mile Island*. Berkeley, CA: The University of California Press.
Wallis, Roy, ed. 1979. *On the Margins of Science: The Social Construction of Rejected Knowledge*. Staffordshire: University of Keele.
The War History Unit of the National Defense College of the Defense Agency, ed. 1969. *Kaigun Gunsenbi* (The Military Equipment of the Navy). Tokyo.
Weber, Max. (1921–1922)1976. "Soziologische Grundkategorien des Wirtschaftens", in Max Weber, ed. *Wirtschaft und Gesellschaft*, Bd. 1. Tubingen: J. C. B. Mohr.
Weber, Max. (1921–1922)1978. "Burokratie (Grundriss der Sozialokonomie, III. Abteilung, Wirtschaft und Gesellschaft, Verlag von J. C. B. Mohr [Paul Siebech], Tubingen, Dritter Teil, Kap. IV, S. 650–678)", in Guenther Roth and Claus Wittich, eds., E. Fischoff, H. Gerth, A. M. Henderson, F. Kolegar, C. W. Mills, T. Parsons, M. Rheinstein, G. Roth, E. Shils, and C. Wittich, trans. *Economy and Society*. Berkeley, CA: The University of California Press.
Weber, Max. (1922)2004. "*Wissenschaft als Beruf* (Gesammelte Aufsatze zur Wissenschaftslehre, Verlag von J. C. B. Mohr [Paul Siebeck], Tubingen, S. 524–555), Science As Vocation", in David Owen and Tracy B. Strong, eds., Rodney Livingston, trans. *Max Weber, The Vocation Lectures*. Indianapolis, IN: Hackett Publishing, pp. 1–31.
Weichselgartner, Juergen and Emilie Brévière. 2011. "The 2002 Flood Disaster in the Elbe Region, Germany: A Lack of Context-Sensitive Knowledge", in Rachel A. Dowty and Barbara L. Allen, eds. *Dynamics of Disaster: Lessons on Risk, Response and Recovery*. London: Earthscan, pp. 141–157.
Weick, Karl E. 2001. *Making Sense of the Organization*. Oxford: Blackwell.
Weick, Karl E. 2009. *Making Sense of the Organization: The Impermanent Organization*. Chichester: John Wiley & Sons.
Werskey, G. 1978. *The Visible College*. London: Allen Lane.
White, Harvey L. 1998. "Race, Class, and Environmental Hazards", in David E. Camacho, ed. *Environmental Injustices, Political Struggles: Race, Class, and the Environment*. Durham, NC: Duke University Press, pp. 61–81.
Wildavsky, Aaron. 1995. *But Is It True? A Citizen's Guide to Environmental Health and Safety Issues*. Cambridge, MA: Harvard University Press.
Wilson, Geoff A. 2014. "Community Resilience: Path Dependency, Lock-in Effects and Transitional Ruptures", *Journal of Environmental Planning and Management* 57(1): 1–26.
Winner, Langdon. 1993. "Upon Opening the Black Box and Finding It Empty: Social Constructivism and the Philosophy of Technology", *Science, Technology and Human Values* 18(3): 362–378.
Wolsink, Maarten. 2007. "Wind Power Implementation: The Nature of Public Attitudes: Equity and Fairness Instead of 'Backyard Motives'", *Renewable and Sustainable Energy Reviews* 11: 1188–1207.
Woolgar, Steve and Javier Lezaun, eds. 2013. "Special Issues: A Turn to Ontology in Science and Technology Studies?", *Social Studies of Science* 43(3): 321–462.

Woolgar, Steve and Dorothy Pawluch. 1985. "Ontological Gerry-Mandering: The Anatomy of Social Problems Explanations", *Social Problems* 32(3): 214–227.

Worms, F. 1996. "Risques Communs, Protection Publique et Sentiment De Justice", *L'Anee sociologique* 46(2): 287–307.

Wynne, Brian. 1982. *Rationality and Ritual: The Windscale Inquiry and Nuclear Decisions in Britain*. London: The British Society for the History of Science.

Wynne, Brian. 1987. *Risk Management and Hazardous Wastes: Implementation and Dialectics of Credibility*. Heidelberg: Springer.

Wynne, Brian. 1996. "Misunderstood Misunderstandings: Social Identities and Public Uptake of Science", in A. Irwin and B. Wynne, eds. *Misunderstanding Science? The Public Reconstruction of Science and Technology*. Cambridge: Cambridge University Press, pp. 19–46.

Yamaguchi, Kazuo. 2006. "Rationality of Tolerance: An Insight into the Parent-Child Relationship", *Rationality and Society* 18(3): 275–303.

Yamazaki, Masakatsu. 1994. "Wagakuni niokeru Dainijitaisenki Kagakugijutsudoin: Inoue Tadashiro Monjo nimotozuku Gijutsuin no Tenkaikatei no Bunseki (The Wartime Mobilization of Science and Technology in Japan during WWII)", *Tokyo Kogyo Daigaku Ronso* 20: 171–182.

Yamazaki, Masakatsu. 2011. *Nihon no Kakuk Kaihatsu: Genbaku kara Genshiryoku e* (Nuclear Development in Japan from 1939 to 1955: From Nuclear Bomb to Nuclear Energy). Tokyo: Sekibundo Shuppan.

Yearley, Steven. 1982. "The Relationship between Epistemological and Sociological Cognitive Interests: Some Ambiguities Underlying the Use of Interest Theory in the Study of Scientific Theory", *Studies in History and Philosophy of Science* 13(4): 353–388.

Yearley, Steven. 1996. *Sociology, Environmentalism, Globalization*. London: Sage.

Zachary, G. Pascal. 1999. *Endless Frontier: Engineer of American Century*. Cambridge, MA: The MIT Press.

Ziman, John. 1968. *Public Knowledge: An Essay Concerning the Social Dimension of Science*. Cambridge: Cambridge University Press.

Ziman, John, ed. 2000. *Technological Innovation as an Evolutionary Process*. Cambridge: Cambridge University Press.

Index

Note: Page numbers in italic indicate a figure and page numbers in bold indicate a table on the corresponding page.

academic sector 36
Act on Special Measures Concerning Nuclear Emergency Preparedness 105–106
actor network theory (ANT) 29–31
actors: sectors and 39–41; as supplementary device 41; types of 40, **40**
Agency for Natural Resources and Energy 144
Agency of Technology 69, **69**
airfoil development trajectory *43, 44*
Asahi Glass Manufacturing Co. Ltd. 122–123
Association for Considering Toyocho's Tomorrow 181
Atomic Energy Basic Law 76–77
Atomic Energy Society of Japan 83

belief effect 49, 150–152, 197
Bernal, J. D. 34
bystanders 40

Callon, Michel 29–31
certainty trough 209–212, *210, 211*
CFCs Problem Liaison Council 127–128
chlorofluorocarbon (CFC): manufacturing of 123–124; ozone hole and 125–127; production capacity of manufacturers of **124**; stratospheric ozone depletion by 128;
as working fluid for OTEC program 119–121, 128, 196
choreographed outsiders 161–163, 198
Chubachi, Shigeru 124–126
citizen sector 36, 38, 178–180, 182, 188–189, 213
Claude, Georges 117
clean energy technology 113
closed-cycle OTEC system 117, 133
collective trust 200
common-pool resources 37
creeping aspects of structural disasters 51

d'Arsonval, Jacques A. 117
decision-making process: circular arguments in 212–214; development trajectory of technology and 140–142; distribution of power in 209–212; exhibiting structural disaster 129–135; formal influences 153; geological disposal and 168–170; HLW disposal and 168; informal influences 153; quality of 164–165, 198; related to energy technologies 152–153
decontamination policy of Japan 13–14
development trajectory of technology 43–45, *43, 44*, 89–93, 109, 140–142
disaster matrix 19–21, **20**
distribution of power 209–212, *211*, 213
dual underdetermination 3–5, 168–175, 189–190, 201

electricity consumption, users' responsibilities for 187–188
Electro-Technical Laboratory 131
environmental radiation 10, **10**
epistemological and ontological dimensions: in public sphere 37–39; in science-technology-society interface 31–32
explosive aspect of structural disasters 51
extreme events, definition of 1

Farman, J. C. 126–127
Federation of Economic Organizations 130
feedback-for-learning channel 127–129, 135–136, 196–197, 213
formal decision-making processes 153
Fourth Squadron incident 94
Fukuda, Kanjiro 94
Fukushima Daiichi Nuclear Power Plant, nuclear reactor specifications at **89**
Fukushima nuclear accident: institutionalized secrecy 194–195; investigation committees 54–56, **54**; Rinkicho accident compared to 87–90, 108–109, 195; as self-reliant failure 102; sociological implications of 102–105, 110; as structural disaster 110; victim inequality 167
functional disintegration: of science-technology-society interface 110; of SPEEDI 105–108

geared turbine failures **91**, 92–93, 96–98
General Headquarters of the Allied Forces (GHQ) 81–82
generalized dynamic mechanisms 45–50
generalized reflexivity 30
generalized symmetry 30
geological disposal: of high-level waste (HLW) 168–169; policy 169–170
Geological Disposal Technology Working Group 181
global warming 137
Governmental Investigation Committee 54–56, *57*
government decontamination policy 13–14

government secrecy, behavioral pattern of 9–10
government sector 35, 36, 182
grants-in-aid 59, 175–176
Grants-in-Aid for the Promotion of Power Source Location 59, **62**, **63**
Greater East Asia Co-Prosperity Sphere 73
Great Kanto Earthquake of 1923 16, 22, 64–66, 83, 194
Guideline for Monitoring Environmental Radiation 10, 53, 105

Hatamura, Yotaro 55
Hatoyama, Ichiro 77
high-level waste (HLW) disposal: configuration of agents 184; economic effects expected from **176**; financial state of local governments 177; geological disposal 168–169; imposed on citizen sector 188–189; infinite responsibility 175–177, 198–199; institutionalized secrecy and 12–13; opposition movement articles **179–180**; policy underdetermination 171–172; responsibility imbalance 187–191; retrievability 170; reversibility 170; sector asymmetry 190; siting failure in Toyocho **178**; social acceptance of 181–182; social decision-making process and 168, 184–185; social model assumed in 172–175; social model failure in 178–182; social model implicating infinite responsibility for 175–177; type-two underdetermination in 168–175
Hiroshige, Tetsu 42
Hokudan-machi 158–160
Hokuriku Electric Power Company (HEPCO) 154

industrial sector 36
infinite responsibility 24–25, 168–170, 175–177, 181–182, 184–191, 198–199
informal decision-making processes 153
initial cost effect 49
initial divergence 49
institutional inertia 12–14

institutionalized inaction 54–55, 58–63, 82–85, 194
institutionalized secrecy: definition of 103; Fourth Squadron incident 94; Fukushima nuclear accident 194–195; as implied by structural disaster 85; institutional inertia and 12–14; of Rinkicho accident 93–94, 103–104, 109; Shibuya Archives 96; SPEEDI and 9–12; during wartime mobilization period 93–96
institutional trust 200
interactions, as social characteristic of social system 33
International Ozone Symposium 126
Investigation Committee on the Accident at the Fukushima Nuclear Power Stations 54
Ishikawa, Ichiro 80

Japan Atomic Industrial Forum (JAIF) 74–75
Japan Atomic Power Company 75, 80–81
Joint Diet Atomic Energy Committee 77–79

Kamogawa, Hiroshi 116, 129
Kanpon type turbines: development of 90–93; failure of 96–98; improving design of 97–98; plane view of *92*
Kaya, Seiji 77, 80, 82
Kepler, Johannes 38
knowledge commons 37–38
knowledge distribution 187
Kotake, Munio 41–42
Kubota, Yoshio 98–100

Latour, Bruno 30–31
lay experts 84
learning effect 49
libre association 30
linear model of research and development 72
lock-in state 45–47, 140, 150–152

Macfarlane, Allison 171
Maeda, Tamon 67
Maizuru Naval Dockyard 100

marine turbines 90
mild freezing 135–138, 197
military sector 35, 36
Ministry of Economy, Trade and Industry (METI) 15, 22, 53, 181, 184, 187
Ministry of Education, Culture, Sports, Science and Technology (MEXT) 10, 106–108
Ministry of International Trade and Industry (MITI) 113–114, 157
Mitsubishi Atomic Power Industries 75
Mitsubishi Heavy Industries (MHI) 148–150
Molina, M. J. 125
M Project 154
multi-dimensional analysis 50, 193
Murakami, Harukazu 94

Nakasone, Yasuhiro 80
National Diet of Japan Fukushima Nuclear Accident Independent Investigation Commission 54
National Institute for Ship Experiments 64–67
National Mobilization Law 71
naval turbines: development of 90–93; failure of 96–98; turbine blade breakage 98–100, *99*
network effect 49, 151, 197
new energy, definition of 113
New Energy and Industrial Technology Development Organization (NEDO) 144
new energy technology development 112–115, 196 *see also* Sunshine project
Nippon Atomic Industry Group Company 75
Nojima Fault Preservation Museum 158–159
non-experts 84
non-rationality 45–50
normal accidents 20
normalization of deviance 20
NPOs 185–186
N Project 156–158
nuclear energy: budget for 82; departments and graduate schools **81**

nuclear energy bills: disclosures 76–77; parties in creation of 74–76; Radioactive Substance Control Bill 78–79; structural disaster and 76–79
nuclear energy industry 75–76, *76*
nuclear power reactors 79–80
nuclear power stations: Grants-in-Aid for the Promotion of Power Source Location 59, **62**, *63*; public expenditure for **60–61**; siting process 59
Nuclear Safety Commission 10, 53, 105
nuclear technology 140
Nuclear Waste Management Organization of Japan (NUMO) 168

ocean energy development project 116
ocean thermal energy conversion (OTEC) technology: chlorofluorocarbon (CFC) as working fluid for 119–121, 196; closed-cycle OTEC system 117, 133; concept of *118*, *120*; development of 116–118, 130; high technology element 131; irreversible global environmental change and 112; open-cycle OTEC system 117, 133; patents related to 122–123, **123**, **132–133**, 137; pilot plant 117, *120*; prospects for 117; quantitative analysis of working fluid for *119*; resurgence of 132–133; sea wreck statistics in the expected sea areas for OTEC siting **122**; stagnated development 131; working fluid for 119–121
Office of Civilian Radioactive Waste Management 171
open-cycle OTEC system 117, 133
OTEC Research Association 131
ozone hole 125–127, *125*
ozone layer, environmental protection and 127

Parliamentary Investigation Committee 54–55
Parsons, C. A. 90
path-dependency theory 45–50, *48*, *50*, 140–142
path-dependent mechanism 11 *see also* path-dependency theory

path-dependent trajectory of renewable energy technologies 139
Phoenix Park 158–159
power distribution 209–212, *211*
precautionary principle 136, 137–138
procedural rationalism 20
Promotion Law for Production of Electricity by Natural Energy 134
public goods, definition of 37
public participation in technology selection 162–163, *163*
public sphere, enhancing science and technology literacy 37–39

quick fixes for problems at hand 58–59, 85–86

Radioactive Waste Working Group of the Advisory Committee on Energy and Natural Resources 181
radiation hazards 78–79
Radiation Hazards Prevention Bill 79
Radioactive Substance Control Bill 78–79
reconstruction in Japan after WWII 67–68
relational sociology 19
relevant outsiders: breaking myth of infeasibility of wind power 154–156, 197; choreographed outsiders vs. 160–163, 198; creating path for wind turbine exports 156–158; Hokudan-machi and 158–160; participating in social decision-making processes 162; role of 165; *see also* stakeholders
renewable energy regime 17
renewable energy technologies 196 *see also* ocean thermal energy conversion (OTEC) technology, wind power
renovated principle of symmetry 199–200, 202
Report of the Special Committee on HLW disposal 12–13
reward systems 33
Rinkicho accident: Fukushima accident compared to 87–90, 108–109, 195; as institutionalized secrecy 93–96, 103–104; military secret instructions issued for **101**; references to 93–94,

93; social context of 104; sociological implications of 102; turbine blade breakage 98–100, *99*
risks, diverging estimations of 6, *7*
risk society: atomic energy and 173; as catastrophic society 2; description of 1–3
role attrition 42
Rowland, F. S. 125

Sanyo Electric Co. 124
Sasaki, Yoshitake 80
Schutz, Alfred 34
science and technology: configurations of sociological explorations of **34**; literacy 37–38; lock-in state of 45–47; public participation in 162–163, *163*; as quick fixes for current problems 72–74; in social model 174; sociology of 33–34; wartime mobilizations 68–74
Science and Technology Agency (STA) 77–78, 81, 117, 145–146
Science Council of Japan (SCJ) 12–13, 80–82
science-technology-society interface: assigning responsibility 213; common-mode failure of 89; decision-making 212–214; distribution of power and 210–212, *211*; dual underdetermination 201; epistemological and ontological dimensions in 29–32; expertise credibility in 84–85; facilitating communication in 15–16; functional disintegration of 110; generating mechanism 161; multi-dimensional analysis in 50; multiple assumptions transparent communication design *203*, 204; multiple assumptions transparent design for public funding for academic research *207*; multiple assumptions transparent expert advice design *205*, 206; policy and participation in 187; pre-war period 15; promoting communication 202; social process solidifying 209; solving problems in 200; structural disaster in 8; terminologies to specific aspects of 33–41

scientific and technological knowledge, as a public good 37
secrecy, description of 2–3
sector model 35–37, 41–42, 183–184
sectors: actors and 39–41; cognition of 37; epistemological and ontological dimensions 36–37; intersectoral relationships of subsectors 183–184, *183*, *185*; types of 35–36
self-denial mechanism 153
Shibuya Archives 96
Shimizu, Yukimaru 146–147
ship experimental station 65–66
Shoriki, Matsutaro 75
social construction of technology (SCOT) 29
social decision-making process *see* decision-making process
social determinism 213
social model 172–175
social responsibility 200
sociological path-dependency, as dynamic theory of structural disaster 42–45
sociology of science and technology 33–34
sociology of scientific knowledge (SSK) 29–31
Special Law for the Promotion of the Utilization of New Energy 113
Specific Substances Restriction Law for Ozone Layer Protection 136–137
SPEEDI 9–12, 18, 105–108, *106*
stakeholders 40, 42, 54, 165 *see also* relevant outsiders
steam turbines *see* naval turbines
stochastic process 49
stress test, as quick fix for safety declaration 58–59
structural disaster: applicability to other kinds of disasters 14; decision-making process and 129–135; definition of 6–8, 15–16, 192; disaster matrix 19–21, *20*; dynamic and static categories of 17–18, 28; elements of 51; erroneous precedents and secrecy before WWII 65–68; integrating static/dynamic parts of 50–51; as lock-in state 45–47, 150–152; multiple assumptions

approach to 201–208; nuclear energy bills and 76–79; path-dependency and 140–142; quick fixes for problems at hand 58–59; sociological implications of 14–19, 186–189; sociological path-dependency as dynamic theory of 42–45; during wartime mobilization period 68–74
structural integration: in science-technology-society interface 110; of SPEEDI 105–108
structural reform 208–209
structure: definition of 28; localized settings of 19
Sugata, Seijiro 76
Sugata Documents 76–77
Sumitomo Atomic Energy Industries 75
Sunshine project: accelerated promotion plan for 143; budget for 114, *115*; end of 137; energy areas for 114–115; origin of 112–115; social shaping of 113–114, *114*; wind power generation 145, 197
Swedish Nuclear Fuel and Waste Management Company (SKB) 169
symmetry principle 199–200

Takeshita, Toshio 80
technological determinism 213
technological lock-in 45–47
technological swords to plowshares 67–68, **68**
technology development: fixed trajectory of 140; path-dependent trajectory of 139–140
TEPCO 145
Toyocho case 175–177, **178**, 182–186
Transactions of the Atomic Energy Society of Japan 173, **173**

type-one underdetermination 181–182
type-two underdetermination 4, 168–175, 181–182, 206

Uda, Koichi 80
Uehara, Haruo 116
underdetermination: definition of 3; types of 4, *5*; *see also* type-one underdetermination, type-two underdetermination
United States Department of Energy (DOE) 171

Wartime Mobilization Law 98–100, 104
wartime mobilizations of science and technology 15–16, 41–42, 68–74, 87–88, 93–96, 104–105, 194–196
Weber, Max 34–35
Whig interpretation of history 141
wind power: breaking myth of infeasibility of 154–156; discrepancies in development trajectory of turbines 143–145; exporting domestically produced turbines 156–158, **157**; generation capacity **144**; imported vs. domestic turbines **151**; infeasibility of 145–148; Mitsubishi Heavy Industries (MHI) 148–150; negative outlook of 147–148; outsiders proving feasibility of turbines **155**; relevant outsiders and 154–155; sociological path-dependency and 142–152; wind turbine failures 146–147, **147**; wind turbine manufacturers **149**, 160

yakebutori 65–66
Yoshida, Shigeru 82
Yucca Mountain station 171–172